This book haunts us with more and more about how people live with death. In modern life there are these endless questions that are explored here. Issues of anticipation, of bereavement, or handling of the dead body, of living with its irrevocable fact of mortality. As we ponder what happens before, during, and after death; this book helps us to do that in a rich, highly detailed way.

Sidney J. Levy, *Professor, University of Arizona, USA*

Death isn't what it used to be. The immortality sought by transhumanists may not be new, but their technologies are. Latter day Cartesians may newly attempt to separate mind and body, but issues regarding the former vessel, grief, and memorialization of the spirit remain. Internet immortality, environmentalism, and modern medicine also alter the concerns and possibilities. This important volume pits everlasting questions against new techniques for treating and understanding death.

Russell Belk, *Professor, York University, Canada*

Death comes brilliantly to life in this volume of insightful research. From dark tourism, online memorials, and coffin erotica to eco-funerals, celebrity deaths, corpse carnivalism, and more, Dobscha's *Death in a Consumer Culture* provides a startling and valuable new view about how our culture of markets, media, and money interrelates with the reality and the long shadow of death.

Robert Kozinets, *Professor, York University, Canada*

This lively book provides stimulating new perspectives on death, and should generate productive thinking about how death and dying are central parts of the marketplace. The international cast of contributors offers both practical and theoretical insights into a spirited range of death-related topics that creatively reframes death as a consumer and market practice.

Jonathan Schroeder, William A. Kern, *Professor,*
Rochester Institute of Technology, New York, USA

Death in a Consumer Culture

Death has never been more visible to consumers. From life insurance to burial plots to estate planning, we are constantly reminded of consumer choices to be made with our mortality in mind. Religious beliefs in the afterlife (or their absence) impact everyday consumption activities.

Death in a Consumer Culture presents the broadest array of research on the topic of death and consumer behaviour across disciplinary boundaries. Organized into five sections covering: The Death Industry; Death Rituals and Consumption; Consumption of Death; Death and the Body; and Alternate Endings, the book explores topics from celebrity death tourism, pet and online memorialization, and family history research, to alternatives to traditional corpse disposal methods and patient-assisted suicide. Work from scholars in history, religious studies, sociology, psychology, anthropology, and cultural studies sits alongside research in marketing and consumer culture. From eastern and western perspectives, spanning social groups and demographic categories, all explore the ubiquity of death as a physical, emotional, cultural, social, and cosmological inevitability.

Offering a richly unique anthology on this challenging topic, this book will be of interest to researchers working at the intersections of consumer culture, marketing, and mortality.

Susan Dobscha is Associate Professor of Marketing at Bentley University in Waltham MA, USA. She has written articles for *Harvard Business Review, Journal of Public Policy and Marketing, Journal of Macromarketing, Consumption, Markets, and Culture, Marketing Education Review, Advances in Consumer Research, Developments in Marketing Science, and Advertising* and *Society Review,* and has presented her work at numerous conferences. She recently co-chaired the 9th ACR Conference on Gender, Marketing, and Consumer Behavior.

Routledge Interpretive Marketing Research

Edited by Stephen Brown
University of Ulster, Northern Ireland

Recent years have witnessed an 'interpretive turn' in marketing and consumer research. Methodologies from the humanities are taking their place alongside those drawn from the traditional social sciences.

Qualitative and literary modes of marketing discourse are growing in popularity. Art and aesthetics are increasingly firing the marketing imagination.

This series brings together the most innovative work in the burgeoning interpretive marketing research tradition. It ranges across the methodological spectrum from grounded theory to personal introspection, covers all aspects of the postmodern marketing 'mix', from advertising to product development, and embraces marketing's principal sub-disciplines.

Death in a Consumer Culture

Edited by Susan Dobscha

Routledge
Taylor & Francis Group

LONDON AND NEW YORK

First published 2016 by Routledge

2 Park Square, Milton Park, Abingdon, Oxfordshire OX14 4RN

52 Vanderbilt Avenue, New York, NY 10017

Routledge is an imprint of the Taylor & Francis Group, an informa business

First issued in paperback 2019

British Library Cataloguing in Publication Data
A catalogue record for this book is available from the British Library

Library of Congress Cataloging in Publication Data
Death in a consumer culture / edited by Susan Dobscha. – 1 Edition.
   pages cm. – (Routledge interpretive marketing research)
   Includes bibliographical references and index.
   ISBN 978-1-138-84819-1 (hardback) – ISBN 978-1-315-72617-5
   (ebook) 1. Death–Social aspects. 2. Death care industry.
   3. Consumption (Economics) I. Dobscha, Susan, editor.
   HQ1073.D43 2016
   306.9–dc23   2015023565

ISBN: 978-1-138-84819-1 (hbk)
ISBN: 978-0-367-27895-3 (pbk)

Typeset in Bembo
by Wearset Ltd, Boldon, Tyne and Wear

Contents

Figures

Tables

Contributors

Editor

Susan Dobscha (Ph.D., Virginia Polytechnic Institute and State University) is Professor of Marketing at Bentley University in Waltham, MA. She explores gender issues in marketing, particularly in the context of the Filene's Basement Bridal Event; consumer resistance to marketing tactics; and the role of consumption in a woman's transition into first-time motherhood. She has also studied sustainability issues related to consumer culture. She has written articles for *Harvard Business Review, Journal of Public Policy and Marketing, Journal of Macromarketing, Consumption, Markets, and Culture, Marketing Education Review, Advances in Consumer Research, Developments in Marketing Science*, and *Advertising and Society Review*, and has presented her work at numerous conferences. She recently co-chaired the 9th ACR Conference on Gender, Marketing, and Consumer Behavior.

Contributors

Stacey Menzel Baker is Professor of Marketing at Creighton University in Omaha, Nebraska. She received her doctorate from the University of Nebraska-Lincoln. Her research focuses on consumer attachment, vulnerability, and resiliency in contexts such as disaster recovery, disability, and social services. Her work has been applied by businesses to promote products and to design accessible servicescapes; by policy makers and agencies in the U.S., Canada, and U.K. to help shape public policies; and by scholars inside and outside her discipline, including those investigating the management of disasters and global environmental change.

Courtney Nations Baker is a doctoral student in the Department of Management and Marketing at the University of Wyoming.

Mary Claire Bass is a graduate student in Business Commerce, with a major in Marketing and Consumer Studies from the University of Guelph.

Her interest in Dark Tourism has allowed her to utilize her marketing degree knowledge and apply it to her interests in history and travel. She is employed by the Government of Ontario, and resides in Toronto, Ontario, Canada.

Peter H. Bloch is the Pinkney C. Walker Professor of Teaching Excellence at the Robert Trulaske, Sr. College of Business, University of Missouri, Columbia. He has a doctorate from the University of Texas, awarded in 1981. He currently teaches consumer behavior at the undergraduate and doctoral levels and is known for his innovative use of instructional technology. He is also recognized for his research on consumer responses to product design and the nature of enduring product interests. His current research includes the modern culture of celebrity and the impact of architectural elements on trade show attendees. In recent years, he has presented and consulted on the creation of effective PowerPoint presentations. An avid photographer, he has twice won Columbia's citywide photography competition. He also enjoys attending auto races and watching classic movies.

Gregory W. Boller is Associate Professor of Marketing at the University of Memphis. His current research interests center on empathy, business ethics, and performance ethnography. He teaches creativity and innovation as a core course in the University of Memphis MBA program. In addition to his academic responsibilities, he is a working actor, and has performed in more than 25 stage productions and 4 films in the last 10 years.

Margo Buchanan-Oliver is Professor of Marketing and Co-Director of the Centre of Digital Enterprise [CODE] at The University of Auckland. Her current research focuses on theoretical and socio-cultural perceptions of digital technologies, the semiotics of representation and the politics of gender. She has published in leading marketing journals and is a frequent peer reviewer.

Louise Canning's academic career spans more than two decades during which time sustainability has been one of her central research interests. Her studies of the handling of environmental issues within market relationships includes the examination of the interface between business and consumer markets and most recently the investigation of human disposition as an act of consumption. She is a regular reviewer for international publications and her work has been published in leading journals such as *European Journal of Marketing*, *Journal of Marketing Management*, and *Journal of Services Marketing*. She was appointed Associate Professor of Marketing at Kedge Business School, France, in September 2013, having previously worked at the University of Birmingham, U.K.

Hakan Cengiz is an Assistant Professor of Marketing in the Department of Business Administration at Karabuk University. He served as former Head of Department of Business Administration from 2014–2015, and he also currently serves as Deputy Head of the Department of Business Administration. He received his M.B.A. and Ph.D. in Business Administration with a concentration in marketing from Eskisehir Osmangazi University. His research interests include topics such as consumer culture, consumer lifestyle, social media and digital marketing. He has won a Visiting Scholar Fellowship to attend the Waikato University for the 2015–2016 academic year. He was also a Visiting Scholar at Marshall Business School (USC) between 2012–2014.

Angela Gracia B. Cruz is a Ph.D. Candidate in Marketing at The University of Auckland Business School. Her research follows an interdisciplinary approach and is broadly concerned with understanding consumption at the boundaries: between East and West, between human and machine, and between life and death. She is Senior Scholar in Marketing and in Film, Television and Media Studies and has published in *European Journal of Marketing* and *Advances in Consumer Research*.

Hilary Downey is a Lecturer in Marketing and Consumer Behavior at Queen's University Belfast (N. Ireland). Her research is concerned with those consumers marginalized and vulnerable in society (i.e. ageing, disabled consumers). As a member of the Innovative Research Methodology group (TCR) and co-editor/reviewer of the poetic chapbook at CCT, her consumer vulnerability-related poetry is given a platform. Her work is published in *Journal of Public Policy and Marketing, Journal of Marketing Management, Journal of Business Research, Journal of Consumer Behavior* and *International Journal of Sociology and Social Policy*, amongst others.

Bruce S. Elliott is a Professor of History at Carleton University in Ottawa, Canada, where he teaches a seminar course on gravestones and cemeteries. He has published articles about gravestones of Bermuda and the American Civil War headstone program.

Terrance G. (Terry) Gabel is Associate Professor of Political Economy and Commerce at Monmouth College, Monmouth, IL (U.S.A.). His interest in death-related marketing and consumption began while toiling as a gravedigger in the summers of his undergraduate years. Scholarly manifestations of this interest have included an exploratory analysis of death-related consumption (Gabel, Mansfield, and Westbrook 1996) and a marketing and public policy examination of the life insurance settlement – i.e., "death bonds" – marketplace (Gabel and Scott 2009). Most recently, his death-related and other poetry has been published in booklets produced in conjunction with the three most recent Consumer Culture Theory Conferences.

Pilar Rojas Gaviria has obtained her Doctoral degree in Economics and Management from Solvay Brussels School of Economics and Management

(SBS-EM). Her doctoral research on homecoming tendencies of Latin American migrants living in Belgium integrates philosophical theories, poetry, and research on consumer behavior. It has been published in *Journal of Consumer Behaviour, Research in Consumer Behavior, Advances in Consumer Research* and *La Fabrique de l'Ethnicité: Consommation et Marketing*. Her postdoctoral research focuses on two pillars (i) The interaction between philanthropy and the market in the construction of solidarity bonds among consumers; and (ii) The understanding of aesthetic experiences of consumption in the construction of multicultural collective identities. Pilar is Affiliated Professor at Universidad Esan (Lima-Peru).

James W. Gentry is the Maurice J. and Alice Hollman Professor in Marketing at the University of Nebraska-Lincoln. Jim obtained his doctorate at Indiana University and has taught at Kansas State University, Oklahoma State, and the University of Nebraska-Lincoln. In addition, he has visited at the University of Wisconsin and the University of Western Australia. His current research interests are elderly consumers, gender, family, and cross-cultural issues.

Chris Hackley is Professor of Marketing at Royal Holloway University of London. His Ph.D. from Strathclyde University focused on the creative process in top advertising agencies, and he has subsequently authored or contributed to some 150 journal articles, books, and conference papers on various aspects of critical marketing, advertising management, consumer culture, and media policy.

Rungpaka Amy Hackley earned her Ph.D. from Royal Holloway University of London, and first and second degrees from Chulalongkorn University, Thailand, and the University of Birmingham, U.K. She was Lecturer in Marketing at the University of Surrey and then Durham University before joining Queen Mary University of London. Her teaching and research focus is on marketing communications, brand management, and consumer culture. Her research has been published in various book chapters, conference proceedings and journals including *Journal of Marketing Management, International Journal of Advertising, Journal of Marketing Communications, Business Ethics: A European Review, Marketing Theory*, and *Advances in Consumer Research*.

Eric Krszjzaniek is a doctoral student at the University of Wyoming. His research focuses on the rhetorical forces associated with the creation and sustainability of wilderness spaces.

Ai-Ling Lai is a Lecturer in Marketing at the University of Leicester. She is primarily interested in interpretive consumer research, which draws on cultural and sociological theories to challenge and to explore consumption and marketing issues. Currently, her research focuses on the topic of embodiment, mortality, self-identity, and existential philosophy. In particular, she draws on the concept of mortal embodiment, drawing on the philosophy of Heidegger and Merleau-Ponty to understand potential donor's ambivalence towards organ donation. Recently, she has broadened her research areas looking at Singlehood in the Marketplace as well as Understanding Embodiment in Spirituality. Methodologically, she works within the interpretive tradition. In particular, her work follows a linguistic-based approach inspired by hermeneutics philosophy and discourse analysis.

Sidney J. Levy (Ph.D. Human Development, University of Chicago) was licensed as a psychologist in Illinois. He joined Northwestern University in 1961, taught there for 36 years, and chaired Kellogg School's marketing department from 1980 to 1992. He is Charles H. Kellstadt Emeritus Professor of Marketing. In 1982 he was honored as a Fellow by the Association for Consumer Research and served as the organization's President in 1991. In 1988 he was named AMA/Irwin Distinguished Marketing Educator. In 1997 HEC-University of Montreal named him the first recipient of a Living Legend of Marketing award. He is currently Coca-Cola Distinguished Professor of Marketing at Eller College of Management, the University of Arizona. His articles have been widely recognized for their influence on the world's marketing activity within the concept of brand image, broadening the application of marketing to non-business fields, and the understanding of symbolic and qualitative aspects of consumer culture.

Phylis Mansfield is an Associate Professor of Marketing at Penn State University, the Behrend College. She has published in several journals, including the *Journal of Business Ethics*, *The Journal of Consumer Affairs*, *Psychological Reports*, and the *Journal of Consumer Marketing*. She has also published several book chapters and cases. Her research interests are in consumer protection, sustainability in marketing strategy, and ethics.

Brent McKenzie, Ph.D., M.B.A., is an Associate Professor in the Department of Marketing and Consumer Studies, in the College of Management and Economics, at the University of Guelph, in Guelph, Ontario, Canada. His research interests are in the areas of retail service quality and shopping behavior, international consumer behavior and culture, and dark tourism. He has a special interest in the Baltic State countries of Estonia, Latvia, and Lithuania, and other regions of the former Soviet Union. He has engaged in extensive research fieldwork, and conducted a number of workshops and presentations in these countries. His research has been published in such academic and practitioner publications as the *Journal of Business Research*, *Management Decision*, the *Baltic Journal of Management*, the *Journal of East-West Business*, *International Journal of Management Practice*, *International Journal of Business and Emerging Markets*, *Knowledge Management Research and Practice*, and *The Retail Digest*. He is also a holder of an Academic Research Fellowship with the Estonian Studies Centre, and Tartu College, in Toronto, Canada.

Del Muise retired from a 30-year career of teaching at Carleton University in 2008. After a long preoccupation with Atlantic regional history, his leading research stream in the recent past is heritage issues within Canada, particularly as related to museum policy and practice, but also to the broader area of the politics of memory. The public face of history in Canada continues to inform current research, which led to a collaborative project entitled Canadians and their Pasts. This project, initiated in 2005, featured a survey of several thousand Canadians about attitudes toward the past, the findings of which are summarized in Conrad, M., Ercikan, K., Friesen, G., Letourneau, J., Muise, D., Northrup, D. and Seixas, P. (2013) *Canadians and Their Pasts* (Toronto: University of Toronto Press). More recently the cultural politics of identity in Cape Breton and the question of roots-led tourism have been a preoccupation.

Leighann Neilson is Associate Professor of Marketing at the Sprott School of Business, Carleton University. She is a research associate for the Carleton Centre for Public History and Sprott Centre for Social Enterprise, where her recent research has focused on charity fundraising methods. Her broader research interests include social and cultural influences on consumption; the influence of collective memory on touristic consumption; marketing in nonprofit and cultural institutions and Canadian marketing, tourism and business history. She is one of three cousins tracing her family's Danish, Irish, and Scottish ancestral histories.

Robert A. Neimeyer, is a Professor of Psychology, University of Memphis, where he also maintains an active clinical practice. He has published 27 books, including *Techniques of Grief Therapy: Creative Practices for Counseling the Bereaved* and *Grief and the Expressive Arts: Practices for Creating Meaning*, the latter with Barbara Thompson, and serves as editor of the journal, *Death Studies*. The author of over 400 articles and book chapters and a frequent workshop presenter, he is currently working to advance a more adequate theory of grieving as a meaning-making process. He served as President of the Association for Death Education and Counseling (ADEC) and Chair of the International Work Group for Death, Dying, and Bereavement. In recognition of his scholarly contributions, he has been granted the Eminent Faculty Award by the University of Memphis, given the Lifetime Achievement Award by ADEC, and made a Fellow of the American Psychological Association.

Phillip Olson is Assistant Professor in the Department of Science and Techonology in Society at Virginia Tech. Holding a Ph.D. in philosophy from Emory University, he comes to STS with research interests in normative epistemology and ethics, and he is particularly interested in the ways that these two areas of research intersect. His current research pursues an interdisciplinary study of the cultural, ethical, political, technological, and environmental aspects of funerary practices – especially emerging disposition technologies (e.g., alkaline hydrolysis) and funerary trends (e.g., cremation and "green burial"). In addition to having published several articles in epistemology, applied ethics, and feminist theory, he has published articles on alkaline hydrolysis, funeral waste, and eco-friendly funeral technologies in journals including *Science, Technology, & Human Values* and *Social Epistemology*. His deathcare experience and research have been covered by *The Atlantic*.

Jeff Podoshen is Associate Professor in the department of Business, Organizations and Society at Franklin and Marshall College in Lancaster, PA, U.S.A. His primary area of research relates to death and violent consumption and dark tourism. Fully immersed in a liberal arts environment, he often blends and bridges theory from a variety of disciplines in order to explain phenomena and build theory. His work has appeared in myriad journals including *Consumption, Markets and Culture, Marketing Theory, Tourism Management, Journal of Community and Applied Social Psychology*, and *International Journal of Consumer Studies*.

Ruth McManus is a leading death studies scholar, author of Death in a Global Age (Palgrave Macmillan 2013), and numerous articles on contemporary death practices. She is a senior lecturer in Sociology at the University of Canterbury New Zealand and President of the Society for Death Studies.

Xavier Menaud is an Associate Professor of Marketing and the Head of the Master of Communication and Media at Paris School of Business. He earned his Ph.D. from the University Paris 2 Panthéon Assas. He currently teaches Marketing and Communication at the undergraduate levels. His research explores Taboo issues in the field of Consumer Behavior, as well as the role of Nostalgia in Advertising and Consumer Behavior.

Françoise Passerard is an Assistant Professor of Marketing at PSB Paris School of Business. Her research focuses on the issues of consumer vulnerability, poverty alleviation, and public health. With a background in Social Sciences, she explores these topics across Transformative Consumer Research. Her work has appeared in the *Journal of Marketing Management* and *Advances in Consumer Research*.

Stephanie O'Donohoe is Professor of Advertising and Consumer Culture at The University of Edinburgh. An interpretive researcher, she has long-standing interests in the creation and consumption of advertising, and in consumption experiences during lifecourse transitions. Her research explores the role of consumption in sense-making among dying or bereaved people, and service providers' experiences of dealing with grieving customers. Much of her work concerns books as a source of insight into consumption experiences and/or a source of comfort in bereavement for children as well as adults. Other studies explore consumption experiences among children, emerging adults and new mothers, and the working lives of advertising creatives. She is on several editorial boards and has published in journals including *Human Relations*; *Journal of Marketing Management*; *European Journal of Marketing*; and *Consumption, Markets and Culture*. She co-chaired the 2014 Interdisciplinary Child and Teen Consumption Conference and the 2015 Interpretive Consumer Research Workshop.

Scott K. Radford is Assistant Professor of Marketing at the Haskayne School of Business, University of Calgary, Alberta, Canada. He received his Ph.D. from the University of Missouri and has undergraduate degrees in Environmental Design Studies (Dalhousie) and Philosophy (University of New Brunswick). His work has appeared in the *Journal of Product Innovation Management*, *European Journal of Marketing*, *Journal of Macromarketing*, and *Journal of Consumer Culture*. His current research is concerned with product design, innovation, and popular culture. He teaches undergraduate courses in Marketing Communication and Marketing Arts and Culture and has won several university teaching awards and grants for his innovative teaching approach.

Dennis W. Rook received his Ph.D. from Northwestern University in 1983, where he concentrated his studies in consumer behavior and qualitative research methods. He subsequently published research on impulse buying, ritualized consumption, focus groups, projective methods, and individual depth interviews. He has served on the editorial review boards of the *Journal of Consumer Research* and the *Journal of Marketing*. In 2002 he was the co-chair of the Association for Consumer Research's (ACR) North American annual conference, and he was elected Treasurer of ACR in 2004. Since 1991 his professional home has been the Marshall School of Business at the University of Southern California, where he served as Chair of the Marketing Department from 2007–2014. He has applied his academic orientation to consulting assignments with Anheuser-Bush, General Mills, McDonalds, Brown-Forman, Frito-Lay, Tropicana, Maybelline, and Discover Card.

Cyril Schäfer was a Senior Lecturer in social anthropology at the University of Otago, New Zealand. He died suddenly as this collection was in production. His research and teaching interests included death and dying, ritual, religion, evil, and human cruelty. His previous research examined the professionalization of the funeral directing occupation, the personalization of post-mortem practices, and the emergence of funeral celebrants in Australasia. At the time of his death, he was engaged in research exploring global memorialization practices, attitudes toward organ donation, and death literacy in contemporary society. He was co-founder of the Society for Death Studies and the immediate past editor of the journal, *Sites: A Journal of Social Anthropology and Cultural Studies*.

John W. Schouten is Professor of Marketing at Aalto University School of Business in Helsinki, Finland, and the Center for Customer Insight at University of St. Gallen in St. Gallen, Switzerland. In addition to his research in the consumer culture tradition, he has published a novel, dozens of poems, and a short story.

John Sherry, Jr., Herrick Professor and Chair of Marketing, Notre Dame, is President of the Consumer Culture Theory Consortium, past President of the Association for Consumer Research, and Fellow of both the American Anthropological Association and Society for Applied Anthropology. He studies brand strategy, experiential consumption and retail atmospherics. His work appears in numerous journal articles and books. He has won awards for his scholarly work and poetry.

Laurel Steinfield is Assistant Professor of Marketing at Bentley University. Her PhD from the University of Oxford focused on critiquing the current conceptualization of materialism, reframing the accusation of materialism as a mode of discursive power. Prior to coming to Bentley she lived in South Africa for almost ten years, undertaking numerous studies that looked at consumerism as well as women empowerment in Africa.

Isabelle Szmigin is Professor of Marketing at the University of Birmingham. Her research interests lie in the areas of conceptualizing consumer behavior and the social and policy issues associated with consumption. 2015 saw the publication of her *Consumer Behaviour* textbook co-authored with Professor Maria Piacentini of Lancaster University. She has published in a wide range of academic journals including *Sociology, Psychology and Marketing, The European Journal of Marketing*, and the *Journal of Business Research and Sociology*. She is on the editorial advisory board of the *International Marketing Review*, and the editorial board of the *European Journal of Marketing* and the *Journal of Advertising Research*.

Cathy Vaessen studied advertising and marketing in Belgium and the United Kingdom respectively, and worked for the European Wind Energy Association as a media planning officer from 2011–2013. She was recently appointed marketing analyst for the Belgian print manufacturer C.P. Bourg. Her interest in environmental sustainability led her to examine this in relation to human disposition for her postgraduate studies at the University of Birmingham.

Christina Welch is a senior Lecturer in Theology and Religious Studies at the University of Winchester where she leads a Masters degree programme on Death, Religion, and Culture, and convenes the Centre for Gender Studies. She has research interests in the connections between religion and culture with a particular interest in visual/material culture. She has publications on the European representations of North American Indians and their spirituality, expressions of spirituality at Greenham Common Peace Camp, and late-medieval British carved cadaver sculptures. She is currently co-writing a book on slow deaths and disease.

Acknowledgments

This book was nothing more than an idea in my head three years ago. I would like to thank those people who helped turn this idea into something concrete and excellent. First, I would like to thank the participants of the first Roundtable on Death at the North American ACR Conference (several of whom are contributors to this volume) in 2012. Their willingness to share rather personal experiences with attendees inspired me to move forward with this project. Cele Otnes was extremely helpful in the proposal stage of the process. I would also like to thank my associate editor, Sinead Waldron, for encouragement at every stage and her ability to keep me on track when I was feeling overwhelmed. I would also like to acknowledge my administrative assistant, Lorraine Johanson, who was instrumental in keeping track of all the documents as they came and went during the course of the final stages of the book. I would also like to thank Bentley University and especially the chair of the Marketing Department and my "work husband" Andy Aylesworth, for their ongoing financial support of my research through grants, travel funds, and my sabbatical in 2013–2014.

On a personal note, I would like to thank all my family and friends who listened to me and shared their very personal stories as I developed the idea for this book: to my amazing friend of 36 years and the best copyeditor in marketing, Christine Douglas; to my longest friend of 38 years, Sabra Fugate, for constantly encouraging me; and to my strongest friend, Natalie Burt Lahr, for being a constant source of inspiration and strength to me. And finally, I would be nothing without my two incredible children. Haven, you are the keel that keeps this family steady even in the choppiest of waters; and Gage, you are a wonder to behold with your combination of magnetic personality and boundless intellect. I am truly honored and humbled every time you call me Mom.

Susan Dobscha
Marblehead, MA

A brief, abbreviated introduction to death

Susan Dobscha

> Sociologically, death can be viewed as the nucleus of a particular culture complex involving a group of interrelated cultural traits which function together in a more or less consistent and meaningful way. The study of the specific areas which make up this complex, such as the culturally defined meaning of death, the roles of the functionaries, bereavement, death rites and practices, and the effect of attitudes toward death upon the general life organization of the individual, could be made more meaningful by viewing these areas as aspects of a larger configuration surrounding death.
>
> (Faunce and Fulton 1958, 205)

I am no expert on death. Yes, I have a layman's understanding of it. I have experienced it in many forms in my personal and professional lives. I have felt bereaved, visited tourist sites where death is commemorated, and made the heartbreaking yet humane decision to euthanize a beloved family pet. To date, however, I have not endeavored to undertake significant academic research that studies the many consumption- and marketing-related aspects of death I find so fascinating. I was initially drawn to the topic of death, and specifically to how consumption and marketing set up shop in the previously extremely private act of dying, when I was asked in 2008 to consult with a green burial organization in Massachusetts. The director had a dilemma: how to promote green (sustainable, eco-friendly – different terms, same coin) burials to consumers whose burial rituals were so firmly entrenched in their Christian beliefs that they remained intact, even through rituals detached from formal religious dogma; specifically, the ritual of dressing and enclosing their dead. This dilemma led to a consumer research question: How do we persuade Christian consumers to re-think the traditional rituals of clothing their loved ones in non-biodegradable garments and then burying them in polyurethane coffins? How do we get these same consumers to change deeply rooted, yet very toxic, burial practices in favor of more sustainable measures that at first glance will make them very uncomfortable, i.e., burying their loved ones without clothing or perhaps in a shroud; encasing them in a pine box; eliminating granite markers. The question piqued my intellectual curiosity so I turned to academic texts to give me some historical perspective and insight into the phenomenon of death as a cultural construct. People of course have been writing about death since the first writers took pen to parchment, but what was heavily dissected in art form (books, plays, paintings, etc.) was noticeably absent in academic inquiry – what I found did not provide clarity. Faunce and Fulton (1958) noted several lacunae in sociology regarding death research but a curious overabundance of research that described and compared funeral rites and rituals of "other" cultures existed, particularly the fetishization of "nonwestern and nonliterate societies (p. 205)." Also during this time emerged an interesting sociological fascination with the "funeral director." It seemed sociologists were comfortable studying death intermediaries because they were "safe." They did not grieve for family members but instead provided a market mechanism for customs previously handled "in-house" or privately (cf. Barnhart, Huff, and Cotte 2014). The "death-care" industry has also been broached by economists and marketing researchers (Banks 1998; Kemp and Kopp 2010; Kopp and Kemp 2007; Quilliam 2008; Schwartz, Jolson, and Lee 2001) who analyzed the costs of burial and the regulations designed to protect consumers from unscrupulous practices. Beyond describing death rituals and dissecting the roles of intermediaries in the funeral business, social scientists have largely shied away from "messier" topics. Samuel claimed that

> over the past century, death and sex have battled it out to be the number one unmentionable in America; these two topics are most reflective of our shame and embarrassment when it comes to all corporeal matters. But death has surged way ahead of sex as a "forbidden quotient"
>
> (Samuel 2013, p. xiv)

and the literature acknowledges that "on a deeper level, death is a rich, metaphysical stew combining elements of philosophy, psychology, religion, anthropology, and sociology; its close relationship with theories about the afterlife makes the subject yet more intriguing (p. x)." The subject of death is rich, yet the taboo surrounding it prevents it from being copiously dissected. Manceau and Tissier-Desbordes (2006) found that 65 percent of French consumers believe it is unacceptable to show death in advertisements. Women are more likely than men to label death as taboo and age increases this discomfort.

Death, like sex, has largely been ignored as a topic of inquiry within the field of marketing and consumer research, with the exceptions of Gabel, Mansfield, and Westbrook (1996); Gentry et al. (1995a; 1995b); O'Donohoe (2015); O'Donohoe and Turley (2000; 2007); Turley (1997; 2005; 2015); and Turley and O'Donohoe (2006; 2012), several of whom appear in this edited volume. This avoidance may be attributed to our general distress with the notion of death and dying; indeed, when I embarked upon this project I received many strange looks and comments like "how depressing!" and "that's morbid." Strangely, the taboos surrounding death (similar to the topic of sex) were just as prevalent in our field as they were with the general public. I found this particularly fascinating given the media's wide ranging coverage on death-related marketing and consumption. Consumers visit celebrity gravesites, write negative obituaries about a parent who abused them, attempt to clone a beloved pet, contest wills and estates, use all manner of tactics to dispose of a deceased loved one's possessions, consider sustainable burials, choose to grieve in public and on the internet, and curiously, hire strippers to perform at funerals ("Strippers perform at funerals in rural China," April 24, 2015). As such, I was compelled to create a larger dialogue on the topic of death, specifically as it relates to consumer behavior and cultural practices. I envision this book as a "touchstone," a starting point, for those scholars interested in studying death, and this introduction as a scholarly map of the broad terrain death occupies in consumer culture (think treasure map vs. Google Maps™).

Five general research themes emerged as a result of canvassing the literature on death: *(1) mortality salience; (2) rituals and rites; (3) bereavement; (4) disposition of possessions; and (5) death consumption*. Being that these themes are similar to those introduced by Turley and O'Donohoe (2012) in their much more comprehensive review of the literature on death, I will briefly introduce each as a service to scholars interested in learning more. First, *mortality salience* is a psychological construct that measures the degree to which subjects fear death. Disturbingly, it is typically "manipulated" in a lab setting, i.e., subjects are made to feel like death is either impending or remote, and it has been linked to a variety of consumption behaviors (see Ferrarro, Shiv, and Bettman 2005). Death Anxiety is a related construct that is also manipulated in lab studies. It represents a corollary to mortality salience in that it reflects the degree to which someone fears the state of not existing (Tomer and Eliason 2006). For example, Gale (2014) found that depictions of death in ads amplified consumers' feelings of worry, catastrophe and negative stereotyping.

As mentioned earlier, sociologists and anthropologists have studied *rituals and rites* ad nauseam. However, the focus of these studies has been on the death rituals practiced by remote tribes in developing countries to the complete exclusion of the death rituals practiced by western and other literate societies. Bonsu and Belk (2003) provided a notable exception by focusing less on the uniqueness of Ghanan customs and more on the ways in which death consumption rituals were part of a person's identity project that survived, and even changed, upon the person's death. They also contributed to the discourse on death and consumption by linking death-related consumption to what Metcalfe (1981) identified as "the ritual economy," a term that describes how consumers will expand or contract the "range of social and cultural capital" they expend on a specific ritual depending upon their actual or aspirational social class. The ritual itself does not structurally change but "telescopes in scale, to expand or contract in the grandness with which it is celebrated, without any essential change in format or rationale (p. 563)."

Bereavement is the process by which people grieve, before, during, and after the death of a loved one. Gentry *et al.* (1995a) noted that

> family transitions caused by events such as divorce, death and accultura-
> tion are associated with high levels of stress and pain for family members,
> and they represent discontinuities in the manner in which the household
> interacts with the marketplace. Changes in behavioral patterns in the
> short run are nearly always present, and frequently long-term behavioral
> patterns change as well.
>
> (p. 67)

A state of liminality is inevitable during bereavement and, as previous research shows, when consumers are in a liminal state they are more vulnerable, thereby compelling them to seek out market solutions that may or may not make them feel better (The VOICE Group 2010). Grieving "restricts a person's ability to note when he or she is being mischarged or overcharged (intentionally or unintentionally), as well as limits his or her ability and desire to share such information when such practices are noted" (Gentry *et al.* 1995b). Darmody and Bonsu (2008) found that consumers experienced ambivalence during the bereavement process, and that they felt the less-acceptable positive emotions creep into the more-acceptable negative emotions felt during grieving. I direct the interested reader to Turley and O'Donohoe (2012) for a comprehensive review of the bereavement literature.

Despite Jacoby, Berning, and Dietvorst asking, "What About Disposition?" back in 1977, the *disposition of possessions* is still an understudied subject in marketing and consumer research, even though it constitutes one of the three stages of consumption (Solomon 2014). In 2000, Curasi, Price, and Arnould stated,

> the topic of disposition and the distribution of possessions will play an
> increasingly prominent role in society in the coming decades and should
> be a topic of interest to professionals dealing with estate planning and
> other end of life issues.
>
> (p. 370)

Recently, Lastovicka and Fernandez (2005) sought to extend our understanding of how consumers dispose of their possessions to strangers. Their studies focused on how sellers "employed rituals to renew, reverse, obscure, remove, lose, retain, or transfer intact their meaningful possessions' public and private meanings (p. 822)." Both articles show the transition from the perspective of "me" to "not me." For example, the disposition chain changes following a family member's death, from "him/her/them" to "not him/her/them;" or, in the case of a wedding ring, to "us." Gentry *et al.* (1995a) found the disposition of a wedding ring upon the death of a spouse to be compelling terrain.

Discussions regarding the disposition of a spouse's wedding ring after divorce and those dealing with the disposition of a spouse's wedding ring after his or her death were treated quite differently. Dialogue surrounding the living spouse's ring incited a heated debate concerning whether the living spouse should retain, dispose of or repurpose the artifact while the same dialogue surrounding a deceased spouse's ring was civilly discussed.

The final theme, *consumption of death*, comprises several areas of inquiry. How do consumers "consume death?" Funerals, online memorials, public shrines, and dancing strippers are but a few of the ways. Commemoration could further be considered one of this theme's major areas of research, and typically concerns commemorating the "public dead," e.g., soldiers who died in battle or citizens who died in some simultaneous tragic event. Visiting the locations of violent events is another type of death consumption, e.g., visiting the setting of JFK's assassination, the concentration camps, New Orleans after Hurricane Katrina, or the killing fields of Cambodia. Stone (2006) described

> the phenomenon by which people visit, purposefully or as part of a broader recreational itinerary, the diverse range of sites, attractions and exhibitions which offer a (re)presentation of death and suffering, is ostensibly growing within contemporary society. As a result, the rather emotive label of "dark tourism," and its awkward, if not more precise, sister term of "thanatourism," has entered academic discourse and media parlance.
>
> (p. 146)

The consumption of violent or abject events is not a violent act in itself. However, some consumers have built physically violent components into their dark tourism experiences, as evidenced by the emergence of Black Metal subculture in the 1990s (Podoshen 2013).

This book is divided into five parts. These parts reflect the themes discussed above with some notable additions. The parts *The Death Industry*, *Death Rituals and Consumption*, and *The Consumption of Death* extend our current understanding of these subjects while the parts *Death and the Body* and *Alternate Endings* serve to expand our understanding of and to stimulate future research on the death/consumption relationship. The following are brief descriptions of the parts and chapters included in this book.

The first part entitled, *The Death Industry*, extends discussions beyond the funeral directors and federal regulations that are designed to protect consumers from unscrupulous practices. Chapter 1 by Elliott sets the stage with an historical account of the cemetery monument industry in a newly industrialized U.S.A. Elliott's analysis of the advertising, sales promotion, and branding techniques used by the competing granite and marble marker manufacturers of Vermont provides an interesting first look at marketing's creep into the death industry. In fact, the marketing of grave markers proved to be one of the first steps in the process of "distanciation" that enabled the death industry to take hold and thrive. The death industry currently continues to thrive through the burgeoning practice of "dark tourism." In Chapter 2, McKenzie introduces the reader to this concept and then centers his analysis on the strategies that marketers use to promote these tourist destinations. Similar to the distanciation that permits the contemplation of one's own death, marketers of the abject, like the sieges of Leningrad and Sarajevo, must present these events in ways that are simultaneously historically accurate but pleasing to consume. Dark tourism sites must negotiate the degree of authenticity they portray in their marketing materials and their merchandise. In Chapter 3, Welch examines the death industry by looking at the curious connection between death and erotica. Welch draws parallels between the "death and the maiden" art movement of the fifteenth and sixteenth centuries and this period's use of erotic art in calendars advertising coffins. Not unlike the Dolce and Gabbana rosary campaign (Rinallo *et al.* 2013), the seemingly contradictory connection between the spiritual (death) and the profane (sex), while seemingly common in western culture, may provide insights into death/sex connections in other cultural contexts (e.g., strippers at Chinese funerals). Chapter 4 examines the returning trend of private funerals. This chapter is written by Schäfer and McManus, and studies the practices of some consumers who choose to plan nontraditional, personalized, often quirky, sometimes therapeutic funerals. Much like the nontraditional wedding, the nontraditional funeral allows consumers opportunities to craft end of life "celebrations of life" where privacy and personalization somehow represent authenticity. Finally, Chapter 5 details how introducing new disposition technologies, like alkaline hydrolysis, can disrupt funeral professionals' claims to the exclusive professional custody of the human corpse. The author, Olson, examines funeral professionals' efforts to manage both their professional identities and the identities of alkaline hydrolysis technologies in order to maintain control over their unique occupational jurisdictions.

Part II expands our understanding of *Death Rituals* by looking at three very different types of ceremonies. In Chapter 6, Hackley and Hackley explore a Thai "hungry ghost" festival in answer to Bonsu and Belk's (2003) call to examine death rituals that occur outside of traditional western contexts, and Faunce and Fulton's (1958) directive to look at these rituals in "literate" societies. They accomplish this by considering how these festivals present opportunities for participants to reconcile the tensions that exist in their daily lives due to the cultural norms affixed to them. Materialism dances with aestheticism and the strict rules that guide behavior are temporarily and actively broken. In Chapter 7, Radford and Bloch tackle consumers' complex relationships with celebrities by examining how these relationships intensify when favored celebrities die. Consuming celebrities' deaths allows consumers to grieve in ways that may be considered inappropriate for family members or friends. Public memorials and overly emotional displays of grief stand in stark contrast to the private and reserved ways most westerners grieve. Grieving the passing of celebrities allows consumers opportunities to express their extreme devotion to celebrity culture without fear of ridicule. The waste and toxicity associated with modern death rituals is called into question in Chapter 8 by Henzgin and Rook. The voluntary simplicity movement has left an indelible mark on how some people choose to consume, through initiatives like the food mile movement, buying locally produced goods, downsizing their homes and raising chickens in urban settings. This chapter also explores how the movement is changing how consumers consume death by looking at the less harmful burial rite of cremation. While not a fully sustainable option due to the emissions produced during the cremation process, it is much better than the traditional embalming/casket option still chosen by the majority of consumers.

Part III, entitled, *Consumption of Death*, is comprised of five chapters that all broadly deal with how consumers consume death, particularly within certain consumption contexts. Chapters 9 and 10 both deal with memorialization. In Chapter 9, author Gabel uses a very personal experience, the death of a friend, to observe the process of online memorialization. This type of commemoration allows us to effectively "cheat death" by creating a virtual and social space through which mourners can share memories about the deceased that will live indefinitely on one of several dedicated online sites. In Chapter 10, Mansfield extends current thinking about the memorialization of pets by documenting the increasing importance humans have placed on pets since their introduction to the home thousands of years ago. A significant consumption element has expanded this importance, with consumers spending almost as much for a pet funeral as a human one. Chapter 11 has Neilson and Muise exploring our compulsion to document our families' pasts. Ancestry.com has made this process infinitely easier with its online database. What compels consumers to research their genealogy? The authors posit that, similar to the online memorialization practices studied by Gabel, consumers are looking for ways to hedge the finality of mortality. In Chapter 12, Passarard and Menaud examine a very taboo subject, even within the socially liberal country of France: assisted suicide. Despite the fact that it is a highly regulated activity, more and more consumers seek potential suicide solutions. By examining existing texts from online support forums, documentaries, and films, the authors try to make sense of a marketplace where consumers are willing to "purchase" a suicide solution when the medical community and government are unwilling to "supply" it. In the end, whose needs will prevail? Chapter 13 ends this part with Turley and O'Donohoe's piece about pathographies, or written autobiographical accounts of those "facing or witnessing terminal illness or grieving for the loss of a loved one." They conclude by contending that the marketplace has become a place where terminally ill people can assert their agency. By "living well" until the end, the authors of the pathographies' were better able to navigate the inevitability of their diagnoses. This chapter, read in conjunction with Passarard and Menaud's chapter on assisted suicide, provides a thought-provoking contrast in how consumers enact or perform their "denouement."

Part IV, *Death and the Body*, is comprised of chapters that focus on the materiality of death. What has historically been discussed within the realm of the spiritual or religious is actually in the end a very embodied, corporeal experience. Archeologists Fredrik Fahlander and Terje Oestigaard state,

> There may be some that actually include the human body in the concept of material culture, but the majority would probably not see it that way. The body is, however, often an important materiality that has great effect on the outcome of social practice. The body as an actant has very little to do with the individual or person, but emphasises the appearance and bodily constitution in the process of subjectivation and categorisation as well as in practical ways of getting certain tasks done.
>
> (2008; p. 4)

This part breaks new ground by connecting the consumption of death with the physical elements that may force us to consume death in the first place. In Chapter 14, Baker, Baker, and Gentry shed light on the changing nature of body disposal. In modernity, how bodies are disposed of upon death is typically a foregone conclusion; the process is either formally or loosely based on spiritual or religious requirements. What emerges when someone chooses to disengage from spiritual rhetoric in favor of constructing a disposal plan that is based on other factors? The authors studied consumers who chose alternative burial options like barrier reef disposal. They found that disengagement from "protocol" was difficult for some living family members who viewed disposal options that did not leave a visible mark (i.e., a gravestone) as a disruption of their mourning experiences. In Chapter 15, Canning, Smzigin, and Vaessen provide another perspective on the materiality of death: the environmental impact traditional burial practices have on pollution and land use. Their study of Belgian burial practices demonstrates that overcoming obstacles that relate to body materiality leads to sustainable burials. If ever there was one, The "Body Worlds" exhibit is a cultural movement that validates such an assertion. Drummond and Krszjzaniek discuss this fascinating consumer spectacle in Chapter 16, which is the most successful traveling museum installation of all time. The human corpse is on display but staged in a way that is palatable to the average museum patron. Not surprisingly, the curator of the exhibit, Dr. von Hagens, is a Barnum-esque character with a flair for the theatrical, couched within the scientific. Drummond and Krszjzaniek speculate that the exhibit's success is largely due to its ability to juxtapose our distaste for the horrible with our fascination with (and desire to achieve) immortality.

Part V, entitled *Alternate Endings*, forces our gazes toward future research with three chapters that more broadly explore death's role in consumer culture. In Chapter 17, Lai calls for an expansion of our understanding of the role consumer culture plays in the creation, maintenance and disruption of the self. The body has been ignored in key theoretical discussions about consumer culture that have covered topics like self, identity, materiality, sharing, and gift-giving (Joy and Venkatesh 1994). This omission or avoidance is remarkable given that consumer culture scholars seem to embrace and reproduce Baudrillard's provocative writing in their own work yet they mysteriously omit and/or ignore his views on the relationship between death and the popular concept of "symbolic exchange." Turley (1997) acknowledged this omission and called for consumer culture scholars to include death as part of the consumption landscape and not just as a physical "omega point" at the end of a life lived. In Chapter 18, Buchanan-Oliver and Cruz use the lens of posthumanism to confront the role of death in a culture where boundaries between human and machine are increasingly blurred. Marketers have begun to embrace this ambiguity in their promotional materials (the Playstation 3 "Baby" ad), and consumers have begun to do the same by espousing the possibility of immortality that the tangled technology-human debate dangles in front of them like a carrot – seemingly achievable but just out of reach. In the final chapter, Gabel curates a selection of poems that focuses on death and dying. These poems were written by scholars as part of the Consumer Culture Theory Poetry Initiative, which was inspired by Schouten and Sherry (2002). It is fitting that the final chapter in this book about death be filled with voices of the living.

References

Bonsu, Samuel K., and Belk, Russell W. (2003) "Do not go gently into that good night: Death-ritual consumption in Asante, Ghana," *Journal of Consumer Research*, vol. 30, no. 1 (June), 41–55.

Curasi, Carolyn Folkman, Price, Linda L., and Arnould, Eric J. (2003) "Understanding the intergenerational transmission of cherished possessions: Insights for estate planning, trust officers and other end-of-life professionals," *Journal of Financial Services Marketing*, vol. 7, no. 4, 369–383.

Darmody, A., and Bonsu, S. K. (2008) "Ambivalence in death ritual consumption," *European Advances in Consumer Research*, vol. 8, no. 51.

Fahlander, F., and Oestigaard, T. (eds.) (2008) *The materiality of death: bodies, burials, beliefs*. Archaeopress. pp. 1–16.

Faunce, W. A., and Fulton, R. L. (1958) "The sociology of death: A neglected area of research." *Social Forces*, 205–209.

Ferraro, R., Shiv, B., and Bettman, J. R. (2005) "Let us eat and drink, for tomorrow we shall die: Effects of mortality salience and self-esteem on self-regulation in consumer choice," *Journal of Consumer Research*, vol. 32, no. 1, 65–75.

Gabel, Terrance G., Mansfield, Phylis, and Westbrook, Kevin (1996) "The disposal of consumers: An exploratory analysis of death-related consumption," in NA – *Advances in Consumer Research* Volume 23, Kim P. Corfman and John G. Lynch Jr. (eds.), Provo, UT: Association for Consumer Research, pp. 361–367.

Gale, J. (2014) "Lethal consumption: an exploration into the use of death anxiety within advertising communications," *Journal of Promotional Communications*, vol. 2, no. 1, 6–30.

Gentry, J. W., Kennedy, P. F., Paul, C., and Hill, R. P. (1995a) "Family transitions during grief: Discontinuities in household consumption patterns," *Journal of Business Research*, vol. 34, no. 1, 67–79.

Gentry, J. W., Kennedy, P. F., Paul, K., and Hill, R. P. (1995b) "The vulnerability of those grieving the death of a loved one: Implications for public policy," *Journal of Public Policy and Marketing*, 128–142.

Hallam, E., and Hockey, J. (2001) "Death, memory and material culture." Bloomsbury Academic. *Mortality: Promoting the Interdisciplinary Study of Death and Dying*, vol. 1, no. 1, 1996.

Hallam, Elizabeth A. (1996) "Turning the hourglass: Gender relations at the deathbed in early modern Canterbury," *Mortality*, vol. 1, no. 1, 61–82.

Jacoby, Jacob, Berning, Carol K., and Dietvorst, Thomas F. (1977) "What about disposition?" *Journal of Marketing*, vol. 41 (April), 22–28.

Joy, A. (2001) "Gift giving in Hong Kong and the continuum of social ties," *Journal of Consumer Research*, vol. 28, no. 2, 239–256.

Kastenbaum, R. (1986) *Death, Society, and Human Experience*. CE Merrill Publishing Company.

Kemp, Elyria, and Kopp, Steven W. (2010) "Have you made plans for that Big Day? Predicting intentions to engage in funeral planning," *Journal of Marketing Theory and Practice*, Winter 2010, vol. 18, no. 1, 81–90.

Lastovicka, J. L. and Fernandez, K. V. (2005) "Three paths to disposition: The movement of meaningful possessions to strangers," *Journal of Consumer Research*, vol. 31, no. 4, 813–823.

Manceau, D., and Tissier-Desbordes, E. (2006) "Are sex and death taboos in advertising? An analysis of taboos in advertising and a survey of French consumer perceptions," *International Journal of Advertising*, vol. 25, no. 1, 9–33.

O'Donohoe, S. (2015) "Consuming childhood grief," in K. Hamilton, S. Dunnett and M. Piacentini (eds) *Vulnerable Consumers: Conditions, Contexts and Characteristics*, London: Routledge [forthcoming].

O'Donohoe, S. and Turley, D. (2000) "Dealing with death: Art, mortality and the Marketplace" in Stephen Brown and Anthony Patterson (eds.), *Imagining Marketing: Art, Aesthetics and the Avant-Garde*, chapter 5, London: Routledge, pp. 86–106.

O'Donohoe, S. and Turley, D. (2007) "Fatal errors: Unbridling emotions in service failure experiences," *Journal of Strategic Marketing*, February, 15, 17–28.

Rinallo, D., Borghini, S., Bamossy, G., and Kozinets, R. V. (2012) "When sacred objects Go B®a(n)d: Fashion rosaries and the contemporary linkage of religion and commerciality," *Spiritual and Sacred Consumption*, London: Routledge, 29–40.

Turley, D. (1997) "A Postcard from the very Edge," in Stephen Brown and D. Turley (eds.), *Consumer Research: Postcards from the Edge*, London: Routledge, chapter 12, pp. 350–377.

Turley, D. (2005), "Death where is thy sting? Mortality and consumer motivation in the writings of Zigmunt Bauman" in David Mick and S. Ratneshwar (eds.), *Inside Consumption: Consumer Motives, Goals, and Desires*, chapter 4, London: Routledge, pp. 67–85.

Turley, D. (2015), "Asking for trouble: Reflections on researching with bereaved consumers" in Kathy Hamilton, Susan Dunnett and Maria Piacentini (eds.), *Consumer Vulnerability: Conditions, Contexts and Characteristic*, London: Routledge, pp. 55–65.

Turley, D. and S. O'Donohoe (2006) "Profit and loss: Service encounters and bereaved consumers," *Human Relations*, vol. 59, no. 10, 1429–1448.

Turley, D. and S. O'Donohoe (2012) "The sadness of lives and the comfort of things: Goods as evocative objects in bereavement", *Journal of Marketing Management*, 28, 11/12: 1331–1353.

Part I
The death industry

1 Proclaiming modernity in the monument trade

Barre Granite, Vermont Marble, and national advertising, 1910–1932[1]

Bruce S. Elliott

Advertisements for cemetery monuments have been a feature of national mass market magazines for just over a century, but they were the product of a specific modernizing moment: a late realization that gravestones could be advertised as consumer products. Some in the stone trades thought monuments "non-advertisable" to the general public. This was not primarily because they were associated with death, for the nineteenth-century "rural cemetery" movement and Victorian gravestone iconography of hands pointing heavenward with the affirmation "Gone Home" evidence a long-standing sentimentalization of death and a focus on memory and heavenly reunion. It was a marketing problem: monuments were a product acquired once in a lifetime when death precipitated need (Hirschbaum 1927). There was a "progressive" faction within the industry, however, who were convinced of the value of advertisement (*Printer's Ink* 1919: p. 41; *American Stone Trade* 1916: p. 29). They would not only move gravestone advertising into the national consumer marketplace, but shift its content beyond the ubiquitous Victorian assurances of quality and economy to the commodification of sentiment and memory, in the more comfortable window of pre-need sale.

Giddens has argued, however, that central to modernity was the discomfiting distanciation of social relations over time and space and with their disembedding from local face-to-face contexts a growing dependence on impersonal mechanisms and expert systems (Giddens 1990: pp. 21, 26–28). In the monument trade, consumer trust in local craftsmen who learned the business through apprenticeship gave way uneasily to industrial production and national corporate structures. (Elliott 2011: p. 16) Wholesalers in quarry towns were supplying distant stonecutters with finished monuments, lacking only the inscriptions, by the 1870s. Local materials and iconographic forms gave way to white marble, then granite, as transportation improvements, metropolitan taste, and new technologies standardized monument types (Gilmore 1956: p. 16; Elliott 2011: p. 39).

Distanciated relationships among producer, retailer, and consumer were mediated by new communications mechanisms: trade publications, business associations, and credit reporting mitigated the uncertainties of business relationships disembedded from local contexts, and fostered trust in professional expertise and technological innovation. Late additions were the professional advertising agency[2] and the mass market consumer magazine. Though the bulk of production was now taking place further up the supply chain, local monument dealers required reassurance that retail sales would remain their preserve when retail advertising, too, went national. This chapter explores the roots of corporate branding and national consumer advertising in the monument trade in the context of growing corporate hegemony and the mediating influence of advertising professionals. An equally important factor in the adoption of national campaigns, however, was the competition for market share that underlay the marble/granite transition. This chapter therefore will compare the marketing strategies adopted by the Vermont marble and granite interests.

David Nye postulated that marketing most products relied upon personal connection or recommendation until the 1880s, when monopolies and corporations emerged that were large enough to manage a nation-wide distribution system (Nye 1985: p. 113). In the monument trade, however, national advertising was pioneered not by the industry's closest thing to a monopoly, the Vermont Marble Company, but by the upstart Barre, Vermont, granite industry. The marble and granite industries were differently structured. The newer granite industry was more fragmented, but its corporate leaders proved more willing to adopt modern marketing innovations to increase their market share at the expense of the older, more consolidated marble trade.

Antecedents of Vermont Marble were wholesaling white marble slabs via the expanding rail network by the 1850s. Aggressive entrepreneur Redfield Proctor consolidated a number of quarry firms and finishing plants to create the vertically integrated Vermont Marble Company in 1880. By 1912 VMC controlled 45 percent of American marble production, but its third president, Frank Partridge, was much less expansionist and aggressive. Lacking a Redfield Proctor, the granite industry remained less integrated. The railway, moreover, came to Barre only in 1875, 25 years after it reached Proctor (Busdraghi 2012: pp. 26–28; Gilmore 1957: 17), and it was only in the 1890s that pneumatic tools streamlined the carving of the harder and more durable granite (Elliott 2011: pp. 37–38). In 1915 some 30 quarry firms supplied rough granite to 160 manufacturers who in turn sold to dealers (*Printers' Ink* 1919: pp. 43–44). Only in 1930 would the largest Barre quarry firm enter the wholesale monument trade itself as a vertically integrated corporation (Clarke 1989, 62; *Boston Herald* 1930: p. 30).

Most Barre manufacturers did belong to a local Association, founded in 1886 as a response to unionization (Wishart 1911: p. 9). As production consolidated, advertising agencies convinced the manufacturers to brand their products and advertise direct to consumers. The Manufacturers Association adopted Barre Granite as a trademark in December 1910, aspiring to achieve the kind of national dominance Vermont Marble enjoyed (*Monumental News* 1911: p. 94), and taking inspiration from a new federal law of 1905 that facilitated the registration and protection of trademarks (Nye 1985: p. 119). One of the largest Barre producers, Boutwell, Milne & Varnum Co., launched its own national campaign in 1912, and then helped the Association launch a broader Barre Granite campaign in 1916. This campaign foundered on apportioning costs during the difficult years of the Great War. Boutwells then remounted its own campaign to promote its Rock of Ages brand in 1919. The more conservative Vermont Marble Company only began advertising in trade journals in 1912, in response to the Barre initiative, and it was only in 1927 that they made a belated entry into national consumer advertising to defend their declining market share.

The Barre Granite campaigns, 1910–1917

In 1910 the Barre Granite Manufacturers Association adopted a trademark and announced its intention to launch an advertising campaign targeting the public and aiming to educate the consumer to request Barre Granite from their local dealers. It was made clear that the wholesale firms would not retail directly to consumers. (Wishart 1911: p. 9). By the summer of 1912 the Manufacturers Association was urging retailers to purchase from a list of their members printed in industry trade journals (*Monumental News* 1912c: p. 581). The manufacturers also worked with the local Board of Trade to brand Barre as the "Granite Center of the World" through road signs and muslin signs for railway flatcar shipments (*Monumental News* 1912b: p. 494; 1912d: p. 990; *Barre Granite* 1917a: p. 3). The branding of the city became a general effort, but the major push to sell Barre Granite would come through the BGMA working with the quarry owners, and through one of the latter operating independently.

   Boutwell, Milne & Varnum Co., one of the largest quarry companies, was able to implement a national campaign of its own in 1912. The Hays agency of Burlington devised a three-pronged campaign involving: (1) trademarking Boutwells' dark Barre Granite with the now century-old logo with the words "Rock of Ages" inside a circle; this trademark was first used on 1 August 1913, and was registered in October (USPTO, TESS, serial number 71073570); (2) an elaborate two-tone advertising booklet entitled *The Rock of Ages*; and (3) advertising that publication to consumers through national magazines. The flagship magazine for this campaign was the *Literary Digest*, which had a larger circulation and less original content than the traditional literary magazines, but it was read by a higher income clientele than the truly mass market serials (Lamson Collection 1913).

   The self-styled progressives within the Granite Association, including Boutwell, were responsible for hiring H.P. Hinman as Secretary in 1915. Hinman was a devotee of the advertising journal *Printer's Ink*, which he devoured cover to cover every week (Hinman 1919: p. 156). The association's offices were redesigned to facilitate the work of Hinman and a staff of four, who communicated through speaking tubes and desk-top telephones (Hinman 1917: p. 3), and in September 1916 they launched *Barre Granite*, a monthly in-house bulletin for the member companies (BGMA minutes 1916, 13 September).

Under Hinman's direction, a national promotional campaign was inaugurated in March 1916, planned by a national rather than a local advertising agency (*Granite, Marble and Bronze* 1916b: p. 38). Though Taylor-Critchfield-Clague had a New England branch office in Boston, it appears much of the work was done at its Chicago headquarters (*Barre Granite* 1917b: p. 2). They planned a four-pronged assault: (1) advertising in mass market magazines, (2) circular letters to dealers explaining the campaign and enclosing proofs or reprints of the month's advertisements, (3) a free promotional publication (similar to Boutwells' *Rock of Ages* but touting the theme of the campaign), and (4) a special issue of one of the national trade journals, to pitch the Barre industry in general and to further educate retailers on the advantages to them of the advertising program. The Association's first circular letter was mailed to 6,000 North American retail monument dealers to explain the magazine blitz that would follow. Then came a proof sheet of the first advertisement in the *Saturday Evening Post*.

This was not the first use of national advertising in the monument industry, as the Hays agency had advertised the "Rock of Ages" booklet in the *Literary Digest*, and the trade journal *Granite, Marble and Bronze* noted that "this was the first of what is known as consumer campaigns in the monument business that has been launched since the days of the consumer campaigns of the Georgia Marble interests and the Winnsboro Granite Corporation" (*Granite, Marble and Bronze* 1916a: p. 42). In a circular letter to dealers the Association introduced what appears to have been the "most radical departure ... in the monument industry": the manufacturers would advertise nationally but continue selling only through retail dealers (de Carle/Grant fonds 1916).

The campaign was not given a name in the literature, but we can call it, as the advertising agency likely did, the *Memorial Masterpieces* campaign. This was the title of the lavish, large-format 32-page picture book that constituted the third prong of the publicity effort. The newspaper ads reprinted its soft-focus photographs and expanded on its theme: "to dignify and glorify a worthy industry" (*Memorial Masterpieces* 1916: p. 2). The first advertisement pictured the mausoleum of Charles Fleishmann (1835–1897), the Cincinnati yeast and vinegar tycoon (Lamson Collection 1916). *Memorial Masterpieces* dominated the first year of the campaign, but in the second a greater variety of imagery appeared. In August 1917, a proof went out to dealers that was accounted "DIFFERENT" and "dramatic", though it was similar in many respects to the images traditionally employed in the trade journals to impress the retailers: a view of 300 quarry workers perched on a huge ledge of rock 200 feet long and weighing 69,000,000 pounds. The Association thought it had "real news value" and urged dealers to "HANG IT IN A FRONT WINDOW!" Though unidentified, it was a view of the Boutwell, Milne & Varnum Co. "Rock of Ages" quarry (Lamson Collection 1917). The fourth element of the campaign was a special May 1916 Barre number of *American Stone Trade* out of Chicago. The prospect of educating 5,100 retail dealers about the advantages of Barre and its product justified the charge of $50 for a double page advertisement in the special number. The real value of course lay in the extensive coverage that counted as news and was therefore cost free (BGMA minutes 1916, 29 April: p. 59).

The four elements of the campaign were mutually supportive. The Barre Association mounted an extensive exhibition of their members' products at the Cleveland convention of the National Retail Monument Dealers Association, but took the unusual step of advertising the exhibition to the general public in the daily press. They then purchased the cover of the trade journal *Granite Marble and Bronze* for a reprint of their Cleveland newspaper ad as a demonstration of their efforts to "help the retail dealer sell more". They claimed that hundreds of "prospects" had attended the Cleveland exhibit, and drew attention of the dealers to their August advertisement in *Saturday Evening Post* promoting pre-need sale (*Granite, Marble and Bronze* 1916c).

The collapse of the Barre initiative

A year and a half into the campaign, the Association circulated a dealer questionnaire, asking whether retailers had experienced positive results. The manufacturers' in-house journal *Barre Granite* reported that hundreds of replies had been received and that the response was "more encouraging than could have been anticipated by the most sanguine members". Sample responses were printed, but there was no attempt at statistical analysis, and because over 160 wholesalers supplied the retail dealers, there was no easy way to measure actual increases in sales on the part of those bearing the costs of the program (*Barre Granite* 1917c: p. 1ff.).

Despite the positive spin put on the campaign by Hinman and his assistants in the monthly issues of *Barre Granite*, doubts were beginning to infect the membership, and the ability of the quarry owners, in particular, to pay in their assessments was affected by the late entry of America into the World War, in 1917.

The quarry owners encountered serious difficulties with coal prices and the availability of railway cars, and faced having to shut down production. In January 1918 they proposed to the manufacturers that the advertising campaign be eliminated for a few months while they met their obligations (BGMA minutes 1918, 7 January). The manufacturers had faced a 25 percent labor shortage and a 47.5 percent increase in stonecutters' wages since the start of the war. Secretary Hinman did the rounds of the dealers' conventions urging retailers to emphasize the "dignity and attractiveness" of simplified, standardized designs. Adoption of the sandblast had increased efficiencies at the time of the last labor contract when both wages and rough stock had increased in price, but there was no new technology to reduce costs now. The manufacturers offered a discount for cash rather than credit as payment delays were hurting cash flows (*American Stone Trade* 1918b: pp. 30–31). As output lagged demand later in 1918, Boutwell gave priority to supplying purchasers who paid in cash (*American Stone Trade* 1918c: p. 32), a practice they would continue. Wartime constraints thus hastened a transformation of business practices, and continuing concern over labor demands would see the bulk of the Barre industry switch to an open shop "American Plan" in 1922. It was not until September 1918 that the Association's circular letters announced to retailers their 1918–1919 campaign. The most interesting aspect, the Association thought, was the addition of *Country Gentleman*, one of the "favorite publications" of "the richest buying class in the world today – the American farmer" (Lamson Collection 1918).

The costs of advertising in the national weeklies had come as something of a shock to some of the Association members. In contrast to the $50 for a double-page spread that would reach the 5,100 industry readers of the trade journal *American Stone Trade* – and that expenditure had been debated at a meeting – the fees for advertising in the national magazines were heartstopping: $6,000 for a full page in *Saturday Evening Post*, though the *Post* enjoyed a circulation of 2,000,000 copies (*American Stone Trade* 1916). The 1916 campaign budget had been increased from $20,000 (BGMA minutes 1916, March) to $30,000, with $20,000 just for four pages in the *Post*. In 1917 what Secretary Hinman called the "strenuous efforts on the part of the progressive members" raised the budget to $50,000 with $30,000 going for a mere six pages in the same magazine. The "progressives" pointed out that this amounted to "less than 1 percent of the sales" but the more recalcitrant members viewed the expenditures with alarm. The pro-advertising faction succeeded in doubling the budget to $100,000 for 1918, as Hinman asserted that the effect of the national campaign was just beginning to be felt in a practical way (*Printers' Ink* 1919: p. 42).

In November, however, the association directors recommended that the national campaign be terminated. The advertising fund was not being supported by "many manufacturers" and "some quarry operators". While everyone agreed about the value of the advertising campaign, the apportionment of the costs was thought inequitable. Some manufacturers thought the quarry owners should be solely responsible for its finance. The resolution to terminate was carried out on 30 November 1918 at a meeting of the manufacturers, by a vote of 30 to 12. As no one wanted the campaign ended, a committee was elected to take up the matter with the quarriers; this time only two opposed (BGMA minutes 1918, 30 November). By December it was clear, however, that no plan could be adopted until the delinquent accounts were paid in (BGMA minutes 1918, 19 December).

The Rock of Ages campaigns 1919–1927

In this atmosphere of frustration and uncertainty, Boutwell, Milne & Varnum Co. decided to relaunch their own campaign for Rock of Ages Dark Barre Granite and to spend the money to "do it right" (*Printers' Ink* 1919, 42). A factor in this decision was probably the hiring of Harold Hinman as their sales and advertising manager (*Monument and Cemetery Review* 1918: p. 70).

There were three key elements in the new campaign that Boutwells launched in January 1919: (1) the Rock of Ages brand, (2) a "Certificate of Quality and Workmanship" which was touted as "impregnable protection: an instrument of honor" and (3) a new national advertising campaign (Lamson Collection 1919a; Bell 1925: pp. 81–90). The firm presented the certificate program as a guarantee to consumers, but the certificates and the inspection system behind them were also a way to control the value of their brand by selling only to companies whose workmanship they approved and who rendered prompt payment. This reduced the number of manufacturing customers from 160 to 50 or so (*Printers' Ink* 1919: pp. 43–44; *American Stone Trade* 1918: p. 14).

The early advertisements for 1919 were lackluster, and Hinman claimed in an interview with *Printers' Ink* that they served primarily to familiarize the public with the name "Rock of Ages". They consisted mostly of text on a background recreating the surface of the granite material, with sometimes a picture of a generic monument at the top, and sometimes none. But the visual quality, and the variety of message, improved as the year went on. Hinman claimed there was a switch to "educational advertisements", but the 1919 campaign was in fact a mixed bag of approaches and appeals (*Printers' Ink* 1919: p. 43). The June advertisement was a view of the Boutwell Rock of Ages quarry intended to impress the public with its magnitude – the same tactic used by the BGMA in August 1917 (Lamson Collection 1919b). Two of the year's advertisements were intended to ingratiate important intermediaries. July saw publication of "The Dealer in Memorials: An Appreciation" (Lamson Collection 1919c) followed in October by a parallel paean to the Cemetery Superintendent (Lamson Collection 1919e).

The campaign also highlighted opportunities and threats to the industry that materialized in the wake of the World War. One circular letter urged dealers to push their community leaders to commission war memorials, and offered a free design service for this purpose (Lamson Collection 1919b). Magazine ads drew attention to the "appropriateness" of erecting personal tributes to relatives and friends who perished overseas, and retailers were sent a brochure explaining cenotaphs: erecting a second monument to a serviceman interred overseas was, if nothing else, good business (Lamson Collection 1919d). The November advertisements countered the "propaganda" for "utilitarian" war memorials: erecting useful structures such as hospitals or libraries instead of granite monuments to a community's war dead. The advertisement featured Lincoln's Gettysburg Address, where the president had "set us the example of an ever-sacred Memorial dedicated to the nation's heroes" (Lamson Collection 1919f).

In July 1923 Boutwell, Milne & Varnum Co. commenced publication of *Rock of Ages Magazine*, a house organ targeting retailers, largely to tout the advantages of the recently adopted open shop or non-union American Plan.

The early numbers vilified the Granite Cutters' National Union and its leadership (*Rock of Ages Magazine* 1923a). But the magazine quickly supplanted the circulars explaining the advertising campaigns, printing advance pulls of the magazine advertisements. The advertising itself remained uninspired: a photograph of a blank headstone with text urging memorialization as a "noble obligation", "a royal tribute", "the perfect monumental granite", and a way to "perpetuate your family name". Another bland headstone was claimed, implausibly, to "express personality". Each ad warned against substitutes, advising consumers to insist upon a "Certificate of Perfection" (*Rock of Ages Magazine* 1924a,b,c,d,f).

These advertisements about advertisements pointed out that the Boutwells ads were "tireless agents", "cutting down sales resistance" and cornering prospects "at odd times in unexpected places" (*Rock of Ages Magazine* 1924e).

A lavish promotional book, Athol Bell's *The Story of the ROCK OF AGES*, was distributed just prior to a 1 July 1925 reorganization when Boutwell, Milne & Varnum Company was purchased by a consortium of Barre, Burlington, and Boston business interests, including Hinman, the former secretary of the Barre Granite Manufacturers Association (*Rock of Ages Magazine* 1925a). The Boutwell firm's offices were moved to Barre from Montpelier and in May 1926 the name of the business was changed to the Rock of Ages Corporation, following other national advertisers in asserting the primacy of the trademarked product (*Rock of Ages Magazine* 1926c).

Rock of Ages Magazine reported a dealer's complaint that advertisements would be more effective with photographs of monuments instead of ink drawings. The editors felt otherwise. The company employed photographs in its pamphlets (*Rock of Ages Magazine* 1925b: p. 18) but their full response came more than a year later when their August 1926 advertisement appeared on the cover of *Advertising and Selling* to illustrate an article about art in advertising (Calkins 1927, cited in *Rock of Ages Magazine* 1927a).

In February 1926 Rock of Ages had rolled out a new campaign masterminded by the Albert Frank & Co. agency with advertisements featuring attractive ink-wash drawings of historic New England churches (*Rock of Ages Magazine* 1926a). They revised their list of consumer magazines to each appeal to different markets. To assist local dealers, booklets, letters, and design books were offered free upon request from a Rock of Ages Service Bureau or from field agents (*Rock of Ages Magazine* 1926b). Rock of Ages had accepted their dealers' view that monument purchases were made most often by wives or widows, and they emphasized that all these magazines were read at home and that women responded favorably to the advertisements depicting historic churches (*Rock of Ages Magazine* 1926d). Yet in terminating the series, the editors concluded that the series had made a "subtle appeal" to the memorial instinct in men's minds. They lauded the 1926 campaign as one of the most successful in the history of advertising (*Rock of Ages Magazine* 1926f). Glen Mitchell, a young Chicago artist, was identified as the creator of the appealing drawings in the second advertisement of the season.

Printers' Ink reproduced a half-tone of one, and Mitchell was awarded a Guggenheim Memorial Foundation Fellowship for study abroad and departed for the Middle East to paint religious subjects en route to Italy (*Rock of Ages Magazine* 1926d).

The February 1927 *Rock of Ages Magazine* devoted unprecedented space to explaining the past and forthcoming campaigns. The journal selection for 1927 had a combined paid circulation of 6 million, read by 25 million adults: *Ladies Home Journal*, *National Geographic*, and *The Farm Journal*, but also *Extension* and *The Christian Herald*, *Architecture*, and *The Spur*, a horse and hounds magazine (*Rock of Ages Magazine* 1926g). August Hirschbaum of the advertising agency explained that a major difficulty with advertising grave markers was that consumers were not in the market for one most of the time. For that reason they would overlook advertisements depicting monuments. The challenge thus was to capture and hold the reader's attention until the name of the company registered. They had decided New England churches would appeal to an educated clientele. Hirschbaum explained that this was the most recent type of advertising, an "indirect appeal" giving an impression of superior lifestyle rather than depicting products and prices. This strategy had been adopted by most of the major department stores (Hirschbaum 1927).

The same issue launched an American History series, with dramatic ink drawings of iconic events and small inset photographs of the gravestones of the chief protagonists. The text, in pseudo-eighteenth-century font, suggested how monuments endured, but the minuscule photographs concealed the fact that some of the heroes were interred beneath monuments of marble (*Rock of Ages Magazine* 1927b). They asserted that the series exerted a strong appeal for both rural and urban residents, and was local advertising in the sense that the advertising media were magazines read in the home (*Rock of Ages Magazine* 1927c; 1927d). The series was intended to maintain interest while stressing the importance of erecting proper memorials (*Rock of Ages Magazine* 1927e).

The Vermont Marble Company campaigns 1927–1932

The late entry into national advertising by Vermont Marble Company at first appears curious. Though granite had surpassed marble as the most common material for grave markers by the turn of the century (*The Reporter* 1898), the marble industry was still an active player and had, moreover, consolidated its sector much earlier, in the 1870s. The Vermont Marble Company in Proctor enjoyed a much greater market share in its commodity than Barre Granite did in its. Vermont Marble had long relied on personal contact with retailers, depending upon hefty monument catalogues and a network of regionally-based travelling agents, who sent postcards to dealers a few days before they arrived to take orders. Though there had been periodicals for the monument trade since *The Reporter* commenced publication in Chicago in 1868, VMC began advertising in trade journals only in 1912 – likely in response to Boutwells' Rock of Ages promotion (See for example *Monumental News* 1912a).

Marble sales were struggling against the competition from granite. An internal analysis by Vermont Marble in 1926 showed that earnings from monument work were shrinking.

Accounting for about a third of sales to the trade before the War, monumental work was their mainstay in the immediate postwar years, rising from 37 to 53 percent of sales in 1918, and to 61 percent the year after, before declining to 54 percent in 1920 and then embarking on a long slide to 24 percent in 1926–1928 (VMC Annual Report 1926: pp. 17–21; 1928, App. C).

Boutwell, Milne & Varnum Co. had recruited Hinman's successor as secretary treasurer of the Barre Manufacturers, Athol Bell, and in 1925 commissioned him to write the lavishly-produced promotional volume that reviewed the company's achievements. Bell detailed the essential strategies of their magazine campaign, effectively setting out a recipe for competitors to follow (Bell 1925: pp. 81–90), and indeed it was followed two years later, in 1927, when Vermont Marble Company finally launched its own campaign. It was likely the wide distribution of Bell's book that inspired a new Boston advertising agency, the Kenyon Company, to approach Vermont Marble in December 1926. They voluntarily undertook a survey of the company's relations with retailers, hoping to be retained to prepare an advertising plan (VMC Annual Report 1926: pp. 14–15). (On the Kenyon agency see *Boston Herald* 1925: p. 24; 1931: p. 6).

What is striking is that Boutwells, which had been aggressively pursuing the consumer in national magazines for more than a decade, had a more tenuous connection with the retailers than Vermont Marble did. In 1925 the granite firm was still engaged only in quarrying: providing rough stone to mostly local manufacturers who produced and wholesaled granite monuments to retailers (Bell 1925: p. 88). The name was changed to Rock of Ages Corporation in 1926 following the retirement of Jim Boutwell and the purchase of the quarries by new partners the year before (*Daily Messenger* 1926: p. 3). It was not until 1930 that they acquired ten Barre manufacturers in a $6 million merger, consolidating a third of the city's granite production, and becoming manufacturers and wholesalers (Clarke 1989: p. 62). Vermont Marble Company by contrast had consolidated the Rutland County marble industry to a remarkable degree a half century earlier, first as the Producers Marble Company trust in 1883, and then through direct takeovers as the Vermont Marble Company, opening a finishing plant that wholesaled not only precut slabs and dimension stone, but three-dimensional monuments ready for local inscription (Gilmore 1956: pp. 11–20). Their expansion rendered unprofitable older but smaller firms in adjoining counties of Vermont and northwestern Massachusetts, effectively ending the marble industry there as VMC extended its own sales throughout the continent (Brainerd 1885; Stott 2008: pp. 187–238; Little 1998: pp. 179–234). Whereas the Barre manufacturers had been attempting to make for themselves a "national name" in 1916, a decade later Vermont Marble was attempting to shore up its existing national market against the competition posed by granite.[3]

In February 1927 VMC agreed to adopt Kenyons' plan. In essentials it mirrored somewhat cautiously the Barre campaign of 1916. The first major innovation was due to technological advances, as the display advertisements proposed for *Ladies Home Journal* were to be in full color. It was only in 1926 that the largest weekly magazine, *Saturday Evening Post*, had offered four-color pages, at a cost of $11,000, nearly double the cost of a black and white page (Marchand 1985: p. 7). Color photographs were not common in magazines till the 1930s (Nye 1985: p. 114). The rest of the Kenyon campaign consisted of half-page advertisements in black and white in *Country Gentleman, Christian Herald*, and *Extension* every second month. These were conservative choices, appealing to middle-class women, prosperous farmers, and readers of the religious press. A memorials booklet *All That is Beautiful Shall Abide Forever* was prepared for distribution through retailers to consumers, equivalent to Barre Granite Association's *Memorial Masterpieces* of 1916, and dealers were to be provided with a plaque identifying them as official agents (VMC Annual Report 1926: pp. 14–15).

They rushed an account of the campaign, likely lifted from the Kenyon proposal, into the February issue of their existing dealer magazine (launched as *Vermont Marble* in August 1925) (Proctoriana Collection, VHS, Doc. 127). Headed "National Advertising in Full Color", it offered local "craftsmen" the opportunity to put the national campaign to work locally. The campaign would open with a Memorial Day advertisement in the *Ladies Home Journal*, a hugely popular family magazine, followed by the rural *Country Gentleman* and the two principal Protestant and Catholic family magazines, with a combined circulation of 5 million households (*Vermont Marble* 1927, n.p.).

The second major innovation had been around for a while but was proliferating in the 1920s: a movement beyond situational or lifestyle advertising that showed products in use (Marchand 1985: p. xvi; Nye 1985: p. 123) to what Marchand has called "social tableaux" in which images and text, according to Nye, attempted to weave a company name into American culture (Marchand 1985: pp. 165–166; Nye 1985: p. 133). Burt has pointed out that though this type of advertising was widely adopted in the 1920s, it was pioneered by Boston's Pettingill Agency for the Lydia E. Pinkham Medicine Company in 1890 (2012: pp. 209–10), and Badaracco has observed from a study of printing trade journals that tableaux advertising was common by 1906 (1990: p. 1046). As Marchand studied the 1920–1940 period he sometimes missed the earlier origins of what he took to be innovations. This form of advertising depended upon an arresting image that would connect with the reader, but it depended upon the text to link the image to the product. The advertisements thus constituted a major step beyond the traditional quarry and monument views that had marked the early days of the Barre campaign and were more akin to Rock of Ages' contemporaneous historical series. The VMC campaign employed an artist, John Newton Howitt of New York, to produce decorous oil paintings for advertisements that exalted the bonds of family (*Vermont Marble* 1927, n.p.).

In April 1927 VMC changed the title of its retailer magazine from *Vermont Marble* to *The Memory Stone*, their belated counter to Boutwell, Milne and Varnum's "Rock of Ages" trademark of 1912. A logo with the words "The Memory Stone" enclosed in a laurel wreath was first employed on 7 December 1928, though it was not filed as a trademark until 1948 (USPTO, TESS, serial number 71556739). The title of the campaign and of its promotional booklet, *All That is Beautiful Shall Abide Forever*, appeared now as a slogan at the bottom of every page. The magazine provided a preview of the bimonthly national advertisements derived from Howitt's canvasses accompanied by romantic and evocative prose (*Memory Stone* 1927a, n.p.).

The June issue provided a preview of the color advertisement that would appear in July, illustrating not a grave marker but the touching tale of a family singing a hymn in an old Colonial church. The father gazes fondly at his daughter with a caption reading "It sounds to him like her mother's voice, singing in Paradise," a quotation from Longfellow's classic New England poem, "The Village Blacksmith." The text below explained how his thoughts turned to her resting place, marked by a monument of marble. It then made the link to Vermont Marble as "America's noblest memory stone", selected as the material for Arlington's Tomb of the Unknown Soldier (*Memory Stone* 1927b, n.p.), to which Howitt was already bound with his paintbox (*Memory Stone* 1927d, n.p.). Using the most modern technologies and advertising agency associative techniques, the content paradoxically referenced upscale traditional America and recalled the New England roots of the American character. September's illustration was of an elderly woman reading on her porch while a well-dressed young couple walked by with their dog. The wreath enclosed the caption "The heart that has truly loved never forgets", a quotation from the Irish poet Thomas Moore. The text below contained a gentle reminder of the obligation to mark the resting places of those dear to us. The New England context of the art continued, with Howitt explaining that the doorway was based on one in Salem, Massachussetts (*Memory Stone* 1927c, n.p.).

The success of the campaign depended upon the image being sufficiently compelling or sympathetic as to cause the viewer to move beyond the caption and read the text that alone identified the product. Perhaps the company already had misgivings about the dominance of atmosphere over association, for in December 1927 the advertisement in *Country Gentleman* and *Extension* was, much less subtly, an advertisement for the new consumer booklet, with the cover reproduced two-thirds actual size and resting upon a wreath of laurel and oak. This, as the *Memory Stone* observed, turned the whole page into a coupon (*Memory Stone* 1927e, n.p.).

The company had set sales targets: a 10 percent increase over average sales in each state over the preceding three years. Nationally the quota was undersold by 13 percent, with only New York exceeding it. Monument sales were off more in 1927 than during the year before, despite the expensive national campaign (VMC Annual Report 1927: pp. 10–11; chart 1928, App. C). Vermont Marble's branch managers and salesmen reported, however, that a propaganda push was vitally necessary. Many dealers were giving pride of place to granite markers in their showrooms (VMC Annual Report 1927: p. 8). The company was also having to contend with a growing list of cemeteries nationwide that restricted or prohibited the use of marble monuments in favor of the more durable granite (VMC Annual Report 1927: pp. 10, 13).

By February 1928 they were becoming aware of the problem that had bedeviled the original Barre Granite campaign of 1916: that consumer inquiries for the booklet and unsolicited anecdotal reports from retailers were the only evidence that the campaigns were worth the considerable expenditure: only 20 orders could be directly attributed to the campaign (VMC Annual Report 1928: pp. 13–14).

By June 1928 the national campaign had changed direction, reflecting a view on the part of the company that its message was too subtle and not reflected in increased sales figures. The decline in marble sales to the trade in fact had been slowed but the advertising nonetheless was changed to highlight the actual product. Instead of the sentimental advertisements evocative of middle-class family relations set in a bucolic and iconic New England landscape, the June and July advertisements reverted to depicting gravestone designs which it was hoped would be more efficacious in their simplicity. None of this advertising would be in color, and none occupied a full page (*Memory Stone* 1928, n.p.).

The reversion to more prosaic and literal advertising may have been a mistake as the sales figures for 1929 showed a further drop of $178,966, nearly as much as in 1927, the year the campaign had been inaugurated, and reversing the improved figures of the year before. As the Great Depression began only in the autumn of 1929 it is unlikely that it was solely responsible for the dip. In future years the Depression would have a chilling effect on the industry, for gravestones were a purchase that could readily be deferred in hard times. VMC's monument sales continued to drop, to a third of their 1928 levels by 1933, when they accounted for a record low of only 17 percent of company sales to the trade, building stone carrying the company through the thirties (VMC Annual Report 1928, App. C). Though the efficacy of national advertising was far from clear, dropping it entirely now appeared suicidal.

As monument sales continued to fall, the 1932 campaign assumed a more dramatic posture. "Murdered by the Savages" read the first advertisement of the year. The concept was to present compelling Vermont headstones of 150 years previous, both to catch the eye and to make the case for the durability of the material. The other innovation was that the advertisements would now be running in the rotogravure sections of major city dailies, and 4, 6, and 10-inch sizes were made available for use over the dealers' own names (*Memory Stone* 1932, n.p.). Over the next five years no further articles on national advertising appeared in *The Memory Stone*.

Aftermath

By 1930 Rock of Ages had picked up the full page color advertising that Vermont Marble had abandoned. The Barre Granite Association at last recommenced advertising in consumer magazines, in 1931, a year after the Rock of Ages quarries bought out ten Barre manufacturers and finally entered the manufacturing and wholesaling line (Clarke 1989: p. 62). Recognizing that collective action by the smaller firms was necessary to compete with the new corporate giant, the Granite Manufacturers Association held meetings with the independent manufacturing firms and signed up virtually all of them, doubling the Association's membership, and negotiated the participation of the six remaining independent quarry companies. They launched a publicity campaign paid for by subscription, and planned to employ Barre Granite as a trade name (*Barre Daily Times* 1931, n.p.).

Ironically in 1940 Barre Granite's advertising agency, the H.B. Humphrey Co. of Boston, received the advertising industry's national medal for excellence in copy for an advertisement that took the focus off gravestones and told a story about people: the type of advertising the Vermont Marble Company had experimented with and abandoned 13 years earlier. The image was an ink drawing of a woman in Edwardian dress waving goodbye to a departing train. The header read "Aunt Meg ... who never married". The text devoted four meandering, narrative paragraphs to the story of Aunt Meg, whose beau Jim Foster never came back from the war. The fifth transitioned from short story to the need for a suitable memorial for a departed loved one.

The Aunt Meg advertisement came to be regarded as a classic example of advertising technique practiced since the 1920s: turning consumer need into a case history (Schwartz 1966: p. 38). The Barre Granite advertisement was included in Julian Watkins's 1949 book *The 100 Greatest Advertisements* (Watkins 1949).

Thus in the monument industry, advertising agencies, product branding, and mass market magazines were late additions to the modern communications strategies adopted to negotiate distanciated and disembedded social relations, as the Vermont marble and granite industries moved from being suppliers of dimension stone to providers of finished monuments, and extended their geographical reach across North America. As the more integrated Vermont Marble Company lost market share to the more durable granite, it remained conservative in the techniques it adopted to extend media advertising both to the trade and to consumers. The less centralized Barre Granite interests stepped in where conservative Vermont Marble feared to tread, and adopted innovations Vermont Marble abandoned.

Notes

1 The author is grateful to Karen Lane of Aldrich Public Library, Barre, Vermont; Paul Carnahan, Librarian of the Vermont Historical Society; Ed Larson, executive director

of the Barre Granite Association; the staff and volunteers of the Proctor Free Library in Proctor, Vermont; Anne Tait; June Hadden Hobbs; and David Gerber.

2 Hower (1949: p. 7) and Sivulka (1998: p. 35) explain the advantages of advertising agencies in this context, but Tim Vos (2013) has recently provided a more contextualized institutional explanation of their origin.

3 Rotundo attributes the demise of white bronze monuments partly to the success of the Barre Granite advertising campaign (Rotundo 1992: 283).

References

Archival materials

Barre Granite Manufacturers Association minutes 1915–1917, Barre Granite Association, Barre, VT.

Barre Granite Manufacturers Association minutes 1918, Directors meetings, Barre Granite Association, Barre, VT.

de Carle/Grant fonds (1916), correspondence, March, DEC-056, Archives and Research Collections, Carleton University Library, Ottawa, Canada.

Lamson Collection (1913), "Before you buy a memorial, get this book", *Literary Digest*, 13 September, BHC-283, Barre History Collection at the Vermont Historical Society, Barre, VT.

Lamson Collection (1916), *Saturday Evening Post*, 25 March, BHC-321.

Lamson Collection (1917), H. Hinman to the monument trade, 4 August, BHC-321.

Lamson Collection (1918), H. Hinman to the monumental trade, 20 September, BHC-321.

Lamson Collection (1919a), circular letter, 25 January, BHC-283.

Lamson Collection (1919b), circular letter, 14 June, BHC-283.

Lamson Collection (1919c), *Saturday Evening Post* proof sheet, 26 July, BHC-283.

Lamson Collection (1919d), circular letter, 16 August and attachments, BHC-283.

Lamson Collection (1919e), *Saturday Evening Post* proof sheet, 25 October, BHC-283.

Lamson Collection (1919f), circular letter, 15 November and attachments, BHC-283.

Proctoriana Collection, Doc. 127, *Vermont Marble/The Memory Stone*, Vermont Historical Society, Barre, VT.

Rock of Ages Magazine, Vermont Historical Society, Barre, VT.

USPTO, TESS (Trademark Electronic Search System), http://tess2.uspto.gov (Accessed: 24 March 2013).

Vermont Marble Company (VMC), Annual Report 1926, Proctor Free Library, Proctor, VT.

Vermont Marble Company (VMC), Annual Report 1927, Proctor Free Library, Proctor, VT.

Vermont Marble Company (VMC), Annual Report 1928, Proctor Free Library, Proctor, VT.

Printed materials

American Stone Trade (1916), May.

American Stone Trade (1918a), "All winter meetings demonstrate confidence", March: p. 14.

American Stone Trade (1918b), H. Hinman, "A message of the Barre Manufacturers", March: pp. 30–31.

American Stone Trade (1918c), "Granite Producers organization", September: p. 32.

Badaracco, C. (1990) "Alternatives to newspaper advertising, 1890–1920: Printers' innovative product and message designs", *Journalism Quarterly*, 67 (4): pp. 1042–1050.

Barre Daily Times (1931), 7 May, n.p., typescript in Lamson Collection, BHC-321.

Barre Granite (1917a), "Annual Report of Secretary", January: p. 3.

Barre Granite (1917b), "Advertising conference", 1 (10), July: p. 2.

Barre Granite (1917c), "Dealers express themselves on advertising campaign", 2 (1), October: p. 1ff.

Bell, A. (1925), *The Story of The Rock of Ages*, Boutwell, Milne & Varnum Co., Montpelier, VT.

Boston Herald (1925), "To meet needs of advertiser", 14 June: p. 24.

Boston Herald (1930), "Granite merger involves $6,000,000", 8 February: p. 30.

Boston Herald (1931), "Kenyon Co., Inc., joins N.Y. firm", 5 January: p. 6.

Brainerd, E. *et al.* (1885), *The Marble Border of Western New England*, Middlebury Historical Society, Middlebury, VT.

Burt, E. (2012), "From 'true woman' to 'new woman'", *Journalism History*, 27 (4): pp. 207–217.

Busdraghi, I. (2011), "Proctor and Barre: The marble and granite quarries and the Italian stoneworkers in Vermont, 1865–1915" in Bianco, R. and Broucke, P. (eds.) *Nature Transformed: Edward Burtynsky's Vermont Quarry Photographs in Context*. Hanover and London: University Press of New England: pp. 24–35.

Clarke, R. (1989), *Carved in Stone: A History of the Barre Granite industry*. Barre, VT: Rock of Ages Corporation.

Daily Messenger (1926), "Rock of Ages Corporation", 24 May: p. 3, St Alban's, VT.

Elliott, B. (2011), "Memorializing the Civil War dead: Modernity and corruption under the Grant administration", *Markers*, 27: pp. 14–55.

Giddens, A. (1990), *The Consequences of Modernity*. Stanford: Stanford University Press.

Gilmore, R. (1956–7), "The Vermont Marble Company: An entrepreneurial study, 1869–1939", *The New England Social Studies Bulletin*, 14 (2): pp. 11–20 and 14 (3): pp. 14–20.

Granite, Marble and Bronze (1916a) "Barre advertising campaign", 26 (4), April: p. 42.

Granite, Marble and Bronze (1916b), "News from the granite centers", 26 (6), June: p. 38.

Granite, Marble and Bronze (1916c), September, cover and p. 42.

Hinman, H. (1917), "Annual report of Secretary", *Barre Granite*, 1 (4): p. 3.

Hinman, H. (1919), letter: *Printers' Ink*, 108: p. 156.

Hirschbaum, A. (1927), "Some of the whys of Rock of Ages advertising", *Rock of Ages Magazine*, 4 (8), February: pp. 18–20.

Hower, R. (1949), *The History of an Advertising Agency: N.W. Ayer & Son at Work, 1869–1949*. Cambridge: Harvard University Press.

Little, M.R. (1998), *Sticks and Stones: Three Centuries of North Carolina Gravemarkers*, University of North Carolina Press, Chapel Hill and London.

Marchand, R. (1985), *Advertising the American Dream: Making Way for Modernity 1920–1940*, University of California Press, Berkeley, CA.

Memorial Masterpieces in Barre Granite from the Granite Centre of the World (1916). Barre: Barre Quarriers and Manufacturers Association.

Memory Stone (1927a), "Changing the name", 2 (5), April, n.p.

Memory Stone (1927b), "Looking ahead in the magazines", 2 (6), June, n.p.

Memory Stone (1927c), "The next full-color page", 3 (1), August, n.p.

Memory Stone (1927d), "The artist in Arlington", 3 (2), October, n.p.

Memory Stone (1927e), "Expanding the coupon to fill the page", 3 (3), December, n.p.

Memory Stone (1928), "New advertisements feature memorials", 3 (6), June, n.p.

Memory Stone (1932), "Dramatic story of Vermont Marble vividly told in 1932 advertising" 7 (4), February, n.p.

Monument and Cemetery Review (1918), "Items of General Interest", December: p. 70.

Monumental News (1911), "Barrie, VT. Special correspondence", January: p. 94.

Monumental News (1912a), "Twenty centuries between them", May: p. 361.

Monumental News (1912b), "New Barre Granite trademark", June: p. 494.

Monumental News (1912c), "Barre Granite Manufacturers' Association", July: p. 581.

Monumental News (1912d), "One of the Barre Granite sign posts", December: p. 990.

Nye, D. (1985) *Image Worlds: Corporate Identities at General Electric, 1890–1930*. Cambridge, MA, The MIT Press.

Printers' Ink (1919), "Elevating a trade through advertising", 108, 28 August: pp. 41–44.

The Reporter (1898), "The passing of marble", September: p. 25.

Rock of Ages Magazine (1923a), "One result of the American Plan", 1 (1), July, n.p.

Rock of Ages Magazine (1924a), "To be read by twenty million", 1 (12), June, n.p.

Rock of Ages Magazine (1924b), 2 (1), July, n.p.

Rock of Ages Magazine (1924c), 2 (2), August, n.p.

Rock of Ages Magazine (1924d), 2 (3), September, n.p.

Rock of Ages Magazine (1924e), 2 (4), "Your sales partner", October, n.p.

Rock of Ages Magazine (1924f), 2 (6), December, n.p.

Rock of Ages Magazine (1925a), 3 (1), "The Rock of Ages changes hands", July: pp. 8–10.

Rock of Ages Magazine (1925b), 3 (6), "Photos or designs": p. 18.

Rock of Ages Magazine (1926a), "More than 900,000 readers", 3 (8), February, [p. 21].

Rock of Ages Magazine (1926b), "Your half of a half-made sale", 3 (9), March: p. 14.

Rock of Ages Magazine (1926c), 3 (12), "It's the Rock of Ages Corporation", June: pp. 3–4.

Rock of Ages Magazine (1926d), "Rock of Ages painter honoured", 4 (2), August: p. 13.

Rock of Ages Magazine (1926e), "Who buys the memorial?", 4 (2), August: p. 14.

Rock of Ages Magazine (1926f), "Closing a notable series", 4 (5), November: p. 34.

Rock of Ages Magazine (1926g), "To help you sell more memorials in 1927", 4 (6), December: pp. 16–17.

Rock of Ages Magazine (1927a), "Art in advertising", February, 4 (8): pp. 21–22.

Rock of Ages Magazine (1927b), "Linking American history", 4 (8), February: p. 30.

Rock of Ages Magazine (1927c), "Both urban and rural populations", 4 (9), March: p. 29.

Rock of Ages Magazine (1927d), "Rock of Ages advertising is local", 4 (10), April: p. 28.

Rock of Ages Magazine (1927e), "How the public reacts", 5 (3), September: p. 25.

Rotundo, B. (1992), "Monumental bronze: A representative American company", in R.E. Meyer (Ed.), *Cemeteries and Gravemarkers: Voices of American Culture*, Utah State University Press, Logan, UT: pp. 264–291.

Schwartz, E. (1965), *Breakthrough Advertising*, Prentice-Hall, New York.

Sivulka, J. (1998), *Soap, Sex, and Cigarettes: A Cultural History of American Advertising*. Belmont, CA: Wadsworth.

Stott, A. (2008), *Pioneer Cemeteries: Sculpture Gardens of the Old West*, University of Nebraska Press, Lincoln, NE, and London.

Vermont Marble (1927), "National advertising in full color", 2 (4), February, n.p.

Vos, T. (2013), "Explaining the origins of the advertising agency", *American Journalism*, 30 (4): pp. 450–472.

Watkins, Julian (1949), *The 100 Greatest Advertisements* (Moore Publishing).

Wishart, C. (1911), "Address of Chas. H. Wishart", *The Reporter*, February: p. 9.

2 The marketing of a siege

Leningrad vs. Sarajevo – memorializing death and despair

Brent McKenzie and Mary Claire Bass

Introduction

A growing area of tourism interest has focused on the field of Dark Tourism, or research examining the desire for people to visit sites of death and the macabre. Although research on this topic is not new, there exists a need to better understand how to compare the "performance" of the resulting museums and memorials that have been established to commemorate these sites. For instance, previous research has studied museums that focused on specific forms of death, such as the Holocaust and genocide museums, while others examined death at battlefield sites, as well as prisons. A commonality of previous studies has been to better understand the supply and demand for such sites, particularly why formalized sites exist and why people choose to visit them. What appears to be missing from the literature is critical examination of the ways of measuring the success of the marketing and commercialization of such sites.

In order to address the gap in knowledge, this chapter wishes to extend the understanding of how dark tourism sites are marketed. This examination is taken from two perspectives. The first is to examine a specific type of memorializing, one that centres on the concept of the siege of a city. Although a siege has a direct military connection and directive, a siege also includes a greater emphasis on the impact upon the citizens and society in which these military and political actions occurred. In other words, in additional to the military deaths, a siege also includes civilian deaths, deaths that may or may not result directly from physical conflict, but also starvation, exposure to the elements, etc.

The second perspective is to better understand how the military and civilian deaths resulting from a siege are emphasized or minimized for political and economic gain by way of attractions, museums, and other revenue-generating activities. Thus this research takes a case study approach to compare and contrast how two cities with similarities in terms of death and despair in the twentieth century, by way of living through a siege. Respectively, the sieges are Leningrad (Saint Petersburg) in the then Soviet Union, now Russia, in 1941–1944 (872 days), and Sarajevo, in Bosnia and Herzegovina (previously part of Yugoslavia) from 1992–1996 (1,425 days). The research examines how these cities have "succeeded" in the commercializing of such horrific events.

To examine this question, multiple methods are employed. The first takes a secondary data approach by examining the major marketing literature related to how to best evaluate the performance, both economic and political, of sites of death and despair. The second places the two sieges within a dark tourism framework under the guise of the authenticity of the attractions as they relate to the siege. The final method presents the finding of personal interviews conducted by one of the authors with knowledge experts of this topic in Saint Petersburg (Monument to the Heroic Defenders of Leningrad) and Sarajevo (survivor of the siege). These findings are linked with the research literature to develop a greater understanding of how to best measure the commercialization of such sites. This study helps to advance the understanding of a growing field of business, the consumption of death, with ongoing political and societal debate as to the appropriateness of such sites.

Background – the Siege of Leningrad and the Siege of Sarajevo

A siege is defined as a military operation in which enemy forces surround a town or building, cutting off essential supplies, with the aim of compelling those inside to surrender (Oxford 2014). The history and details of a siege must first be understood before the methods of packaging and placement on the scale of darkness can be analysed (Stone 2006). The background of these sieges is first discussed to provide an overview of the root causes and players of the war, and the way in which the siege was lifted.[1]

The Leningrad Siege lasted 900 days, starting on September 8, 1941. It is remembered by the city as a "period full of suffering and heroism" (City of St. Petersburg 2014). Nazi Germany's goal when attacking Leningrad was to eliminate the population of and take control of the city. The root purpose of obtaining control of Leningrad was for militaristic gains. The city had a large amount of artillery camps that the Nazis could use to their advantage, and the Nazis, with the assistance of Finnish troops, encircled the city to isolate communication and starve the inhabitants of the city to death. The Leningrad Navogord strategic offensive and defensive, also known as the Red Army, protected and fought to prevent the city from falling to the enemy. Estimates suggest that there were over 600,000 fatalities directly attributed to the siege. In order to stave off starvation, strict rations of food that would equate to 125 grams of bread per person per day were required (Siege of Leningrad 2014). Ultimately, the siege was broken on January 27, 1944, when the Red Army successfully fought off the Nazis. Thus, from a strategic standpoint, the City of Leningrad was victorious in outlasting the Nazis' military aims of the siege.

In contrast, the Siege of Sarajevo is most often remembered as a site of conflict and tragedy. With the death of Marshall Josip Tito in 1980, the socialist leader of Yugoslavia, the subsequent two decades saw the breakup of

Yugoslavia into a number of independent nations. The region of Bosnia and Herzegovina declared their independence in 1992, from Yugoslavia. Almost immediately after this declaration a siege was imposed first by the Yugoslav People's army, which was made up of Serbian-Croatian forces, and then by the Army of Republika Srpska whose soldiers were predominantly Bosnian Serbs. In total, the siege lasted from April 5, 1992, until February 29, 1996. At 1,425 days, the siege of Sarajevo lasted just over 1.5 times longer than the siege of Leningrad. The strategy by the mainly ethnic Serbian forces, mirrored that of Leningrad in that the aim was to isolate the city from all communication, and access to food, with the added peril of constant snipers, due to the relative proximity of the siege line to the city, firing at those who would venture into the streets.

The result was a total of 13,952 casualties, 11,541 of which were Sarajevo civilians. Unlike the military end to the siege of Leningrad, the siege of Sarajevo cease-fire was a result of brokered agreement, officially known as the General Framework Agreement for Peace in Bosnia and Herzegovina, but commonly referred to as the Dayton Accords led by international community, and also led by the government of President Bill Clinton of the United States (Palmer and Posa 1999). The result was newly negotiated territories on the conditions that the Serbian forces would surrender Sarajevo (Šarcevic 2008). As noted by Šarcevic (2008), there has been a continued question as to what degree this ethnic conflict continues to challenge Sarajevo to this day.

The marketing of the Sieges of Leningrad and Sarajevo

As noted, Leningrad and Sarajevo are both cities that were the focus of military sieges that caused mass casualties, primarily civilian. Both cities though, are arguably better known for other events and attractions. Leningrad, formerly, and currently, known as Saint Petersburg, was founded by Czar Peter the Great and is home to many world famous museums such as the Hermitage and the Winter Palace, while Sarajevo was the site of the assassination of Archduke Franz Ferdinand (a cited contributing factor to the start of World War I) and the 1984 Winter Olympics. For this study it is their shared history as being subjected to the two most well known sieges of the twentieth century that is of interest.

From a marketing perspective, the sieges are remembered and the memorials, materials, and ephemera related to the sieges have been packaged as dark tourism sites in different ways. The siege of Leningrad has been positioned as a tourist attraction, with the primary goal of focusing on the heroes that defended and fought to protect the city from Nazi Germany. This has been accomplished by commemorating the strengths of the citizens of the city, and extensive documentation and exhibits related to preserving the memory of their role in the ultimate lifting of the siege.

Alternatively, the siege of Sarajevo has been packaged and remembered as a site of conflict between different ethnic groups, but more tellingly, it is the pain and suffering that can still be felt by the people of the city that is the focus of its existence as a site of dark tourism (Burke 2011). This can be partially attributed to the fact that in Sarajevo three ethnic groups, Serbs, Croats, and Bozniaks, influenced the start of the war, and these same groups continue to live in close proximity to one another in Sarajevo to this day. What is interesting to note is how the two cities could endure such similar military-based atrocities and be presented to tourists in intensely different ways. Furthermore, the success of packaging and commodification of both sites has influenced their success as dark tourism attractions.

The scope and framework of dark tourism

One way in which to better understand the role that the sieges play in tourist-related sites in these two cities, is by way of dark tourism categorization. It is important to grasp that dark tourism is certainly not the sole form of tourism in Leningrad and Sarajevo, but rather that by taking a dark tourism perspective there is the opportunity to utilize a "siege" as another way to advance the understanding of the realm of dark tourism research.

As noted in Stone and Sharpley (2008), dark tourism is defined as visiting "sites, attractions or events linked in one way or another with death, suffering, violence or disaster" (p. 574). Travel to dark sites is not new, but in many societies, visiting sites associated with death is, and has been a considerable part of the tourist experience; this can be seen with the existence of pilgrimage, one of the earliest forms of travel. However, the commercial marketing of such locations to encourage tourist visitations is justly debated. The term itself is credited to Lennon and Foley (2000), which itself has built from the term "thanatourism" (Seaton 1996) or the study of tourism related to death. Sites of dark tourism can be at the actual location that tragedy occurred, or a site that commemorates deaths that have occurred somewhere else (Wight 2006).

According to Dr. Philip Stone, founder of the Institute for Dark Tourism Research (http://dark-tourism.org.uk/), dark tourism sites can be classified based on a relative scale from "darkness" to "lightness". There are six levels in this scale and it incorporates the following factors: the purpose of the site; proximity to the tragedy; level of tourist infrastructure: time since the event: and manner of remembrance used at the dark tourism site (Stone 2006). The darkest site's sole purpose is to memorialize and educate, in comparison to lighter sites whose primary goal is to entertain (Stone 2006). Furthermore, the darkest sites are often considered the most authentic as they are located at the actual sites of death, while lighter sites focus more on being a tourist attraction with death being the feature that is marketed.

Authenticity and dark tourism

Although of the same ilk as Stone, the researchers Heuermann and Chhabra (2014) have focused on the scope of the authenticity of the dark tourism site.

There has been a growth in research on authenticity and heritage in tourism (Chhabra, Healy, and Stills 2003) as there is a growing interest by tourists seeking an authentic experience. Authenticity for the tourist is achieved when the attraction, or site, is as realistic as possible. Conveying authenticity is often achieved by providing the visitor with original buildings, artefacts, and sites where actual events related to death occurred (Apostolakis 2003). The research of Heuermann and Chhabra (2014) categorized the different types of authenticity as it relates to tourism in five ways. The first classification is that of an objectivist site. These sites rely on the site's actual heritage with low tourism infrastructure (Chhabbra 2010). The second level of authenticity is the constructivist site. These sites have a higher tourism infrastructure and are packaged and stylized to appeal to the general public (Heuermann and Chhabbra 2014).

The third level of authenticity is called a negotiation site, which represents a balance between objectivist simplicity and constructivist infrastructure authenticity (Chhabbra 2010). The fourth level of authenticity is called an existentialist site and these sites focus on providing a uniform front, aimed to illicit certain emotional responses and a resulting state of mind for the tourist viewing it. Finally, the last level of authenticity is named theoplacity. This classification represents a balance between the emotional aspect of existentialism and the simplicity of an objectivist site (Chhabbra 2010). As the work of Heuermann and Chhabra (2014) represents a relatively unexplored framework for analysing different types of dark tourism sites, one has the ability to classify the different siege-related tourist sites of Leningrad and Sarajevo within this scale of authenticity.

Authenticity and the Siege of Leningrad and the Siege of Sarajevo

The official tourist website of both these cities along with tourism social media sites were examined to analyse the way the cities and tourist attractions are packaged to attract tourists. The way these dark tourism sites are packaged is derived from the tourism website of the city or the individual web page of the site itself. The packaging perspective was extracted from the way the city or the site communicates the story of the siege. Tourist experiences, by way of web site postings, were used to measure the "success" of the dark tourism site and were analysed by using reviews from the site "TripAdvisor" (TripAdvisor.ca) to find common themes in positive reviews and poor reviews. This analysis thus provides data to align with Chhabbra's (2010) levels of authenticity. The analysis resulted in the classification of dark tourism sites into the two categories of authenticity labelled negotiated authenticity, and theoplacity authenticity.

Negotiated authenticity

The first sites compared and contrasted are two different museum sites in each city that are related to the sieges. They are dark tourism sites that have a negotiated authenticity. In Leningrad, The State Memorial Museum of Leningrad Defense Blockade commemorates the history of the citizens, defenders, and offensive soldiers who lived and fought through the siege (City of St. Petersburg 2014). St. Petersburg's pride in their victorious battle is seen in their description of the memorial museum, "The sacrifice and the extraordinary endurance of the survivors is etched on the conscience of the city, a source of immense pride and profound sorrow" (City of St. Petersburg 2014). Common themes among reviews by visitors to this attraction stated that it had a large emotional effect on them, and that it was a compelling site that did not sugar coat the events during this period in order to please a wider audience.

A related site in Sarajevo was the City Hall, which was destroyed during the siege and only recently re-opened. Inside the building one sees the bullets shot into the wall during the siege. The Serb forces frequently shelled the building throughout the siege. The official tourist site of Sarajevo does not define its relevance to the siege, but merely only says it was damaged when the city was under siege (City of Sarajevo 2003). Reviewers commonly stated though, that the ethnic nature of the conflict is clearly visible when visiting the City Hall.

Taken together, both of these sites have similar memorial and educational purposes for life during the sieges, but their packaging differs. Sarajevo would be relatively darker than Leningrad from the objectivist authenticity perspective as it is more dominant in the negotiated authenticity, due to the remaining shell damage at the site. Sarajevo's main tourist site does not market City Hall as a site of pride and resilience, as is the case of Leningrad's, but merely identifies it for potential visitors as a building damaged during the war.

A second set of dark tourism sites, which would be classified as dark resting places, also fall within the category of negotiated authenticity. The purpose of the Monument to Heroic Defenders of Leningrad (discussed in greater detail below) was to commemorate the heroic efforts of civilians and soldiers of the Leningrad Siege (City of St. Petersburg 2014). The related "Eternal Flame" in Sarajevo, is a memorial to all the citizens lost in the siege. Reviewers found that the site made a powerful statement about the conflict in the past, and now is a popular spot filled with important history. These sites would be identified as dark resting places because they are sites that honour the dead through memorial. But both sites are also "negotiated", because they are true memorial sites, but have had construction, such as statues at the Monument, and the creation of an "eternal flame" for those who perished during the siege.

Theoplacity authenticity

The second category of authenticity, in terms of dark tourism sites in these cities, was placed with the realm of theoplacitly authenticity. The reason being was that they provide insight to the history of the siege and attempt to bring the stories of the siege to life by creating an experience. In Leningrad, the "Histours Siege of Leningrad Battlefield" (www.histours.ru) tour takes tourists around Leningrad and tells the story of battles, death, and disaster during the siege. It also takes tourists to the road to life, which was Leningrad civilians only way of transporting in artillery and supplies during the siege.

For Sarajevo, The Sarajevo War Tunnel takes visitors to see the (www. sarajevoinsider.com) only way for Sarajevo citizens to escape the city during the siege and the only way to transport food and supplies into the city during the siege. These sites could be classified as darker than those of the Negotiated Authenticity because they are sites where actual disaster and death occurred.

Primary data collection

As noted, the sieges of Leningrad and Sarajevo can be placed within existing frameworks in terms of the authenticity of some of their dark tourism attractions. This placement and classification of sites that relate to the sieges of Leningrad and Sarajevo provide insight as to their assignment within the field of dark tourism. To compliment these findings, primary research was also explored based on interviews conducted by one of the authors with those living in the two respective cities. With respect to the siege of Leningrad, the curator of the most prominent dark tourist site of the siege of Leningrad, The Monument to the Heroic Defenders of Leningrad, was interviewed. For Sarajevo, due to the relative recent occurrence of the siege, an interview was conducted with a citizen of Sarajevo who lived through the siege. The purpose of the inclusion of this type of data for this study was to provide insights that directly relate to personal interpretations of the relativity of the respective sieges to dark tourism. For both cases a series of questions were asked with the stated aim of better understanding the sieges as sites of dark tourism.

As early as 1942 there was a desire to create a memorial to the siege of Leningrad (or blockade as it is referred to in Russia). Since the war was still going on, this was deemed impossible and it was on the 30th anniversary of the end of the siege in 1972 that several competitions to create a memorial commenced. The aim was to work with artists, sculptors, and architects on the creation of such a memorial, and on May 9, 1975 (the 30th anniversary of the end of World War II for the Soviet Union) it was determined that the site would be on a main street circle 9 km from the location of the front line. The three selected to create the memorial were an architect, a sculptor, and an artist, who all were defenders of the city. The upper part of the memorial was the first to open (see Figure 2.1). It was to be the central monument and museum about the siege. It was also the sight of annual events memorializing the siege.[2] People place flowers, bow down in remembrance, hold concerts, and conduct intellectual competitions for children to learn about the blockade.

Figure 2.1 Monument to the heroic defenders of Leningrad (Brent McKenzie).

The memorial itself is specifically designed to not just house memorabilia and materials about the siege, but also as an artistic expression. There are many symbols. The ceiling depicts the Leningrad sky during the war, and there are 900 lamps surrounding the exhibits. The 900 represents the days of the siege, and they are made from shell cartridges that fell upon the city; thus "light from the darkness of the blockade" (see Figure 2.2). This memorial is a tourist site for those outside of the Saint Petersburg area, and international tourists, but its relevance is mostly for the survivors of the siege, and their relatives.

The second interview was with a resident of Sarajevo who lived through both the War as well as the siege, and in fact was injured by shell shrapnel in her apartment. What was interesting from the interview was the focus on living through the period by creating a new "normal" or the creation of a different reality. The interviewee talked about continuing to go to University, study for exams, etc. during the siege, but that it was very hard to know

Figure 2.2 "Shell casing" lamps (Brent McKenzie).

what was going on. Because of the lack of, or inconsistent access to, electricity, any news was received by way of a car radio or the local newspaper, "Oslobodjenje" (Liberation) which managed to publish during the first two years of the siege.

As life was just day to day, because of the ongoing shelling and constant threat of snipers, there was a need to hide in closets and the interior of buildings, and even when there were some "nice moments" such as receiving UN rations and clean water, you could not dwell on them. The interviewee eventually escaped from Sarajevo through the aforementioned tunnel to the airport, and made her way to relatives who had previously escaped to Croatia. Although when meeting people who want to talk about the siege, she has a willingness to share these types of stories, but most tourists want to focus on more widely known events such as the assassination of Archduke Franz Ferdinand in 1914, and the 1984 Winter Olympics. One additional dark tourism site of interest mentioned by the interviewee, was something generally only discovered once visitors had arrived in Sarajevo. These are the cemeteries related to the siege. There are military cemeteries located right in the town (see Figure 2.3), and people often had to bury their dead wherever they could because of the ongoing conflict.

A final comment of interest was about the "awkward politics" that continue to exist in Bosnia and Herzegovina. For many there is a belief the war

Figure 2.3 Kovaci – Martyrs' memorial cemetery – Sarajevo (Tamir Mostarac – permission given by author).

is not completely over, thus challenging the creation of permanent memorial and siege-related attractions.

Discussion and conclusions

Based on this analysis of major dark tourism sites in Leningrad (Saint Peters-burg) and Sarajevo, one can conclude that these cities have packaged the sieges as memorial and dark conflict sites that fall within the scope of dark tourism. Through this analysis and research it is evident that sites in Lenin-grad are both packaged and received as sites of dark tourism where heroism occurred. For Leningrad, there is pride in remembering the soldiers who defended and fought Nazi Germany to protect their city. This packaging can be attributed to a straightforward remembrance of the protection of the "Motherland" from foreign forces. The soldiers of Leningrad were addition-ally victorious in battle and were able to fight off this enemy. This fact can help us to better understand how tourism surrounding the siege in Leningrad is packaged.

In contrast, although many of the dark tourism sites related to the siege in Sarajevo are also packaged and received as sites of conflict, they represent a more complicated interpretation and sense of remembrance. This result may be ascribed for those in Sarajevo as having lingering feelings of conflict, feelings that in comparison to those that survived the siege of Leningrad, are less unifying. This social environment as noted by Mikhailova (2014), in Bosnia and Herzegovina, has created a current state that is not at war, or at peace, but rather somewhere in between. Unlike in Leningrad, the residents of Sarajevo did not experience a clear resolution, or sense of victory resulting from the siege, since the Dayton Accord was imposed on those involved.

Consequently, it is suggested that in terms of dark tourism, Sarajevo would be viewed as a "darker" city than Saint Petersburg (Leningrad) in terms of how the siege is remembered and marketed. As noted, the level of objectivist authenticity is very high. The damage from artillery attacks can still be seen throughout the city. The tragedy that occurred within Sarajevo is communicated into the way the sites are marketed and at the tourist sites themselves. The proximity of the event to present day also results in darker experiences in comparison to the tragedies in Sarajevo, versus Leningrad, regardless of the fact the personal atrocities in Leningrad were on a much grander scale.

Thus the packaging strategies or marketing practices that exist today are influenced by the way that each of the sieges has been depicted and thus remembered. The history and story of the respective wars creates a sentiment within each city that had been besieged. In Leningrad, the victorious action of the soldiers is communicated through tourist sites and can be seen through tourist feedback provided in online sites such as TripAdvisor. In contrast, tourist feedback and commentary on these forums on the siege of Sarajevo is often conflated with the war itself. The devastation that resulted from the war is often placed within the context of more well-known tourism sites in Sarajevo, such as the locations of the 1984 Winter Olympics. From this analysis, it appears that the root causes and players in the siege, combined with the ending of the war, can influence how dark tourism sites are communicated and "packaged" into tourism experiences.

Dark tourism, as an identifiable form of tourism, has a relatively short period of existence. It can be argued that because of the ongoing debate as to the exact nature of what constitutes dark tourism, it can be considered a fragile framework. It is suggested that one of the contributions of this chapter is to continue to advance the understanding of dark tourism, through a comparative study of another site of death and destruction, the siege. Although no definitive conclusions about how the sieges of Sarajevo and Leningrad advance the understanding of the concept of dark tourism are suggested, by taking a comparative approach, does provide some key insights as to how a siege can be marketed from a dark tourism perspective. From a theoretical perspective, the comparative nature of this study advances the understanding of the role of dark tourism taxonomies and particularly for a relatively new form of classification of the role of authenticity and dark tourism as advanced by Heuermann and Chhabra (2014). Secondly, this research suggests that utilizing multiple research perspectives can add to the confidence in the classification of both the category of dark tourism, as well as the specific sites or attractions themselves.

In terms of contribution to practice, the findings of this chapter can be used by both tourism attraction providers as well as other affected stakeholders such as governmental agencies in two ways. The first is being able to better communicate the value of such sites not only in terms of historical perspectives, but also in terms of their impact on the tourism sectors in these cities today. Second, for those charged with operating, maintaining, and marketing such sites, there is a greater understanding of taking a multi-message perspective on how these sites can be made more attractive not only to visitors, but to those directly and indirectly linked to the history of the events that occurred. Future research should examine these same issues for other types of dark tourism, in other countries.

Notes

1 For a more thorough history of the siege of Leningrad one can look to "The 900 Days: The Siege of Leningrad" (Salisbury 1969). For more detail on the events of the siege of Sarajevo, look to "Sarajevo under siege: Anthropology in Wartime". (Ek 2009).
2 There are memorial events every year on September 8, 1941, start of the siege, the May 9 end of war, January 27, the end of the siege "Leningrad day of liberation" and February 23, the "Day of Defenders of Our Motherland" in honour of military personnel.

References

Apostolakis, A. (2003) "The convergence process in heritage tourism", *Annals of Tourism Research*, 30/4, pp. 795–812.

Burke, S. (2011) "Sarajevo Rose". Retrieved from www.theharvardadvocate.com.

Chhabra, D. (2010) "Back to the Past: A sub-segment of Generations Y's perceptions of authenticity", *Journal of Sustainable Tourism*, 18/6, pp. 793–809.

Chhabra, D., Healy, R., and Sills, E. (2003). "Staged Authenticity and Heritage Tourism", *Annals of Tourism Research*, 30/3, pp. 702–719.

City of Sarajevo (2014) "Tourism Association of Sarajevo Canton – The Culture and History – Unique Spirit Space". Retrieved from www.sarajevo-tourism.com/sarajevo-through-history.

City of St. Petersburg (2014) "The 900-day Siege of Leningrad". Retrieved from www.saint-petersburg.com/history/great-patriotic-war-and-siege-of-leningrad/.

Ek, I. (2009) *Sarajevo Under Siege: Anthropology in Wartime*, Philadelphia: University of Pennsylvania Press.

Heuermann, K., and Chhabra, K. (2014) "The darker side of dark tourism: An authenticity perspective", *Tourism Analysis*, 19, pp. 213–225.

Lennon, J. and Foley, M. (2000) *Dark Tourism: The Attraction of Death and Disaster*, New York: Continuum.

Mikhailova, A. (2014) "The Darkest Page of the Hermitage Museum's History". Retrieved from http://sputniknews.com/in_depth/20141108/1014517833.html.

Oxford Dictionary (2014) "Definition of a siege". Retrieved from www.oxforddic
tionaries.com/us/definition/american_english/siege.

Palmer, L. and Posa, C. (1999) "The best-laid plans: Implementation of the Dayton
Peace Accords in the courtroom and on the ground" *Harvard Human Rights Journal*,
Spring, vol. 12, pp. 361–383.

Salisbury, H. (1969) *The 900 Days: The Siege of Leningrad*, New York: Harper &
Row.

Šarcevic, E. (2008) "Bosnian Institute News: Ethnic Segregation as a Desirable Con-
stitutional Position?" Retrieved from www.bosnia.org.uk/news/news_body.cfm?
newsid=2528.

Seaton, A.V. (1996) "Guided by the dark: From thanatopsis to thanatourism", *International Journal of Heritage Studies*, 2/4, pp. 234–244.

The Siege of Leningrad (2014). Retrieved from www.historylearningsite.co.uk/world-
war-two/world-war-two-and-eastern-europe/the-siege-of-leningrad/.

Stone. P. (2006) "A dark tourism spectrum: Towards a typology of death and macabre
related tourist sites, attractions and exhibitions", *TOURISM: An Interdisciplinary
International Journal*, 54/2, pp. 145–160.

Stone, P., and Sharpley, R. (2008) "Consuming dark tourism: A thanatological
perspective", *Annals of Tourism Research*, 35/2, pp. 574–595.

Wight, C. (2006) "Philosophical praxes in dark tourism: Controversy, contention,
and the evolving paradigm", *Journal of Vacation Marketing*, 12, pp. 119–129.

3 Marketing death through erotic art

Christina Welch

This chapter will explore the recent phenomenon of erotic coffin calendar art produced to advertise funeral caskets manufactured by the Italian company *Cofani Funebri* since 2003, and the Polish company *Lindner* since 2010. The calendars of both companies were developed especially for promotion purposes and typically feature a company coffin and a scantily-dressed young woman in a sexually suggestive pose. The use of erotically posed young women is not unusual in advertising terms, and frequently such tactics are used to make goods attractive to hetero-normative men. Adverts for expensive cars, tobacco, designer clothing and aftershave typically intimate that the men who purchase the products will increase their sex appeal (Reichert and Lambert, 2003). However, the coffin calendars as a form of marketing do not seem to conform to the 'sex sells' marketing ploy; few people purchase their coffin before death, and even fewer would find this purchase increases their sexual appeal, plus one is simply never sexy when dead.

Thus, the question arises as to where calendars sit in terms of contemporary consumer culture. In exploring this issue this chapter examines the juxtaposition in these calendars of a symbol of death (a coffin) with a symbol of fecund life (a young woman erotically presented) through the notion of iconicity. Messaris has described iconicity as a form of 'persuasive communication' that stems from the emotional response elicited by presented images (1997, pp. viii–xv). Two time periods and genres of representation will be considered in relation to iconicity and the use of death to 'sell' a message.

The first time period of this chapter explores the artistic background to, and iconicity of, the coffin calendar photographs through proto- and early-Reformation artworks produced in the Death and the Maiden genre (1495–1550). It will highlight how the iconicity of these Early Modern artworks was used to emphasize concerns over mortality during a time of religious change in Europe (from Roman Catholicism to Protestantism), and then compare and contrast this with current concerns over mortality during the present period of religious change in Europe (from a period of Christian domination in public life to increased institutional secularization from the late twentieth century onwards).

The second time period examines the 1960s onwards in relation to Vidal's notion of death and desire in contemporary culture, a culture she argues is obsessed with cars and especially car-crashes. Drawing on the concept of Futurism, and the work of Bauman, and Baudrillard, she examines the 'close connections between cars and culture', and details how car crashes can be read to 'recover a certain degree of control over death' (2012, pp. 4, 17) in a culture which is largely 'death denying' (Becker, 1973).

This chapter then provides an overview of the coffin calendars themselves, an exploration of the two distinct ways in which they can be contextualized, before concluding that whilst sex sells most things, even eroticism struggles to make death palatable. It is important to note that the reading of the visual representations is based around Northern European society's historical and contemporary hetero-normative Christian-based culture. Further, sexualized and highly eroticized representations of young woman signify life and the soft-fleshiness of womanhood in its most fecund state, juxtaposed with images of death; whether a skeleton, a decomposing body, or a coffin (the modern signifier of mortality), all, by drawing on the work of Lefebvre (1991), can be read as cold, rigid and inherently phallic (Welch, 2013, p. 2).

The first company to market funeral caskets through the use of scantily-clad young women posed erotically with a company coffin was *Cofani Funebri*. Their initial foray was in 2003[1] and featured six bi-monthly photographs of angels and coffins together with life-affirming poetic cantos; five of the photographs were of women dressed as angels, and one featured a man. The images were all soft focus and mildly erotic. The cover shot of the 2003 Calendar, which was entitled 'Angels' (*sic*),[2] featured two bare-shouldered women in scarlet dresses laying on a scarlet sheet strewn with white lilies. With its birds-eye gaze, the viewer looks down on the two women in tight frocks with bare shoulders, and cleavage on show; it is not clear what the calendar is promoting. Although white lilies are often seen as a symbol of death, there are echoes of the bed of roses scene from the film *American Beauty* (1999), which juxtaposes the pale skin of a naked young woman with the scarlet of roses.[3] The hint of sexuality continues throughout the calendar although each of the six images does include a coffin. The five shots that feature women typically show them in skimpy clothing exposing large amounts of cleavage, or a lot of leg (and often both). May/June is the only poetic canto to be explicit about death. '...It is life in quest of life in bodies that fear the grave'. November/December is the page that features a male model; imaged as an angel there is little of him as a sexual body (unlike the female models). In terms of publicity, the calendar hints at death but seems more intent on flaunting female sexuality. But whatever its intent the calendar gave the company publicity with worldwide sales (Anon 2003).

The sexy-woman theme continued in the 2004 edition,[4] which retained to bi-monthly format but used Italian for the typescript. The cover image foregrounded the torso of a woman in a skimpy white bikini posed beside a coffin with a metal crucifix on the lid. January/February featured a women dressed as a schoolgirl sitting on a coffin; the coffin order details featured on this and every other page. March/April showed a young woman dressed in a company T-shirt in the act of undressing; she looks down at the crucifix on a coffin whilst her hands hold the material of her T-shirt just below her breasts. May/June featured a slightly older woman crouched beside a company coffin who looks directly at the camera, her outfit making the most of her cleavage. The remaining photographs are in the same vein and appear to advertise the women as much, if not more so, than the coffins; notably the models were the wives, friends, and/or girlfriends (WAGS) of the coffin makers (Anon, 2003; Anon, 2009).

The 2005 Calendar[5] shifted to a monthly format allowing for a cover shot and twelve photographs; there was a return to English typescript that continues into the present. This edition largely depicted models engaged in aspects of coffin manufacture. For instance, Miss July is shown holding with a chisel sitting astride an elaborately carved coffin, she is shot wearing black strappy heels, black bikini-style lingerie and an unbuttoned white shirt. Miss August, in similar garb, sits on top of a coffin and uses a power sander with her right hand, whilst her left thumb is hooked into the top of her panties, and Miss December, in a revealing black dress, drills holes into a coffin to fix a name-plaque in place. Miss April however, is shown in a crucifixion pose standing against a coffin. She wears the unbuttoned white shirt and black lingerie of her compatriots, but stands with her arms outstretched on the lid of a coffin which rests on a trestle. The coffin acts as the crosspiece of crucifixion cross, and the lighting of the scene gives it ephemeral feel. It is clear in this edition that the *Cofani Funebri* calendars are designed to shock. By erotically posing scantily-clad young women in the company of coffins, this funeral casket manufacturing firm is juxtaposing sex and death, and is unafraid to use religious symbolism to add additional layers of meaning to its annual promotional material.

The 2006 Calendar[6] has a raunchy look, and the typescript and lighting give the images a gothic feel. Several photographs depict a woman (or women) with chains (April, June), whilst others show the models by candle light. All the models are WAGS and are dressed in lingerie of varying kinds; all are posed against a company coffin. By 2007[7] there is a clear move away from the WAGS calendar, to a more professional looking marketing campaign. The cover shot to the 2007 Calendar notes a change in style by clearly stating that the photographs were taken by Maurizio Matteucci, a fashion photographer and co-owner of the company. By this stage the calendars had gained an international cult-following and whilst their effect on casket sales was negligible, they had raised the international profile of the firm (Matteucci in Anon, 2007)

The 2007 Calendar was also explicit in its connection with death. Entitled 'The Last 2 Let You Down', the photographs featured 'charming undertakers'. These undertakers were young women dressed in a black top hat with black lingerie (black heels, black hold-up stockings, and a black bra and briefs set). The shots featured a company coffin, the same for every shot, and either one or two young woman in erotic poses. The 2008 Calendar[8] reverted to the WAGS style of presentation, with the models bearing less flesh and posed in less overtly erotic positions; whereas December 2007 featured two young women seemingly caught just before a lesbian encounter (one women lay on top of a coffin whilst another bent over her), the 2008 calendar marked a brief return to the soft eroticism of the earlier editions with women in skimpy dresses leaning on coffins.

The 2009 Calendar[9] pushed at the boundaries of coffin marketing. The first calendar to be shot outdoors, every image in the 2009 edition featured a model in corsetry posed with the same casket; the side panel of the coffin engraved with the head and torso of the crucified Christ, his arms outstretched, and the head tilted slightly to the right. The cover image echoed the April 2005 photograph, and played on crucifixion imagery with the model standing in front of the coffin with her arms outstretched, the coffin again acted as the crosspiece of the crucifixion-cross. Jesus' outstretched left arm is visible on the coffin behind her, and the five stages of grief made famous by Kübler-Ross (1969) are superimposed onto the image; Denial, Depression, Acceptance, Bargaining and Anger. Four photographs take the death, Christianity and eroticism mix further.[10] April and October both show a corseted woman posed with the Jesus coffin; Miss April sits on the coffin with her legs apart fondling her breasts, Jesus' outstretched right hand points up to her crotch, and Miss October sits with her legs apart so Jesus' head is between her splayed legs. Both July and August show the models posed suggestively with a processional cross, and this unorthodox use of Christian symbolism has meant that Matteucci has kept these images for private viewing only (available by purchase); it is not entirely clear however, why these images are deemed more controversial than the posed crucifixion-style shot on the front cover, or having a carving of the crucified Christ pointing towards female genitalia.[11] Unsurprisingly though, there has been some controversy about this particular calendar (Gillies 2011).

The 2010 Calendar[12] pushed the eroticism of the imagery further still, with a Bondage and Domination (BD) theme. A male model was included in several of the photographs but he typically took the role of a gravedigger. The female models wore fetish wear, and several were chained to coffins. There was also an increase in scenes of two women engaged in, or about to engage in, BD activity giving the calendar a Swingers Club edge.[13] Given the subject matter, the coffins often took a marginal role in the photographs. The 2011 Calendar[14] included for the first time fully exposed naked breasts. Several shots echoed the previous year's fetishism theme with black vinyl clothing, and suggestions of BD, although one month (December) had a bridal theme. The coffins were again barely visible. Indeed, their role as a mere prop for glamour photography had become increasingly evident as the years had progressed.

The 2012 Calendar[15] took the marginalization of the coffin to a new level, as it did not feature a single coffin that the company sells. Titled 'La Petite

Morte', the French euphemism for an orgasm, each of the photographs showed a skeleton in a see-through Perspex coffin reacting to the suggestive actions of female models. Miss January tickles the skeleton's groin with a feather duster and he appears to giggle; it is evident the skeleton is meant to be male from the hetero-normativity of the posed scenes. Miss October holds a riding crop, and the skeleton (in an upright coffin) positions his hands over his crotch, mouth aghast in mock horror at the anticipated whipping. Miss July pleasures herself and the skeleton tries to escape his coffin, whilst Miss December, crouched over a horizontal Perspex coffin similarly touching herself, incites the skeleton to similarly masturbate; grinning broadly his bony hands are positioned where his genitals would have been.

Ten years after the first coffin calendar, the 2013 offering goes back to its roots and features angels.[16] Explicit in its portrayal of sex and death, this calendar was called '2013 Sexy Coffin Calendar' and featured for the first time a model of colour; five shots showing a Black-skinned angel with black wings, and seven shots showing Caucasian angels with white wings. There were no poetic cantos this time, but the soft eroticism of the 2003 Calendar was evident with less flesh on show, and only a minimal use of BD props such as whips and chains. This calendar effectively celebrated a decade of *Cofani Funebri* marketing death through the use of erotic art.

In 2010 another casket manufacturer entered the coffin calendar market, *Lindner* of Poland. *Lindner's* calendar was a direct response to *Cofani Funebri*, and from the start they sought to out-do the competition; the director of the Polish firm stated that, 'in Poland we manufacture the best coffins and our girls are more beautiful, so why not do better than them?' (*TVSpain.tv*, 2010). *Lindner's* calendars were in larger format and more glossy, and they went for a 'sort of Hollywood feel with a darker edge' (Lindner in Anon 2010[17]).

The 2010 *Lindner* Calendar[18] featured twelve photographs of young women in different outfits, all posed against a company coffin; a sexy bride sitting on a coffin, a farmhand in a corset hay-baling against a coffin, a gypsy in a skimpy dress pushing a coffin into the sea – each month had a story theme. It was clear that the calendar was advertising both sex and death, although some months pushed Freud's twin *eros/thanatos* (1924; 1962) theme to the limits with the female model holding a weapon; Miss April in a camouflage design bikini, strappy high heels and a army-style peaked cap, lies on top of a coffin holding a rifle; Miss June in a red tartan bikini holds a pistol as she leans against a coffin: Miss October is sat on a coffin dressed in a skimpy black one-piece resting her arm on a large sword, and Miss August stands in a hay meadow wearing a black basque holding a scythe in a Grim Reaper pose.

The 2011 Calendar[19] had a 1930s Hollywood gangster-movie theme; Miss January tries to stop a shooting; Miss March defends her stash of whiskey; May shows two women at a card table, and Miss August photographs a crime scene. Again foregrounding and juxtaposing *eros* and *thanatos*, the back cover photograph shows a couple seemingly having sex on a coffin; a woman is perched on a nature-themed funeral casket, one stockinged leg is wrapped around a man; her arms hold his waist and neck. The front cover image meanwhile shows just a woman's bottom in a frilly thong, her hands are behind her back and in one hand she holds a pistol, whilst wrapped around her wrist is a pearl bracelet with a small coffin hanging off it.

The 2012 Calendar[20] coincided with the football World Cup and each month featured a naked young woman body-painted in outfits that spoke of the competing nations; a company coffin was a prop in every shot. February's model wore a bear-skin hat and was body-painted in a skimpy representation of a Buckingham Palace guard (England); May's model was body-painted as Marilyn Monroe (USA); and September featured a model body-painted in the colors of Israel's flag. This calendar could be seen to echo the words of England footballing legend Bill Shankley, who, in 1981, stated that football was 'a matter of life and death' (in Wilson, 2012: 173).

The 2013 Calendar[21] took a surrealist turn, focusing on fantasy photo-shopped landscapes. Several images had Biblical themes such as February depicting a (Jacobs) ladder of coffins reaching into the sky, March echoing the Fall narrative with a snake wrapped around a naked woman, and September's image being reminiscent of the Tower of Babel; unsurprisingly the Polish Church spoke out (Student, 2012). November's scene had a vampiric edge showing a woman removing the heart from her male victim, and in several images, the line between fecund woman as life, and as a symbol of life and death, was blurred, as it was in the 2010 Calendar with the weaponry.

The calendars from both *Cofani Funebri* and *Lindner* have clearly been produced to market funeral caskets through the use of 'sex sells' promotion; young women in erotic clothing and poses making the coffins appealing to a male hetero-normative audience. However, the women acting as a symbol of fecund life and sex, stand in contrast to the funeral caskets, a signifier of death. As such, the calendars can be seen to stand as recent additions to the long artistic tradition of representations of death (Llewellyn, 1991; Guthke, 1999; de Pascale, 2007; Townsend, 2008). However, the use of the coffin as an allegory for death resonates with many death studies theorists, such as Walter (1991; 1994), Bauman (1992), and Davies (2002), who argued that contemporary Western society is increasingly one where death is hidden or denied. In contrast, materiality, commercialization, secularization, and the quest to hold onto youth and fecundity for as long as possible, are all aspects of a society that tries to hold onto life and living. Notably, both Poland and Italy, where the coffin calendars are produced, are traditionally Roman Catholic countries undergoing a decline in the institutional authority of the Church (Halman and Drauland, 2006). This has resulted in a change in religious observance with young Poles and Italians moving away from traditional religious practices and beliefs (Sansonetti, 2009, p. 138; Arnold, 2012, p. 204), and both countries reflecting the general modern pan-European uncertainty on what happens after death (Ipsos Mori, 2011).

In order to explore the coffin calendars as a response to dramatic shifts in society, and as a continuation of death represented in art, an examination of proto- and early-Reformation (herein proto/early Reformation) Death and the Maiden (D&M) artworks is pertinent. During this period, as previously noted, Roman Catholicism was being challenged by Protestantism and nowhere was the battleground more contested than in death and after-life beliefs. In D&M images, erotic representations of women as objects of sexual and worldly desire (*eros* and *vanitas* respectively) were juxtaposed with a signi-fier of death (*thanatos*); although, given this period of history predates the common use of coffins, death here is symbolized by a body or a skeleton.

The potent links in Western culture between *thanatos* (mortality) and *eros* (sexual desire) are long standing, and have their roots in the Biblical Fall nar-rative, but rarely, if ever, has erotica been used to sell death despite both being potent themes in artworks throughout the ages. Perhaps the closest form of promoting the importance of thinking about death (*Memento Mori*) via erotic imagery dates to the proto/early Reformation-era and a group of Northern European artists who developed the Death and the Maiden artistic genre. Here, a maiden, the signifier of this-world and material sensuality (*vanitas*), and especially the sin of concupiscence (lustful desire), stood in stark contrast to the symbol of death in the form of the Grim Reaper. The juxta-position of the two characters potently informed the early-Modern viewer that a focus on the pleasures of this-life, would likely lead to a most unpleasant after-life. This form of representation acted as a *Memento Mori* highlighting that death was inevitable and one's post-mortem place of eternal residence was decided on how one chose to lead their mortal life (Welch, 2013, p. 11).

Religion grounded the Death and the Maiden visual trope, with the key artists using their imagery to, in effect, publicize the Protestant notion that at death each person accounted for their own sins. Protestantism categorically removed the Roman Catholic post-mortem safeguard of Purgatory. In Pur-gatory, one accounted for ones own sins, but prayers could be said for the dead-in-purgatory by the living to help alleviate the pain of purgation, and indulgences purchased before death could speed up the process by which a mortal cleansed their soul before unification with God. Although the notion of Original Sin (the sin of disobedience and concomitant sexual awareness in the Fall narrative) was important in Roman Catholicism, it came to increas-ing prominence in Protestant theology, and it is that theology that permeated the proto/early Reformation D&M artworks.

Initiated by Albrecht Dürer, the proto/early Reformation D&M images typically featured death as a predatory male with the maiden somewhat ambiguous about his sexual advances. In his *Young Woman attacked by Death; or The Ravisher* (1495)[22] a young woman turns away from her ravisher (a wild looking naked man), yet her right hand lies lightly on his right arm, and she sits perched on his lap with her legs wide apart. The maiden may not embrace Death advances but she is not denying him either. This piece by Dürer's is notable as Death is not only personified in the engraving, but named in the title. Prior to this period, typical representations of death were of anonymous, featureless, ungendered skeletons or body shapes, such as those in the Three-Living/Three-Dead images, and Dance of Death murals (Welch, 2013, p. 4).

The shift in representation from an anonymous image of death to Death personified reflects the increasing importance of Augustinian theology in proto/early Reformation thought. Augustine (354–430 CE) in his work *City of God* (14:21), claimed that before the Fall of Adam and Eve from the Garden of Eden, sexual intercourse would have occurred without concupiscence, and therefore Eve, despite bearing children to Adam, would have remained a virgin; lustful sex rather than procreative sex was therefore sinful. He also argued that the sin of disobedience came from eating the fruit of The Tree of Knowledge of Good and Evil, and that it was this sin that brought lust and death to the human condition. He noted that Genesis 3:17–19 situates Adam as entirely responsible for bringing death into the world (13:23)[23]; through his disobedience, we return to dust after a life of toil. Meanwhile, Augustine noted that biblically Eve was linked with lust as she encouraged Adam to eat of, and give into his desire for, the forbidden fruit; for this sin she was punished with painful childbirth and concupiscence for her husband (Gen 3:16). Thus, in the proto/early Reformation, a dualistic mode of thinking equated Adam as male with death, and Eve as female with life and lust.

In Europe at this time, women were typically perceived as signifiers of wantoning, of pleasure, and the 'unruly' (Purkiss, 1992, p. 74, 78); strongly associated with concupiscence, females were generally regarded as dangerous. Luther (commonly considered the father of the Reformation) firmly believing only sex within marriage was blessed (1995, vol. 1: 134), any non-marital sex (including homosexual relations) was deemed depraved, and therefore bad for one's soul, family and honor (1966, vol. 44: 8).[24] Further, whilst sexual desire was natural and God-given (Gen 1:28), concupiscence was sinful, and unmarried women, as autonomous females, were considered especially dangerous by those of Reformist persuasions (Wiesner-Hanks, 2000, p. 64). This understanding of women is clear in two proto/early Reformation artworks.

In 1517 Niklaus Manuel (Deutsch) (c. 1484–1530) engraved *Der Tod und Das Mädchen* (Death and the Maiden)[25] which powerfully clarifies his feelings toward worldliness, and pedagogically situates the vanity of beauty and the sin of lust. Death (as a rotting body) is depicted ravishing a young woman; he is kissing the maiden, his hand holding up her baroque-style dress to display her bare legs and the playful garter-ribbons at her knees, she meanwhile is holding his decomposing hand at her genitals. The image is an allegory; humanity may have its tempting earthly pleasures, but at death we must each account for our sins before God. This theme is echoed in an engraving by Hans Sebald Beham entitled *Three Nude Women and Death* (1546–1550),[26] Death is depicted as a leering skeleton staring wide-eyed at a ritual of female mutual masturbation. Although skeletal, Death is clearly male and the engraving shows the circle of life (youth, maturity, old age and death), whilst didactically representing women as signifiers of unnatural fleshly desire.

The engravings of Niklaus Manuel and Sebam Beham inform visually, that it is to the after-life, not this-life, that one should turn one's attentions. That the images are so pornographic is deliberate. They potently resonate with Messaris' notion of iconicity, an artistic trope designed to stimulate the 'lustful thoughts [they] supposedly [were] intended to discourage' (Sekules, 2001, p. 170). Only by engaging the viewer in body and mind, could the soul take precedence and ensure that it was heavenly, not earthly, pleasures, which were the center of one's lived experience.

Thus, the D&M imagery of the proto/early-Reformation sought to foreground the after-life by utilizing the fecund maiden as a negative symbol of this-life, with its immoral sensuality (*eros*), materiality (*vanitas*), and concupiscence, with Death acting as a potent signifier of one's accepted mortality. However, the coffin calendars in contrast foreground this: life, utilizing the maiden as a positive symbol of earthly sensuality, materiality and concupiscence. Where proto/early Reformation society discouraged *vanitas*, contemporary society embraced it. Death now signified by a coffin, the current acceptable signifier of one's unacceptable mortality is just a prop, a background to physical pleasures of this-life. Although both D&M images exploit iconicity, where once they reminded the viewer to be careful of the pleasures of this-life as an eternal after-life beckoned, today the pleasures of this-life are celebrated, for as part of the outcome of secularization, religious notions of the after-life hold less sway.

However, the coffin calendars can also be explored through the lens of Futurism. Vidal notes that 'Futurist visions were quite close to our contemporary reality when it comes to the close connection between cars and culture' (2013, p. 4). This has certainly been the case in terms of advertising with, since the 1960s, a notable rise in the linking of sexuality and desirability with automobiles (Lewis and Goldstein, 1983; Bayley, 1986; Stevenson, 2004). As Bishop notes:

> We are all familiar with scantily clad women in ads for ... cars ... for the most part these ads are aimed at straight males and the stereotypical sexy woman – sexy, that is, in the minds and fantasies of straight males ... huge breasts, clad only in a bikini and posed in a sexually suggestive fashion.
>
> (2012, p. 130)

The link between the marketing of cars with sex, and the marketing of funeral caskets with sex is evident in both the *Cofani Funebri* and *Lindner* calendars. However, a deeper connection between the calendars and contemporary culture is evident through Futurism's notion 'to conquer and dominate nature', and through the movements rejection of emotional sentimentality and otherworldliness (Vidal, 2013, p. 13). Death is part of nature, and just as Futurism sought to conquer, if not death itself, then the fear of death, by an appeals to technology, the industrial, and youth, these calendars do likewise. As Walter has noted, with the advent of modern culture, death has become increasingly professionalized (1994, p. 48). Funeral directors have largely taken over from priests as figures of authority for all things death-related, and, as a consequence, death has become increasing privatized and industrialized. The otherworldliness of clerical rites for the dead, and the emotional sentimentality of a personal contact with the deceased, have typically been replaced by bureaucratic formalities, and a coffin replacing the corpse as the focus of attention. Death in modern times has become imbued with the tenets of Futurism.

Vidal draws on two specific theorists to argue that Futurism has allowed modern society 'to recover a certain degree of control over death' (2013, p. 17). She draws on Bauman's (1992) notion that cultural creativity is a force driven by the knowledge that humanity is mortal, and in creating endlessly, life becomes a 'string of evanescent moments where nothing lasts' (Vidal, 2013 p. 164). With nothing immortal, the mortal has no meaning, and thus for Bauman, whilst we are 'busy making life … preserv[ing] the past and creat[ing] the future', we are busy denying death (Bauman, 1992, p. 170). For Bauman, death is defied through the 'counter-mnemotechnic … of culture' (1992, p. 31) with culture acting as a device to forget mortality. Baudrillard too, Vidal notes, sees an increasing denial of death in modern culture, although he takes a different perspective (2013, p. 164). Rather than forgetting death by creating culture, Baudrillard argues that as society has moved away from symbolic ceremonies, death becomes devoid of meaning, an anomaly, even an abnormality (1993, p. 126). As death and dying rituals have become disconnected from their traditional religious roots (Walter, 1994, p. 48), and funerals increasingly echo Futurism, modern society it seems pushes ever harder to deny death, and the coffin calendars echo this notion with their inherent foregrounding of *vanitas*.

Vidal pushes her Futurism argument further though, and notes that Futurism was fascinated by the phenomenon of the car crash, and captivated by speed. With Futurism's ambition to dominate nature, speed and the crashed car, she argues, has great symbolic value (2013, p. 17). For Vidal, speed defies natural limits (2013, p. 159) and with its testosterone-fuelled inferences, driving cars fast denotes sexual arousal (Bayley, 1986, p. 77). The link between the car and masculinity has been powerfully expressed by Lefebvre who understood cars as inherently phallic objects through his notion of abstract space where cars were 'extensions of the body' (1991, p. 50), acting as an 'objectal "absolute" … symbolising force, male fertility, [and] masculine violence' (1991, p. 287).

With cars then a phallic symbol, signifying hardness, aggression, and power, even power over nature through speed and technology, the car crash/crashed car acts potently as a symbol of Futurism's desire 'to recover a certain degree of control over death' (2013, p. 17); death is not brought about by natural causes in a car crash, but through human-created technology. The potent link between violence, even death, brought about by technology appeared as a plot-line in Zola's *The Human Beast* (1890), but the link between sexual arousal and violence has a long history, and was integral to the philosophy of de Sade (1740–1814) (Clack, 2002, p. 82). Notably, since 1929, studies have noted how violence, especially the violence of car crashes, has been known to effect sexual arousal in men (2013, p. 141), and Vidal argues that the novel (1973) and film (2004) *Crash* take this to its extreme. Vidal sees as a heady mix of sex and death in the symbol of the car, with speed and the car crash resonating with the ideals of Futurism.

The link between the Futuristic phallic car and the coffin are clear; both are rigid, industrial, and connected with death and violence. Not only are both objects expressions of cultural creativity, but both are items deliberately designed to obscure the natural processes of the world. Thus both aid humanity in providing some control over the natural processes of this world, including death. A car allows the driver to toy with death, surviving death or bringing death prematurely; vast numbers of deaths are brought about by road traffic accidents (WHO 2013). It is perhaps no surprise then that just as cars are advertised through appeals to sex, promoted by fecund women, erotically dressed and provocatively posed, that modern society, with its increased attempts to deny death, should find companies marketing coffins likewise. The calendars with their overtly sexy models and this-life remit, speak of Futurism's desire to control, if not death itself, then the reality of death. The calendars resonate with the Futuristic desire of technologically triumphing over mortality; like automobile advertising, the calendar images are designed to impart the importance of earthly pleasures. They promote sensuality, fecundity and human creativity, they highlight the erotic and the life-giving, they resonate with *vanitas* and *eros*. Yet death is an ever-present reality even in these contemporary calendars, which note that *thanatos* drives us onwards to make the most of this-life, especially in a time when understandings of the next-life are ambiguous.

This chapter then has explored the erotic coffin calendars in terms of Death and the Maiden art, and argued that the contemporary coffin calendar D&M images reverse the usual artistic trope of *Memento Mori* – remember you will die. They draw on the proto/early Reformation genre that, through the use of iconicity, reminded viewers to live this-life with their after-life destination in mind. But in their modern context, the coffin calendar D&M works, reflect contemporary society's view that one should live this-life with little thought to one's demise. It has also examined the coffin calendars through the lens of Futurism. Drawing on Vidal's analysis of cars and car crashes, these unusual marketing ploys echo much of Futurism's desire to control, as much as possible, death. Both Bauman and Baudrillard have argued that modern society is death denying, and these coffin calendars resonate strongly with this sentiment; death in the modern Western world is marginalized, whilst fecund life is foregrounded. Yet, notably only two of

Europe's funeral casket companies market their products in this manner, and thus it must be remembered that despite their advertising to a consumer culture-driven society where sex sells, even eroticism struggles to make death widely palatable.

Notes

1 See www.trovatuttoedicola.it/index.php?mod=calendari&act=show_calendario& c=2&id=43 (last accessed 24 November 2014).
2 Despite being an Italian calendar, the cover title, the month names and the poetic cantos were all in English.
3 For an image of the bed of roses scene from American Beauty (1999) see http:// media-cache-ec0.pinimg.com/736x/a0/ab/ca/a0abcadd317eba1c1e736a5ad11c-fe5e.jpg.
4 See www.trovatuttoedicola.it/index.php?mod=calendari&act=show_calendario_ mese&id=462 (last accessed 24 November 2014).
5 See www.qnm.it/bellezze/calendari/calendari_2005/calendario_cofani_funebri_2005/ (last accessed 24 November 2014).
6 See www.qnm.it/bellezze/calendari/calendari_2006/calendario_cofani_funebri_2006/ (last accessed 24 November 2014).
7 See http://calendari.excite.it/2007/donne/cofani (last accessed 24 November 2014).
8 See http://calendari.excite.it/2008/donne/cofanifunebri (last accessed 24 November 2014).
9 See http://ww2.arezzoweb.it/calendari/calendario.asp?calendario=2009_cofani_ funebri (last accessed 24 November 2014).
10 All bar the two offensive months are available to view here www.trovatuttoedicola. it/index.php?mod=calendari&act=show_calendario_mese&id=368 (last accessed 1 October 2014).
11 Despite the 2005 and 2009 calendars clearly drawing on religious symbolism, in 2011 Matteucci claimed that any form of censorship of the calendars was inappropriate as religious imagery was not present – see https://mysendoff.com/2011/08/ selling-death-with-sex-appeal/.
12 See http://foto.ilgazzettino.it/italia/calendario-cofani-funebri-2010-foto-da-cofanifunebri.com/7–3812.shtml (last accessed 24 November 2014).
13 Rome, where *Cofani Funebri* are based, has a Swingers Venue called Flirt, where couples can wear fetish gear and/or engage in BD activity with like-minded others; Vanilla Alternatives in the UK, Fun For Two in the Netherlands, and Lava Club in Poland are just three of the many similar clubs across Europe. Matteucci has a Gothic edge to his so-called 'pre-mortem' photography and as can be seen from his portfolio (www.fotocommunity.it/fotografo/matteucci-maurizio/foto/ 1760123) there is an overlap between these adult clubs and his photographic interests. His models frequently wear fetish style clothing, and are often posed in situations reminiscent of adult sexual behaviour.
14 See www.qnm.it/bellezze/calendari/calendari_2011/calendario_cofani_funebri_2011/ (last accessed 24 November 2014).
15 See http://ww2.arezzoweb.it/calendari/calendario.asp?calendario=2012_cofanifu-nebri (last accessed 24 November 2014).
16 See http://mag.sky.it/mag/life_style/photogallery/2012/10/15/calendario_belle_e_ bare_2013.html (last accessed 24 November 2014).
17 Interestingly the images used to illustrate this story about *Lindner* are from the *Cofani Funebri* calendar; it would seem that sex and death might bring publicity to

the coffin calendar companies but only on a homogenous level – there are several examples where the images from the competitor calendar are used.

18 See www.kalendarzlindner.pl/2010-en/ (last accessed 24 November 2014).
19 See www.kalendarzlindner.pl/2011-en/ (last accessed 24 November 2014).
20 See www.kalendarzlindner.pl/2012-en/ (last accessed 24 November 2014).
21 See www.kalendarzlindner.pl/2013-en/ (last accessed 24 November 2014).
22 See www.wikiart.org/en/albrecht-durer/young-woman-attacked-by-death-1495 (accessed 24 November 2014).
23 For a fuller exploration of Augustine on sin, sex, and death, see Clack, 2002, pp. 21–37.
24 See Reggio (2012) for further details on Luther on marriage.
25 See *Der Tod und Das Mädchen* (Deutsch 1517) http://commons.wikimedia.org/wiki/File:Niklaus_Manuel_Deutsch_003.jpg (Last accessed 24 November 2014).
26 Hans Sebald Beham reworked (in 1546–50) a woodcut by his brother Bartel http://commons.wikimedia.org/wiki/File:Death_and_Three_Nude_Women.jpg (Last accessed 24 November 2014).

Bibliography

Anon. (2003) 'Mortician sexes up death with racy coffin calendar', *Taipei Times*, 3 November 2003 www.taipeitimes.com/News/feat/archives/2003/11/03/2003074485 (last accessed 24 November 2014).

Anon. (2010) 'Topless coffin calendar sparks controversy in Polish church' *Metro online* 5 November 2010 http://metro.co.uk/2010/11/05/drop-dead-gorgeous-calendar-sparks-controversy-in-polish-church-572108/ (last accessed 24 November 2014).

Arnold, M. (2012) 'How does religion matter in Poland today? Secularisation in Europe and the "Causa Polinia Semper Fedelis"'. In Malik, A. and Przemysław, Ł. (eds.) *Europe and America in the Mirror: culture, economy, and history*. Krakow: NOMOS 199–238.

Augustine. A. (1998 [*c*.413]) *City of God* (translated by R.W. Dyson). Cambridge: Cambridge University Press.

Baudrillard, J. (1993) *Symbolic Exchange and Death* (translated by I.H. Grant). London: Sage.

Bauman, Z. (1992) 'Survival as a Social Construct', *Theory, Culture and Society*, 9 (1), 1–36.

Bayley, S. (1986) *Sex, Drink and Fast Cars: the creation and consumption of images*. London: Faber & Faber.

Becker, E. (1973) *The Denial of Death*. New York: Free Press.

Bishop, J.D. (2012) 'Advertising Ethics'. In Shaw, L. (exec. Ed.) *A Brief Guide to Marketing Ethics*. London: Sage: 122–136.

Clack, B. (2002) *Sex and Death: a reappraisal of human mortality*. Cambridge: Polity.

De Pascale, E. (2007) *Death and Resurrection in Art* (translated by Shugaar, A.). Los Angeles: Getty Publications.

Davies, D. (2002) *Death, Ritual and Belief: the rhetoric of funeral rites*. London: Continuum.

Freud, S. (1924) *Beyond the Pleasure Principle*. New York: Boni and Liveright.

Freud, S. (1962) *The Ego and the Id*. New York: W.W. Norton.

Gillies, M. (2011) 'Selling Death with Sex Appeal' *Mysendoff.com*, August 2011 https://mysendoff.com/2011/08/selling-death-with-sex-appeal/ (last accessed 24 November 2014).

Guthke, K.S. (1999) *The Gender of Death: a cultural history in art and literature*. Cambridge: Cambridge University Press.

Halman, L. and Draulans, V. (2006). 'How Secular is Europe?' *British Journal of Sociology*, 57 (2), 263–288.

Ipsos Mori. (2011) *Views on Globalisation and Faith*. https://www.ipsos-mori.com/Assets/Docs/News/ipsos-global-advisor-views-on-globalisation-and-faith.pdf (last accessed 24 November 2014).

Janusz. (2010) 'Sexy video trip to the afterlife in Lindner coffins' *TVSpain.tv* 22 November 2010 www.tvspain.tv/blog/?p=2706 (last accessed 24 November 2014).

Kübler-Ross, E. (1969) *On Death and Dying*. New York: Macmillan.

Lefebvre, H. (1991) *The Production of Space*. Oxford: Blackwell.

Lewis, D.L. and Goldstein, L. (eds.) (1983) *The Automobile and American Culture*. Michigan: University of Michigan Press.

Llewellyn, N. (1991) *The Art of Death: visual culture in the English death ritual, c.1500–1800*. London: Reaktion Books.

Luther, M. (1966). 'Christian in society I'. In Atkinson, J. (ed.) *Luther's Works Vol. 44*. Minneapolis, MN: Augsburg Fortress Press.

Luther, M. (1995) 'Lectures on Genesis 1–5'. In Pelikan, J. (ed.) *Luther's Works Vol. 1*. Minneapolis, MN: Augsburg Fortress Press.

Messaris, P. (1997) *Visual Persuasion: The role of images in advertising*. London: Sage.

Purkiss, D. (1992) 'Material Girls: the seventeenth century woman debate' In Brant, C. and Purkiss, D. (eds.) *Women, Text and Histories, 1575–1760*. London: Routledge; 69–100.

Reichert, T., and Lambert, J. (eds.) (2003) *Sex in Advertising: perspectives on the erotic appeal*. Mahwah, N.J.: Lawrence Erlbaum.

Sansonetti, S. (2009) 'Social indicators of secularisation in Italy'. In Kosmin, B.A. and Keysar, A. (eds.) *Secularism, Women and the State: the Mediterranean world in the 21st century*. Hartford, CT: ISSSC: 137–153.

Sekules, V. (2001) *Medieval Art*. Oxford: Oxford University Press.

Stevenson, H. (2004) *British Car Advertising of the 1960s*. Jefferson: McFarland & Co. Inc.

Student, J. (2012) 'Church angry at Polish coffin maker's use of topless models in calendar' *GuySpeed* 3 November 2012. http://guyspeed.com/church-angry-at-polish-coffin-makers-use-of-topless-models-in-calendar/ (last accessed 24 November 2014).

Townsend, C. (2008) *Art and Death*. London: I.B. Tauris.

TVSpain.tv (2010) '*Sexy video trip to the afterlife in Lindner coffins*', 22 November 2010 www.tvspain.tv/blog/?p=2706 (last accessed 24 November 2014).

Vidal, R. (2013) *Death and Desire in Car Crash Culture: a century of romantic Futurisms*. Oxford: Peter Lang.

Walter, T. (1991) 'Modern death: taboo or not taboo?' *Sociology*, 25 (2), 293–310.

Walter, T. (1994) *The Revival of Death*. London: Routledge.

Welch, C. (2014) 'Death and the erotic woman; the European gendering of mortality in times of major religious change'. *Journal of Gender Studies*: 1–20. www.tandfonline.com/loi/cjgs20 (last accessed 24 November 2014).

Weisner-Hanks, M.E. (2000) *Christianity and Sexuality in the Early Modern World: regulating desire, reforming practice*. London: Routledge.

WHO (2013) Global Status Report on Road Safety 2013. www.who.int/violence_injury_prevention/road_safety_status/2013/en/ (last accessed 24 November 2014).

Wilson, M, R. (2012) 'Anxiety: Attention, the Brain, the Body, and Performance'. In Murphy, S. (ed.) *The Oxford Handbook of Sport and Performance Psychology*. Oxford; OU Press: 173–190.

4 Authenticity, informality and privacy in contemporary New Zealand post-mortem practices

Cyril Schäfer and Ruth McManus

Introduction

Personalised funerals have emerged as a global post-mortem trend in recent decades. While substantive national and regional variations in these mortuary practices exist, personalised, celebratory rituals are typically correlated with late-modern processes of secularisation and individualisation. These funerals are integrally linked to the biography and personality of the deceased and accentuate informality and mourner participation. Frequently juxtaposed with the traditional religious practices of the past, personalised funerals are described as creative productions that offer mourners a more therapeutic bereavement experience. This shift to new ritualisations of death has been associated with an increasing variety of funeral products and services that underscore personal choice, control and identity.

This chapter elucidates some of these mortuary transformations and specifically assesses the current shift to increasingly private responses to death in New Zealand, which problematise some of the simplistic connections between individualism, capitalism and funeral options (Dickinson 2012). By analysing funeral professional discourse, as well as media representations of personalisation, we argue that these discussions of contemporary funerary practices frequently elide the experiences of the bereaved and privilege a discursive construction of society that equates these putative changes with more enlightened (and "healthy") attitudes to death in the twenty-first century. Bereaved participants in this project, on the other hand, mobilised a competing discourse which recognised not cultural and societal mourning obligations, but privileged authenticity and privacy as key concerns shaping funerary practices. Rather than consuming funereal goods and services as symbolic and experiential products (Sanders 2010: 64) or linking consumption to immortality ideologies (Turley 2005), bereaved participants emphasised a desire to resist post-mortem products and services which they regarded as incompatible with biographical authenticity.

Personalisation and the ethos of openness

Much of the current literature examining the process of personalisation in North America, Europe and Australasia emphasises that funerary practices have undergone a remarkable transformation in the last three decades. In his study of funeral practices in the United States, Rasmussen (2007: 16), for example, asserts that there has been a proliferation of personalised funeral options, noting that the term "life appreciation" is indicative of a trend to preserve the peculiarities of mourners and the deceased. Garces-Foley and Holcomb (2006) emphasise that these new rituals not only express personal values and beliefs, but that they allow for active mourner engagement and the reinforcement of community bonds. Kearl and Jabobsen (2013: 74) describe these personalised celebrations as "therapeutic entertainment" that assesses post-mortem biographies as measures of completeness. In addition to accentuating the individuality of the deceased and the progression to personal expression (Roberts 2010), these celebrations can also be productively linked to the transformation and wellbeing of mourners, who – in their co-creation of post-mortem memories – affirm the continuing significance of social relationships in the face of death (Long and Buehring 2013: 97). While some authors have argued that personalised constructions indicate a certain death denial or grief avoidance (Ramshaw 2010), significant shrift has reiterated the meaningful and empowering characteristic of personalised funerary forms. These changes are typically juxtaposed not only with the impersonal religious practices of earlier periods, but also the bureaucratic medicalisation of death and dying in the twentieth century. Rather than the sequestration intrinsically associated with the modern depersonalisation and over-professionalisation of death (Dickinson 2012), celebratory rituals can be located in a framework of neo-modern death that prioritises self-determination and control (Staudt 2014). These changes similarly reflect a death revival (Dickinson 2012: 152) that signals increasing engagement with questions of mortality and prioritises the emotional needs of the living (Wilce 2009).

Researchers in UK and Europe have observed a similar shift to celebratory rituals. In a study of Scottish funeral practices, for example, Caswell (2011) stipulates that these post-mortem rituals feature references to the life and personality of the deceased and provide scope for mourner involvement in funeral arrangements. She goes on to note, however, that representations of this shift to personalisation frequently obscures the complex realities of funeral construction and that contemporary rituals continue to demonstrate a significant degree of standardisation. An English study by Holloway *et al.* (2013: 50) elucidates this assessment and reveals that rather than a simplistic post-modern plethora of post-mortem opportunities, contemporary funerals represent psycho-social-spiritual events that demand "the active participation by all actors in the co-creation and enacting of the funeral as a meaningful event". Similar themes have been expounded on other parts of Europe. Winkel (2001: 75), for example, states that individuality in the funeral context is inextricably linked to the involvement of friends and relatives and that this shift is itself related to an emerging emotionalisation and psychologisation of the self in German society. While such analyses have accentuated the processes of meaning-making, other European studies have reiterated the continuing significance of funeral professionals in the collaborative construction of rituals. In their assessment of Dutch mortuary traditions, Venbrux, Peelen and Altena (2009) assert that increasingly informal approaches to death have been accompanied by a concomitant proliferation of death specialists offering a bricolage of post-mortem services.

Authors exploring Australasian funeral practices have noted similar transformations. Jalland (2006) has traced the history of death and grief in Australia, noting that a new form of expressive emotionality has accompanied the diverse rituals that emerged in the twentieth century. Other authors have equated secularisation and individualisation with a loss of meaningful, communal ritual. Crouch (2004: 135), for example, has asserted that celebratory rituals avoid the realities of death and instead provide a superficial construction, which "merely papers over the fragmentation of our existence, our terror and ignorance of death, and our inability to accept the actuality … of suffering and pain". Such critiques frequently draw on the seminal work of scholars such as Gorer (1965) and Aries (1974), who argue that death in the modern era was denied or taboo. In the New Zealand context these death-denying attitudes have been reiterated by authors such as Schwass (2005), who accentuate an increasing unfamiliarity with death. Other authors such as Thomas (2013) have outlined some of the fundamental differences between Maori and Pakeha (non-Maori inhabitants of European descent) approaches to death, emphasising that Maori death is traditionally a public event characterised by openly expressed grief, while Pakeha practices typically prioritise privacy. Assessments such as those by Crouch (2004) and Schwass (2005), however, fail to expound on the complexities of funeral change and the various tensions inherent in the personalisation process. While funeral experts typically emphasise creativity, individuality and the realisation of an efficacious grief process (Schäfer 2012), bereaved families focus on negotiating inimical funeral expectations and composing an appropriate post-mortem biography of the dead.

Significant for this chapter exploring funerary practices is that these changes are occurring against a wider revival of death, or what Wilce (2009) terms a "bereavement movement". The media is filled with features acclaiming a new ethos of openness transforming death-related practices, while a plethora of internet sites proclaim a new awareness and democratisation of death. The prominent themes in this discourse are the diversity of contemporary funeral options accompanied by a new attitude to death typified by honesty and transparency. As this chapter will demonstrate, this attitude is itself a discursive construction (Frith *et al.* 2013) that emphasises a particular form of responsibilisation and model of grief that is not entirely consistent with the assessments proffered by bereaved participants. Ethnographic interviews similarly revealed that these putative changes do not capture the complexity of contemporary funerals and that bereaved participants articulated a discourse of resistance that critically evaluated the relevance of post-mortem products and services, as well as predominant models of bereavement, and emphasised instead the overarching desire for authenticity.

Methodological note

The themes presented in this chapter emerged from 65 qualitative, semi-structured, ethnographic interviews conducted around New Zealand. The interview component was complemented by participant observation at a number of funeral homes and funeral professional conferences over a two-year period (2012–2014). A purposive sampling approach was implemented to ensure data saturation (Guest *et al.* 2006), as well as socio-economic, religious and ethnic variability. The present project includes participants from a range of socio-economic and ethnic backgrounds, including gentrified urban neighbourhoods, underprivileged rural communities and cosmopolitan city suburbs. Participants came from a variety of personal and religious backgrounds, with the majority (85 per cent) identifying themselves as non-religious or secular. The study included 42 bereaved individuals (33 Pakeha, five Maori, two Pacific Islander and two Asian), as well as clergy, celebrants, funeral directors and funeral service providers (23). The majority of participants were female (42), with most bereaved participants involved in post-mortem arrangements for older parents or partners. Although not suggesting that the participants in the study are representative of the entire New Zealand population, it is possible to claim with some confidence that the views presented are typical and demonstrate a significant degree of homogeneity.

Informed by a grounded theory approach (Charmaz 2006; Adamson and Holloway 2012), the analytical aim of this project was to decipher potential patterns and diversities in the ways in which people organise and negotiate post-mortem arrangements and assess the personalisation process. The constant comparative method was used to examine similarities and differences in participant responses and the research data was coded using systematic, computer assisted qualitative data analysis software (*Atlas.ti*). Initial inductive, line-by-line coding was followed by focused coding and the elaboration of analytically significant themes. The codes were clustered into categories, and memos were generated to document code definitions, relationships between codes and the emerging themes that form the basis of the ensuing discussion.

Responsibility, cost and funeral options

Even a cursory assessment of the aforementioned "episteme of death" (Staudt 2014: 13), or death revivalism promoting an enlightened approach to mortality, reveals a number of substantive contextual issues relevant to the ensuing evaluation. One clear theme in this discourse is the connection between funeral options, openness, cost and responsibility. The media is replete with reports describing idiosyncratic instances of personalisation represented as exemplifying a new attitude to death and dying. These stories reiterate the shift to individualised, celebratory practices and underscore the variety of funeral options currently available in New Zealand (for example, Arnold 2012; Heather 2014, Chapman and O'Neil 2014; Harvey 2012; Carville 2013). In addition to emphasising that personalised practices signify a substantive societal shift, media reports frequently focus on calls to demystify death, drawing on earlier, traditional (as well as indigenous) practices that incorporated a prosaic familiarity with mortality. This theme is particularly prevalent in reports describing developments such as the Death Café[1] which provide fora for people to "confront" mortality and consider funerary options (Colvin 2013).

Funeral options and the possibilities of participating in post-mortem identity construction are also evident in the increasing number of pre-planning internet sites and software applications. Sites such as www.mywonderfullife. com, for example, provide an online service that enables individuals to plan and personalise funerals to reflect the life and wishes of the arranger, while www.finalfling.com offers "life planning tools" for people who prefer to "be in control of life and death decisions". A comparable New Zealand site (www.bettersendoff.co.nz) provides a range of resources to allow people to personalise funeral rituals. Funeral pre-planning and memorialisation applications such as "iFuneral" and "Legacy Organiser", as well as innumerable funeral director apps and websites, emphasise that pre-planning relieves bereaved families of further anxiety and stress, while ensuring that the preferences and funeral options of an individual are clearly articulated before death.

Explicit in many of these accounts is the association between funerals, finances and post-mortem planning. Although funeral costs and the more recent corporatisation of the funeral industry have long been the subject of media critiques and exposés (McManus and Schäfer 2014), the contemporary reports emphasise the need for individuals to assume a significant degree of personal responsibility for post-mortem preparations. Emotive news stories proclaiming that a significant number of New Zealanders are "too poor to die" (Stock 2012) are interspersed with stories that stipulate the need to openly discuss funeral arrangements and costs (for example, Meadows 2013; Simpson 2014; O'Sullivan 2014). Such discussions are described as promoting autonomy, preventing irrational funeral expenditure, and alleviating potential financial burdens for the living. These expressions emphasising the need to confront the societal "death taboo" are accompanied by concomitant stories highlighting the plight of unprepared or destitute individuals unable to afford rudimentary funeral arrangements. One illustrative example includes a news story reporting the difficulties of a pensioner forced to leave his rented accommodation after spending his limited savings on a funeral for his wife (Blundell 2014). This story generated hundreds of reader comments balanced between frustration at perceived funeral director esurience, and incredulity that the pensioner had not saved or prudently planned his funeral finances.

These discussions of funeral costs and arrangements were framed as demanding a certain degree of effort and honesty. In one media story about pre-planning, for example, the CEO of the Funeral Directors Association of New Zealand was reported as stating that a "combination of poor financial literacy and an unwillingness to talk about death" contributed to the very small number of people who had arranged funeral insurance or set aside adequate finances to pre-fund funerals (Stock 2014). Such media examples also resonate with the writings of a number of academics who have recently emphasised that a paucity of post-mortem pre-arrangements is problematic, and emphasised the need for a "culture of financially preparing for death" (Valentine and Woodthorpe 2013; Woodthorpe 2014). As Frith *et al.* (2013: 429) have noted in their discussion of media representations of dying in Britain, such representations constitute instructional tales that privilege autonomy and consumer choice, and further, that planning post-mortem pre-arrangements can be "taken as indicative of the person's moral strength of character". Conway (2013) reiterates that control associated with death and dying reflects a late modern emphasis on self and individual autonomy but that this portrayal of post-mortem practices privileges a particular cultural experience that is not universally relevant.[2]

A second substantive factor alluded to in the aforementioned discussion is the role of the funeral professionals. Although alternative funeral services (such as DIY services and direct disposal funeral providers) are affecting the provision of conventional funeral services in New Zealand, most people continue to utilise the services of funeral professionals (funeral directors and celebrants). Funeral expert discourse emphasises a need for honesty, sincerity and transparency in the construction of post-mortem arrangements. This honesty and openness applies not only to discussions of death and funeral pre-arrangement, but assessments of grief and mourning. Funeral professionals in our project emphasised the significance of genuine emotion and the need to elicit appropriate emotional expression for the realisation of a healthy grief process, and this process was itself integrally linked to honesty and transparency. Although few of the funeral professionals had formal psychological training, grief theories emphasising stage or phase theories of grief, as well as linear processes requiring confrontation and "grief work" for healthy resolution, found common expression in professional interview responses. These responses resonate with the seminal findings of Wortman and Silver (2001) who noted that medicalised, essentialised understandings of grief continue to inform prescriptive grief myths.

In their evaluations of funerary changes, funeral specialists emphasised the diversity of current practices but also accentuated the saliency of authenticity and transparency. Celebrants and funeral directors reiterated that there was a need to recognise the superficiality that characterised much of human life in modern ("Western") society and the quest for a deeper form of authenticity only discoverable under the surface of social life (Theodossopoulos 2013: 344). As one celebrant clearly articulated: "there's always that missing factor

I've found at a lot of funerals, is that lack of transparency, I suppose. There's this big privacy thing around a person's life, and it's almost like a bit of a cover-up" (Valerie[3]). Discussions often centred on a perceived lack of honesty and "realness", with one funeral provider noting that traditional funeral firms were themselves "distant and cold and un-emotive" – with a new generation of funeral directors described as "human and emotional and real" (Danielle, funeral director). Emotion, authenticity and natural grief were also frequently conflated in these assessments of funerary practices, with one participant asserting that there had a been a significant shift towards "being natural and authentic" (Catherine, funeral director). Reiterating the media representations of an emerging societal confrontation with mortality, she went on to suggest that her funeral company focused on "responding to death naturally: death is a natural occurrence ... we're responding to families and their grief processes and loss processes as being a very natural thing" (Kaylene, funeral director). Celebrants and funeral directors espoused a common sentiment that funerals were one of the few existing opportunities for honesty and unconcealed emotional expression in contemporary life.

Professional participants emphasised that their role was not simply to construct a funeral ritual (or "celebration of life") but to encourage families to discover the important (but occasionally unrecognised) grief resource located in the articulation of the biographical story of the deceased. These narratives formed the focus of many celebratory funerals and demanded that the bereaved survivors identify events or moments in the person's life that satisfactorily (and honestly) encapsulated the authentic identity of the deceased individual. These notions of authenticity assumed that there was a "real" self awaiting discovery and that superficiality concealed an inner reality (Theodossopoulous 2013: 340–342). Capturing the "essence" of an individual and presenting this biographical narrative in a funeral setting was closely linked to therapeutic goals, including the realisation of a healthy grief process. Funeral professionals in this study felt that one of their fundamental tasks was to negotiate barriers to authenticity and encourage families to prioritise transparency. Professionals further articulated that the personal and familial transparency associated with the construction of life-centred funerals was intrinsically linked to a societal shift promoting greater openness around death and dying.

These participant responses are clearly linked to the aforementioned discussion of openness and choice, with both factors presented as predominant post-mortem concerns. Invitations to engage with mortality by exploring post-mortem preferences were pervaded by calls for individuals to consider the potential impact of their inevitable demise, pre-plan their funerals and participate in the construction of post-mortem identities. The augmentation of funerary choices is represented as a positive societal development linked to empowerment, agency and independence and contrasted with the religious paternalism of earlier decades. At the same time, transparency – in the context of funeral arrangement – is associated with the well-being of bereaved individuals. Transparency is not only coupled with confession and authenticity, but is also a source of moral authority emphasising Birchall's (2011: 8) contention that transparency is a virtue, "the secular version of a born-again cleanliness that few can fail to praise". What is relevant to our present discussion is that both choice and transparency focus on individual autonomy and reduce potentially complex funerary arrangements to simple matters of choice and honesty. What the ensuing section reveals, however, is that while bereaved participants were acutely aware of the discourse privileging honesty, an increasing number of people were choosing to forgo the celebratory funerals described by funeral professionals and selecting private, informal forms of disposal. This emerging trend highlights a number of important themes that elucidate the aforementioned shift to personalised funerary practices.

The realities and practicalities of funeral arrangement

An increasing number of people in New Zealand are choosing private funerals or direct disposals. Although both post-mortem practices take various forms, they commonly have few of the formalised components associated with conventional clergy-led or celebrant funerals. Some funeral professionals felt that these forms of disposal failed to fulfil the perceived funeral function noted above, and others equated the practice with a continuing form of denial in contemporary society that ignored enlightened understandings of grief. An increasing number of funeral directors offered various forms of direct disposal and a number of direct cremation operators have emerged in urban centres around New Zealand emphasising minimal-service and minimal-cost cremation services. Most funeral directors provided private funerals (which are generally attended by a smaller number of mourners), and a few bereaved participants also noted that these funerals were cheaper than traditional funeral services and allowed the bereaved family to organise disposal with limited professional involvement. One funeral director described some of the key elements of these two forms of disposal:

> Direct cremation is driven by cost. We normally work with the family with the direct cremation and see what we can accomplish and generally it turns out to be, that we will still have – they don't call it a service – we just call it a gathering, they are just going to drop Dad off at the crematorium, but they normally sit there for forty minutes and the fundamentals of what they are doing there are basically the same as a service but it's not formalized. They'll sit there and talk about their memories, they'll have some photos, they'll take flowers out. They have an opportunity to say good-bye but it's not called a funeral because Dad didn't want a funeral and it's a private thing so they feel quite safe in their expressions … When I first started, a private service was literally five or ten people at the crematorium, two minutes, it was literally the committal prayer and that was it. Now, you'll have a private service, but you'll still have, there will be twenty or thirty people there and they'll still have service sheets, they'll still have slide

shows, so basically, all of the elements of a full service, just with invitations. Sometimes that can go on longer than a normal funeral service.

(Brian, funeral director)

Informality, privacy and control over attendance emerged as integral features of these post-mortem practices and their significance will be explored further below. Funeral directors and celebrants in this project asserted that there had been a significant rise in the number of direct disposals and private funerals over the decade, with professional participants estimating that between 10–30 per cent of total disposals could now be categorised as alternative funeral services.

Although funeral professionals frequently stated that public emotional expression in a funeral setting was intrinsically linked to an efficacious grief process, bereaved participants asserted that protection from the expectations of performative grief provided significant motivation to avoid public funerals. Bereaved participants emphasised that their grief would be on display and that they had a particular aversion to the surveillance of grief by peripheral mourners. Funeral directors and celebrants attributed this development to insincerity and a continuing denial of death in contemporary society. As one professional participant explicitly noted, death had been sequestered and people had lost their traditional knowledge of appropriate bereavement practices:

I think the problem is that people aren't really prepared for the whole thing about death and grieving and I think the biggest issue is that people are not taught how to grieve. They are not taught that they are allowed to grieve and they are not taught the different expressions of grief.

(Michael, funeral celebrant)

In the absence of this traditional knowledge and overarching religious framework, funeral directors and celebrants proffered that their position as funeral professionals was inextricably linked to broader educational roles that promoted societal understanding of bereavement.[4]

Although bereaved participants in this project noted that funerals were ideally "for the living", many lamented the complexities associated with constructing appropriate forms of funerary ritual. The overarching concern for bereaved participants was achieving an acceptable level of congruity between the biography of the dead and the accompanying ritual. Strategies for achieving this symbolic form of coherence (Prendergast *et al.* 2006: 889) included implementing any express wishes articulated by the dead, but more generally, it comprised efforts to identify authentic biographical attributes. Some participants noted that alternative disposal options were particularly appropriate for people that had led private lives with limited social engagement:

We looked at [my daughter], looked at her and thought, "Right, this is a girl who is a very private girl". Therefore, it was just going to be private.

> I think for me, I like to personalise things, for me I looked at her, those who knew her would be there anyway. Even our advertisement [in the local newspaper], we thought we'd make it private.
>
> (Sonya, bereaved parent)

As a Maori family with "respect for things Maori", she noted that there were clear cultural expectations surrounding funerary practices, but that taking the body to the family home (rather than the community Marae) and organising a small family funeral (rather than a public tangihanga) were more appropriate forms of burial that authentically reflected the life of her daughter.

One clear theme that appeared in discussions of private funerals was that an increasing number of people described New Zealand attitudes incommensurate or inconsonant with predominant forms of existing ritual. Participants frequently referred to processes of secularisation, reiterating Belich's (2001) contention that a discernible secular tone has historically been evident in levels of church attendance, the secular orientation of the state, and the acceptance of religious pluralism. Participants specifically identified the decline of institutional Christianity and the concomitant rise of "religionless" New Zealanders during the twentieth century. These participants noted the minimal religious content evident in family funerals and that mortuary practices were predominantly "down-to earth", "simple" and "honest" affairs. While notions of Pakeha identity remain contested (see, for example, Bell 2009), "informality" emerged as a leitmotif in descriptions of Pakeha funeral practices. Although secular funeral celebrants[5] have emphasised the development of personalised, less formalised celebratory funerals (clearly distinguished from earlier, religious funerals), some participants stated that these personalised funerals retained important elements of standardisation that were not necessarily concordant with the life of the deceased.

Bereaved participants also noted that they were protecting the dead from further indignity or scrutiny by organising small funeral gatherings that avoided surveillance and judgement. A number of participants, asserted, for example, that the deceased had suffered various forms of illness and led difficult lives that would remain incomprehensible to most mourners. The daughter of a Dutch immigrant similarly noted that the lives of her parents were characterised by isolation and remoteness and there was no way of meaningfully translating these experiences into a form of ritual understandable to friends and extended family. As Pauline elaborated, the life of her sister had been extremely difficult and a private funeral gathering was the only perspicuous post-mortem option:

> We didn't have to put up a front, in a sense. It was a very … I never thought about that, but we didn't have to put on a show. We didn't do any pretend. Patricia had a sad and difficult life and everyone who loved her knew that. We didn't have to polish it up. It was lovely.
>
> (Pauline, death of her sister)

Funerals which extoled the virtues of the dead in such situations were particularly problematic as they epitomised the superficiality and meaninglessness of conventional post-mortem rituals for bereaved interviewees. Related to this feature of private funeral services was the need for intimacy. Participants in this project often engaged in careful assessments of who they considered legitimate mourners, based on their relationships with the dead. Potential motivations for attending the funeral were scrutinised by mourners organising the funeral with inessential (or tangential) attendees described as diluting the desired intimacy and detracting from the required authenticity. Participants stipulated that the uncertain, difficult period associated with dying was particularly significant as it revealed those that shared the requisite level of intimacy with the dead individual:

> I think people have lots of reasons for having private funerals, but I think part of it is they don't want a lot of folk coming who have never been there for them up until that time and they just come for the show.
>
> (Jacqui, funeral celebrant)

The placement of ashes following cremation was described by many participants as the most meaningful component of the post-mortem process. Although authors such as Holloway *et al.* (2013) have clearly explicated the meaning-creating and meaning-taking processes integrally involved in the construction of funerary rituals, some participants in our study emphasised that funerals were little more than perfunctory obligations that held limited personal relevance. Cremation rates in New Zealand currently exceed 80 percent of total disposals, and most of the participants described the significance of ash disposition linked to private funerals and direct cremation. Even for participants who had arranged celebrant funerals, many felt that the placement of ashes offered a level of authenticity and meaning absent in personalised funeral rituals. In addition to providing bereaved family and friends with a process to disengage from the materiality of the dead, ash disposals allowed these individuals to contribute to the biographical narrative of the dead in a creative and participative way. Ash disposal was intrinsically informal and free from the institutional restrictions (Prendergast *et al.* 2006) or the lingering influence of Christian beliefs that the bereaved families felt often permeated funeral arrangements. Not subject to some of the temporal restrictions associated with the funeral itself, ashes were both divisible and versatile allowing the bereaved to engage in deliberations surrounding identity and transcendence. Rather than the rhetoric of a grief process that culminated in various forms of closure, bereaved participants emphasised the temporally indefinite dimension of ash disposition.

Ash disposition allowed bereaved participants to do something for the dead by ensuring that this disposal was congruent with the authentic identity of the dead. Rather than the authenticity articulated by funeral professionals – which privileged emotional expression and the realisation of a healthy grief process –

bereaved participants described a process of identifying and substantiating the essence of the dead. By placing the ashes in personalised spaces connected with the biographical history of the dead, the bereaved individuals were finding a place for the dead and memorialising their essence in a very potent way. Not only was the placement of ashes linked to a retrospective fulfilment of identity (Davies 2002), but it also allowed the dead to remain relevant in the lives of the living by permeating the spaces of everyday life. Some participants noted that the scattering of ashes in personalised locations was comforting precisely because it created an intimacy with the dead not possible in spaces such as churches and cemeteries which felt unfamiliar to the bereaved interviewees. Some participants explained that it was the informal and mundane tenor of the dispersal which was particularly appropriate. One participant, for example, described the disposition of her parents' ashes:

> We know where the tree is. And of course with Mum being there, Dad in life said a few times over this year said he wanted to go to the same place as Mum. So no, there is no significance to anyone else, only us that know … We literally just met at the park, scattered the ashes, said "Goodbye Dad," and then we went out for afternoon tea as well … Scattering the ashes was nice both times. It was funny and it was personal and private, and nobody else around us knew what we're doing.
>
> (Tina, death of her parents)

The disposal described by the participant was an act of memory that reunited her parents, as well as a particularly intimate, personal event congruent with the biography of her parents (who had led quiet, private lives). While a few participants had not returned to the scattering site, others structured a range of memorial activities around the site noting that the visitations constituted continuing relationships with the dead as well as self-reflexive assessments of the grief process.

While the distinction between immanence and transcendence may no longer be clear in personalised funerary practices (Quartier 2013), private ash scattering and personalised forms of memorialisation do not focus solely on the worldly achievements of the deceased. Although New Zealand is frequently described as a secular country[6] with an "areligious habitus" (Schröder 2011: 44), bereaved participants described the presence of the dead in natural landscape settings as transcendent and infinite. Authors such as Hornborg (2012) have argued that emerging forms of spirituality are conceptualised as timeless, universal human essences located inside each individual and similar (essentialised) notions of spirituality were articulated by numerous participants. While some participants included spiritual or religious content in their post-mortem practices to assuage religious family members, most emphasised that such inclusions held limited personal relevance. Funeral directors and celebrants also noted that discussions of spirituality were difficult and potentially incongruous with non-religious approaches to life and death. Bereaved participants asserted that discussions of spirituality were potentially "awkward" and "embarrassing" and that it was difficult to articulate the meaning of ash disposition but that these practices had broader meaning. The mother describing the scattering of her son's ashes in the mountains stated:

> We talked about putting a wee plaque up on that rock [where the ashes are scattered]. It is way off the track … no one is ever going to find it. Every year when we go up, we take a piece of crystal or a rosebush or something and in the rock there is a sort of a little ledge, and every year we just put a little stone there and the next year when we go back we check to see that it is still there and of course it is always is still there, and that has got significance.… I wanted to have some marker that he had been on the earth, but I don't have an urgency about that now. I just sort of seem to know that he has his rock and we know that it's his rock.
>
> (Elizabeth, death of her son)

Descriptions of ash disposition were also suffused with symbolic notions of regeneration, renewal and ecological sustainability. These responses reiterate the findings of authors such as Rumble *et al.* (2014) who have argued that remains are increasingly dispersed back into environments that sustain the living – rather than being sequestered in specialised spaces for the dead – and that emerging forms of disposal are themselves intrinsically connected to new modes of spirituality. Significant in the New Zealand context was that participants identified natural settings as sites emblematic of transcendence, with links to Romantic representations of nature uncontaminated by the coercive conventions of modernity. Parks, beaches and rivers invoked the essence of the dead as well as signifying a certain timelessness and source of spiritual nourishment. While such claims may be inextricably linked to Pakeha attempts to secure their place in New Zealand (McAra 2007: 99), natural spaces exuded a continuity that was not only familiar but made participants feel that they were a part of something more significant by revealing the relentless cycles of birth and decay, and the immateriality of (individual) human lives.

Concluding comments

This brief examination of funeral practices in New Zealand critically assesses contemporary representations of personalisation. What becomes evident in this evaluation is that professional discourses not only privilege an emotional authenticity aligned with notions of honesty and transparency, but also underscore the role of funeral professionals in the realisation of this process. Together with wider media representations proclaiming a fundamental shift in attitudes to death, this portrayal elaborates the significance of individualisation, funeral choices and autonomy. What becomes very clear in this analysis is that a discussion of post-mortem possibilities and shifting societal sentiments obscures the lived experiences of bereaved individuals, as well as eliding the prescriptive assumptions inherent in this discourse. Rather than consuming funeral options that acclaimed the individuality of the deceased, bereaved participants mobilised a discourse that carefully assessed the value and suitability of these funeral options, and emphasised the significance of post-mortem practices that reflected the authentic essence of the deceased. In contrast to popular thanatological suppositions that conflate personalisation with transparency, bereaved participants emphasised the appeal of privacy and informality, noting that these priorities contributed to the biographical integrity of the dead. Rather than framing such actions as a denial of death, bereaved participants felt that this was one final act to establish an authentic memory of an individual that also conferred a form of transcendence to the dead.

At a theoretical level, the competing discourses of authenticity evident in this discussion draw attention to the discursive struggles that occur and the relationships of power that produce both the professional and the consumer in contemporary society. These discourses also structure the social context of funeral options in consumer society, resisting the easy hegemony that underpins the assumption that the commodification of funeral options is an uncontested social trend. Instead, the divergent discourses of authenticity elucidated above speak to the complexity and multi-layeredness of funerary practices and demonstrate how discourses of disposal are continually constituted and re-constituted.

Notes

1 Death Cafés are a social franchise developed in England which provide individuals with the opportunity to discuss death and dying. The objective of this development is described as increasing "awareness of death with a view toward helping people make the most of their (finite) lives" (http://deathcafe.com/what/). There are a number of international developments with related goals. Fora such as the Death Salon in the United States (www.orderofthegooddeath.com/death-salon#.VEH-FLecfVBI), Dying Matters in England and Wales (www.dyingmatters.org/) or The Groundswell Project in Australia (www.thegroundswellproject.com/) aim to promote open dialogue (and death literacy) around death, dying and bereavement. Some of these groups explicitly link openness with a need to make plans for the end of life. Deathoverdinner.org, for example, states: "How we want to die – represents the most important and costly conversations America isn't having" (http://deathoverdinner.org/).

2 Conway (2013: 336) specifically asserts that this interpretation of personalisation represents middle class expressivism.

3 Pseudonyms have been used to protect participant anonymity.

4 There is a clear link between the augmentation of funeral services and the professionalisation of the funeral directing occupation. See, for example, Emke (2002) and Rasmussen (2007).

5 Secular funeral celebrants (also known as civil celebrants or humanist officiants in the UK) presently conduct more than 60 per cent of all funerals in New Zealand.

Celebrants emerged in the 1970s and were closely associated with increasing secularisation and diversification of beliefs and lifestyles during this period (Macdonald 2011: 239).
6 Although this definition, as well as the broader debates about the nature of secularity and the historical processes involved in this shift, continue to be contested (Baldacchino and Kahn 2011).

References

Adamson, S., and Holloway, M. 2012. Negotiating sensitivities and grappling with intangibles: experiences from a study of spirituality and funerals. *Qualitative Research*, 12(6): 735–752.

Aries, Philippe. 1974. The reversal of death: changes in attitudes toward death in Western societies. *American Quarterly*, 26(5): 536–560.

Arnold, Naomi. 2012. It's about dying, naturally: alternative burials on the rise. *Nelson Mail*. www.stuff.co.nz/nelson-mail/lifestyle-entertainment/weekend/7556969/Its-about-dying-naturally [Accessed 4 February 2014].

Baldacchino, Jean-Paul, and Kahn, Joel S. 2011. Believing in a secular age: anthropology, sociology and religious experience. *The Australian Journal of Anthropology*, 22(1): 1–13.

Belich, James 2001. *Paradise reforged: A history of the New Zealanders from the 1880s to the year 2000*. Auckland: Penguin Press.

Bell, A. 2009. Dilemmas of settler belonging: roots, routes and redemption in New Zealand national identity claims. *The Sociological Review*, 57(1): 145–162.

Birchall, C. 2011. Introduction to "secrecy and transparency": the politics of opacity and openness. *Theory, Culture and Society*, 28(7–8): 7–25.

Blundell, Kay. 2014. Funeral costs overwhelm widower. *The Dominion Post*. www.stuff.co.nz/national/9751156/Funeral-costs-overwhelm-widower [Accessed 23 March 2014].

Carville, Olivia. 2013. Kiwi funerals go global online. *Fairfax Media*. www.stuff.co.nz/national/9168340/Kiwi-funerals-go-global-online [Accessed 14 February 2014].

Caswell, Glenys. 2011. Personalisation in Scottish funerals: individualised ritual or relational process? *Mortality*, 16(3): 242–258.

Chapman, Katie, and O'Neil, Andrea. 2014. Dealing with death in a Kiwi way. *The Dominion Post*. www.stuff.co.nz/dominion-post/capital-life/9934484/Dealing-with-death-in-a-Kiwi-way [Accessed 15 May 2014].

Charmaz, Kathy. 2006. *Constructing grounded theory: A practical guide through qualitative analysis*. London: Sage.

Colvin, Kirsten. 2013. Preparing for death with a coffee and a chat. *Daily Life*. www.stuff.co.nz/life-style/life/9289702/Preparing-for-death-with-a-coffee-and-a-chat [Accessed 15 February 2014].

Conway, S. 2013. Representing dying, representing class? Social distinction, aestheticisation and the performing self. *Mortality*, 18(4): 327–338.

Crouch, Mira. 2004. Last matters: the latent meanings of contemporary funeral rites. In *Making sense of dying and death*, edited by Andrew Fagen. Amsterdam and New York: Rodopi, pp. 125–140.

Davies, Douglas. 2002. *Death, ritual, and belief: The rhetoric of funerary rites*. London: Continuum.

Dickinson, George E. 2012. Diversity in death: body disposition and memorialization. *Illness, Crisis, and Loss*, 20(2): 141–158.

Emke, I. 2002. Why the sad face? Secularization and the changing function of funerals in Newfoundland. *Mortality*, 7(3): 269–284.

Frith, Hannah, Raisborough, Jayne, and Klein, Orly. 2012. Making death "good": instructional tales for dying in newspaper accounts of Jade Goody's death. *Sociology of Health and Illness*, 35(3): 419–433.

Garces-Foley, Kathleen, and Holcomb, Justin S. 2006. Contemporary American funerals: personalizing tradition. In *Death and religion in a changing world*, edited by Kathleen Garces-Foley, pp. 207–227. Armonk (New York): M. E. Sharpe.

Gorer, Geoffrey. 1965. *Death, grief, and mourning in contemporary Britain*. London: Cresset.

Guest, Greg, Bunce, Arwen, and Johnson, Laura. 2006. How many interviews are enough? An experiment with data saturation and variability. *Field methods*, 18(1): 59–82.

Harvey, Sarah. 2012. Funeral fireworks … why Kiwis go out with a bang. *Sunday Star Times*. www.stuff.co.nz/national/6867468/Funeral-fireworks-why-Kiwis-go-out-with-a-bang [Accessed 14 February 2014].

Heather, Ben. 2014. Don't wear black – the new funeral traditions. *The Dominion Post*. www.stuff.co.nz/dominion-post/news/9673518/Don't-wear-black-the-new-funeral-traditions [Accessed 13 March 2014].

Holloway, M., Adamson, S., Argyrou, V., Draper, P., and Mariau, D. 2013. "Funerals aren't nice but it couldn't have been nicer". The makings of a good funeral. *Mortality*, 18(1): 30–53.

Hornborg, Anne-Christine. 2012. Are we all spiritual? A comparative perspective on the appropriation of a new concept of spirituality. *Journal for the Study of Spirituality*, 1(2): 249–268.

Jalland, P. 2006. *Changing ways of death in twentieth-century Australia: War, medicine, and the funeral business*. Sydney: Uiniversity of New Wouth wales Press.

Kearl, Michael C. and Jacobsen, Michael H. 2013. Time, late modernity and the demise of forever: from eternal salvation to completed bucket lists. In *Taming time, timing death: Social technologies and ritual*, edited by Dorthe R. Christensen and Rane Willerslev, pp. 59–78. Farnham: Ashgate.

Long, S. O., and Buehring, S. 2014. Searching for life in death: celebratory mortuary ritual in the context of US interfaith families. *Mortality*, 19(1): 80–100.

McAra, Sally. 2007. Land of beautiful vision: making a Buddhist Sacred Place in New Zealand. Honolulu: University of Hawai'i Press.

Macdonald, Julie. 2011. *Contemporary ritual-makers: A study of independent celebrants in New Zealand* (Unpublished doctoral dissertation). Massey University, Palmerston North.

McManus, R., and Schäfer, C. 2014. Final arrangements: examining debt and distress. *Mortality*, 19(4): 379–397.

Meadows, Richard. 2013. Funeral expenses a fact of life. *Fairfax Media*. www.stuff.co.nz/business/money/9471177/Funeral-expenses-a-fact-of-life. [Accessed 14 February 2014].

O'Sullivan, Patrick. 2014. Death planning a part of life. *Hawkes Bay Today*. www.nzherald.co.nz/hawkes-bay-today/news/article.cfm?c_id=1503462&objectid=11237987 [Accessed 13 March 2014].

Prendergast, David, Hockey, Jenny, and Kellaher, Leonie. 2006. Blowing in the wind? Identity, materiality, and the destinations of human ashes. *Journal of the Royal Anthropological Institute*, 12(4): 881–898.

Quartier, T. 2013. On the border of death dimensions of Dutch mourning rituals. In *Changing European death ways*, edited by E. Venbrux, T. Quartier, C. Venhorst, and B. Mathijssen. Zurich and Berlin: Lit Verlag, pp. 191–211.

Ramshaw, E. J. 2010. The personalization of postmodern post-mortem rituals. *Pastoral Psychology*, 59(2): 171–178.

Rasmussen, Shane E. 2007. *Arbitrary traditionality: Cultural authenticity and modern mainstream American deathways*. Unpublished PhD, University of Louisiana at Lafayette.

Ritchie, Jenny, Morrison, Sandy, and Vaioleti, Timote. 2013. Transgressing boundaries of private and public: auto-ethnography and intercultural funerals. *Studies in Symbolic Interaction*, 40: 95–126.

Roberts, Pamela. 2010. What now? Cremation without tradition. *OMEGA–Journal of Death and Dying*, 62(1): 1–30.

Rumble, H., Troyer, J., Walter, T., and Woodthorpe, K. 2014. Disposal or dispersal? Environmentalism and final treatment of the British dead. *Mortality*, 19(3): 243–260.

Sanders, G. 2010. The dismal trade as culture industry. *Poetics*, 38(1): 47–68.

Schäfer, Cyril. 2012. Corpses, conflict and insignificance? A critical analysis of post-mortem practices. *Mortality*, 17(4): 305–321.

Schröder, Ingo W. 2011. Preliminary anthropological reflections on secularism and secularity. *Kultūra ir visuomenė*, 2(3): 37–47.

Schwass, Margot. 2005. *Last words: Approaches to death in New Zealand's cultures and faiths*. Wellington: Bridget Williams Books.

Simpson, Heather. 2014. Treating death as taboo risks bills stress. *Marlborough Express*. www.stuff.co.nz/marlborough-express/news/9716415/Treating-death-as-taboo-risks-bills-stress [Accessed 14 April 2014].

Staudt, Christina. 2014. Introduction: a bird's eye view of the territory. In *Our changing journey to the end: Reshaping death, dying and grief in America*, edited by Christina Staudt and Harold Ellens. Santa Barbara: Praeger, pp. 3–24.

Stock, Rob. 2012. Are we too poor to die. *Sunday Star Times*. www.stuff.co.nz/business/money/6867599/Are-we-too-poor-to-die [Accessed 2 February 2014].

Stock, Rob. 2014. More Kiwis paying for funerals in advance. *Sunday Star Times*. www.stuff.co.nz/the-press/business/9858533/More-Kiwis-paying-for-funerals-in-advance [Accessed 1 April 2014].

Theodossopoulos, D. 2013. Laying claim to authenticity: five anthropological dilemmas. *Anthropological Quarterly*, 86(2): 337–360.

Tomas, N. 2013. Recognizing collective cultural property rights in a deceased – Clarke v. Takamore. *International Journal of Cultural Property*, 20(3): 333–348.

Turley, D. 2005. Mortality and consumer motivation in the writings of Zygmunt Bauman. In *Inside consumption: Consumer motives, goals, and desires*, edited by S. Ratneshwar and D. G. Mick. Abingdon: Routledge; 67–84.

Valentine, C., and Woodthorpe, K. 2013. From the cradle to the grave: funeral welfare from an international perspective. *Social Policy and Administration*. 48(5): 515–536.

Venbrux, Eric, Peelen, Janneke, and Altena, Marga. 2009. Going Dutch: Individualisation, secularisation and changes in death rites. *Mortality*, 14(2): 97–101.

Wilce, James M. 2009. *Crying shame: Metaculture, modernity, and the exaggerated death of lament*. Chichester: Wiley-Blackwell.

Winkel, H. 2001. A postmodern culture of grief? On individualization of mourning in Germany. *Mortality*, 6(1): 65–79.

Woodthorpe, K. V. 2014. *I can't afford to die: Addressing funeral poverty*. International Longevity Centre.

Wortman, C. B., and Silver, R. C. 2001. The myths of coping with loss revisited. In *Handbook of bereavement research: Consequences, coping, and care,* edited by M. S. Stroebe, R. O. Hansson, W. Stroebe, and H. Schut. Washington, DC: American Psychological Association, pp. 405–429.

5 Custody of the corpse

Controlling alkaline hydrolysis in US death care markets

Philip R. Olson

Controlling funeral technologies

In the preface to *This Republic of Suffering*, Harvard historian Drew Gilpin Faust writes:

> It is work to deal with the dead … to remove them in the literal sense of disposing of their bodies, and it is also work to remove them in a more figurative sense. The bereaved struggle to separate themselves from the dead through ritual and mourning. Families and communities must repair the rent in the domestic and social fabric, and societies, nations and cultures must work to understand and explain unfathomable loss.
>
> (2008, p. xiv)

Funeral work is performed by a wide variety of actors, each of whom has different roles and responsibilities in the collaborative processes of caring for the dead and the bereaved. In antebellum America, the decedent's family was typically responsible for performing most of this work – though the dying, too, were expected to do the work of preparing themselves psychologically and spiritually for a "Good Death." Additional funeral work was dispersed across a variety of trades, including clergy, carpenters, liverypersons, blacksmiths, surgeons, druggists, and chemists, each of whom performed specific types of funeral work ad hoc (Laderman, 2003; Plater, 1996, pp. 41–49). After the Civil War, growing numbers of entrepreneurial undertakers perceived the social and economic advantages of consolidating funeral work, thereby initiating the process of professionalizing funeral work.

Today, funeral professionals play a prominent role in both the literal and figurative removals of the dead from the world of the living in the US, providing goods and services intended to manage both the decomposition of dead bodies, as well as the decomposition of social ties. These two forms of removal roughly correspond to two broad categories of funeral work, which sociologist George Sanders labels "front stage" and "back stage" work (Sanders 2010, p. 56). According to Sanders, this distinction captures "a division of labor in which the front-staff are mostly comprised of salespeople and bereavement counselors ... while embalmers work behind the scenes," preparing dead bodies for their separation from the living (2010, p. 56). Several death studies scholars rightly note that US funeral professionals today seek to de-emphasize their "back stage" work, and to promote their "front stage" work (Sanders, 2010; Schäfer, 2007; Laderman, 2003; Emke, 2002; Prothero, 2001; Cahill, 1995). Indeed, funeral industry marketing executive Dean Lambert (2011, p. 48) urges funeral directors to focus less on the disposition of corpses and more on "new and creative ways to celebrate lives and help people grieve."

Funeral professionals' preferment of their own "front stage" work feebly disguises the fact that physically working with dead bodies continues to occupy a central place in the funeral professions. Funeral consumers may turn to grief counselors, event planners, and merchants located, as Lambert puts it, "outside the traditional funeral industry" (2011, 48); but as Howarth (1996, p. 15) reminds us, "[m]odern funeral directors acquire control over the funeral service via their custody of the corpse." Moreover, funeral professionals' commercial custody of the corpse has been achieved by way of funeral professionals' control over the *technological* means of body preparation and disposition. It is well known that embalming technologies played a powerful role in the professionalization of funeral work in the US. Through the appropriation and standardization of embalming, US undertakers transformed the care of the corpse into a technical skill, the practice of which continues to be controlled by professional funeral directors and embalmers. As Lambert acknowledges,

> [t]he average consumer neither has the skills nor the desire to perform the technical function for which funeral directors receive training. It is a highly specialized trade, which is a barrier to entry into the realm of embalming and restorative arts.
>
> (2011, p. 48)

Technological shifts and innovations can unsettle any number of boundaries that work to organize and define communities of practice, giving practitioners reason to confront anew the prevailing practices, technologies, norms, professional identities, divisions of labor, and social relations that have become routine over time. The funeral industry is no exception. Consider the case of cremation's increasing popularity in the US since the last half of the twentieth century. Early in their concurrent histories, embalming funeral directors and cremationists viewed themselves as belonging to distinct communities of practice. Until the end of the twentieth century, funeral directors viewed cremationists as industry outsiders, portraying cremation as undignified, irreligious, and even un-American (Prothero, 2001, pp. 174–182). Today, cremation is decidedly mainstream, and more and more US funeral homes now house cremation retorts of their own, though many crematoria operate independently of any funeral home. To accommodate cremation, funeral professionals have had to do more than simply make way for new machines, tools, and techniques; they have also had to welcome new funeral actors, and retool their own professional identities. Indeed, funeral directors' de-emphasis of back stage work is itself a retooling of professional identity in response to the ongoing supplantation of a once identity-conferring technique (embalming) by a once disparaged process (cremation).

This chapter examines funeral actors' efforts to control a very new disposition technology that has begun to enter North American funeral markets (and *only* North American funeral markets) over the last four years, namely, alkaline hydrolysis (AH). The introduction of AH technologies into US funeral work involves more than the presence of new machines upon the funeral stage; it also implicates established funeral actors in new ways, while introducing new actors who wish to create a place for themselves within the funeral industry. Drawing upon intensive interviews with funeral professionals and AH system developers, industry literature, death studies literature, and historical resources, I argue that US funeral professionals' ongoing efforts to control AH technologies involve the management of a number of professional boundaries, including the dissociation of funeral contexts and funeral technologies from non-funeral contexts and non-funeral technologies; the separation of professional funeral expertise from other kinds of expertise; and the distinction between funeral industry "insiders" and industry "outsiders." Industry debates about AH afford us an opportunity to witness funeral professionals' efforts to manage their professional jurisdiction, identity, and occupational expertise in relation to a potentially disruptive technology.

Alkaline hydrolysis in focus

AH is a reductive chemical process through which tissues are dissolved in a heated (sometimes pressurized) solution of water and strong alkali. In funerary contexts,[1] a single body is sealed in a cylindrical, stainless steel vessel into which the alkali solution is added. The design of the vessel and the duration of the process vary, depending upon the temperature and pressure at which the process is carried out. Low temperature, unpressurized systems can hydrolyze a human body in about 12 hours. At higher temperatures and pressures the process can take as little as three to four hours. The process yields an inert, sterile effluent and brittle bone material. The effluent can be disposed of through municipal sewer systems, provided the fluid is cooled and the pH adjusted to meet local requirements. The brittle bone material is cooled, dried, and crushed, and may be returned to the decedent's family. AH remains legal in only in nine US states and one Canadian Province since its initial introduction into US death care markets in early 2011, and today only a handful of funeral service providers offer AH disposition as an option to their customers.

The story of AH originates in non-funerary contexts nearly 20 years before its introduction into US and Canadian funeral markets. In the early 1990s, two biomedical researchers at Albany Medical College, Dr. Gordon Kaye and Dr. Peter Weber, used AH to dispose of dead laboratory animals. In 1994, Kaye and Weber's now-defunct company, Waste Reduction by Waste Reduction (WR²), was awarded a patent that describes an apparatus² that is now widely known as a "tissue digester" or "caustic digester." Versions of this apparatus continue to be used internationally in a variety of non-funerary contexts, including bio-containment facilities, biomedical and veterinary research facilities, diagnostic centers, the food service and pharmaceutical industries.³ Many of these digesters are designed to hydrolyze large amounts of animal waste (between 1,500 and 10,000 pounds) in a single cycle. But in 2005, WR² also designed and built the first single-human-body digester for the Mayo Clinic's anatomical bequests program. It was this machine that paved the way for AH's introduction into the funeral industry. By processing human bodies one at a time, the Mayo Clinic's AH system fit with a prevailing Western funerary norm that prohibits the comingling of multiple human remains, in the interest of showing respect (materially and symbolically) for the individuality of the human person even after death. After the collapse of WR², Joe Wilson and Sandy Sullivan (chiefs of WR²'s US and UK operations, respectively) each formed their own, separate companies devoted to developing AH technologies, and to building a market for AH within the funeral industry. Wilson's Indiana-based Bio-Response Solutions, Inc. (BRS) and Sullivan's Scotland-based Resomation, Ltd. are the leading manufacturers of single-body AH systems for commercial funeral application.

Despite the fact that AH technologies entered funeral markers only after they were first put to use in a variety of non-funerary contexts, some funeral professionals are keen to insist upon industry jurisdiction over AH disposition technologies, and to establish regulations that would allow only licensed funeral professionals to offer funerary AH. For example, Ohio funeral director and AH pioneer Jeff Edwards urges regulators to keep AH within the funeral industry, and to prevent industry outsiders – Edwards mentions tire shop owners – from "taking a form of disposition from the industry" (Parmalee, 2011b, p. 24). Edwards was the first funeral director to offer AH disposition to his customers, and over the course of roughly two months he hydrolyzed 19 bodies, before the Ohio Department of Health (ODH) ordered him to stop. While Edwards views AH as a disposition technology that falls squarely within the occupational jurisdiction of licensed funeral directors, from the point of view of the Ohio Board of Embalmers and Funeral Directors (OBEFD), Edwards' use of AH jeopardized his standing as a legitimate funeral professional, "[s]pecifically for using an unauthorized method of disposition on dead human bodies…" (Parmalee, 2011b, p. 25). Without speculating about the motives behind the ODH and OBEFD's resistance to Edwards adoption of AH, Edwards' case makes clear Bowker and Star's observation that membership within communities of practice "largely revolves around the nature of the relationship with the *objects*" that members view as belonging to that community, and that "[a]cceptance or legitimacy derives from the familiarity of action mediated by member objects" (2000, p. 299). Indeed, the transition of AH from laboratory contexts into funeral contexts involves both a transformation of the material and symbolic identity of AH systems themselves, as well as disruption of the social and professional identities of funeral directors.

Technologies and identities in transition

A comparative history of the funeralization of arterial embalming in France and the US illustrates how jurisdictional claims to a particular technology can shape death care markets, as well as professional and technological identities. Pascale Trompette and Mélanie Lemonnier (2009) point out that, in nineteenth-century France, physicians proclaimed exclusive jurisdiction over embalming. Resisting the efforts of French embalming pioneer J. N. Gannal (1791–1852) to create "a new occupation ('embalmers'), distinct from the health profession," physicians reproached Gannal "for practicing without the slightest medical diploma" (Trompette and Lemonnier, 2009, p. 13). In France, it was not until the late twentieth century that embalmers began "to build their occupation as an independent body of experts" (Trompette and Lemonnier, 2009, p. 18) with "control over the corpse" (Trompette and Lemonnier, 2009, p. 16). In the US, however, the professionalization of embalmers took place much more rapidly. Spurred on by the exigencies of dealing with corpses produced by the US Civil War (Faust, 2008), and unencumbered by vigorous resistance from physicians, embalming undertakers swiftly formed the material infrastructure and professional networks upon which to build a unique professional identity and to direct a consolidated death care market.

At the same time that embalming helped to create a unique social and professional space for funeral professionals, this space also transformed embalming techniques themselves.

For example, before suffusing the corpse with embalming fluids, the funeral embalmer, unlike the anatomical embalmer, "sets" the body's facial features in preparation for ritual viewing. Furthermore, the arterial embalming fluids used in typical funerary contexts are much less concentrated than those used to preserve corpses for anatomic study. A less concentrated fluid yields a more "lifelike" softness in the tissues of a corpse that is intended for viewing within the brief interlude between death and final disposition (usually burial or cremation). Furthermore, funeral embalming standardly involves the aspiration (suction-removal) of organ material from the body cavity – a procedure that is obviously not performed upon bodies whose cavity organs are to be preserved for study. Thus, while embalming technologies helped to create a unique social space of professional death care, distinct from, albeit intimately connected to, domestic, medical, and clerical domains, embalming technologies were themselves transformed to fit the uniqueness of the spaces they helped to create.

Alkaline hydrolysis in transition

The uniqueness of funeral contexts from other professional, commercial, and industrial contexts is maintained not only by managing the boundaries of professional identity, but also through the management of the boundaries of technological identity. Consider for example Swedish biologist Susanne Wiigh-Mäsak's interest in controlling the technological identity of her innovative disposition technique, Promession. In 2001, Wiigh-Mäsak founded Promessa Organic, a company devoted to developing a method of freeze drying dead human bodies and processing them into compost. According to science writer Mary Roach, Wiigh-Mäsak is decidedly against the idea of marketing Promession as a technology for the disposal of dead animals. Paraphrasing Wiigh-Mäsak, Roach writes, "[i]f Promessa becomes known as a company that disposes of dead cows or pets ... it will lose the dignity necessary for a human application" (2003, p. 274). Given that AH technologies entered funeral markets *after* they were first used in non-funerary contexts to dispose of animal carcasses, we might expect to observe efforts, on the part of funeral stakeholders, to control and transform the identities of AH technologies as they transition into funerary contexts. The record does not disappoint those expectations. Samantha Wilson, a biologist with AH system manufacturer BRS, states the problem clearly: "The scientific community has been using the [AH] process for well over a decade, but this [the funeral industry] is an entirely different industry that requires utmost sensitivity" (Kenevich, 2011, p. 17).

One way in which funeral veterans and newcomers alike have sought to control the identity of funerary AH is by renaming the technologies. Today, funerary AH technologies go by a variety of names, including alkaline hydrolysis, flameless cremation, and by the cremation-signaling trade names Bio-Cremation, Resomation, and Aquamation. But in 2003, when Mary Roach's bestseller, *Stiff*, was published, AH had not yet debuted on the funeral scene, and had not yet acquired a distinctive funerary appellation. In her book, Roach refers to envisioned funerary AH systems as "mortuary digesters," adopting a version of the names standardly given to AH systems in non-funerary contexts (i.e., "tissue digesters" or "caustic digesters"). Yet, as Roach points out, the AH system used by the Florida State Anatomical Board (FSAB) to dispose of donated human cadavers has since 1998 operated under the name, "reductive cremation," a classification that facilitated AH's implementation under Florida law (2003, p. 254). As I have indicated elsewhere, several other states that have legalized AH for the disposition of dead human bodies have elected to classify or regulate AH as a form of cremation (Olson 2014, 682–683). With respect to the funeralization of AH technologies, this renaming is much more than a matter of legal classification and regulation; it is also essential for distinguishing non-funerary AH systems from funerary AH systems (regardless of whether AH is viewed as a form of cremation or as an alternative method of disposition), and for distinguishing the professional identity of funeral service providers from laboratory workers. First, the names given to funerary AH visually and aurally link the technology to cremation, thereby shaping the identity of the technology by associating it with technologies already internal to the funeral industry. Second, as AH system developer Joe Wilson puts it, "the laboratory term 'tissue digester' did not bear any sensitivity to the funeral industry" (Wilson, 2011, p. 32). In particular, use of the laboratory term in funerary contexts would overlook funeral professionals' unique expertise in overseeing the *sacred* rite of preparing and disposing of human remains. Joe Wilson's company, BRS, Inc. (BRS), which manufactures both funerary AH systems and non-funerary AH systems, enforces the distinctiveness of professional funeral expertise, and the distinctiveness of funerary AH systems, by establishing a separate web domain for its funerary systems, and by using the terms "digester" and "tissue digester" only in reference to its laboratory systems" (Bio-Response Solutions, Inc., 2008a; Bio-Response Solutions, Inc., 2008b).

It is not only naming practices that are used to distance funerary AH systems from non-funerary AH systems. AH system developers also distance funerary and non-funerary systems from one another by adapting the design of AH systems to both fit and reinforce the distinctiveness of funerary contexts. In *Stiff*, Roach reports on her encounter with a large non-funerary AH system operated by a veterinary school to dispose of large amounts of biological material. The type of system she observes is common in non-funerary contexts. In systems like these, the vessels in which the AH process takes place look like huge, stainless steel pressure cookers, with a stainless steel lid that is latched to the top of the "pot" when the system is in operation. Depending on the size of the digester, large systems can process up to four thousand pounds of biological material at once. The material to be hydrolyzed is lowered into the vessel from above, and in non-funerary contexts the remains of multiple organisms are routinely processed simultaneously. While providing a graphic description of the veterinary AH system at work, Roach perceptively reassures her reader, "Of course, for mortuary digestions, some alterations will be made in the name of dignity" (2003, p. 256). *Stiff* was published two years before the design of AH systems began to adapt to the unique social and professional spaces of US death care culture, but Roach rightly identifies the principal consideration that continues to guide the redesign of funerary AH systems, namely, morality.

Critics who categorically oppose funerary AH commonly contend that AH fails to demonstrate proper respect for the sacred human corpse. A variety of concerns about the dignified treatment of human remains have been raised in the name of public morality in general and religious ethics in particular. Adversaries of AH commonly express disgust at the thought of sacred human remains being flushed down the drain like everyday bodily waste, and at the thought of those remains somehow finding their way back into the bodies of the living through food and water (Olson, 2014). But even amongst proponents of funerary AH, the moral character of funerary AH systems is a matter of serious concern. Disputes about the morality of funerary AH are played out discursively and materially in relation to a number of AH system design features that are laden with moral significance. One design feature immediately stands out as the most obvious (and most important) feature that sets funerary AH systems apart from non-funerary systems; funerary AH systems are *always* designed to process only one human body at a time. The exclusive use of single-body systems within funerary contexts is morally requisite, as this design feature demonstrates respect for a widely recognized moral revulsion to the idea of comingling human remains. Some AH proponents argue that funerary systems do more than simply conform to the normative injunction against comingling, they conform more perfectly than cremation systems. In an article published in *The National Catholic Bioethics Quarterly*, Sister Renee Mirkes writes, while "cross-contamination of bodily remains between cremations is unavoidable … [t]he alkaline hydrolysis unit is completely cleaned between cycles, so there is no cross-contamination of one body's remains with another" (2008, pp. 687–688).

A second design feature that distinguishes funerary AH systems from non-funerary AH systems has to do with the position or orientation of the body when it is placed in the AH cylinder, and while the AH process takes place. In non-funerary systems, and in systems designed for *pet* funerals, the remains are lowered into the vessel from above. But in systems designed for human funerals, bodies are always slid into the vessel horizontally, thereby conforming to the normative body orientation of traditional cremation and earth burial. As pointed out (Olson 2014, pp. 685–686), the orientation of the body during the AH process is a point of contention amongst AH system designers. For example, Steve Schaal, president of the North American Division of Matthews Cremation has criticized the design of competitor BRS's funerary systems because the BRS systems tip the vessel at an angle during the AH process. According to Schaal, BRS's systems fail to respect the dignity of the human corpse by tipping it at an angle during the AH process.[4]

In preparation for their introduction into sacred funerary contexts, the technological identities of AH systems have reconfigured and purified of their preexisting associations with laboratory animal disposal. This reconfiguration and purification have taken place both through the renaming AH technologies, and by adapting the design of AH systems to fit the uniqueness of funerary contexts. Efforts to separate funerary AH from non-funerary AH conform to and facilitate broader interests in insulating the social spaces of death from other social spaces. In the mid-nineteenth century, Gannal appealed to the separateness of the world of the dead from the world of the living as grounds for liberating embalming from the exclusive control of physicians, and for creating a new occupational identity. "[W]hat," Gannal asks,

> is the subtle link between the art of healing a person who is ill and that of embalming a dead man. – As far as I'm concerned, I can't see any worth mentioning. You ask me what right I have to embalm corpses…

Why, I have the right of an embalmer; the answer is simple.

(1845 cited in Trompette and Lemonnier, 2009, p. 5)

In the US today, funeral professionals routinely and rapidly remove dead bodies from domestic or medical spaces, transporting the dead to specialized funeral spaces (typically funeral homes or crematoria) in which, and through which, funeral professionals assert expert authority over the bodies of the dead. The case of AH reveals that the management of disposition technologies continues to be an important part of the work that funeral professionals do to create and maintain a unique professional identity within a distinct social space.

Professional identity in transition

Death care scholar Spencer Cahill argues, based on his ethnographic study of a cohort of mortuary science students, that the professional identity of occupational neophytes is grounded in

> an occupation's publicly recognized claim to a distinctive and definitive occupational jurisdiction.... [O]ccupations with a definitive license to "carry out activities rather different from other people" have a foundation on which to build neophytes' professional identities.
>
> (1999, p. 117)

One key way in which funeral professionals maintain control over the dead human body (and thus death care markets) is by defining a unique social space over which they themselves have authoritative, expert jurisdiction. The present study demonstrates that one important way in which funeral professionals manage the boundaries of their professional jurisdiction is by exercising control over the identities of the technologies that are used to perform work that is specific to their professional identity. Yet new technologies are not simply passive in relation to fixed professional identities; new technologies also act to change professional identities. In what follows I will examine the impact of funerary AH on US funeral professionals' social and occupational identity as moral authorities and technical experts with respect to the disposal of dead human bodies.

Through the standardization of funeral embalming, US undertakers transformed the care of dead bodies into a technical occupation that required specialized knowledge, practical training, and skill. The link between embalming and the professional identities of US funeral directors is evident in the words of one mortuary science student interviewed by Cahill: "[T]he only time you feel like a real funeral director is in the embalming lab. The rest of the time, you just memorize things you're gonna forget" (1999, p. 115). One crucial reason for why embalming has been so integral to US funeral directors' professional identity is that embalmers *themselves* are the ultimate authorities on the skilled techno-artistry of embalming. Recall that Lambert specifically identifies embalming, but not cremation, as unique to funeral directors' "technical function" and "specialized trade." Moreover, by disdainfully referring to direct cremation as "bake and shake" (Prothero, 2001, p. 175), funeral directors' have evoked the artless expediency of a familiar convenience food to criticize cremation.

As is the case with cremation, one need not have highly specialized knowledge or technical training to operate a funerary AH system. As funerary AH provider Mike Phillips of Central Florida Casket Store and Funeral Chapel puts it, "I could pull someone in off the street, given them this manual, and they could operate it themselves. Anybody could do this."[5] And while giving me a tour of the Resomation-built AH system he operates at Anderson-McQueen Funeral Home, John Anders referred to the pipes that feed and relieve the AH system as a "plumber's nightmare." Similarly, he referred to the system's circuit panel as an "electrician's nightmare." To funeral professionals like Anders, the technical details of the AH system are not only unknown but also somewhat intimidating. Anders is content to consign responsibility for the plumbing and electrical details to specialists outside his profession. As is the case with funerary incineration technologies, deep technical expertise is inessential as a basis for claiming professional authority over funerary AH technologies. Lamenting cremation's consumer status as an *alternative* to funeral services centered on the skillfully embalmed corpse (Parmalee 2011a, p. 12), Edwards also explicitly articulates concern about the professional consequences of further deskilling funeral work through AH. Without strict regulation, Edwards worries, unskilled business persons outside of the funeral profession (Edwards mentions a shop owner) could begin offering AH to funeral consumers (Parmalee 2011b, p. 24), thereby weakening funeral professionals' exclusive jurisdiction over the commercial care of dead human bodies.

The introduction of AH technologies into US funeral markets involves more than the presence of new machines upon the funeral stage; it also implicates established funeral actors in new ways, and introduces new actors who wish to create a place for themselves within the funeral industry. Indeed, the status of funeral actors as professional "insiders" or "outsiders" is intimately bound up with the "insider" or "outsider" status of the technologies they use. Edwards has every reason to be sensitive to the ways in which the indeterminate status of AH technologies can destabilize the boundaries of funeral professionalism. Although Edwards was no newcomer to the funeral profession, having enjoyed professional status as a licensed funeral director for several years prior to offering AH, his work with AH technologies threatened his status as a member in good standing of the community of funeral professionals – at least in the eyes of the OBEFD, which accused Edwards of engaging in "immoral or nonprofessional conduct…" (Parmalee 2011, p. 25). It is understandable, then, that Edwards insists upon the insider status of funerary AH, for if AH technologies were internal to the funeral industry, then Edwards' use of those technologies would not threaten his professional status. More-over, the national media attention given to Edwards' controversial use of AH triggered concern amongst subsequent adopters of AH technologies. One early adopter expressed disappointment about the way in which AH was introduced into Ohio funeral markets. "It caused some other states to dig in right away," states Jason Bradshaw, "and this one [Edwards] is kind of a rogue person out there doing this, and it gave it [alkaline hydrolysis] more of this rogue status."[6] Bradshaw worries that AH's status as a legitimate funeral tech-nology could be damaged if AH is used by rogues, "out there," whose out-sider status rubs off on the identity of the technologies themselves.

The perceived legitimacy of funerary AH depends not only on the rela-tionship between AH technologies and the professional status of AH service *providers*, but also on the relationship between AH technologies and the professional status of AH system *engineers, manufacturers,* and *distributors.* Estab-lished funeral professionals who offer AH depend upon *new actors* who possess a techno-scientific expertise regarding AH systems. This expertise enters into funeral work partly in the form of skills that are designed into or embedded in AH systems themselves: skills that funeral professionals who operate AH systems need not (and most often do not) possess. Established actors' new-found dependence generates uncertainties about the grounds upon which authority over funerary AH may be claimed, and blurs the boundaries of funeral professionalism in general. Established funeral professionals' lack of technical expertise may provide new actors, who possess no formal funeral training, with grounds for claiming status as funeral industry experts or insiders. BRS's Joe Wilson considers himself "part of the funeral industry," and his company has plans to offer AH disposition for pets by establishing a pet-loss center in the company's new plant – though Wilson states that BRS currently has no interest in moving into the human disposition business.[7] BRS is a funeral newcomer, and the company's relationship to the funeral industry is mediated only through the funerary AH systems it manufactures. Meanwhile, BHS continues to manufacture AH systems for use in pharma-ceutical and bio-containment contexts, pointing out that BRS is "all about killing microbes."[8] Lacking formal training as a funeral director, Wilson understandably positions himself as a techno-scientific expert with "35 years' experience in designing and building biohazardous processing systems for medical facilities and biocontainment laboratories," adding that BRS has "the most experienced engineering team in the industry" (Wilson, 2012, p. 1). Yet according to early funerary AH adopters Jim Bradshaw and his son Jason, of Minnesota-based Bradshaw Funeral Homes, Wilson is "not connected with the industry," and is "sort of an industry outsider."[9] For the Bradshaws, the professional identity of an AH system supplier can affect the legitimacy of the technology itself. "I think we felt," states Jason Bradshaw, "that we are doing something that was outside the norm enough where we wanted our own legitimacy coming from a company that was connected in the industry."[10] In 2011, the Bradshaws purchased an AH system built by Resomation, Ltd., but distributed by the one hundred year old funeral giant, Matthews International, a leading manufacturer of cremation retorts, and a supplier of a wide range of memorialization products and funeral industry services.

Resomation, Ltd. distances its funerary AH systems from non-funerary precursors in two ways: first by availing itself of the decidedly insider status of Matthews International, which Resomation has appointed as the sole distributor of Resomation systems in North America; second by manufacturing *only* funerary AH systems. One of the leading public proponents of Resomation's AH systems, Dean Fisher, appeals to his own funeral pedigree to reinforce Resomation's funerary fitness. Fisher, who heads UCLA's anatomical donations program (which operates a Resomation-built AH system), grounds his AH expertise primarily in his status as a funeral industry insider. In a 2012 article about AH regulation published in a leading funeral trade journal, *The Director*, Fisher proposes a number of regulatory policies from his position as "a licensed funeral director for 27 years," but secondarily as someone who has "a strong working knowledge of alkaline hydrolysis" (Fisher, 2012, p. 34). Fisher does not emphasize his technical expertise, but instead draws particular attention to moral concerns regarding the regulation of AH systems, notably, concerns about the dignified treatment of the human corpse, the prevention of the comingling of human remains, and the purity of the bone matter to be returned to decedents' families (Fisher, 2012). Fisher's insistence upon the moral purity of funerary AH systems both fits and reinforces funeral professionals' belief in the importance of maintaining a unique professional identity within a distinct social space.

Conclusions

US funeral professionals' sense of their own identities is changing. Funeral professionals have traditionally justified their custody of the corpse both by way of their technical expertise in caring for the bodies of the dead, and by way of their perceived moral authority regarding the dignified handling of human corpses. But the increasing division of funeral labor into "front stage" and "back stage" work signals a willingness amongst funeral professionals to tolerate a somewhat fractured professional identity. And in light of the elevation of front stage work, the sentiment expressed by one mortuary science student interviewed by Cahill – "the only time you feel like a real funeral director is in the embalming lab" – is undoubtedly losing some professional power. Nevertheless, tolerance for diversity or ambiguity within the boundaries of funeral professionalism does not imply tolerance for ambiguity at the fringes of funeral professionalism. "If we start deciding we're going to play on the fringes, that's where any industry gets into trouble," notes early AH adopter Jim Bradshaw.[11] I follow Cahill in maintaining that a key way in which funeral professionals maintain control over the dead human body is by defining a unique social space over which they alone have jurisdiction. I offer that the introduction of AH technologies into US funeral markets obligates funeral professionals to perform the professional labor of simultaneously managing the boundaries of their professional identity, as well as managing the technological identities of funerary AH systems. Indeed, AH developers and AH providers are currently working out their professional identities on the very surfaces of the AH systems they design and use. Funerary AH technologies may allow actors who possess no formal training as embalmers or funeral directors to claim inclusion as funeral professionals or experts. On the other hand, the funeral industry's current de-emphasis of back stage work could supply funeral professionals with grounds to resist the inclusion of these actors, though possibly at the expense of marginalizing the back stage work (and workers) upon whom front stage funeral professionals largely rely in order to retain control over the dead human body in US death care markets.

Notes

1 I use the term "funerary" specifically to refer to *human* funeral contexts.
2 US Patent Office, Patent No. 5,332,532.
3 Telephone interview with Joe Wilson, CEO of Bio-Response Solutions, Inc. (Conducted 6 January 2014).
4 Interview with Stephen Schaal, President, North American Region, Matthews International Cremation Division. (Conducted in Charlotte, NC, 10 November 2012).
5 Telephone interview with Mike Phillips, Funeral Director and Owner, Central Florida Casket Store and Funeral Chapel. (Conducted 15 January 2014).
6 Interview with Jim and Jason Bradshaw of Bradshaw Funeral Services. (Conducted in Stillwater, MN, 3 July 2013).
7 Telephone interview with Joe Wilson, 6 January 2014.
8 Telephone interview with Joe Wilson, 6 January 2014.
9 Interview with Jim and Jason Bradhsaw, 3 July 2013.
10 Interview with Jim and Jason Bradshaw, 3 July 2013.
11 Interview with Jim and Jason Bradshaw, 3 July 2013.

References

Bio-Response Solutions, Inc. (2008a). Tissue digester models. Available at: www.bioresponsesolutions.com/Digestermodels.html (Accessed: 29 December 2014).

Bio-Response Solutions, Inc. (2008b). Alkaline hydrolysis disposition. Available at: www.bioresponsefuneral.com (Accessed: 29 December 2014).

Bowker, G.C. and Star, S.L. (1999). *Sorting things out: classification and its consequences.* Cambridge: MIT Press.

Cahill, S. (1995). "Some rhetorical directions of funeral direction: historical entanglements and contemporary dilemmas," *Work and Occupations*, 22 (2), pp. 115–136.

Cahill, S. (1999). "The boundaries of professionalism: the case of north American funeral direction," *Symbolic Interaction*, 22 (2), pp. 105–119.

Emke, I. (2002). "Why the sad face? secularization and the changing function of funerals in Newfoundland," *Mortality*, 7 (3), pp. 169–84.

Faust, D. (2008). *This republic of suffering: death and the American civil war.* New York: Random House.

Fisher, D. (2012). "Creating policy and legislation for alkaline hydrolysis," *The Director*, 84 (1), pp. 34–36.

Howarth, G. (1996). *Last rites: the work of the modern funeral director*. Amityville, NY: Baywood Publishing Company.

Kenevich, T. (2011). "Suppliers of alkaline hydrolysis," In *The funeral director's guide to alkaline hydrolysis*. Wall, NJ: Kates-Boylston Publishers, pp. 15–18.

Laderman, G. (2003). *Rest in peace: a cultural history of death and the funeral home in twentieth-century America*. Oxford: Oxford University Press.

Lambert, D. (2011). "Alkaline hydrolysis: why are we talking about it?" In *The funeral director's guide to alkaline hydrolysis*. Wall, NJ: Kates-Boylston, pp. 48–49.

Mirkes, Sr. R. (2008). "The mortuary science of alkaline hydrolysis," *National Catholic Bioethics Quarterly*, 8 (4), pp. 683–695.

Olson, P. (2014). "Flush and bone: funeralizing alkaline hydrolysis in the US," *Science, Technology, and Human Values*, 39 (5), pp. 666–693.

Parmalee, Thomas. (2011a). "NFDA Takes a Stand on How to Classify Alkaline Hydrolysis," In *The funeral director's guide to alkaline hydrolysis*. Wall, NJ: Kates-Boylston, pp. 11–14.

Parmalee, Thomas. (2011b). "Jeff Edwards: Trailblazing Professional Remains a Controversial Figure," In *The funeral director's guide to alkaline hydrolysis*. Wall, NJ: Kates-Boylston, pp. 23–26.

Plater, M. (1996). *African American entrepreneurship in Richmond, 1890–1940: the story of R.C. Scott*. Brunchey, S. (ed.) *Garland studies in entrepreneurship*. New York: Garland Publishing.

Prothero, S. (2001). *Purified by fire: a history of cremation in America*. Berkeley: University of California Press.

Roach, M. (2003). *Stiff: the curious lives of human cadavers*. New York: W. W. Norton and Company.

Sanders, G. (2010). "The dismal trade as culture industry," *Poetics*, 38 (1), pp. 47–68.

Schäfer, C. (2007). "Post-mortem personalisation: pastoral power and the New Zealand funeral director," *Mortality*, 12 (1), pp. 4–21.

Trompette, P., and Lemonnier, M. (2009). "Funeral embalming: the transformation of a medical innovation," *Science Studies*, 22 (2), pp. 9–30.

Wilson, J. (2011). "How I've spent my career promoting alkaline hydrolysis," In *The funeral director's guide to alkaline hydrolysis*. Wall, NJ: Kates-Boylston, pp. 31–36.

Wilson, J. (2012). Unpublished letter to Mr. Ed Defort, Editor of *The Director*, dated 3 January 2012.

Part II

Death rituals and consumption

6 Death, ritual and consumption in Thailand

Insights from the Pee Ta Kohn hungry ghost festival

Rungpaka Amy Hackley and Chris Hackley[1]

Introduction

A consequence of the precipitous rise of Asian economies in recent decades and, in particular, the emergence of China as a global economic power, has been increased research into Asian consumption (Fam *et al.*, 2009). However, there are still relatively few studies that use qualitative methods (Eckhardt and Dholakia, 2013; Hackley and Hackley, 2013), and fewer still that focus on ritual. In this chapter we seek insights into Asian consumer culture by examining the ritual elements of a hungry ghost festival held annually in Thailand, South East Asia.

Asian brands and consumer practices in food, martial arts, music, electronic games, high fashion and many other areas, have made significant inroads into Western markets (Kniazeva and Belk, 2012; Hong and Kim, 2013; Seo, 2013; Kuang-Ying Loo and Hackley, 2013) yet the nuances of Asian consumer culture remain an enigma to many in the West (McGrath *et al.*, 2013; Venkatesh *et al.*, 2013). Asian consumer culture is perhaps most noted in the West for the stereotypically ostentatious consumption and display of luxury brands by the rapidly growing middle and upper classes (Chadha and Husband, 2007; Lu, 2008). From an anthropological perspective, brand consumption is implicated in identity work, group identification and class distinction (Belk, 1988), although the cultural, historical, political and economic contexts of consumption differ profoundly around the world. Western style consumption carries many tensions and contradictions within the West: this is also true for Eastern consumers who try to assimilate to Western consumer culture (Tiwsakul and Hackley, 2012). Consumption cannot be regarded as an unproblematic practice in any context: it is a site for the negotiation of power, status, social class and identity through practices that differ in local cultural contexts. There is a need for more consumer research that focuses on the many local contexts of Asian consumer culture, and rituals around death and the hereafter offer rich potential sources of consumer cultural insight.

Since Rook (1985) first introduced ritual into the consumer research field, various commentators (e.g. Arnould, 2001) have remarked on the relatively small number of follow-up studies. Amongst the studies of ritual consumption, rituals connected to death are even more neglected. Yet, rituals surrounding death are intimately bound up with consumption practices of various kinds, from the burning of paper models of consumer goods to placate ancestors in Asian death rituals, to the ritualized gift-giving and feasting in some Western and African funeral rituals, and onward to the carnivalesque festival consumption of Dia de Meurtos, the Mexican Day of the Dead, or its counterpart, All Souls Day, and other death festivals such as Halloween, the Japanese Bon festival, the South Korean Chuseok, Qingming in China, or the many varieties of ghost festivals held around the Asian world. In this chapter our empirical focus falls on one particular example of a death ritual – the hungry ghost festival held annually in Dansai Province, North-East Thailand.

The hungry ghost is an enduring feature of East, South-East and North Asian religious and folk mythology, representing the negative spiritual consequences of earthly desire. Paradoxically, many rituals that invoke the hungry ghost also seem to embrace the overt materialism that, to Westerners, characterizes much Asian consumption, for example, in the form of burnt offerings of paper versions of Louis Vuitton bags, Mercedes-Benz cars and Gucci wrist watches to be consumed by the dead in the afterlife. Paper burning rituals have been in existence in China for 1000 years (Blake, 2011) but the uses of paper models of branded goods, though, dates from the emergence of Western-style consumption in the East. Many hungry ghost rituals have feasting, dancing, music, entertainment performances and other consumption practices at their core, including food and other offerings for visitors, and for the ghosts themselves.

In this chapter, our study of the hungry ghost religious mythology reveals the uneasy assimilation of traditional Asian values and Western consumer culture by connecting the present, the past, the living and the dead. The mythological figure of the hungry ghost can be seen to work not only to oppose the values of individualism and materialism with which Western consumer culture is often associated, but to assist in their cultural assimilation. Our aim in the chapter is twofold. First, we wish to progress the use of ritual in consumer research with a focus on an area of death ritual that has not been previously the subject of research in the field. Second, we use insights from death ritual to open up a new perspective in Asian consumer culture research. Specifically, we draw attention to the role of death ritual in an apparent paradox. Rising Asian economies are known in the West for the ostentatious brand consumption often indulged in by the new middle and upper classes, yet in these very same cultures there are long standing traditional values of prudence and modesty. We suggest that not only does consumption feature significantly in the examples of Asian death ritual we describe, but it serves to reconcile the deep contradiction between Western-style brand consumption, and Eastern-style modesty and religious asceticism. Finally, we suggest that our empirical focus on the unique tradition and spectacle of the Dansai hungry ghost festival permits a striking insight into the role of ghosts in Buddhist consumer culture in general, and in the Thai Theravāda tradition in particular.

We will begin with a brief overview of ritual as it has been addressed in consumer research, including some of the examples of work focusing on death ritual. We will then outline the cultural background for our empirical study of a Thai hungry ghost festival before describing our research method. We then delineate our key findings and discuss the implications. Overall, we aim to contribute new insights from a novel empirical setting to the growing body of work dealing with ritual, death, and Asian consumer culture.

Ritual and death in consumer research

Rituals connect individuals with common beliefs and values; they mark transformational events or incidents, and they re-instantiate rules, norms and practices that underlie the social order (Driver, 1998). They may be connected to calendrical rites such as the summer solstice, harvest or new year celebrations, and they may be undertaken to mark rites of passage such as those from single to married, from child to adult, or from living to dead. In all their various forms, rituals carry symbolic meanings (Rook and Levy 1983; Gainer 1995) and the study of ritual has played a key role in advancing understanding of the symbolic aspects of consumption (Rook, 1985; Belk, 1994; Stanfield and Kleine, 1990; Wallendorf and Arnould, 1991; Holt, 1992; Houston, 1999; Ustuner *et al.*, 2000; Minowa, 2008).

Studies of death ritual have hitherto tended to focus on the consumption activities connected to funeral rites, both in the West (e.g. Price *et al.*, 2000; Metcalf and Huntington, 1991) and beyond (Bonsu and Belk, 2003: see also Bond, 1980; Goody, 1962). The consumer research literature on death and consumption has begun to contribute valuable insights into theories and practices of how consumers manage the experience of the death of loved ones and the rituals which accompany the fundamental rite of passage from life, to death (O'Donohoe and Turley, 2005, 2000; Bonsu and Belk, 2003; Bonsu and DeBerry-Spence, 2008; Gentry *et al.*, 1995; Davies, 1997). In addition, studies have provided insights into the linkage between the achievement of secular immortality and consumer affluence (Hirschman, 1990), and the meanings and practices of the disposition of possessions of the dead (Kates, 2001; Price *et al.*, 2000). Three consumer culture studies in particular look into death rituals and death consumption in a non-Western context: Bonsu and Belk (2003) (and a subsequent work by Bonsu and DeBerry-Spence, 2008); Zhao and Belk's (2003; 2008) study of Chinese death ritual consumption; and Wattanasuwan's (2005) research on the paper burning ritual in Thailand.

In anthropological studies, death ritual as a sub-category of ritual can take many forms, some of which reflect local traditions and myths. They can evolve into spectacular, and, sometimes, commercially inflected, tourist attractions. Death rituals might celebrate life or death, and they might serve to distil fears and superstitions into a single time period and event, thereby dissipating their power to instill fear or dread (Driver, 1998). In the Western tradition, death ritual may be focused on funeral rites that enable the living to come to terms with the loss of loved ones and also, perhaps, with their own mortality. These strategies of grief management are sometimes grouped under the category terror management theory (TMT) (Bonsu and Belk, 2003). Death ritual around funeral rites have different meanings in the East and West. In the West, death marks the end of life, and therefore, of consumption (Borgmann, 2000: Hirschman *et al.*, 2013). In Eastern death ritual, though there is no such finality, reflecting the different eschatologies between Buddhism and Taosim in the East, and the Western Judeao-Christian-Islamic tradition. Asian Buddhist death rituals celebrate death as a natural progression on the Wheel of Life. For Buddhists, the dead are always with us, as a literal presence in everyday life, especially at propitious times. The dead may be mischievous or may be malign, if they are tormented ghosts, or they may be benign and contented ancestors who bring blessings to the living. The destinies of the dead and the living are inter-twined in Buddhist death rituals, and the intimacy of this connection is evident in many Asian death rituals.

In rituals connected to death, the possessions of both the deceased and the living assume symbolic importance (see, for example, Belk *et al.*, 1989; Belk, 1988, 1991; Gentry *et al.*, 1995; Turley, 1995, 1998; Carroll and Romano, 2010). For example, the possessions of the dead might have special status conferred upon them, to be preserved, gifted to special individuals, or eliminated, while some mourners will offer gifts to the bereaved, or for the benefit of the dead themselves. Symbolic exchange can be socially visible in death ritual, such as when gifts are given to the bereaved (Bonsu and DeBerry-Spence, 2008; Bonsu and Belk, 2003; Langer, 2007). In Asian death ritual, exchange can also occur within liminal spaces, for example where ghosts or the deceased are placated with offerings such as food or models of consumer goods or money to be ritually burned, for use in the after life. These symbolic exchanges serve to maintain relationships between the living and the dead, fulfilling Driver's (1998) 'gifts' of order and community within transformation.

We will now outline the role of the hungry ghost mythology across parts of Asia and, in particular, in the Thai Theravāda Buddhist tradition. We will then briefly describe the method, followed by an account of selected features of the festival that we focus on for this chapter, before discussing the main themes that emerged from the analysis of the various data sets. Finally, we discuss the insights that emerge to contour our understanding of the role of death ritual in Asian consumer culture.

Hungry ghosts and Thai Theravāda Buddhist tradition

The hungry ghost is an entity that inspires countless folk myths, rituals and festivals in countries such as China, Tibet, Thailand, Taiwan, Singapore, Japan, Malaysia and Hong Kong. The hungry ghost is typically a feature of Buddhist spiritual mythology, although there are different nuances in the differing traditions of Buddhism, and hungry ghost stories are also inflected by local history, tradition and mythology. Theravāda Buddhism is the dominant religious tradition in Thailand (Kolm, 1985) and is also practiced in other Southeast Asian countries including Thailand, Sri Lanka, Burma, Laos and Cambodia, whereas Mahāyāna Buddhism is practiced in East and North Asian countries such as Tibet, China, Japan, Taiwan and Korea (though Confucianism and Taoism exert some influence on this branch of Buddhism in this region). Thai Theravāda Buddhism is inflected with many animistic, Brahamistic, and local folklore beliefs, along with regional emphases drawing from Taoist, Mon and Khmer traditions. This amounts to a highly variable and localized system of beliefs, behaviors and myths. There have been some previous consumer research studies that touch upon the hungry ghost cosmology within the Tibetan Mahāyāna Buddhist tradition (e.g. Gould, 1991, 1992) and in Chinese Taosim (Zhao and Belk, 2003; 2008) but none of which we are aware that explore the tradition in Thai Theravāda Buddhism.

The hungry ghost is stuck between levels on the Wheel of Life, tormented by earthly desires. It may be a human who lived immorally or died badly, or who did not have relatives to perform the necessary rituals to enable him or her to progress from being an unhappy ghost in Hell to being a content and benign ancestor. Hungry ghosts must be placated or distracted lest they create mischief and disrupt the happiness and equanimity of others (Zhao and Belk, 2003). Gould (1991) refers to a hungry ghost in the Tibetan Mahāyāna tradition as a 'preta', using an Anglicization of the Sanskrit word to mean a recently dead ghost (Oates, 1974; Langer, 2007). In the ghost infused Thai Theravāda religious tradition (McDaniel, 2006) a hungry ghost (Anglicised as a 'pred') can subsist in that form on the Wheel of Life for an indeterminate time, depending on the circumstances, so may not necessarily be recently deceased and could be an ancient spirit.

There are many different types of ghosts in Thai mythology. Some cannot let go of their loved ones, others cling to their former homes or to sensory pleasures. All are hungry in some way or other, most are tormented and some are malicious. They are described vividly in stories, often as a frightening entity with huge hands, long limbs and a tiny pin-hole sized mouth so it cannot feed itself to assuage its distress. Conveniently for adults, the first author recalls, children are told that they too will become a hungry ghost in their next life if they are disrespectful to their parents. But the spirits of the dead are not just sources of frightening stories for Thai Buddhists. A ghost is a liminal entity in Buddhism as it is in a transitional state towards other incarnations on the Wheel of Life. When loved ones die, the living have a duty to take part in rituals that will assist the transition of the deceased spirit from tormented, yearning ghost to happy and placated ancestor.

Hungry ghost festivals

Hungry ghost festivals usually occur around the 15th day of the 7th lunar month in the Chinese calendar, although this can vary somewhat according to timezone and local custom. According to the typical mythology, this is a time when the gates of the Hell realm are opened and for a short space of time the hungry ghosts are able to escape to roam the physical world. In this, hungry ghost festivals share some common mythology with many other festivals of life and death around the world such as Samhain, Halloween, Purim and el Dia de los Muertos, (e.g. Belk, 1994; Santino, 1995).

Festivals involving hungry ghosts in different regions can have a different character, and draw on differing histories and formats. For example, the 'Portor' hungry ghost festival in Phuket province, Thailand, is intended to earn merit for the living by offering food to 'Por Tor Kong' (the Devil spirit in charge of the hungry ghosts' realm) and to other hungry spirits. Por-tor (this is an Anglicized spelling which approximates the Thai word) derives from the Chinese heritage in Southern Thailand when the first immigrants from China and Malaysia came to work in the tin mines of Phuket. In the Por-tor festival the consumption of food is prominent, especially of red turtle cakes that are symbolic of long life and good fortune. The festival is held to worship the ghosts who have been released from their realm by the goddess 'Gwan Yin' to return to their former homes. The living assist the dead in their transition from ghosts to ancestors by inviting the ghosts to come and eat, and in return for their solicitous merit making the ghosts will bless the people and give luck to their various undertakings in the town. In another example, at the Ge Tai festival in Singapore the ghosts are assumed to be physically present at the performance and attendees leave seats for them then strain to see the show around the imaginary ghosts on the front row, performing their respect to the ontologically present spirits.

Hungry ghost festivals, then, can entail various ritual practices, some of which are intimately connected to consumption. There can be feasting, music, trading, gift-giving, and many involve the ritual burning of paper offerings in the form of imitation money, or paper models of branded goods such as watches, cars, handbags, mobile phones and even Viagra tablets. The ritual burning of paper offerings echoes the ancient practice in Chinese Taoism (Blake, 2011) of the Joss paper burning ritual (Wattanasuwan, 2005). The paper offerings are intended to be re-animated in the afterlife for the use of the dead, in spite of hungry ghosts having committed the sin of materialism. The offerings are intended to be of benefit to the dead as practical assistance in the afterlife, and also to reflect the respect and solicitous observance of ritual of their living relatives, thereby assisting the ghosts' passage on to the next stage of the Wheel of Life. The corporeal participants also have a stake in the observance of death rituals since they earn merit for themselves and their families by engaging in the process. Placated ghosts will return blessings to the living. Merit is often conceived in varieties of Buddhism as a spiritual concept that has a material dimension – the faithful hope for a more favorable transition to their next existence on the Wheel of Life, but they also hope to benefit from greater luck and material comfort in this life. The benefits of merit in the here and now are often bound up with superstition and folk belief, such as when monks are asked to provide auspicious lottery numbers or to bless new cars or businesses. We will now discuss the method of this study before examining the Pee Ta Khon festival in greater depth.

Method

We use a multi-method approach to arrive at a tentative interpretation of some of the cultural meanings of one example of a hungry ghost festival, the Pee Ta Khon. This event was not one of those we observed directly in Thailand, for logistical reasons: the event is a bus and pick-up truck journey of some 14 hours from Bangkok, and attendance is made more difficult because the precise timing of the event is decided, often at the last minute, by local 'black magicians' (literally translated) or spiritual leaders, and can be anywhere between March and June. We chose to focus on it because it is a particularly vivid and uniquely carnivalesque enactment of the hungry ghost mythology.

Our examination of the Pee Ta Kohn hungry ghost festival draws on elements of discourse analysis, visual semiotics and cultural anthropology. Our discourse analysis (Potter and Wetherell, 1987) is applied to three semi-structured interview transcripts (translated from Thai by the first author) with an official at the Thai Authority of Tourism, with the leading local festival organizer, and with a local expert on the festival in Bangkok. The transcribed texts are sifted and coded for structure, function and variation (Potter and Wetherell, 1987) and the resulting themes assimilated with themes from the other data sources. Second, we conducted a visual semiotic analysis (Hodge and Cress, 1988; Culler, 1985; Pink, 2006; Buckingham, 2009) of selected publicly available video ethnographies of the festival (of which there are many on social media). In so doing we attempt a mediated version of naturalistic observation (Belk and Kozinets, 2005). Third, we sought an ethnomethodologically informed 'rich' description (Geertz, 1973) by contextualizing this information with the first author's first-hand knowledge of the ways in which hungry ghost mythology is subsumed into everyday Thai life, and also with informal sources such as archive material about the festival on Thai tourism websites, and informal observations and conversations with other Thai nationals with knowledge of these events. Assimilating and coding the various sources of data, we collated a number of sub-themes that we distilled into two main meta-themes or 'interpretive repertoires' (Potter and Wetherell, 1978), discussed below.

We believe our analysis to be well-informed but do not claim that it is definitive. There are not only logistical and interpretive but linguistic issues to deal with in the study. Thai language consists of differing dialects and vocabularies in different regions. A person raised and educated in Bangkok can only communicate with great difficulty with compatriots from the regions who speak only the local dialect. There will be contradictions and inconsistencies in accounts of the origin and meanings of particular death ritual practices, and we do not seek to gloss over these to present a tidier analysis. We offer what we believe is a well-informed outsider's interpretation which, as we note, cannot be regarded as definitive.

The Pee Ta Khon festival

In the following account, we draw on our transcribed interviews, archive material on Thai tourism websites, and our analysis of the video data, and we contextualize all this with the first author's native understanding of how the folk beliefs and mythologies celebrated in the ritual percolate through to everyday Thai life. It is important first to describe the mythical foundation, ritual practices and local meanings entailed in this unique ritual.

The 'Pee Ta Khon' or hungry ghost festival is held annually for three days in Dansai district in the north-central Loei province of Thailand. Dansai is regarded as a sacred place and this festival, like all such festivals, is unique to this district and cannot be held anywhere else in this form. It is considered essentially local and central to the identity of the local people, although today it attracts an international tourist audience because of promotion by the Tourism Authority of Thailand (TAT). The festival is one of the most important Thai merit-making ceremonies in the 'Heed Sib-Song Klong Sib-Si' tradition of the Theravāda Buddhist calendar (Ruangviset, 1996). It also serves as a fertility festival calling on the relevant spirits to bless the forthcoming harvest.

'Pee Ta Khon' is part of the larger event called 'Bun Luang', and includes the 'Pee Ta Khon' festival (hungry ghost festival), the 'Prapheni Bun Bung Fai' (rocket festival) and 'Bun Pra Wate' (a merit making ceremony). Originally known as 'Pee Tam Khon', which is literally translated as 'ghosts follow the living', the festival is based on an old folklore tale. According to the tale, the procession of ghosts in the Pee Ta Kohn re-enacts the last and tenth incarnation of the Buddha, Prince Mahavejsandon, leaving his banishment in the forest to return to the village, accompanied by the ghosts who wish to escort him safely back to the town. The Prince is welcomed back to the village with much rejoicing from his parents, family, friends and from the respectful ghosts, all of whom join in the festival celebrations to mark his return.

The first day of the festival is an assembly day, precursor to the main events, and is called 'Wan Ruam'. In the early morning the town's residents invite the Spirit known as 'Phra U-Pakut' from the 'Mun River' to protect the area where the festival is held, in order to bless the festival. There is a small parade at this stage. Later in the morning the parade goes to the house of the black magician or wizard, called 'Ban Chow Guan' in order to perform the ritual 'Bai Sri Soo Kwan' (the ritual of bringing back spirits). When this is finished, 'Chow Guan' (the black magician who takes care of a ghost named 'Pee Hor Luang'), Nang Tieam, Kana San, and Nang Tang (the black magician's helpers), a dancing group of Pee Ta Khon and some local residents would be invited to join the parade. The parade then moves to 'Phon Chai' temple and more local residents in their ghost outfits join the parade.

The main procession, and the centre piece of the festival, begins on the second day. It consists of hundreds of elaborately costumed giant 'ghosts' with fierce masks, all dancing, laughing and waving giant phalluses as they mischievously and joyously move through the village toward their final destination, the temple. The town's residents put great effort into the elaborate and complex giant ghost costumes. Masks made of rice husks or coconut leaves are worn, with hats made from sticky-rice steamers. Most, but not all, of the ghost actors are men, even though many female ghosts are represented with the costumes, evidently from their exaggerated sexual characteristics. Female ghost actors have been present for the past ten years, reflecting the prominence of female ghosts in Thai tradition, and also illustrating a softening of the patriarchal character of such rituals. The ghost performers in the parade are not 'real' ghosts, but they are, in a sense, part of the contemplation of death that is so central to Theravāda Buddhist belief, and is also echoed in other festivals around the world, such as the Mexican Dia de los Muertos, the Day of the Dead. Unlike some other merit making festivals, such as Por Tor and Ge Tai, the ghosts are not regarded as literally present during the Pee Ta Khon parade. The festival is thought to be under the protection of, and in honor of, spirits, and this is reinforced in the merit ceremonies at the temple towards the end of the festivities.

The general sense of a temporary dissolution of social hierarchy is assisted by much alcohol consumption and ribald fun, as onlookers are often teased by the ghosts waving the giant phalluses in their faces. Western pop music and American stars-and-stripes national flags add to the carnivalesque sense of a cultural hiatus. The parade continues until the afternoon when the ghosts welcome the Prince Mahavejsandon and his family back to the earth (this part is called 'Hae Phra'). The third day is the day of virtue. Local people attend a grand sermon and follow Buddhist rituals at the temple. The exuberance of the previous days gives way to solemn piety, and the behavior of the 'ghosts' changes accordingly.

Findings

Sifting, coding and assimilating the various data sets resulted in a number of themes that we subsumed into two superordinate interpretive repertoires, expressed as polarities: spiritual/material and sacred/profane. The overlapping themes comprised practices and discourses that nuanced the ways in which consumption and spirituality interacted in the ritual context of Pee Ta Kohn.

Spiritual/material

The coded belief system of Pee Ta Khon festival is evolving in line with social changes. The interviews with organizers were notable for their emphasis on the pious spiritual observance within the events and there seems to be no evident tension between the commercial or profane elements of the festival, and the spiritual and sacred elements (Belk *et al.*, 1989). To the Western observer, the festival seems to have a party atmosphere that, on the face of it, belies its serious meaning. Lady Gaga's songs were sometimes played as the hungry ghosts danced, and American flags were part of the costume of some hungry ghosts. An element of cultural globalization seemed present, as has been observed in other non-Western death rituals (Bonsu and Belk, 2003). To the outsider, the juxtaposition of symbols of Western-style consumption with ancient myths and deep religious symbolism seems discordant. The levity sits oddly with the ostensible piety, and yet the whole effect seems thoroughly normalized. None of the interview participants suggested that the religious significance of the festival was in any way compromised by influences of marketization or detraditionalization (McAlexander *et al.*, 2014). The spiritual elements seemed thoroughly inscribed into the material culture surrounding the events. There may be more tensions than interviews acknowledged, but this would be difficult to assess in a culture in which harmony tends to be prized. The Pee Ta Khon provides a ritual setting in which the spiritual and the material seem juxtaposed and assimilated. Our interpretation was that the carnival aspects of the parade signify that this mutual accommodation is special and exceptional and stands outside of typical everyday social interaction in Thailand, which is normally respectful of the social status of the speakers.

The festival itself is a consumption event not only with regard to its value to tourism (some other hungry ghost events are limited to local or ethnic attendees) but also as an occasion to sell food, beer, souvenirs and other goods from stalls set up along the parade route. The local people are proud of the event and they invest significant amounts of time and money into preparing the costumes and staging the event (and some of course earn revenue from sales at the street stalls). The festival also references the cultural belief that the living must offer sustenance to ghosts in the form of food or other items of value. In return, the ghosts dispense spiritual merit and reciprocal material advantages for their living benefactors. It seems that in partaking in such ritual exchange, the living are acknowledging their own liminal states on the Wheel of Life. Consumption and consumerism are merely aspects of the earthly landscape. Their moral status is relative to other aspects of a person's life, circumstances and behavior, and indeed to their previous lives. Many Buddhists believe that good material fortune in this life is a consequence of moral virtue shown in a previous life. Consequently, a person can be wealthy, fortunate and successful in this world, and also morally virtuous and pious, because of their conduct in a previous life. The ontological continuity between past and present lives means that material benefits can translate from one to the other. Prudence and material asceticism are seen as moral virtues in Buddhism, as they are in many other religions, but their counterparts, ostentatious wealth and material abundance, may not necessarily be moral vices.

Sacred/profane

None of the interviewees remarked on the oddness of the ribaldry and sexual symbolism in the parade alongside the deeply serious religious symbolism. It appears to be unique to this festival and highly unusual in Thai cultural representation, notwithstanding the elements of fertility ritual that may have been absorbed into Pee Ta Khon. Mainstream Thai culture is deeply conservative yet the hungry ghost figures flaunt their genitalia and use them to tease local residents, other participants and tourists. In addition, models of exaggerated genitalia and priapic figures are also available for sale from streetside stalls, as they are, for example, in parts of Greece. Playfulness is present in other Thai festivals, such as Songkran in which water is sprayed at strangers, but without the sexual ribaldry.

This unique character gives the Pee Ta Kohn a Rabelasian, carnivalesque (Bakhtin, 2009; Belk, 1994) flavor. The levity that can often be an important part of ritual (Minowa, 2008) is in this case designed to entice the ghosts from their realm and encourage them to join in the fun. The juxtaposition of sacred and profane is especially noticeable since the crude behavior of the ghosts gives way to solemn piety and decorum in the last phase of the festival. They attend a grand sermon at the local temple and behave in accordance with Thai norms of social deportment. The contrast with the earlier impish behavior is striking, and symbolizes the re-instantiation of social norms. As with Bakhtinian (2009) carnival, ribald behavior parodies and subverts norms of social relations and values within ritually designated times and places. Part of Pee Ta Khon's ritual purpose seems to be to both legitimize and contain the transgression of social norms of polite behavior. The sense of renewal engendered through ritual has an added resonance in death ritual, since the immanence of death for the living is openly acknowledged and celebrated, rather than sublimated. In this case, profanity, in the form of ribald behavior by the ghosts, is a means of temporarily subverting social norms and structures in order to re-instantiate them.

Discussion

The water-throwing in the famous Songkran festival (celebrated throughout Thailand, it entails splashing water at friends and strangers alike) and the waving of genitalia in Pee Ta Khon hint at the 'grotesque bodies' of Bakhtin's (2009) medieval 'festival of fools' in which urine and excrement were thrown and sexual ribaldry indulged. For Bakhtin (2009) carnival time represented a permitted transgression of the imposed social and moral order into one condensed event, for the purpose of re-inscribing that same order. The subversive tone of Pee Ta Kohn, then, can be seen in such a light. As the gates of the ghosts' realm are opened for a time, they can move beyond their usual limits to wander the earth and interact with the living. Similarly, the human participants in Pee Ta Kohn are able to enjoy the festival levity as a 'time out' from the normal social hierarchies and rules of everyday Thai life.

Consumption is central to the ritual celebration, in the form of stalls that sell alcohol, souvenirs and food to tourists along the parade route, and also in the form of offerings made to the spirits of the festival. Consumption is a set of practices that sit uneasily with some religious traditions since it can result in the marketization and the subsequent detraditionalization (McAlexander *et al.*, 2014) of the religion, diluting its spiritual value for adherents and damaging its historical integrity. In contrast, the consumption practices that are central to Pee Ta Kohn seem to cohere with its ritual meaning and are not seen to damage its spiritual integrity. The ritual seems to have a role in exposing, and also reconciling, what is on the face of it an ideological dilemma of spiritual asceticism versus material consumption. Abstentation from material comforts is a route to spirituality in Buddhism, and individuals who display excessive adherence to material desires risk becoming a hungry ghost after death, and wandering in torment with unsatiated desires. Yet the distinction is more nuanced than this: ghosts are thought to need material goods in the afterlife, even branded items that are burned symbolically for them in the form of paper models. They also need food, while merit making death rituals often entail feasting, music, dancing and other consumption practices. Furthermore, as we note, material good fortune in this life can be enjoyed by a pious person who earns many blessings by observing religious rituals, or who has earned their good fortune through exercising piety and virtue in a previous incarnation on the Wheel of Life.

The 'ghosts' in the Pee Ta Kohn festival, although a figurative rather than a literal presence in this ritual, are heralded as liminal entities (Turner, 2009) on a physical and a spiritual journey, but fully present neither in their destination nor in their place of origin. Individuals and groups taking part in the festival could be said to detach themselves from their normal 'fixed point in the social structure' (Turner, 2009, p. 94) – that is, from their normal roles, status and ranks in Thai society to join in the irreverent and subversive levity. As the subversive behavior gives way to more solemn piety during the final stage, the moral order is thus renewed and reinstated, as in Carnival and Mardis Gras.

Transgression is permitted in certain ritual settings: the taboo is immanent in the transgression, and is re-instantiated through it (Bataille, 2007). The subversive sexualized ribaldry in Pee Ta Kohn reflects a taboo in the sense that sexual liberality, like excessive desire for material goods, can condemn a person to the bleak spiritual destiny of the hungry ghost. Within the ritual setting, the violation of normal codes of polite social interaction represents a permitted transgression. The subversive and mischievous character of the ghost procession speaks to the role of ghosts in Thai life as a source of mischief and danger and adds to the sense of the carnivalesque as the normal, everyday world is turned upside down and inside out. The normal concern in Thai society for respect, politeness, social hierarchy and delicate social behavior is temporarily suspended as the procession weaves through the town in a spirit of transgressive exuberance.

The event as a whole dramatizes a cultural myth (Campbell, 1972; Harrison, 1912; Rook, 1985), in this case, the cultural myth of the Prince Mahavejsandon and his return from exile in the forest. It makes an intense and colorful spectacle of the usually hidden beliefs about hungry ghosts that are so prevalent in everyday Thai life. The living seek to neutralize the potential of the ghosts to cause mischief and harm by honoring them with ritual offerings, and in so doing they link the present with the past (Durkheim, 1912). The dead are beings who, like the living, subsist on the Wheel of Life, but at different levels. The existence of hungry ghosts is a stark warning of the bleak spiritual destiny that awaits those who cling to the desires of the material world, yet consumption practices, both symbolic (paper burning) and material (feasting) are used to connect dead and living, and to generate virtue (and merit) from evil. The ideological dilemma of materialism versus spiritual asceticism is thus resolved through consumption ritual. The Pee Ta Khon illustrates the cultural significance of death ritual to consumption, and of consumption to death ritual, and nuances the understanding of Asian (specifically, Thai) consumer culture beyond simplistic notions of unproblematically ostentatious material consumption. The tensions underlying Western-style consumption practices in the East are both revealed, and, to an extent, reconciled, through the ritual performance of religious belief.

Concluding comment

We offer this tentative and provisional reading of the Pee Ta Kohn hungry ghost festival as a potential source of insight into the way death ritual can both reflect and assimilate some of the underlying tensions of Asian consumer culture, specifically the dilemma between spiritual asceticism and ostentatious material consumption. The field would benefit from further research focusing on other death rituals, including fully immersive ethnographies. The hungry ghost is a powerful mythological figure across the Buddhist world but the nuances of meaning surrounding hungry ghost rituals of differing kinds in different regions and under differing religious and folk mythologies need further close investigation. Death ritual can serve to symbolically connect contemporary society with pre-capitalist forms of exchange (Blake, 2011) and the Pee Ta Kohn is suggestive of an accommodation between the values of contemporary consumerism and traditional, pre-capitalist values of spiritual asceticism.

Note

1 The authors would like to thank Professor Russ Belk for kindly commenting upon an earlier draft of this chapter.

References

Arnould, E. J. (2001), 'Ritual three gifts and why consumer researchers should care', *Advances in Consumer Research*, Vol. 28, pp. 384–386.

Bakhtin, M. (2009), *Problems of Dosteovsky's Poetics* (11th ed.), (C. Emerson Trans.), University of Minnesota Press, Minneapolis (original work published in 1984).

Bataille, G. (2007), *The Accursed Share* Volume I, (R. Hurley Trans.), Zone Books, New York (original work published in 1989).

Belk, R. W. (1988), 'Possessions and the Extended Self', *Journal of Consumer Research*, Vol. 15 No. 2, pp. 139–168.

Belk, R. W. (1991), 'Possessions and the Sense of Past', in Belk, R.W. (Ed.), *Highways and Buyways: Naturalistic Research From the Consumer Behavior Odyssey*, Association for Consumer Research conference proceedings, pp. 114–130.

Belk, R. W. (1994), 'Carnival, Control, and Corporate Culture in Contemporary Halloween Celebrations', in Santino, J. (Ed.), *Halloween and Other Festivals of Death and Life*, University of Tennessee Press, Knoxville, TN, pp. 105–132.

Belk, R. W. and Kozinets, R. V. (2005), 'Videography in marketing and consumer research', *Qualitative Market Research: An International Journal*, Vol. 8, No. 2, pp. 128–141.

Belk, R. W., Wallendorf, M., and Sherry, J. F. Jr. (1989), 'The sacred and the profane in consumer behaviour: theodicy on the Odyssey', *Journal of Consumer Research*, Vol. 16, No. 1, June, pp. 1–38.

Blake, F. (2011), *Burning Money: The Material Spirit of the Chinese Lifeworld*, University of Hawaii Press, Hawaii.

Bond, G. D. (1980), 'Theravāda Buddhism's meditations on death and the symbolism of initiatory death', *History of Religions*, Vol. 19, No. 3, pp. 237–258.

Bonsu, S. K. and Belk, R. W. (2003), 'Do not go cheaply into that good night: death-ritual consumption in Asante, Ghana', *Journal of Consumer Research*, Vol. 30, No. 1, June, pp. 41–55.

Bonsu, S. K. and DeBerry-Spence, B. (2008), 'Consuming the dead: identity and community building practices in death rituals', *Journal of Contemporary Ethnography*, Vol. 37, No. 6, pp. 694–719.

Borgmann, A. (2000), 'The moral complexion of consumption', *Journal of Consumer Research*, Vol. 26 No. 4, March, pp. 418–422.

Buckingham, D. (2009), 'Creative visual methods in media research: possibilities, problems and proposals', *Media Culture Society*, Vol. 31, No. 4, pp. 633–652.

Campbell, J. (1972), *Myths to Live by*, Viking, New York.

Carroll, E. C. and Romano, J. (2010), *Your Digital Afterlife: When Facebook, Flickr and Twitter Are Your Estate, What's Your Legacy?*, New Rider's Press, Berkeley, CA.

Chadha, R. and Husband, P. (2007), *The Cult of the Luxury Brand: Inside Asia's Love Affair with Luxury*, Nicholas Brealey International, London.

Collins, S. (1982), *Selfless Persons: Imagery and Thought in Theravāda Buddhism*, Cambridge University Press, Cambridge, UK.

Culler, J. (1985), *Saussure*, Fontana, London.

Davies, D. J. (1997), *Death Ritual and Belief: Rhetoric of Funerary Rites*, Continuum, London.

Driver, T. F. (1998), *Liberating Rites*, Westview Press, CO.

Durkheim, E. (1912), *The Elementary Forms of the Religious Life*, Allen and Unwin, London.

Eckhardt, G. M. and Dholakia, N. (2013), 'Addressing the mega imbalance: interpretive exploration of Asia', *Qualitative Market Research: An International Journal*, Vol. 16, No. 1, pp. 4–11.

Fam, K. S., Yang, Z. and Hyman, M. (2009), 'Confucian/Chopsticks Marketing', *Journal of Business Ethics*, Vol. 88, pp. 393–397.

Gainer, B. (1995), 'Ritual and relationships: Interpersonal influences on shared consumption', *Journal of Business Research*, Vol. 32, No. 3, pp. 253–260.

Geertz, C. (1973) 'Thick Description: Toward an Interpretative Theory of Culture', in Geertz, C. *The Interpretation of Cultures: Selected Essays*, Basic Books, New York.

Gervais, K. G. (1986), *Refining Death*, Yale University Press, New Haven.

Gentry, J. W., Kennedy, P. F., Paul, C., and Hill, R. P. (1995), 'Family transitions during grief: discontinuities in household consumption patterns', *Journal of Business Research*, Vol. 34, No. 1, September, pp. 67–79.

Goody, J. (1962), *Death, Property and the Ancestors: A Study of Mortuary Customs of the Lodagaa of West Africa*, Stanford University Press, Stanford, CA.

Gould, S. J. (1991), 'An Asian approach to the understanding of consumer energy, drives and states', in Hirschman, E. C. (Ed.), *Research in Consumer Behaviour: A Research Annual*, Vol. 5, Jai Press Inc., London, pp. 33–59.

Gould, S. J. (1992), 'Consumer materialism as a multilevel and individual difference phenomenon – an asian-based perspective', in *Special Volumes – Meaning, Measure and Morality of Materialism*, Association for Consumer Research, pp. 57–62.

Hackley, A. R., and Hackley, C. (2013), Television product placement strategy in Thailand and the UK, *Asian Journal of Business Research*, Vol 3 No. 1, pp. 97–110.

Harrison, J. E. (1912), *Themis: A Study of the Social Origins of Greek Religion*, Cambridge: Cambridge University Press.

Hirschman, E. C. (1990), 'Secular immortality and American ideology of affluence', *Journal of Consumer Research*, Vol. 17, June, pp. 31–42.

Hirschman, E, C., Ruvio, A., and Belk, R. (2013), 'Death Styles and the Ideal Self,' in Ruvio, A. and Belk, R. (Eds.), *Identity and Consumption*, Routledge, London, pp. 215–224.

Hodge, R. and Cress, G. (1988), *Social Semiotics*, Polity, Cambridge.

Holt, D. B. (1992), 'Examining the descriptive value of ritual in consumer behaviour: a view from the field', *Advances in Consumer Research*, Vol. 19, pp. 213–218.

Hong, S. and Kim, C. H. (2013), 'Surfing the Korean wave: a postcolonial critique of the mythologised middlebrow consumer culture in Asia', *Qualitative Market Research: An International Journal*, Vol. 16 No. 1, pp. 53–75.

Houston, R. H. (1999), 'Through pain and perseverance: liminality, ritual consumption and the social construction of gender in contemporary Japan', *Advances in Consumer Research*, Vol. 26, January, pp. 542–548.

Kates, S. M. (2001), 'Disposition of possessions among families of people with AIDS', *Psychology and Marketing*, Vol. 18, No. 4, pp. 365–387.

Kniazeva, N. and Belk, R. W. (2012), 'The Western Yogi: consuming Eastern wisdom', *International Journal of Consumer Research*, Vol. 1, No. 1, pp. 1–27.

Kolm, S. C. (1985), 'The Buddhist theory of "No Self"', in Elster, J. (Ed.), *The Multiple Self*, Cambridge University Press, Cambridge, UK, pp. 233–265.

Kuang-Ying Loo, B. and Hackley, C. (2013), 'Internationalisation strategy of iconic Malaysian high fashion brands', *Qualitative Market Research: An International Journal*, Vol. 16, No. 4, pp. 406–420.

Langer, R. (2007), *Buddhist Rituals of Death and Rebirth: Contemporary Sri Lankan Practice and its origins*, Routledge, New York.

Lu, P. X. (2008), *Elite China: Luxury Consumer Behavior in China*, John Wiley & Sons, Singapore.

McAlexander, J., Leavenworth Dufault, B., Martin, D. M., and Schouten, J. W. (2014), The marketization of religion: field, capital and consumer identity, *Journal of Consumer Research* DOI 10.1086/677894.

McDaniel, J. (2006), *The Map and the World in Buddhism*, Thai digital monastery, Available at http://tdm.ucr.edu/index.html.

McGrath, M. A., Sherry, J. F. and Diamond, N. (2013), 'Discordant retail brands strategy in the house of Barbie', *Qualitative Market Research: An International Journal*, Vol. 16, No. 1, pp. 12–37.

Metcalf, P. and Huntington, R. (1991), *Celebrations of Death: Anthropology of Mortuary Practices*, Cambridge University Press, New York.

Minowa, Y. (2008), 'The importance of being earnest and playful: consuming the rituals of the West Indian American Day Carnival and Parade', *European Advances in Consumer Research*, Vol. 8, pp. 53–59.

Oates, C. (1974), *The Hungry Ghosts*, Black Sparrow Press, Los Angeles.

O'Donohoe, S. and Turley, D. (2005), 'Till death us do part? Consumption and the negotiation of relationships following a bereavement', *Advances in Consumer Research*, Vol. 32, pp. 625–626.

O'Donohoe, S. and Turley, D. (2000), 'Dealing with death: art, morality and the marketplace', in Brown, S. and Patterson, A. (Eds.), *Imagining Marketing: Art, Aesthetics and the Avant-Garde*, Routledge, London, pp. 86–106.

Pink, S. (2006), *Doing Visual Ethnography*, 2nd ed. Sage, London.

Price, L., Arnould, E. J., and Curasi, C. F. (2000), 'Older consumers' disposition of special possessions', *Journal of Consumer Research*, Vol. 37, September, pp. 179–201.

Potter, J. and Wetherell, M. (1987) *Discourse and Social Psychology: Beyond Attitudes and Behaviour.* Sage London.

Rook, D. W. (1985), 'The ritual dimension of consumer behavior', *Journal of Consumer Research*, Vol. 12, No. 3, December, pp. 251–264.

Rook, D. W. and Levy, S. J. (1983), 'Psychosocial themes in consumer grooming rituals', in Bagozzi, R.P. and Tybout, A.M. (Eds.), *Advances in Consumer Research*, Vol. 10, Association for Consumer Research conference proceedings Ann Arbor, pp. 329–333.

Ruangviset, P. (1996), *Heed Sib-song Klong Sib-si of Loei People*, Feature, Bangkok.

Santino, J. (1995), *All Around the Year: Holidays and Celebrations in American Life*, University of Illinois Press, Urbana, IL.

Seo, Y. (2013), 'Electronic sports: a new marketing landscape of the experience economy', *Journal of Marketing Management*, Vol. 29, No. 13–14, pp. 1542–1560.

Stanfield, M. A. and Kleine, R. E. (1990), 'Rituals, ritualised behaviour and habit: refinements and extensions of the consumption ritual construct', *Advances in Consumer Research*, Vol. 17, pp. 31–38.

Tiwsakul, R. A. and Hackley, C. (2012), 'Postmodern paradoxes in Thai-Asian consumer Identity', *Journal of Business Research*, Vol. 66, No. 4, pp. 490–496.

Turley, D. (1995), 'Dialogue with the departed', in *European Advances in Consumer Research*, Vol. 2, F. Hansen (Ed.), Association for Consumer Research conference proceedings, Provo UT, pp. 10–13.

Turley, D. (1998), 'A postcard from the very edge: mortality and marketing', in

Brown, S. and Turley, D. (Eds) *Consumer Research: Postcards from the Edge*, Routledge, London, pp. 350–377.

Turner, V. (2009), *The Ritual Process: Structure and Anti-structure*, Aldine Transaction, New Brunswick.

Wallendorf, M. and Arnould, E. J. (1991), 'We gather together: consumption rituals of Thanksgiving Day', *Journal of Consumer Research*, Vol. 18, No. 1, June, pp. 13–31.

Wattanasuwan, K. (2005), 'Remembering you, remembering your brands: immortalising the decreased through the paper-burning ritual in Thailand', 3rd workshop on interpretive consumer research, Copenhagen Business School, Denmark.

Ustuner, T. Ger, G., and Holt, D. B. (2000), 'Consuming ritual: reframing the Turkish henna-night ceremony', *Advances in Consumer Research*, Vol. 27, pp. 209–214.

Venkatesh, A., Khanwalkar, S., Lawrence, L., and Chen, S. (2013), 'Ethnoconsumerism and cultural branding: designing "nano" car', *Qualitative Market Research: An International Journal*, Vol. 16, No. 1, pp. 108–119.

Zhao, X. and Belk, R. W. (2003), 'Money to burn: consumption by the dead in China', (abstract), in Keller, P.A. and Rook, D. (Eds.), *Advances in Consumer Research*, Vol. 30, p. 4.

Zhao, X. and Belk, R. W. (2008), 'Desire on fire: a naturalistic inquiry of Chinese death ritual consumption', *European Advances in Consumer Research*, Association for Consumer Research conference proceedings, Vol. 8, p. 245.

7 Ritual, mythology, and consumption after a celebrity death

Scott K. Radford and Peter H. Bloch

Celebrity watching in the twenty-first century has been magnified by extensive coverage in both conventional and online media. Today, nearly every aspect of celebrities' lives is visible to the public (James, 1993; McCutcheon, Maltby, Houran, and Ashe, 2004). We know where they vacation, when they are pregnant, and the current state of their weight. In this context, modern celebrities are known not so much for their accomplishments, but for the lives they lead (McCutcheon, Lange, and Houran, 2002; McCutcheon *et al.*, 2004) – they are famous for being famous. As a result, reality television stars are often more famous than highly talented artists, musicians, or actors. Although celebrity watching is often portrayed as trivial (Jenkins, 2006), the connection to a celebrity is genuine and can provide an important component in self-definition (O'Guinn, 1991; Radford and Bloch, 2012).

Through media consumption, people form vicarious relationships with celebrities that add meaning to their lives and enhance the self (McCutcheon *et al.*, 2002; Rojek, 2001). An active identification with a celebrity leads many fans to feel that they have a personal relationship with the media figure (Giles, 2002); the celebrity may be even be considered a 'friend.' (Caughey, 1984). Recently, celebrities have strengthened these relationships by encouraging people to follow the details of their life through real time Twitter feeds (Greenberg, 2009) and personal revelations in media interviews (Rojek, 2007).

Of particular interest here is the case where public fascination with a famous individual intensifies with death. The end of an important person-celebrity relationship may result in a profound sense of loss and feelings of grief. This chapter will investigate the intersection of the public realm of celebrity with the private realm of grief and mourning. This intersection has become increasingly relevant because the rise of celebrity culture has coincided with the reduction in public visual iconography of death (Aries, 1985). Increasingly in western society, expressions of grieving and mourning have become more subdued and increasingly viewed as inappropriate (Clark and Franzmann, 2006).

However, fans of celebrities have become surprisingly comfortable in expressing their grief publicly. Tributes range from depositing gifts at the site of the stars' home, to impromptu ceremonies, to posting emotional messages on Facebook or Twitter. Public displays of mourning, such as those spontaneously enacted for celebrities, provide mourners with the opportunity to deal with loss in a culture where open mourning has been discouraged (Franzmann, 1998; Haney, Leimer, and Lowery, 1997). In other words, fans can engage in more dramatic mourning responses with celebrities than would be deemed appropriate with family or friends.

These death rituals (Bonsu and Belk, 2003) serve as a means of dealing with the shared grief that fans feel for the loss of celebrities. These rituals demonstrate the traditional five stages of grief (Kubler-Ross and Kessler, 2005), but in the realm of celebrity, they also include the memorialization of the deceased through product consumption (Gentry, Kennedy, Paul, and Hill, 1995; Radford and Bloch, 2013) as well as the mythologizing of the celebrity through storytelling and shared experiences (Radford and Bloch, 2012; Wang, 2007). The current chapter provides an overview of what we know about consumer responses to celebrity death and identifies some of the process that influence these responses.

Celebrities and celebrity worship

As long as there have been heroes and accomplishments, there has been fame, where individuals are set apart for some ability, characteristic, or accomplishment. Celebrities in the twenty-first century are known for their artistic accomplishments, their attractiveness, and lifestyle (McCutcheon *et al.*, 2002; McCutcheon *et al.*, 2004). As explained by James (1993, p51) 'The celebrity was yet another pioneering American contribution to twentieth-century fame. Celebrities weren't just famous for what they did. They were famous for the lives they led while they did it.' This manifestation of celebrity has been created and perpetrated by the increasingly prevalent commercial and social media (Boorstin, 1962) and increasingly, there is a recognition that celebrities must manage and control their identities. Celebrities provide small unguarded glimpses of their lives and this authenticity engages fans on a deeper level, to the point where they are engaging in emotional labor (Nunn and Biressi, 2010). This can include personalized messages from celebrities to fans, tweets and retweets that respond to fans' comments, or taking selfies with them at fan conventions.

Connected to the idea of celebrity are the commodities and products associated with the famous person. In addition to the products that are directly related to the reasons for being famous – such as music tracks and concert programs for a singer or DVDs for a movie star – there are a host of additional products that are associated with the celebrity and are part of the marketing engine that commodifies the celebrity into a marketable product. Rein and colleagues (1997) suggested that celebrity is mostly about the commercial value that can be generated by an individual. Therefore, celebrity at its core is about being able to generate money. This may come from large speaking fees such as those commanded by popular psychologist Dr. Phil, multi-million dollar movie contracts for Hollywood stars such as Robert Downey Jr., or the salary and endorsement deals paid to sports stars like David Beckham. In addition to the direct salaries commanded by these individuals, they also have the ability to market a range of complementary products for which they receive some additional remuneration. Celebrities may market themselves, as Oprah did with her magazine 'O', they may market products associated with themselves, such as Phil Mickelson golf courses, or they may act as endorsers for other products such as Brad Pitt's endorsement of Chanel. Many celebrities who are well past the prime of their careers travel around the globe to sell autographs and photos at conventions organized by firms such as Wizard World and Creation Entertainment. Research on celebrity endorsement has noted that there is a transfer of meaning between the celebrity and the consumer good, and then from the good to the consumer (McCracken, 1989). This same transfer of meaning should also take place when the celebrity is connected in any meaningful way with a particular good. The engagement and associated connection with the celebrity may render goods as sacred to the consumer.

Para-social relationships

Horton and Wohl (1956) coined the term *para-social relationship* to describe the manner in which individual users of mass media interact with representations of people appearing in the media. They suggested that the media create the illusion of a face-to-face relationship with the public figure. Subsequent research suggests that media consumers evaluate celebrities using similar criteria as they would use to evaluate individuals in person. It has been argued that not only are the evaluations of these figures similar to those made in person, but in fact that the subjects may even view the media figure as one with whom they have a personal relationship (Giles, 2002).

These socio-affective relationships between fans and celebrities are characterized by the pleasure that is derived from the activity of engaging with a celebrity, the shared enjoyment of the celebrity that one can derive from communicating with others, and the centrality of fan status to the individual (Courbet and Fourquet-Courbet, 2014). Fans of the celebrity begin to identify with the celebrity and in some cases they even take on the attitudes and beliefs of the celebrity (Brown, Basil, and Bocarnea, 2003). This identification with the celebrity can also influence the behaviors of the fans and can equate to greater pro-social behaviors towards causes that are important to the celebrity (Bae, Brown, and Kang, 2011; Brown, 2010; Brown et al., 2003). Celebrities are getting more organized now in managing the causes that they can support with their names. Kevin Bacon recently launched *Sixdegrees.org*, that is a portal to help celebrities identify a cause that they want to support in a specific area and *Omaze.com* allows consumers to contribute to charities with their names being entered into drawings for once in a lifetime experiences with top level celebrities. In addition to a personal identity that is formed through interaction with the celebrity, fans also exhibit a shared identity with other fans. Group identification has been facilitated by the availability of online communities and social media contexts and this shared identity may be characterized both as belonging to a group and identifying shared features and characteristics (i.e. groupal identity) (Courbet and Fourquet-Courbet, 2014).

There is a broad spectrum of fans identifying with a celebrity which can range from casual interactions to a more passionate engagement. Maltby and colleagues (2006) noted that consumers may engage in increasingly intense forms of celebrity worship that begins with simple attraction and at its most extreme is borderline pathological:

> There is *entertainment-social* celebrity worship that reflects an attraction to a favorite celebrity because of their perceived ability to entertain and social focus. There are *intense-personal* attitudes reflecting intensive and compulsive feelings about the celebrity. The most extreme expression of celebrity worship is *borderline-pathological*, thought to reflect an individual's social-pathological attitudes and behaviors.
>
> (Maltby *et al.*, 2006, p. 274)

These increasing levels of engagement with the celebrity are also character-ized by higher involvement and identification with celebrity-related products (Brown *et al.*, 2003). People who are particularly involved with celebrities will seek out media material and products associated with the celebrity. We contend that owning products associated with the celebrity is a normal course of engagement. For example, buying products that are directly associated with the celebrity's source of fame, such as Taylor Swift's new album, would be a normal form of engagement, and is in fact necessary to the source of fame. However, it is when products that are only tangentially associated with the celebrity are sought, such as a used dinner napkin, that celebrity idolization begins.

Belk and his colleagues (Belk, Wallendorf, and Sherry, 1989; O'Guinn and Belk, 1989) introduced the concept of *sacralization*, to describe how products (as well as entities such as celebrities) become especially revered. Past research has examined the phenomenon in the context of sacred collections or heir-looms and the increased value that they derive from their history and personal connection (Curasi, Price, and Arnould, 2004; Grayson and Shulman, 2000). The veneration of products, events, or places at the group or subculture level has also been investigated. For example, O'Guinn and Belk (1989) studied the consumption of sacred experiences at a religious theme park and Belk and Costa (1998) and Kozinets (2001) looked at this phenomena among the sub-cultures of mountain man re-enactors and Star Trek fans, respectively.

When celebrity worship moves to higher levels, the goods associated with a famous individual also may acquire sacred status through the process of *contamination* (Belk *et al.*, 1989) or *contagion* (Newman, Diesendruck, and

Bloom, 2011). Under these processes, the immaterial characteristics of a person are transferred to an inanimate object. Particularly revered are those objects that actually have some remnants of the person such as the bones of a medieval saint, a sweat-stained scarf from Elvis, or an autograph from James Gandolfini. Therefore, their contagion has led to a subsequent desire for and higher value placed on objects that are directly associated with a revered individual or event. For example, one can go to a sporting goods store and purchase a Major League quality baseball for a few dollars, but a home run baseball associated with a famous hitter may lead to violent outfield scrambles and in one case to a fan's death (CNN.com, 2011).

This perceived relationship may emerge in a particularly salient manner with the death of the celebrity. While the relationship was mostly one-sided, the end of that relationship for the consumer may result in a profound sense of loss. This is likely to be greater for celebrities with whom the individual felt a greater attachment. While it has been noted that individuals feel some connection to celebrities, most often that relationship has been likened to the relationship with a friend or neighbor, not a familial or romantic relationship (McCutcheon et al., 2002). However, grief may be exhibited and a sense of loss felt when these individuals, who the subject feels are a part of their social relationships, are lost. Therefore, it is certainly conceivable that consumers will exhibit grieving behaviors for a celebrity with whom they have no actual physical contact, and with whom they have only developed a one-sided parasocial relationship, similar to the manner in which they would grieve for the death of a friend, a neighbor, or an acquaintance. A natural part of death and grieving are the consumption rituals that are associated with both the public and private process of mourning.

Death and grieving

Death is a particularly intense life event which may motivate varying behaviors in different individuals. It is possible that consumers will engage in meaning transfer to compensate for the loss of a loved one (Richins, 1994). That is, consumers will imbue a material good with some form of meaning that acts as a surrogate for the relationship with the individual. In addition to the meaning of goods, the loss of a related other also may lead to the feeling of a loss of some part of the self. "The prior possessions of the deceased can be powerful remains of the dead person's extended self" (Belk, 1988, p. 144). The loss of self and the rituals of death may result in a need to cling to items that have been contaminated by contact with the deceased. More traditionally, individuals in Western cultures will often react to death by spending money (Gabel, Mansfield, and Westbrook, 1996). Following a house and a vehicle, the third largest purchase that consumers usually make is a funeral. As such, individuals have come to associate death with spending money. As noted by Gabel and colleagues (1996, p. 363) "the meaning of death [is] reduced to the spending of money, possibly in order to demonstrate how much one cared for the deceased." Grieving consumers are more vulnerable because less thought and planning go into death-related consumption decision making. Funeral parlors have been known to exploit this consumption disability. In some cases markups of 900 percent have been found on death-related goods and services (Gabel *et al.*, 1996). In addition to the need to find meaning by acquiring an object related to a celebrity is the fact that consumers may not be acting in the most rational and deliberate manner and may easily be exploited by marketers who are trying to take advantage of their grief. This has led to a common understanding that death offers an avenue for the exploitation of grieving consumers and that consumers will often pay higher prices for art, memorabilia, and other products associated with the focal celebrity.

The idea of post-death sacralization of a person or an artifact is not new, nor is it restricted to celebrities as defined above. The veneration of holy relics associated with saints and martyrs was common in the Middle Ages (McCane, 1991; Rollason, 1989). More recently popular media has suggested that there is a 'death effect' for fine artists, such that their works are valued more highly after their death then when they were alive. Some have gone so far as to propose that the only way for an artist to truly become wealthy is to die tragically. However, an artist's death does not typically make them famous and the value of work only tends to increase after death if the artist was known or recognized prior to their death (Grant, 1991). This comes with a caveat; for artists that have some fame prior to their death, there is, in fact, a positive death effect. Economic research has proposed that supply and demand factors can explain price variances following an artist's death, e.g., certain works of lesser known Mexican painters (Ekelund, Ressler, and Watson, 2000), as well as well-known painters like Picasso (Czujack, 1997). Ekelund *et al.* (2000) indicate that in the basic artist–patron relationship there is an unwritten contract that the artist will continue to produce quantities of art in a consistent manner, so that the system remains in equilibrium. The artist will not flood the market with work, nor will they cease selling their paintings, thus maintaining market equilibrium.

However, when the artist dies, this equilibrium is interrupted since there is no longer any conceivable future supply. Therefore, the tendency is for the demand to increase for the remaining works as a reaction to the termination of supply. The increase in demand and decrease in supply means that there is an immediate and sudden price increase for all works by the artist. These increased prices will tend to entice collectors to sell their works. This serves the function of restoring supply to the prior level in turn lowering the price. So, following an artist's death there is an immediate spike in the price. Shortly after, the availability of their work increases and the market gradually returns to an equilibrium level that tends to be higher than the level prior to the artist's death. The death effect though is not as drastic as many think. The immediate increase is quite short lived and the long term increase is not particularly large. Moreover, while the work of artists is heavily influenced by the limited supply of products created by the artist, works associated with a celebrity do not have the same limitations. There are no limits on the number of songs that iTunes can sell after a celebrity death, or the number of memorial t-shirts, or even the number of DVD copies of a celebrity's movies. Therefore, with a few exceptions, most of the products associated with a celebrity are reproducible and do not exhibit the same limitations of supply and demand. Instead the attraction or desire for products to memorialize and remember the deceased cannot simply be explained by the cessation of supply.

Consumption as a response to celebrity death

While celebrity is often seen as trivial, for many there are significant implications for both self and group identity formation. Fans of celebrities exhibit varying levels of involvement with celebrities and they often use products as a means of constructing and supporting this self-identity. However, the end of the relationship can be hard on fans and the grief and mourning responses they exhibit can be intense with implications for the individual and their construction of identity. In the wake of this loss, products can often been used as a means of remembering or maintaining an attachment to the celebrity and providing stability or meaning to consumers when they are in a liminal state around death (Gentry *et al.*, 1995b).

We now present a summary framework to further illuminate the nature of consumer responses to a celebrity death (see Figure 7.1). At the left is the triggering event, the death of a celebrity. For a given individual, only certain celebrities will evoke a noticeable response upon their deaths. Thus, strong responses derive from the death of a celebrity where there was a strong pre-existing attachment. In cases where the attachment was strong, the death will elevate the sacred status of both the celebrity and related products or relics. Attachment theory suggests that when people feel strong attachments to others a proximity-seeking system is engaged, which causes them to seek ways of being close to the relevant other (Bowlby, 1978; Shaver, Hazan, and Bradshaw, 1988). This attachment to a familiar or desirable other is really no different when it is directed towards a face-to-face relationship or one that is consumed only through media (i.e. parasocial) (Stever, 2011). Once fans have formed an attachment with a celebrity, they will seek proximity in a number of ways such as looking at photographs, being avid consumers of the creative work, and seeking vicarious proximity by collecting memorabilia (Stever, 2011). When the celebrity dies, just as in a traditional relationship, the grieving fan may engage in instrumental and cognitive efforts to maintain a sense of continuing attachment with the celebrity and counteract the pain felt from the loss (Schuchter and Zisook, 1993). Fans will seek to both hold on to items to remember the celebrity and seek out new items to memorialize the celebrity. The possessions of the deceased can serve both as a means of moving through the grief process and maintaining a sense of connection to the lost loved one (Gentry *et al.*,

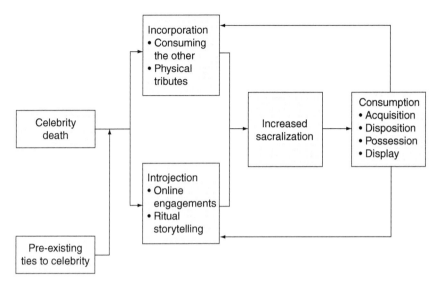

Figure 7.1 Responses to celebrity death.

1995), but can also be used as a device for avoidant coping (Field, Nichols, Holen, and Horowitz, 1999).

When a person loses a significant other, they tend to grasp at pieces of that other and take them into themselves. Johnson (1997) notes two stages of incorporating the other into the self as a part of mourning: *introjection* and *incorporation*.

> In introjective modes, the subject takes the Other by verbal means. The Other is embodied in the self imaginarily, through practices like the writing of poems. While introjection is a more or less conscious process, incorporation works secretly through unconscious means. It involves ingestion of objects – literally things – rather than the embodiment of the Other through words or images. These forms of 'eating the other' are more or less transformed or verbalized, more or less metaphorical.
>
> (Johnson, 1997, p. 238)

Following the death of a loved one, an individual also may feel a loss to their extended self (Belk, 1988) and consumers try to compensate with the acquisition of material goods (Wicklund and Gollwitzer, 1982). Thus, as shown in the figure, demand for celebrity products and associated buying activity increases. Material objects, places, or activities associated with the deceased become means of enhancing memories (Johnson 1997). Objects are often used as a means of preserving the memory of the deceased and they are incorporated into the person's life. In the case of race car driver Dale Earnhardt

Sr., fans sought relief through consumption and, just as they did when he was alive, they continued to measure their self-worth as a fan based on the gear that they owned (Radford and Bloch, 2012). Grieving persons may retain the items that belong to a loved one as means of avoidant coping and not fully accepting the loss (Gorer, 1965). Some fans refuse to accept the death and continue to wear their gear and look for the driver on the track (Radford and Bloch 2012). However, products may be natural and positive tools that assist in the grieving process. Yet, as noted above, people in a liminal state of grief are often vulnerable and do not always make the most rational decisions. While, many celebrities are supported by an extensive marketing program of memorabilia, there seems to be a clear disdain for persons who seek solely to compensate from the death of a celebrity. This creates an interesting dichotomy, as the demand for celebrity memorabilia is heightened by the death of a celebrity, while at the same time there are strong critiques of those who sell it. As noted by Radford and Bloch (2012) fans were highly interested in Earnhardt merchandise, but its purchase or sale for profit was criticized. Consider the following quote.

> He stopped at this truckstop to get gas and he overheard a cashier telling this lady that was trying to purchase an Earnhardt car that she couldn't sell her that until her manager got there 'cause they had to adjust the price – of course higher – man that burns me up . . .
>   He was a person, a human being – and his death should not be treated like it was just some damn TV show – to make money off of – people that do stuff like this – will have their day – what goes around comes around.
>
> (*IFC* Levi – Reported in Radford and Bloch 2012)

As fans sacralize a celebrity and associated goods, marketers become aware of this phenomenon and related increases in demand. This stimulates market entry among those with celebrity goods. In today's world of online commerce, such entry can occur only minutes after a celebrity dies, unlike the weeks required in earlier decades. While there has always been a market for memorial items, such as plates from the Bradford Exchange, or commemorative spoons, there has typically been a lag between the death of a celebrity and the ability of marketers to bring these objects to market. More recently, however, it has become easier for consumers to acquire goods online, both from existing marketers and from other consumers through consumer to consumer exchanges such as ebay or kijiji. This means that there is now a more readily available marketplace to fulfill the demand for celebrity-related goods that occurs immediately after death. This speed to market creates unprecedented opportunities for sellers to profit and allows consumers to seek consumption-related relief when it is most desired (Radford and Bloch, 2013). The grief reaction and increased sacralization of the celebrity is also often associated with a desire to acquire items associated with the celebrity

(Zaidman and Lowengart, 2001). At the same time sellers can anticipate increases in demand for celebrity-related goods and bring these items to market. Memorabilia sellers are motivated to get their goods to market as soon as possible to achieve first mover advantages and to take advantage of the high emotion levels that immediately follow a celebrity's death (Kerin, Varadarajan, and Peterson, 1992).

Just like the death effect in art, empirical evidence has indicated that there is an increased demand and supply for celebrity memorabilia immediately after death, but that this effect is not long term. The market is energized by the death of a celebrity as both buyers and sellers rush to market. The response occurs quite suddenly, merely minutes after death, but it is relatively short lived and demand begins to recede almost as quickly as it began (Radford and Bloch, 2013). What is perhaps most interesting, though, is that there is very little evidence of a price increase following a celebrity death. While many buyers are afraid that prices will rise, and many sellers are counting on this, the reality is that there is little change in the price paid at auction (Radford and Bloch, 2013). This may speak to the fact that celebrity deaths do not exert the same kind of vulnerability from grieving as has been evidenced in more traditional relationships. It may also suggest that because marketers are so quick to respond to the increased demand that there are not the perceptions of shortages that have been evidenced by the death effect in art.

What is interesting though is that the type of death and the type of memorabilia both have an effect on the demand for products. When a celebrity dies suddenly, fans are much more driven to seek memorabilia and exhibit public grieving behaviors (Radford and Bloch, 2013). For example, the sudden deaths of Michael Jackson, Amy Winehouse, and Robin Williams all led to very public displays of grief and grieving. While the deaths of equally famous figures such as Farah Fawcett and Ronald Reagan, who were both stricken with long-term illnesses, led to much fewer public displays of mourning. Finally, there is also evidence that consumers actively seek products that hold an indexical connection to the celebrity, that is directly contaminated by contact, than items that are iconic, that is representative of the celebrity (Grayson and Martinec, 2004; Radford and Bloch, 2013).

As shown in the figure, grieving fans have another way to express their emotions outside the consumption of celebrity products. Today, fans may take to various internet venues as places to publicly express their feelings of loss. Forums dedicated to the lost celebrity thrive with activity while social media trends further capture the posts of saddened fans. The voicing of such grief online and gathering responses may feedback to further enhance the sacred status of the celebrity in question. A similar feedback may occur from the acquisition of celebrity goods. The figure also notes that the buying and online reactions may reinforce each other as well.

Conclusion

The process and practices of mourning are important in the maintenance and reconstruction of self following the loss of an important figure in one's life. This is no less important when that figure was known through a parasocial relationship. The means of mourning may be different and,with the absence of the corporal grieving rituals associated with the disposal of the body, the rituals of working through grief are more associated with customs associated with the community (Averill and Nunley, 1993), the memorialization through product consumption or symbols (Cann, 2014) and the mythologizing about the interactions with the celebrity (Radford and Bloch, 2012).

There are a number of different conceptualizations of grief and grieving and the process of mourning, including Kubler Ross's stages of grief (Kubler-Ross and Kessler, 2005), Worden's four tasks of mourning (Worden, 1982), and Streobe and Schutt's dual process model of loss- and restorative-oriented coping (Stroebe and Schut, 2010), each of which can be layered on to the process of mourning for the loss of a celebrity (see Courbet and Fourquet-Courbet, 2014; Radford and Bloch, 2012). However, when considering the role of consumption and related products in the bereavement process for celebrities, consumption seems to serve a dual role of supporting the rituals and constructing the myths that are used to progress through mourning.

The possession, consumption, display, and disposition of products are another important part of the ritual of mourning for fans as they cope with loss. The death of a celebrity serves to create an intersection between public consumption with the private space of death and mourning. Particularly in Western cultures, where death is often a private family affair reserved for close friends, the outpouring of grief exhibited in a very public manner is blurring the boundaries between the private and public sphere (Klaassens, Groute, and Vanclay, 2013). Rituals that surround death are often prescribed by group membership and are even conceived of duties of belonging to the group (Averill and Nunley, 1993). In the past, this group membership was often religious in nature, but with celebrity the group membership is oriented around a community of consumption. As a result, many of the rituals associated with the death of a celebrity involve the consumption of products associated with the celebrity. This may involve binge watching Robin Williams movies, reenacting Michael Jackson dance moves, or depositing cigarettes and whiskey at a makeshift memorial outside of Amy Winehouse's house.

Death creates a mythology around the celebrity that is often greater than that experienced during life (Wang, 2007) and this mythology, like religious ritual, is often associated with special objects or items. In death, mythologizing helps the consumer to construct the identity of the celebrity that they would like to remember. Troubled artists like Amy Winehouse and Kurt Cobain were remembered as tortured geniuses; Johnny Cash and Dale Earnhardt, who were both vilified by fans and media during their lives, were celebrated as rebels after death; and following Michael Jackson's death there were very few mentions of the bizarre behavior and unhealthy relationships that were often discussed when he was alive. As a process of coping, myth-making helps the fan move through the grieving process and incorporate the essence of the source of fame into their own self-conception as fan. It is not necessary that the mythology was always positive though, just that it was true to the identity of the celebrity that is possessed by the fan. For example, fol-lowing the death of Margaret Thatcher, sales of 'Ding Dong the Witch is Dead' soared on iTunes, which likely would have amused the strong-willed politician, and the death of Joan Rivers sparked snappy insulting tweets from Lena Dunham that the star herself would likely have appreciated. The myth constructed around identity is useful to fans if it helps them to restore their self-identities in the wake of the loss by reflecting on the pleasure derived from the celebrity in life.

An interesting outcome of this merging of the private and public in the realm of celebrity is the opportunity that it provides to bring private discus-sions into greater public focus. Following Robin Williams' suicide there were a number of discussions of mental illness in the popular press. Robin Williams' death provided an opportunity for discussions of mental health, which is often stigmatized and private, in the public sphere. This positive outcome of a celebrity death has also been evidence with discussions of sexu-ality (Wang, 2007) and organ donation (Bae *et al.*, 2011). However, as with many issues surrounding celebrity, this attention was fleeting. The myth of Robin Williams as struggling with mental illness served as a totem around which people could make sense of his death, but once the process of mourn-ing was complete, the discussions faded from consciousness.

As fandom is oriented around a community of consumption, the loss of the focus of this consumption will likely trigger a number of responses. Most of these responses are healthy attempts to navigate the process of mourning and dealing with the loss. The groupal identity of belonging to a group which values the celebrity will influence the degree, the type, and the magnitude of mourning and the associated rituals and myths that are enacted and created to deal with this grief. Consumers will seek products as a means of remembering the deceased, demonstrating their devotion to others, compensating for the loss of self, and rebuilding their self-identities in the aftermath of the celebrity death.

References

Aries, P. (1985). *Images of Man and Death* (J. Lloyd, Trans.). Cambridge, MA: Harvard University Press.

Averill, J. A., and Nunley, E. P. (1993). Grief as an Emotion and as a Disease: A Social-Constructionist Perspective. In W. Stroebe and R. O. Hanssson (Eds.), *Handbook of Bereavement*. Cambridge: Cambridge University Press.

Bae, H.-S., Brown, W. J., and Kang, S. (2011). Social Influence of a Religious Hero: The Late Cardinal Stephen Kim Sou-hwan's Effect on Cornea Donation and Vol-unteerism. *Journal of Health Communication, 16*, 62–78.

Belk, R. W. (1988). Possessions and the Extended Self. *Journal of Consumer Research, 15*(2), 139–168.

Belk, R. W., and Costa, J. A. (1998). The Mountain Man Myth: A Contemporary Consuming Fantasy. *Journal of Consumer Research, 25*(3), 218–240.

Belk, R. W., Wallendorf, M., and Sherry, J. F., Jr. (1989). The Sacred and The Profane In Consumer Behavior: Theodicy On the Odyssey. *Journal of Consumer Research, 16*(1), 1–38.

Bonsu, S. K., and Belk, R. W. (2003). Do Not Go Cheaply into that Good Night: Death-Ritual Consumption in Asante, Ghana. *Journal of Consumer Research, 30*(1), 41–55.

Boorstin, D. J. (1962). *The Image: What Happened to the American Dream* (2nd edition ed.). New York: Atheneum.

Bowlby, J. (1978). *Attachment and Loss.* Harmondsworth, UK; Markham, Ont.: Penguin Books.

Brown, W. J. (2010). Steve Irwin's Influence on Wildlife Conservation. *Journal of Communication, 60,* 73–93.

Brown, W. J., Basil, M. D., and Bocarnea, M. C. (2003). Social Influence of an International Celebrity: Responses to the Death of Princess Diana. *Journal of Communication, 53*(4), 587–605.

Cann, C. K. (2014). *Virtual Afterlives: Grieving the Dead in the Twenty-First Century.* Lexington: University Press of Kentucky.

Caughey, J. L. (1984). *Imaginary Social Worlds: A Cultural Approach.* Lincoln, NE: University of Nebraska.

Clark, J., and Franzmann, M. (2006). Authority from Grief, Presence and Place in the Making of Roadside Memorials. *Death Studies, 30*(6), 579–599.

CNN.com. (2011). A souvenir moment becomes tragedy at ballgame. Retrieved November 25, 2014, from http://edition.cnn.com/2011/SPORT/07/07/texas.rangers.game.death.

Courbet, D., and Fourquet-Courbet, M.-P. (2014). When a Celebrity Dies ... Social Identity, Uses of Social Media, and the Mourning Process Among Fans: The Case of Michael Jackson. *Celebrity Studies, 5*(3), 275–290.

Curasi, C. F., Price, L. L., and Arnould, E. J. (2004). How Individuals' Cherished Possessions Become Families' Inalienable Wealth. *Journal of Consumer Research, 31*(3), 609–622.

Czujack, C. (1997). Picasso Paintings at Auction, 1963–1994. *Journal of Cultural Economics, 21*(3), 229–247.

Ekelund, R. B. J., Ressler, R. W., and Watson, J. K. (2000). The 'Death-Effect' in Art Prices: A Demand-Side Exploration. *Journal of Cultural Economics, 24*(4), 283–295.

Field, N. P., Nichols, C., Holen, A., and Horowitz, M. J. (1999). The Relation of Continuing Attachment to Adjustment in Conjugal Bereavement. *Journal of Consulting and Clinical Psychology, 67*(2), 212–218.

Franzmann, M. (1998). Diana in Death – A New or Greater Godness. *Australian Folklore, 13,* 112–123.

Gabel, T. G., Mansfield, P., and Westbrook, K. (1996, 1996). *The Disposal of Consumers: An Exploratory Analysis of Death-Related Consumption.* Paper presented at the Advances in Consumer Research, Minneapolis, MN.

Gentry, J. W., Kennedy, P. F., Paul, C., and Hill, R. P. (1995). Family Transitions During Grief: Discontinuities in Household Consumption Patterns. *Journal of Business Research, 34*(1), 67–79.

Giles, D. C. (2002). Parasocial Interaction: A Review of the Literature and a Model for Future Research. *Media Psychology, 4*(3), 279–305.

Gorer, G. (1965). *Death, Grief, and Mourning* (1st ed.). Garden City, NY: Doubleday.

Grant, D. (1991, Nov 18, 1991). No Death Benefits. *Barron's National Business and Financial Weekly*, pp. 17, 31–32.

Grayson, K., and Martinec, R. (2004). Consumer Perceptions of Iconicity and Indexicality and Their Influence on Assessments of Authentic Market Offerings. *Journal of Consumer Research, 31*(2), 296–312.

Grayson, K., and Shulman, D. (2000). Indexicality and the Verification Function of Irreplaceable Possessions: A Semiotic Analysis. *Journal of Consumer Research, 27*(1), 17–30.

Greenberg, A (2009). Why Celebrities Twitter. Retreived April 23, 2015, from www.forbes.com/2009/03/03/twitter-celebrities-privacy-technology-internet_twitter.html.

Haney, C. A., Leimer, C., and Lowery, J. (1997). Spontaneous Memorialization: Violent Death and Emerging Mourning Ritual. *OMEGA–Journal of Death and Dying, 35*(2), 159–171.

Horton, D., and Wohl, R. R. (1956). Mass Communication and Para-Social Interaction: Observations on Intimacy at a Distance. *Psychiatry, 19*, 215–229.

James, C. (1993). *Fame in the 20th Century* (1st U.S. ed.). New York, NY: Random House.

Jenkins, H. (2006). Star Trek Rerun, Reread, Rewritten: Fan Writing as Textual Poaching. In H. Jenkins (Ed.), *Fans Bloggers, and Gamers* (pp. 37–60). New York: New York University Press.

Johnson, R. (1997). Grievous Recognitions 2: The Grieving Process and Sexual Boundaries. In D. L. Steinberg, D. Epstein and J. R. (Eds.), *Border Patrols: Policing the Boundaries of Heterosexuality* (pp. 232–252). London: Cassell.

Kerin, R. A., Varadarajan, P. R., and Peterson, R. A. (1992). First-Mover Advantage: A Synthesis, Conceptual Framework. *Journal of Marketing, 56*(4), 33.

Klaassens, M., Groute, P. D., and Vanclay, F. M. (2013). Expressions of Private Mourning in Public Space: The Evolving Structure of Spontaneous and Permanent Roadside Memorials in the Netherlands. *Death Studies, 37*(2), 145–171.

Kozinets, R. V. (2001). Utopian Enterprise: Articulating the Meanings of Star Trek's Culture of Consumption. *Journal of Consumer Research, 28*(1), 67–88.

Kubler-Ross, E., and Kessler, D. (2005). *On Grief and Grieving.* New York: Scribner.

Maltby, J., Dayb, L., McCutcheon, L. E., Hourand, J., and Ashe, D. (2006). Extreme Celebrity Worship, Fantasy Proneness and Dissociation: Developing the Measurement and Understanding of Celebrity Worship within a Clinical Personality Context. *Personality and Individual Differences, 40*(2), 273–283.

McCane, B. R. (1991). Bones of Contention: Ossuaries and Reliquaries in Early Judaism and Christianity. *Second Century: A Journal of Early Christian Studies, 8*(4), 235–246.

McCracken, G. (1989). Who is the Celebrity Endorser? Cultural Foundations of the Endorsement Process. *Journal of Consumer Research, 16*(3), 310–321.

McCutcheon, L. E., Lange, R., and Houran, J. (2002). Conceptualization and Measurement of Celebrity Worship. *British Journal of Psychology, 93*(1), 67–87.

McCutcheon, L. E., Maltby, J., Houran, J., and Ashe, D. D. (2004). *Celebrity Worship: Inside the Minds of Stargazers* (1st ed.). Baltimore, MD: PublishAmerica.

Newman, G. E., Diesendruck, G., and Bloom, P. (2011). Celebrity Contagion and the Value of Objects. *Journal of Consumer Research, 38*, 215–228.

Nunn, H., and Biressi, A. (2010). 'A Trust Betrayed': Celebrity and the Work of Emotion. *Celebrity Studies* (1), 49–64.

O'Guinn, T. C. (1991). Touching Greatness: The Central Midwest Barry Manilow Fan Club. In R. W. Belk (Ed.), *Highways and Buyways* (pp. 102–111). Provo, UT: Association for Consumer Research.

O'Guinn, T. C., and Belk, R. W. (1989). Heaven on Earth: Consumption at Heritage Village, USA. *Journal of Consumer Research, 16*(2), 227–238.

Radford, S. K., and Bloch, P. H. (2012). Grief, Commiseration, and Consumption Following the Death of a Celebrity. *Journal of Consumer Culture, 12*(2), 137–155.

Radford, S. K., and Bloch, P. H. (2013). Buyer and Seller Responses to the Death of a Celebrity: The 'Death Effect' online. *Marketing Letters, 24*(1), 43–55.

Rein, I., Kotler, P., and Stoller, M. (1997). *High Visibility: The Making and Marketing or Professionals into Celebrities.* Lincolnwood: NTC/Contemporary Publishing Company.

Richins, M. L. (1994). Valuing Things: The Public and Private Meanings of Possessions. *Journal of Consumer Research, 21*(3), 503–521.

Rojek, C. (2001). *Celebrity.* London: Reaktion.

Rojek, C. (2007). Celebrity and Religion. In S. Redmond and S. Holmes (Eds.), *Stardom and Celebrity: A Reader.* Los Angeles: Sage Publications.

Rollason, D. W. (1989). *Saints and Relics in Anglo-Saxon England.* Oxford: Basil Blackwell.

Schuchter, S. R., and Zisook, S. (1993). The Course of Normal Grief. In M. S. Stroebe, W. Stroebe and O. Hansson (Eds.), *Handbook of Bereavement* (pp. 23–43). New York: Cambridge University Press.

Shaver, R., Hazan, C., and Bradshaw, D. (1988). *Love as Attachment: The Integration of Three Behavioural Systems.* New Haven, CT: Yale University Press.

Stever, G. S. (2011). Fan Behavior and Lifespan Development Theory: Explaining Para-social and Social Attachment to Celebrities. *Journal of Adult Development, 18*(1), 1–7.

Stroebe, M., and Schut, H. (2010). The Dual Process Model of Coping with Bereavement: A Decade On. *Omega: Journal of Death and Dying, 61*(4), 273–289.

Wang, Y. (2007). A Star is Dead: A Legend is Born: Practicing Leslie Cheung's Posthumous Fandom. In S. Redmond and S. Holmes (Eds.), *Stardom and Celebrity: A Reader* (pp. 326–340). London: Sage.

Wicklund, R. A., and Gollwitzer, P. M. (1982). *Symbolic Self-Completion.* Hillsdale, N.J.: L. Erlbaum Associates.

Worden, J. W. (1982). *Grief Counseling and Grief Therapy: A Handbook for the Mental Health Practitioner.* New York: Springer Pub. Co.

Zaidman, N., and Lowengart, O. (2001). The Marketing of Sacred Goods: Interaction of Consumers and Retailers. *Journal of International Consumer Marketing, 13*(4), 5–14.

8 Voluntary simplicity in the final rite of passage

Death

Hakan Cengiz and Dennis W. Rook

Voluntary Simplicity is a value driven consumer lifestyle that was first observed in the post-modern era in the 1970s (Elgin and Mitchell 1977), and which has grown steadily (Shama 1988; Iyer and Muncy 2009), and materialized in various ways. The current societal focus on carbon footprints, sustainability, green lifestyles, food sourcing, and product sharing reflect, to varying degrees, consumers' desires to simplify their lives in socially responsible ways. This chapter presents the results of an exploratory, discovery-oriented examination of the voluntary simplicity lifestyle trend within the context of ritual consumption practices and purchases associated with the final rite of passage: death. We provide evidence of lifestyle simplification and its underlying, motivating factors through examination of the basic ritual elements proposed by Rook (1985): (1) ritual scripts, (2) ritual artifacts, (3) ritual actors and roles, and (4) ritual audiences. Dramatic and recent changes in the consumption of death have materialized from individuals' conscious choices to simplify their own endings, with subsequent profound impact on these four elements. However, like any complex consumption phenomenon, we hypothesize that other demographic and psychographic factors also impact the consumption of death today.

Voluntary simplicity

Since its inception in the 1970s (Wells 1971; Plummer 1974) lifestyle analysis has proven to be a useful tool for better understanding consumers by layering psychographic "flesh" over demographic "bones," thereby humanizing and animating the "target," and often providing more in-depth and subtle consumer insights. Lifestyle analysis is quite dynamic, with new lifestyles emerging over time, with some achieving prominence in popular culture, for example, yuppies, road warriors, soccer moms, couch potatoes, yoga mommas, goths, and many others. One distinctive lifestyle that was first observed in the 1970s includes individuals who have made conscious decisions to pursue Voluntary Simplicity (Elgin and Mitchell 1977). This lifestyle trend has slowly but steadily increased in prominence among consumers and in the consumer behavior literature (Leonard-Barton 1981; Shama 1988; Mitchell 1983; Craig-Lees and Hill 2002; Etzioni 1998; Zavestoski 2002; Huneke 2005; Bekin, Carrigan, and Szmigin 2005;

Cherrier 2009; Iyer and Muncy 2009). Shama (1988) in fact claimed that the consumers who have voluntarily simplified their lives comprise one of the fastest growing segments in America, although empirical evidence of this is lacking.

In their seminal work Elgin and Mitchell (1977) suggested that voluntary lifestyle simplifiers adhere to five basic values: (1) material simplicity, (2) self-determination, (3) ecological awareness, (4) human scale, and (5) personal growth. Shama (1988) similarly defined voluntary simplicity as a lifestyle of low consumption, ecological responsibility, and self-sufficiency. We suggest that limiting expenditures on consumer goods and services, ecological responsibility, and self-sufficiency are the core concepts of simplicity lifestyles today. The lifestyle simplification trend can be examined from numerous theoretical and empirical perspectives, and in a variety of contexts. The approach taken here believes that a universal human rite of passage, death, provides a rich context for exploring simplification trends.

The American way of death

First, we provide a brief overview of traditional death practices in the United States that collectively constitute the funeral industry. We generalize with caution, as religion and cultural factors generate considerable variation in how death rituals are conducted. So, like Jessica Mittford (1963; updated posthumously in 2000) in her groundbreaking classic, *The American Way of Death*, our focus will be on the typical, or average, funerary practices. For much of the twentieth century, death rituals commonly centered around the local undertaker and his funeral home. The deceased would be removed from home or a hospital and delivered to the funeral home where the body would be embalmed, dressed and cosmetically enhanced. Sometimes the body would be returned to its home for a viewing and wake; often the viewing was held in the funeral home. Next, a funeral service would be held, attended by family members and friends, followed by a procession to the cemetery where the body would be buried. The sequence of these events changed little, however, increasing affluence and the marketing efforts of the funeral industry raised the stakes considerably. As Jessica Mittford observed over 50 years ago:

> gradually, almost imperceptibly, over the years the funeral men have constructed their own grotesque cloud-cuckoo-land where the trappings of Gracious Living are transformed ... into the trappings of Gracious Dying. The same familiar Madison Avenue language, with its peculiar adjectival range designed to anesthetize sales resistance to all sorts of products, had seeped into the funeral industry in a new and bizarre guise.
>
> (pp. 13–14)

Funerals received a big upgrade. Undertakers were rebranded as "funeral directors" who encouraged the purchase of solid copper caskets, floral tributes, handmade fashion for the corpse, among numerous other products and services.

Funerals became a new venue for conspicuous consumption, which like earlier expressions of it, elicited critical commentary. Even a Hollywood film, *The Loved One*, was largely based on Evelyn Waugh's 1948 satire, *The Loved One: An Anglo-American Tragedy*, the impetus for which was Waugh's visit to Forest Lawn cemetery in Burbank, California. The 1965 film also drew from Mittford's more recent book, and mocked the upselling of funereal offerings, but with little apparent effect on consumers' death consumption choices.

Value Line divides the funeral services industry into three categories: (1) cemetery owners and operators, (2) funeral homes and (3) manufacturers of burial and memorial products and services (Spencer 2014). *Forbes* magazine recently estimated the annual revenue of the funeral industry to be approximately $20 billion. With roughly 2.5 million deaths per year in the US, this amounts to an average cost per funeral of slightly over $8,000 (Boring 2014). A breakdown of the common funeral items and their costs is provided in Table 8.1. This is a substantial sum for the average household, and an impossible amount for families with more limited means. These financial realities explain the frequency of print and broadcast messages that encourage individuals to purchase term death insurance policies that will protect their survivors from funereal financial burdens.

While Table 8.1 summarizes the most basic elements of a traditional funeral's cost structure, Table 8.2 enumerates myriad detail related to the medical and legal, ceremonial, body disposition, and memorial aspects of death consumption, regardless of whether it involves traditional burial or cremation. Many of these items commonly require incremental expenditures above the basic funeral package, which can easily result in a funeral that costs far more than the $8,300 average.

However, the revenue growth in the funeral industry has been flat for almost ten years. One analyst concludes that four changes are profoundly impacting the funeral industry today: (1) lower-priced products and services

Table 8.1 Cost of an adult funeral – 2012

Item	Price
Non-declinable basic services fee	$1,975
Removal/transfer of remains to funeral home	$285
Embalming	$695
Other preparation of the body	$225
Use of facilities/staff for viewing	$400
Use of facilities/staff for funeral ceremony	$495
Use of a hearse	$295
Use of a service car/van	$130
Basic memorial printed package	$150
Metal casket	$2,395
MEDIAN COST OF A FUNERAL	$7,045
Vault	*$1,298*
Total cost of a funeral with vault	*$8,343*

Source: Spencer (2014), "Industry Analysis: Funeral Services," Value Line, April 28.

Table 8.2 Death-related products and services

Products and services[1]			
Medical and legal	*Ceremonial*	*Body disposition*	*Memorial*

• Embalming
• Death certificates
• Ritual bathing/
  dressing
• Mortuary/
  refrigeration/
  packing the body
  in ice
• Sanitary care of
  un-embalmed
  remains
• Printing services
	• Costumes
	• Cosmetic
	  enhancements
	• Flowers
	• Wreaths
	• Dove or balloon
	  release
	• Candles
	• Graveside
	  services
	• Tents or chairs
	  for graveside
	• Decoration
	• Scattering at sea
	  by airplane or
	  boat
	• Inside pieces for
	  casket
	• Body transfer
	  with limousine,
	  hearse etc.
	• Portrait car
		• Niche or crypt
		  plate
		• Cremation vault
		• Burial vault
		• Burial plot
		• Burial clothing
		• Coffin/casket
		• Urns
		• Container
		• Grave markers
		• Digging the
		  grave
		• Other cremation
		  services
			• Memorial gifts
			• Memorial books
			• Acknowledgment
			  cards
			• Register book
			• Keepsakes/
			  pendants
			• Obituaries
			• Jewelry
			• Printing service
			• Life tribute DVD
			• Remembrance
			  throw
			• Blanket
			• Memorial
			  reception room
			• Thank-you notes
			• Funeral invitations

Note

1 Any single item in the table may fall into more than one category.

purchased over the internet, (2) the growth of national funeral home chains, (3) cultural diversity in the US that demands different funeral ritual practice, and (4) the rising popularity of cremation (Harrington 2007: pp. 201–216). Although disposition of a dead body through cremation has been performed throughout the world for several thousand years, its popularity has only recently increased in the US, and done so with amazing rapidity. As Table 8.3 summarizes, 50 years ago fewer than 4 percent of deaths resulted in cremation; in 2012 the number had risen to over 43 percent.

Cremation changes everything

Such a dramatic and relatively swift change in a core component of life's final *rite de passage* is extraordinary, and begs the question: why? On the website of the Cremation Association of North America (CANA) are the results of a 2006 survey that investigated the reasons that Americans are shifting their preferences from the traditional funeral and burial to cremation. The number one factor that was mentioned was cost savings. In 2013 the National Funeral Directors

Table 8.3 Cremation rates in the United States

Year	Total cremation rate (%)
2012	43.2
2005	32.13
1995	21.11
1985	13.86
1975	6.55
1965	3.87

Source: National Vital Statistics Report.

Association reported that the average cost for a cremation was approximately $1,600, which is roughly one fifth of the cost of a traditional funeral. The second most frequently cited factor was the desire to save land, followed by a preference for a simpler end of life ritual. All three of these factors are strongly correlated with the defining elements of a simplicity lifestyle, which supports the belief that the dramatic increase in cremations in the US is a manifestation of preferences for simplicity, not only in life but also at the end of it. At the same time, it is likely that other factors also contribute to opting for cremation, particularly cost. The post-2008 recession and income stagnation likely have made it more difficult for middle class individuals to afford a traditional funeral, and even if affordability is less of an issue for some, they may have readjusted their economic priorities in ways that would preclude spending large sums on a traditional funeral.

The previously mentioned survey by CANA yields similar findings. Lower cost and environmental impact are the top two cremation motivators. In addition, the CANA study cites the wider range of disposition options that cremation opens up, such as scattering of the ashes over one or more locations, dividing the ashes among family members, or incorporating them into keepsake jewelry or other items. The ease of transporting ashes versus a corpse was also listed as an advantage of cremation. Finally, the acceptance of cremation by religions that had previously frowned on it (e.g., Catholicism) opens up the option to a larger number of individuals. Also, the growing presence of immigrant populations for whom cremation is the cultural norm have likely contributed to its growth.

Cremation has had a profound effect on the ways in which individuals' lives end, and simplifies the experience in various ways. We belief that cremation's impact on end-of-life practices can be further understood in more nuanced ways by deconstructing the cremation-driven ritual. Specifically, as mentioned earlier, our analytic framework relies on Rook's (1985) specification of consumption rituals' structure and content, which include four key elements: (1) scripted behavior, activities, and events; (2) actors and their assigned roles; (3) consumption artifacts and services; and (4) ritual audience, or observers. As these elements are discussed it should be useful to refer to Table 8.4, which illustrates the various products, people, and services that may be consumed within each.

Table 8.4 Death rituals consumption domain

	Medical/legal products/services	Ceremonial products/services	Body disposition products/services	Memorial products/services or merchandise
Artifacts	• Embalming • Body transfer with limousine, hearse, etc. • Portrait car • Death certificates • Refrigeration • Ritual bathing/dressing • Mortuary • Packing the body in ice • Sanitary care of un-embalmed remains	• Costumes • Cosmetic enhancements • Flowers • Wreaths • Dove or balloon release • Candles • Graveside services • Tents or chairs for graveside • Decoration • Scattering at sea by airplane or boat • Inside pieces for casket	• Niche or crypt plate • Cremation vaults • Burial vaults • Burial plots • Burial clothing • Coffins/caskets • Urns • Casket container • Grave markers	• Memorial gifts • Memorial books • Acknowledgment cards • Register book • Keepsakes/pendants • Obituaries • Jewelry • Printing service • Life tribute DVD • Remembrance throw • Blanket • Memorial reception room
Scripts	• Legal scripted activity • Cultural and familial normative scripts	• Visitation • Invocations • Parades/procession/pomp • Several days • Different funeral homes in different countries	• Cremation • Burial (traditional, green and home burial) • Witnessed cremation	

Roles		
• Drivers for hearse, limousine/utility car	• Funeral director	• Casket bearer/pall bearer
• Clerical personnel	• Security staff	• Attendant for crypt entombment
• Cleaning staff	• Priest/clergy	• Other interment personnel
• Coroner	• Undertaker	• Eulogists/speakers
• Cemetery director	• Caterers	
	• Mourners	
	• Music providers	
	• A lady attendant for hairdressing and cosmetic (hairdresser)	
	• Ushers	
	• Aftercare planner	
	• Reception staff	
	• Escorts motorcycle escort	
	• Other staff[1]	

Audiences
• Family members
• Friends
• Representatives of companies and government institutions
• Funeral home staff
• Colleagues
• Neighbors
• Community
• Participation by members of clubs or organizations
• Social media connections[2]

Notes

1 Includes services of staff and clerical personnel, personnel to arrange and coordinate services; funeral service staff at church and place of interment; recorded music, church care and maintenance; service personnel for ushering, care of flowers and accompanying cards from donors; committal service at cemetery.

2 Social media connections refer to the people or organizations that were in contact with the bereaved family members and the deceased one in social networking sites.

Script Elements. Traditional death rituals commonly extended over several days, and were highly scripted. After a corpse was embalmed, dressed, and groomed it was typically transferred to a home or funeral parlor for viewing. At the same time family and friends would visit the deceased's home to offer their condolences and bring a cornucopia of comfort food. This visitation period would last as long as three days. Depending on the individual and the circumstances of his or her death, the tone of the script could vary from tragic (e.g., the sudden death of a child) to downright bawdy (e.g., the classic Irish wake). Things culminated in a funeral service followed by burial in a cemetery, and often concluded with a final gathering at the deceased's home. Today the process of dying often stretches out over several years due to medical protocols that can prolong the inevitable, or as a result of illnesses that can't be staved off but have a long span, such as Alzheimer's disease. When death finally occurs, it has been anticipated, mourned, and planned to varying degrees for a long period of time. In this situation the ritual script's emphasis is more likely to be on dignified disposition rather than elaborate ceremony and extensive consumption. The ritual script tends to be shorter and simpler, with an attendant reduction in expenditures. One can also observe today some shifts in the funeral service venue from the traditional funeral home to the deceased's own residence. Although it is difficult to determine the magnitude of this trend, it reflects voluntary simplicity on both the reduced spending and self-sufficiency dimensions. The steady rise of eco-consciousness has produced green funeral options that provide an ecologically responsible alternative to both traditional burial and cremation. The most simple stripped down script would direct the transportation of the corpse to a cremation facility, followed by a distribution of the ashes, and possibly a memorial service at a later date.

Audience Elements. People are living longer today, but the longer one lives, the greater the decline in one's living cohorts. For example, at the age of 65, 80 percent of one's age cohorts are still alive; at age 85 the figure drops to only 30 percent. Thus, the longer one lives the smaller the pool of age cohorts who are available to attend one's funeral, and even those who are still living may be too infirm to participate. The second author's mother is 93, and this year the number of her Christmas cards that were returned with "whereabouts unknown" designation was the highest ever, illustrating the audience diminishment point. Another reason for smaller funeral audiences is the geographic dispersion of family members and friends due to employment, retirement, and other situational factors. Even if younger family members are around, if someone has been seriously ill and/or institutionalized for years, he or she has been socially removed from the everyday lives of friends and family, so there is likely less motivation to participate in funereal rituals for someone who has been "gone" for some time. When death ritual audiences are small, the events involved will likely be simpler and relatively inexpensive.

Artifact Elements. Cremation is likely to account for close to 50 percent of death dispositions within the next 10 years. As noted earlier, this disposition alternative involves significantly reduced expenditures funereal on goods and services. With an average cost of $1,600 cremation is $6,700 less expensive than the average traditional funeral cost of $8,300 (2010 NFDA General Price List Survey). Using the 2010 cremation rate of 41 percent, approximately 984,000 of the 2,400,000 individuals who died that year were cremated. Multiplying the number of cremations by the $6,700 average cost differential between cremation and traditional funerals results in a loss to the funeral industry of roughly $6.59 billion. Of course, traditional funeral providers are eager to provide cremation services for those so inclined. However, when one examines the funeral artifacts in Table 8.4, it is easy to see where the losses are likely located. Even if someone wants to have Forest Lawn (a high end traditional funeral service provider) conduct a cremation, this is still an end of life simplifying solution, and unlikely to require limousines, caskets, flowers, or a dove release. The role of flowers and floral displays at funerals was damaged some years ago with the emergence of the "in lieu of flowers" request to direct one's condolences toward a favored charity of the deceased. The increasing popularity of cremations has had an equally if not more severe impact on the floral industry.

Actors and Roles. Cremation has had a negative impact on the sales of traditional funeral products and services such as funeral homes, caskets, flowers, printing services, tombstones, limousines, caterers, banquet halls, music providers, religious service providers, among others. Consequently the cast of characters to perform the various roles noted in Table 8.4 is much diminished. These declines reflect both the reduced expenditure and ecological responsibility aspects of lifestyle simplicity. While we have seen the decline of traditional funeral consumption practices, products and services, we have also witnessed the emergence of technology that enables new approaches to the consumption of death.

Online memorial sites

The internet and its proliferating social media sites have provided new avenues for the consumption of death. Online practices affect dying, memorialization, funerals, and other death-related issues in different ways. Users pay their respects publicly by using online communication platforms to not only mourn the deceased person but also to establish relationships with others who are also grieving (Wright, 2014). Online practices can take the form of the transformation of a social media profile (Facebook) into a memorial profile or an online memorial site constructed after death. Social media connections play important ritual roles in spreading news of the death, announcing funeral arrangements and creating a shared biography of the deceased. At the end of 2012, it was estimated that three million Facebook user profiles had become memorialized (Kaleem, 2012). Social media users express grief by sharing audio or video clips, making status updates and comments on photos (Brubaker, Hayes, and Dourish, 2013). Such activities take the place of memorial products or services such as memorial books, acknowledgement cards, register books, and many more which have been important parts of traditional funerals. However, in the online environment, memorial pages and web funerals are mostly created and controlled by virtual friends and people who hardly even knew the deceased (Walter, Hourizi, and Moncur, 2011). The emergence of social media sites affect rituals of mourning on several levels: spreading news of the death, providing a virtual (rather than physical) space in which to display grief, and changing social protocols for roles in collective mourning (Lingel, 2013).

Both social networking sites and online memorial sites allow users to embrace a do-it-yourself (DIY) mourning approach. DIY mourning can be seen as a kind of participatory media communication, where new forms of social interaction are taking place outside of traditional manifestations of mourning (Lingel, 2013: 194). The emergence of DIY mourning suggests that although traditional funeral rites continue to be followed, there is a developing interest, or perhaps even need, to craft, organically and disparately, individual displays, practices and rituals for experiencing loss (Lingel, 2013). There are also online memorial sites which enable people who are grieving to celebrate, remember or commemorate those who died. Such memorial sites are generally created to interact with friends or family members and receive messages of hope and prayer. However, online practices may be seen as another simplification trend in contemporary funerals, although actual expenditures on digital wreaths, headstones, uploaded soundtracks and tablets suggest that the artifactual dimension is expanding in new and different ways. In addition, online memorials and funerals lead to a spatial expansion and dissolve physical barriers to participation (Brubaker *et al.*, 2013). Internet allows mourners to participate in the grieving ceremony. This is a fact that affects ritual elements such as roles and audiences at a funeral. It can be also said that online mourning practices show new forms of ritualized behavior related to death that extend beyond traditional funereal practices (Wright, 2014).

In conclusion, this exploratory research began with a focus on the Voluntary Simplicity Lifestyle and its impact on the American way of death. Clearly, it is a significant contributor to the scaling down of the ritual elements that are associated with the consumption of death. However, as we noted in the beginning, other factors are also involved: economics, demographics, cultural diversity, and secularism, among others. Whether this simplification trend will be adopted in the newly affluent developing nations is uncertain. The *nouveau riche* may be inclined to want to go out with a big bang. Certainly in cultures that traditionally view funeral services as the occasion for public ceremony and spectacle (e.g., India, Bali) simplification seems less likely. Ironically, these two cultures commonly rely on cremation, so perhaps increased income will allow for more elaborate and higher pyres. Also, the desire to personalize and customize one's death ritual may pull away from simplicity. Now in their late sixties, the oldest Baby Boomers are exhibiting their desires for self-determination about their ends, which has given rise to a new professional service category: funeral planners.

References

Bekin, C., Carrigan, M., and Szmigin, I. (2005). "Defying Marketing Sovereignty: Voluntary Simplicity at New Consumption Communities," *Qualitative Market Research: An International Journal*, 8 (4), 413–429.

Bonsu, S. and Belk, R. (2003). "Do Not Go Cheaply into that Good Night: Death-ritual Consumption in Asante, Ghana," *Journal of Consumer Research*, 30 (1), 41–55.

Boring, P. (2014). "Death of the Death Care Industry and Eternal Life Online," *Forbes*, April 24.

Brubaker, J. R., Hayes, G. R., and Dourish, P. (2013). "Beyond the Grave: Facebook as a Site for the Expansion of Death and Mourning." *The Information Society*, 29 (3), 152–163.

Cherrier, H. (2009). "Anti-Consumption Discourses and Consumer-Resistant Identities," *Journal of Business Research*, 62, 181–190.

Cook, G. and Walter, T. (2005). "Rewritten Rites: Language and Social Relations in Traditional and Contemporary Funerals," *Discourse and Society*, C. 16, (3), 365–391.

Craig-Lees, M. and Hill, C. (2002). "Understanding Voluntary Simplifiers," *Psychology and Marketing*, 19, 187–210.

De Witte, M. (2003). "Money and Death: Funeral Business in Asante, Ghana," *Africa-London-International African Institute*, C. 73, (4), 531–559.

Dubisch, J. (1989). "Death and Social Change in Greece," *Anthropological Quarterly*, C. 62, (4), 189–200.

Elgin, D. and Mitchell, A. (1977). "Voluntary Simplicity," *Co-Evolutionary Quarterly*, Summer, 5–18.

Etzioni, A. (1998). "Voluntary Simplicity: Characterization, Select Psychological Implications, and Societal Consequences," *Journal of Economic Psychology*, 19, 619–643.

Harrington, D.E. (2007). "Markets: Preserving Funeral Markets with Ready-to-Embalm Laws," *The Journal of Economic Perspectives*, C. 21, (4), 201–216.

Huneke, M.E. (2005). "The Face of The Un-Consumer: An Empirical Examination of The Practice of Voluntary Simplicity in The United States," *Psychology and Marketing*, 22, 527–550.

Integrity Burial Boxes Ltd. (2011). "The ABC's of Building and Marketing a Columbarium Wall," Author House.

Iyer, R. and Muncy, J.A. (2009). "Purpose and Object of Anti-Consumption," *Journal of Business Research*, 62, 160–168.

Kaleem, J. (2012). "Death on Facebook Now Common as 'Dead Profiles' Create a Vast Virtual Cemetery," *Huffington Post* (December 7), at www.huffingtonpost.com/2012/12/07/death-facebook-dead-profiles_n_2245397.html, accessed April 12, 2015.

Lingel, J. (2013). "The Digital Remains: Social Media and Practices of Online Grief," *The Information Society*, 29 (3), 190–195.

Leonard-Barton, D. (1981). "Voluntary Simplicity Lifestyles and Energy Conservation," *Journal of Consumer Research*, 8, 243–252.

Lieberman, P. (1993). *Uniquely Human: The Evolution of Speech, Thought, and Selfless Behavior*, Harvard University Press.

National Funeral Directors Association (2013). www.nfda.org/media-center/statistics-reports.html, (Accessed on February 5, 2013).

Mittford, J. (1963). *The American Way of Death*, New York: Alfred A. Knopf.

National Funeral Directors Association (2014). http://nfda.org/component/content/article/7.html#trends, accessed on February 20, 2014.

Plummer, J. T. (1974). "The Concept and Application of Life Style Segmentation," *Journal of Marketing*, 38 (1), 33–37.

Rook, D.W. (1985). "The Ritual Dimension of Consumer Behavior," *Journal of Consumer Research*, 12 (3), 251–264.

Shama, A. (1988). "The Voluntary Simplicity Consumer: A Comparative Study," *Psychological Report*, 63, 859–869.

Sher, B. D. (1963). "Funeral Prearrangement: Mitigating the Undertaker's Bargaining Advantage," *Stanford Law Review*, pp. 415–479.

Spencer, Mathew (2014). "Industry Analysis: Funeral Services," Value Line, April 28.

Trigg, A. B. (2001). "Veblen, Bourdieu, and Conspicuous Consumption," *Journal of Economic Issues*, pp. 99–115.

Wells, W. and Tigert, D. (1971). "Activities, Interests, and Opinions," *Journal of Advertising Research*, 11 (August), 27–35.

Walter, T., Hourizi, R., Moncur, W., and Pitsillides, S. (2011). "Does the Internet Change How We Die and Mourn? Overview and Analysis." *OMEGA–Journal of Death and Dying*, 64 (4), 275–302.

Waugh, Evelyn (1948), *The Loved One: An Anglo-American Tragedy*, London: Chapman and Hall.

Wright, N. (2014). "Death and the Internet: The Implications of the Digital Afterlife," *First Monday*, 19 (6).

Zavestoski, S. (2002), "The Social-Psychological Bases of Anticonsumption Attitudes," *Psychology and Marketing*, 19, 149–165.

Part III
Consumption of death

9   Cheating death via social self immortalization

The potential of consumption–laden online memorialization to extend and link selves beyond (physical) death

Terrance G. Gabel

It was a very special feeling. I felt as if I was entering a sanctuary ... I feel affinity to a group of people scattered all over the world, linked by the common human experience of the loss of someone related to them with bonds stronger than death.

> (Bo Jonsson, father of a recently deceased young man, discussing his experience with the first online memorialization website (Golden 2006, paragraph 7))

The prior possessions of the deceased can be powerful remains of the dead person's extended self.

> (Belk 1988, p. 144)

...the memories of Gary ... will remain with me forever. Some of my memories include our late night stocking shelves at Hy-Vee. His cream-colored Javelin ... His Kawasaki motorcycle ... His blue jean jacket that he wore in the winter and his signature big bright smile...

> (Ken, friend of recently deceased Gary, in the latter's online memorial)

The notion of "cheating death" summons visions of avoiding certain demise. "Cheating of death" is, though, ultimately seen as temporary in that all humans must one day die. However, as suggested in the first of the quotes above, online memorialization's unique ability to link the living to deceased loved ones may facilitate at least a partial "cheating of death." The second and third quotes suggest that products and their consumption – and memories thereof – can possibly be intimately involved in challenging the certainty of death.

This possibility of "cheating death" has emerged from research on both a "New Model of Grief" (Walter 1997, 1996) and online memorialization (Lim 2013; Walter *et al.* 2011–12). This research collectively suggests (1) that death has been decoupled into "physical" and "social" components, and (2) that "social immortality" – i.e., eternal life for the *social self* – may now be possible.

Central to "social self immortalization" is online memorialization involving the interactive, communal process of post-mortem identity construction wherein mourners co-author the biography of the deceased – with themselves (autobiographically) in it – as part of the grieving process (Walter *et al.* 2011–12; Carroll and Landry 2010; Roberts 2006; Walter 1996). The role of products and their consumption in this process has not been meaningfully examined.

The purpose of the present exploratory inquiry is to extend understanding of mourning and social self immortality from a consumption perspective. Particularly useful in this regard is Belk's (2013, 1988) conceptualization of the *extended self*, which holds that our possessions are significant contributors to and reflections of who and what we are. I extend this conceptualization beyond the physical lifespan of the consumer via introspectively-aided participatory netnographic analysis of an online memorial. Overall, insight is provided into the potential power of products and consumption to (1) enhance the identities and selves of both deceased persons and mourners, (2) perhaps forever link the living to the dead, and, per Kozinets' (2002) conceptualization of "emancipatory communal consumption" being ironically used to "escape the market," (3) help mourners cathartically and at least temporarily escape from what Walter (1997, 1996) refers to as "the old death" (i.e., the unpleasant market-driven experience of death wherein mourners are to quickly "get over" death and "move on with life" without the deceased in it).

I begin, below, with a review of relevant literature. This is followed by a discussion of methodological approach. Finally, research findings and their implications are addressed.

Literature review

Three areas of research are of prime relevance to this inquiry; postmortem identity construction, online memorialization, and the *extended self*. Review of pertinent literature in each topical domain, with a view toward understanding each in the context of the potential role of products and consumption in online memorialization and social self immortalization, follows.

Postmortem identity construction

Mourning-related sociological and psychological research dating back to the early 1900s suggests that the process of constructing, reconstructing, and preserving representations of the selves of others continues, in earnest, after death (Neimeyer, Prigerson, and Davies 2002; Volkan 1981). Insight into how and why postmortem identity construction projects are undertaken can be gained via consideration of psychological research on mourning. One reason why such projects are undertaken involves "grieving individuals ... struggling to affirm or reconstruct a personal world of meaning that has been challenged by loss" (Neimeyer, Prigerson, and Davies 2002, p. 239). One way in which postmortem identity construction transpires entails anchoring memories of the deceased around their belongings; referred to, in this context, as *linking objects* (Neimeyer, Prigerson, and Davies 2002; Volkan 1981, 1974).

According to Volkan, *linking objects* are inanimate objects employed as a "symbolic bridge (or link) to the representation of the dead person" (1981, p. 20). *Linking objects* can be broken into five not necessarily mutually exclusive categories: (1) personal possessions of – most commonly objects actually worn by – the deceased (e.g., clothing, jewelry, and eyeglasses), (2) objects that were given to the mourner by the deceased as a gift, (3) "something the deceased used to extend his senses or bodily functions, such as a camera (an extension of seeing)," (4) objects realistically or symbolically representing the deceased (e.g., photographs or identification bracelets, respectively), and (5) "last-minute objects," things "at hand when the mourner first learned of the death or saw the dead body" (Volkan 1981, p. 104).

Memories associated with grief linking the dead to the living may be based not only on objects. They may be similarly founded about what Volkan terms *linking phenomena*.

I have also observed in my patients what I call linking phenomena – fantasies, sensations, and behavior patterns that perpetuate the possibility of contact between the mourner and the one he mourns without reference to any tangible object (Volkan 1981, p. 106).

Examples of *linking phenomena* include religious beliefs and other intangible things "with sensory impact" such as music/songs (Volkan 1981, p. 106). These intangible "things of sensory impact" provide the mourner the opportunity to have his or her representation of the phenomenon in question "meet externally the representation of the one he mourns and to keep the circumstances of this meeting under his absolute control" (Volkan 1981, p. 106).

With both *linking objects* and *phenomena*, the foci of the memory linking the living to the dead belongs to both parties. According to Volkan: "The linking object belongs to both the deceased and to the patient himself, as if the representations of the two meet and merge in an externalized way" (1974, p. 190). Most research in this area concerns family members mourning the loss of children wherein what is mutually possessed by the living and the dead are physically existing tangible things of, or otherwise related to, the deceased; most commonly clothing and mementos. Whatever form they take, these *linking objects* are "something actually present in the environment that is psychologically contaminated with various aspects of the dead and the self" (Volkan 1981, p. 101).

From the perspective of the present inquiry, it should be noted that while research on *linking objects* and *linking phenomena* has focused on physically present tangible possessions or mementos of the deceased, a host of other products and various aspects of their consumption commonly examined by consumer researchers could just as easily be posited to serve as the objects or non-tangible phenomena around which mourning, memories, and postmortem identity construction/social self immortalization are anchored. Also, notably not accounted for in Volkan's (1981, 1974) *linking objects* and *linking phenomena* are mourner memories concerning (1) possessions of the deceased that are either not physically accessible and/or no longer in existence, and (2) consumption experiences and other consumption-related activities of the deceased involving possessions of either the deceased or mourners.

Online memorialization

The first interactive grief webpage – www.Webhealing.com – was launched in 1995 (Golden 2006). Although its usage was not exclusively for online memorialization, it was the first interactive social network site (SNS) to facilitate the practice (Sofka 1997). Today, a variety of types of SNSs allow mourners to memorialize deceased persons online. Such sites can be categorized on the basis of whether or not (1) the site is grief-specific, and (2) memorialization transpires intentionally (Walter *et al.* 2011–12). As a result, four possible – albeit only three practical – types of online memorialization SNSs exist. The first type involves intentional memorializing in grief-specific sites (i.e., cyber-cemeteries) wherein the SNS is dedicated to online memorialization. Examples include memorialization pages sponsored by funeral homes as well as webpages such as My Death Space (www.mydeathspace. com/), Online Funeral (www.online-funeral.com), the Eternal Portal (www. theeternalportal.com/), and Legacy.com (www.legacy.com). The second category consists of SNSs where the memorializing is intentional but the site is not dedicated to grief and mourning (e.g., Facebook, most specifically memorial pages created within it). A third form involves any of a wide variety of non-grief-specific sites where unintentional memorialization occurs as a result of the "digital remains" of persons being downloaded and preserved by others (Walter *et al.* 2011–12). The fourth type – unintentional memorialization on grief-specific sites – is not practically possible.

Regardless of SNS form, online memorialization offers mourners unique and meaningful benefits relative to traditional means of mourning (e.g., physically visiting cemeteries or funeral homes or attending funeral services in other locations). These benefits include:

1   Immortalization of the social self facilitating continuation of bonds with the dead (Lim 2013; Walter *et al.* 2011–12; Carroll and Landry 2010; Roberts 2006),
2   Greater freedom of emotional expression during grieving (e.g., celebration and expressing admiration of the deceased and/or their values) (Carroll and Landry 2010; Roberts 2006),
3   Personalization of the grieving process via creation of personal tributes to the deceased in whatever form the mourner chooses (Roberts 2006),
4   Enfranchisement of disenfranchised mourners (Walter *et al.* 2011–12; Carroll and Landry 2010; Roberts 2006; Sofka 1997),
5   Providing mourners an acceptable means of communicating with the dead (e.g., as a form of ongoing dialogue or to realize closure) (Walter *et al.* 2011–12; Carroll and Landry 2010),

6   Management of the digitized "objects of the dead" (e.g., photos and music, which can be uploaded and shared, facilitating better representation of the deceased than can be achieved via words alone) (Walter *et al.* 2011–12),

7   Rendering death and grieving both more public and communal; thus offering mourners a higher level of emotional support and often involving shared, interactive construction of the biography of the deceased over extended periods of time and repeated visitation to the memorial (Walter *et al.* 2011–12; Carroll and Landry 2010; Ryan 2008; Roberts 2006; Sofka 1997),

8   Possible initiation of further – or rekindling of ceased – online or off-line communications between perhaps geographically distant mourners (Roberts 2006), and

9   Greater convenience in that the mourner can visit the memorial whenever they like from the comfort of their own home and without having to physically interact with other mourners (Carroll and Landry 2010; Sofka 1997).

Two of these benefits warrant special consideration; one contained in the list above and another, more general one, not. Per benefit #7 above, Carroll and Landry (2010), echoing the sentiments of other researchers, place special importance on the public, communal, interactive construction of the biography of the deceased (with mourners autobiographically inserting themselves into the deceased's biography).

> …in some ways the most interesting theme concerns the way many posters contribute to and therefore author or coauthor biographies or narratives of the deceased's life, biographies that evolve over time and that in important ways are contested or negotiated by the post writers. These posts include memories and stories the posters shared with the deceased and are recording or writing in a public space. It is important that in these memories the survivor usually has played a central role. As such, these contributions reveal a tension between the need to prominently and uniquely include oneself in the narrative of the life being remembered and the shared goal among posters of uniting in communal grief, or of finding or creating a common theme.
>
> (Carroll and Landry, 2010, p. 345)

Although not explicitly contained in any of the benefits addressed above, Sofka (1997) suggests a more general benefit superordinate to and encompassing of the nine listed. This involves online memorialization's unique ability to "provide cathartic outlets for the expression of grief that are not available through traditional means" (p. 563). Although Sofka provides no further explanation of the nature of this catharsis, her allusion to inadequate "traditional means" of grieving bears great similarity to both Walter's (1997, 1996)

"New Model of Grief" and Wood and Williamson's (2003) "New Acceptance of Death" wherein it is posited that, starting in the mid-1990s, growing numbers of persons in Western nations began actively looking to escape the unpleasant, secular, private, market-driven experience of death and mourning that had been dominant since at least shortly after World War II. According to Walter (1996):

> The dominant model found in contemporary bereavement literature sees grief as a working through of emotion, the eventual goal being to move on and live without the deceased. This article challenges this model ... Survivors typically want to talk about the deceased and to talk with others who knew him or her. Together they construct a story that places the dead within their lives, a story capable of enduring through time. The purpose of grief is therefore the construction of a durable biography that enables the living to integrate the memory of the dead into their ongoing lives; the process by which this is achieved is principally conversation with others who knew the deceased. The process hinges on talk more than feeling; and the purpose entails moving on with, as well as without, the deceased.
>
> (Walter 1996, p. 7)

The advent of communal, interactive online memorialization – within the same mid-1990s timeframe – appears to have provided Western mourners the much-desired opportunity to effectively escape from and purge the various unpleasantries of the then ubiquitous "old death."

From the perspective of the present inquiry, while the unique benefits of online memorialization suggest numerous possibilities for understanding social self immortalization, of equal interest to what *is* found in extant research is what *is not* found. Most notable is the conspicuous scarcity of mentions of products and consumption in the memories of mourners. For instance, in the lone consideration of the topic from a consumption perspective, Lim (2013), in her discussion of "materiality" (i.e., "ways in which individuals and groups enact and perform their relationship to the deceased" [p. 397]), provides only one explicit consumption-related example; a mourner communicating with the deceased by posting about the baking of cakes together in the past. When products and their consumption are mentioned, they are often discussed in derogatory fashion. This is particularly true in the context of memorial posts in which mourners express concern over what they interpret to be other mourners alluding to the "materialistic values" of the deceased (Walter *et al.* 2011–12; Ryan 2008).

What makes this lack of attention to products and their consumption in online memorialization research so conspicuous is the important role that products and consumption are known to play in the lives of consumers. Arguably unrivaled in its exemplification of this importance is Belk's conceptualization of the *extended self*. Attention now turns to a review of this key concept in the context of social self immortalization via online memorialization.

The extended self

The notion of the *extended self* holds that "we regard our possessions as parts of ourselves" (Belk 1988, p. 139). Our identities are thusly defined, in part, by what we presently possess and what we have possessed in the past (Belk 1988). The *extended self* is, however, comprised not only of our physical selves and tangible products possessed. It also includes one's "internal processes, ideas, and experiences, and those persons, places, and things to which one feels attached (Belk 1988, p. 141).

The inclusion of "persons" as a component of the *extended self* has special relevance in the context of the present inquiry. This is due to the fact that online memorialization is primarily engaged in by persons – friends and family members of the deceased – who are likely to have been both constituent of and/or part of the deceased's *extended self* while living. The question arises as to how the involvement of these persons in the *extended self* of the living carries over to the process of online social self immortalization. In this regard, while discussions of the *extended self* are typically confined to focal, living consumers, Belk does hint at the possibility of an "immortal extended self" when contending that our possessions, broadly defined, are used to "seek happiness, remind ourselves of experiences, accomplishments, and other people in our lives, and even create a sense of immortality after death" (Belk 1988, p. 160). This suggests that social self immortalization may involve mourner expression of memories of products and consumption-related experiences associated with the deceased.

Perhaps most importantly with respect to the present inquiry, Belk, in accord with Volkan's (1981, 1974) *linking objects*, but not limiting consideration of them to physically present tangible possessions or mementos of the deceased, contends that "The prior possessions of the deceased can be powerful remains of the dead person's extended self" (Belk 1988, p. 144). Thus exemplified is the notion that possessions – and memories thereof – may serve to help (1) define who and what the person possessing them both *is* – while living – and *was* – after death – and (2) link the living to the dead. Recall, however, that it is not just possessions per se which may function in this manner. This is due to the fact that, as previously alluded to, it is not only products and goods presently or once possessed that constitute the *extended self*. Also included are "ideas, and experiences" and persons and places "to which one feels attached" (Belk 1988, p. 141). Thus, it can be reasoned that perhaps also serving to define who and what a person is or was, as well as serving to link the living to the dead, are memories based on (1) ideas and experiences related to products and their consumption, and (2) the persons with which and the places in which consumption experiences and behaviors have transpired.

Lastly, the original conceptualization of the *extended self* has recently been updated to account for emergent realities of the "digital world" (Belk 2013). Several suggested "digital modifications" are based on changes in self construction and presentation driven by advances in online technology. For purposes of the present inquiry, the most relevant of these updates are *sharing* (i.e., it is now far easier to share digitized possessions and self-presentation with others), and *co-construction of self* (i.e., identity construction is now jointly engaged in with those one interacts with online) (Belk 2013). With regard to the enhanced ability to share aspects of one's self with others online, one suggested "needed update" involves the notion that when possessions are shared and "jointly owned" – as they are in cases of both the *extended self* and *linking objects* and *phenomena* – they "enhance the sense of imagined community and … create feelings of group identity" (Belk 2013, p. 486). Building on this, updates per the *co-construction of self* include the notion that the process of creating this sense of community and group identity based, in part, around shared possessions, is a "joint project resulting in an aggregate self that belongs as much to the others who have helped to form it as it does to oneself" (Belk 2013, p. 488).

Collectively suggested by these two "digital modifications" to the *extended self* is the possibility that this joint project of constructing community and group identity around jointly owned possessions may not only continue but also escalate in magnitude after death. This may be due, for instance, to once close group members having grown apart over time due to geographic relocation or careers and family obligations being "brought back together" via remembrance of the *extended self* – and their roles and places in it – of the deceased. Further suggested is the possibility that one of the things now jointly owned by the group is the *extended self* of the deceased (which may serve as input into the process of interactively co-constructing the biography of the deceased during online memorialization and social self immortalization).

Research methodology

This exploratory inquiry involves an introspectively-aided participatory netnographic analysis of the "cyber-cemetery"-based memorialization of "Gary," a white male who died at the age of 45.[1] Participant netnography, the primary methodological technique employed, is discussed first below. The limited, supplemental role of introspection is then addressed.

Participant netnography

A netnography is an ethnography conducted in the context of understanding online communities of various form via humanistic research techniques (Kozinets 2010). Netnographies can be performed in participant-observational or non-participant-observational fashion depending on whether or not the researcher actively participates in online community activities.

The present research involves participant-observational netnography due to the fact that I, the researcher, am one of the mourners participating in Gary's online memorialization. The online community being researched in the present inquiry is the group of 38 mourners participating in the memorialization. This community is widely geographically dispersed about the United States – from 15 different states – with almost all members having grown up with Gary in or around his hometown in Iowa in the 1960s, 1970s, or 1980s. Seven participants are recognizable as family members. Most non-family members appear to have seen Gary at most several times – if at all – in the 20–25 years prior to his death (due largely to Gary and his immediate family moving from Iowa to southern California in the mid-late 1980s). The SNS-based communications analyzed are the 53 posts interactively made to Gary's 14-page, 7,156-word, 455-line online memorial; commencing two days after his death and spanning a period of three years and three months thereafter. Finally, the communal phenomenon to be understood is the interactive online immortalization of Gary's social self; including his *extended self* within it.

Introspection

Introspection involves the incorporation of the researcher's own personal experience into the research project. This practice has a long history of controversial usage in the social sciences based on the ironic notion that although researcher introspection is necessarily unavoidable, the desire among many social science scholars and publication gatekeepers to attain honorific *objectivity* and *scientific* status for their research and disciplines leads them to view the use of introspection as inappropriate (Levy 1996; Clandinin and Connelly 1994). Introspection has been effectively employed in bereavement research (Walter 1996) and can be seen as particularly applicable to online memorialization research given the autobiographical manner in which mourners "write themselves into the biography" of the deceased (see: Walter *et al.* 2011–12; Carroll and Landry 2010; Roberts 2006).

In the present inquiry, introspection is employed in what Wallendorf and Brucks (1993) refer to as *reflective* fashion in that the researcher is not the central focus of the research but rather merely acknowledges his role in the communal or cultural context being studied. Introspection here assists with development of a keen understanding of the communal context in which the focal phenomenon occurs as a result of the fact that I am an old friend and high school and college classmate not only of Gary's but also of many of the mourners posting to his online memorial. As a result, I have personal knowledge of (1) many of the events in Gary's life that are discussed in the memorial, and (2) many of the interpersonal relationships between Gary and the mourners. This often intimate personal knowledge of the communal context in which Gary's memorialization transpires allows me to interpret and report data and findings with greater validity and veracity than could someone lacking such knowledge.

Research findings

Slightly less than half of the 53 messages in Gary's memorial are relatively short (i.e., 2–5 sentences) and contain simple and generally upbeat condolences and statements of concern for the deceased and his surviving family members and/or brief statements describing the mourner's fondest memories of Gary. The majority of these "simple condolence messages" were posted to the memorial website very early in its existence; shortly after Gary's death and, it is assumed, prior to mourners giving high levels of reflexive thought to the matter of Gary and his passing.

Slightly more than half of the 53 messages are longer – up to 75 lines of text – and more detailed. Many of these longer postings contain often vivid reference to temporally distant (1) products that Gary owned – often ones that he was *known for* possessing – and/or (2) individual or jointly enacted consumption of these or other products. As a result, these postings – specifically the interactively shared memories constituting them – can be viewed as exemplary of "powerful remains of the dead person's extended self" (Belk 1988, p. 144) and/or *linking objects* and *phenomena* (Volkan 1981, 1974). The content of these "consumption-related memories" of Gary are listed in Table 9.1 and discussed below.

Consumption-related memories of Gary

The 53 posts to Gary's online memorial contain a total of 67 *consumption-related memories*; each indicative of an instance wherein a mourner clearly demonstrates that their memories of Gary consist of products, consumption acts, or consumption experiences. Most such references date back 25–40 years to Gary's childhood and high school or college years. These memories fall into seven emergent categories and, upon reflective interpretation, one additional superordinate category encompassing many of the others. Each category is discussed below.

Retail Stores. Four mourners recounted memories of working with Gary at the Hy-Vee grocery store in their mutual hometown during their high school years. Mourners typically stated simply that they had worked with Gary or that he had made working there enjoyable. Exemplary of the latter is the following excerpt from one memorial posting.

> Gary was such a funny person; always a joke followed by his wonderful smile. We had many fun nights at Hy-Vee, singing to the radio and joking around. You will be missed.
>
> (Randy)

Products/Possessions the Deceased Is Remembered By. Twelve data instances suggest that prominent in mourner memories of Gary are products that he used or possessed – as part of his *extended self* – in the distant past. A diverse

Table 9.1 Consumption-related memories of Gary

1	**Retail stores (4 instances):**
	– Hy-Vee grocery store (4)
2	**Products/possessions of the deceased he is remembered by (12 instances):**
	– Cars (6)
	– Home stereo system (1)
	– Motorcycle (1)
	– "Italy" t-shirt (1)
	– Towel over shoulder at pool (1)
	– Black light posters (1)
	– Blue jean jacket (1)
3	**Current products/possessions of mourners (3 instances):**
	– A photo of Gary (3)
4	**Consumption acts or experiences of the deceased (9 instances):**
	– Surfing (1)
	– Music lover or favorite song (3)
	– Loaning money (with interest) (1)
	– Wearing of cowboy boots and personality change (1)
	– Swimming (1)
	– Shooting bottle rockets (1)
	– Stories of "Cruising" (1)
5	**Consumption acts or experiences jointly engaged in with deceased (35 instances):**
	– Listening to or singing music (6)
	– Partying or drinking beer (3)
	– Prom (1)
	– "Cruising"/riding in car (4)
	– Shopping (1)
	– Playing with toys as child (1)
	– Snowmobile riding (1)
	– Taking a boat ride (1)
	– Eating pizza (2)
	– Garage demolition (1)
	– Riding motorcycles (2)
	– Playing sports (7)
	– Sled riding (1)
	– Hiking (1)
	– Trading baseball cards and coins (2)
	– Water balloon raid (1)
6	**Deceased teaching or inspiring others to engage in consumption acts (2 instances):**
	– Teaching mourner to surf (1)
	– Inspiring mourner to go to college and get specific degree (1)
7	**Consumption-related discussions with the deceased (2 instances):**
	– Discussion of product cost or value (1)
	– Discussion of hunger and need to eat (1)

range of these physically extinct yet socially immortal *linking objects* is noted, including black light posters, a towel one mourner remembers him having draped over his shoulder at a swimming pool, his Kawasaki motorcycle, his Levis blue jean jacket, and his home stereo system. The latter is vividly remembered by brand name and with reference to how Gary used to talk about it as "The self proclaimed ground pounding thunder of his Sansui home stereo system" (Craig).

Most notable, however, with regard to these socially immortal *linking object*-based memories of Gary, are five mourners discussing their fond recollections of one of Gary's cars, an AMC Javelin; commonly referred to as "*The Javelin.*" Exemplary are the following quotes.

> The Javelin was a classic that inspired a few unforgettable nights, some that might still get a few of us into trouble.
>
> (Nate)

> My memories and impressions of Gary ... are many and varied ... Unspeakable acts of mayhem in the Javelin ...
>
> (Craig)

> Some of my memories include ... His cream-colored Javelin, not the most glamorous car in the world but certainly a car that made a statement with lots of personality which fit him so well.
>
> (Ken)

Products Presently Possessed by the Mourner. Data also indicate that current products and possessions of mourners serve as reminders of and strong links to Gary (i.e., as *linking objects*). All three such data instances concern pictures/photos of Gary. One mourner, for example, states that he may put a "cherished photo of many of us (with Gary)" from their shared high school days in a newspaper ad the mourner was thinking of placing in the local newspaper in Gary's hometown (where many of their mutual friends from that time still reside today).

Consumption Acts or Experiences of the Deceased. This emergent category involves cases in which mourners recall Gary engaging in specific consumption acts. These memories appear to involve *linking phenomena* in that they are founded upon intangible "things of sensory impact" (Volkan 1981, p. 106). Nine such instances are found in the data and include memories of Gary's music consumption (and discussions thereof), various sporting activities, loaning money to mourners (with interest), and shooting bottle rockets out of a college dorm window. Also included is Gary's mother's vivid recollection of what transpired when her son – the youngest of four siblings – put on a pair of new cowboy boots as a child.

> I was thinking of a funny story which I have retold over the years. When Gary was 5 yrs old we got him a pair of little cowboy boots with pointed

toes. He went through a complete personality change becoming aggressive toward his sister and brother and kicking them with the pointed toes. I guess he finally got the chance to not feel like the little one, but the cowboy boots did have to disappear!

(Susan)

Consumption Acts or Experiences Jointly Engaged in with the Deceased. The most common form of "consumption-related memory" of Gary involves jointly engaged in acts of consumption and/or the sharing of memorable consumption experiences. This category, like the last, exemplifies consumption-laden *linking phenomena* connecting the dead to the living. Such memories were recounted a total of 35 times. Most prominently mentioned co-constructed consumption acts or experiences include playing sports (seven instances), listening to or singing music (six instances), riding in a car (four instances), "partying" or drinking beer (three instances), riding motorcycles (two instances), collecting or trading baseball cards or coins (two instances), and eating pizza (two instances). Several discussions of these memories are quite lengthy and detailed and/or include reference to multiple consumption acts or experiences. Consider, as exemplary, the following verbatim memorial excerpt posted by Gary's cousin, Tina.

> . . . I am thankful that I was able to spend a lot of time with cousin Gary over the past couple of years, it is a good feeling … Of course, as most people know, Gary was a music Fanatic. Just ONE of his favorite songs was "Through the Fire" by Chaka Kahn and when I finally learned how to download music onto my MP3 player, that was one of the songs I added. So, one of the most memorable nights with Gary … I brought my MP3 player. We were laying down, side by side (after consuming a whole large pizza, uuggg…) and I got my player out so I could have him listen to it. We put our heads together so I was able to have one ear plug and he could have the other. We were supposed to sing the song together like we actually WERE the singers and when it came on, neither one of us could get any of it out. That moment had touched us both to a point where we couldn't move or hardly breath and we just layed there and cried together. It felt so good and when it was over, we looked at each other and started laughing and laughing and laughing, it was great! I know, something only him and I could relate to, but it was priceless!!!
>
> (Tina [mourner's original emphases, spelling, and parenthetical statement])

Deceased Teaching or Inspiring Others to Engage in Consumption Acts. Two data instances involve mourner memories of Gary either teaching them or inspiring them to engage in a specified consumption act. One such instance, in a message posted by Gary's cousin Dan, indicates remembering Gary having given him "...the courage to go and pursue getting my engineering degree." In the other instance, another mourner fondly recalls Gary's "failed efforts in teaching me to surf in a day or less during a visit to Cali(fornia)" (Craig).

Consumption-Related Discussions with the Deceased. Two participants in Gary's online memorialization recall memories of at times intense consumption-related discussions. One mourner remembers Gary as having "A curious nature with the propensity to continually inquire as to the cost or value of a particular item" (Craig). The other mourner discusses how Gary had a habit of jokingly telling him, when they would "run into each other" during their days together at college, that he "hadn't had a decent meal in days" as an apparent excuse (and cue) to go "to the nearest convenience store" and ride around (rather than study) (Randy).

In summary, consideration of the seven categories of online memorialization-based data illuminate the heretofore neglected potential of products and consumption experiences to act as *linking objects* or *linking phenomena* that form the basis of high-resonance memories that (1) enhance the identities and selves – and *extended selves* – of both deceased persons and mourners, and (2) perhaps forever link the living to the dead (via social self immortalization). However, reflective interpretation of data suggests the existence of an additional superordinate category encompassing the seven discussed above. This "final category" is discussed below.

Emancipatory communal consumption and cathartic escape via consumption-laden online memorialization

As previously alluded to, Sofka (1997) contends that a key benefit of online memorialization is its unique ability to "provide cathartic outlets for the expression of grief that are not available through traditional means" (p. 563). This, coupled with consideration of both Walter's (1997, 1996) "New Model of Grief" and Wood and Williamson's (2003) "New Acceptance of Death," suggests that online memorialization has provided mourners in Western nations a highly communal, interactive, emotional, and personalized means of escaping the often unpleasant, market-driven experience of death, dominant since at least the end of World War II.

Akin to this notion in the consumer research literature is Kozinets' (2002) discussion of how emancipatory communal consumption is employed at the Burning Man Festival to cathartically escape unpleasant market-driven phenomena. According to Kozinets:

> ...[Burning Man's] emancipatory drive is ... directed at an exploitative ethos that weakens social ties and dampens self-expressive practices. As a complex consumption phenomenon, Burning Man provides people with the experience of living in a sharing, caring community, exemplifying the communal ethos said to be undermined by dominant market logics.
>
> (Kozinets 2002, p. 33)

In the present inquiry, the ability to interactively and communally post "consumption-related memories" of Gary to his online memorial appears to be similarly providing mourners an opportunity to cathartically escape unpleasant death-related phenomena. Specifically, data suggest that the community of mourners here immortalizing Gary's social self – including his *extended self* – are using memorialization to escape the unpleasant market-driven experience of death and mourning that was dominant and pervasive – perhaps even "largely inescapable" – prior to the advent of online memorialization. Borrowing from Walter (1996), online memorialization has provided these mourners a means of both (1) finding a place for Gary in their lives, and (2) interactively co-constructing a representation of Gary; one significantly based on vivid remembrance of products and consumption experiences from 25 to 40 years in the past.

Further, a host of temporal and geographic factors collectively render online memorialization perhaps the only possible means of non-privately mourning and memorializing Gary for the vast majority of the 38 mourners participating in the memorialization. These factors include (1) Gary's sudden and traumatic death occurring in southern California on a Monday, (2) his memorial services being in southern California the following Saturday (as announced in a local CA paper the same day), (3) only five of the 38 participating online mourners residing in California or adjoining states, (4) the majority of mourners living in Iowa and other Mid-Western states, and (5) no mourners mentioning having attended his memorial services. In addition, it appears that the vast majority of online mourners did not become aware of Gary's death until weeks or months after his memorial services. Thus, consistent with Walter *et al.* (2011–12), Carroll and Landry (2010), Roberts (2006), and Sofka (1997), online memorialization has here facilitated the enfranchisement of otherwise disenfranchised mourners.

But the participants in Gary's online memorialization appear to be escaping far more than an unpleasant model of death and mourning. They are, in an important way, at least temporarily escaping an unpleasant, market-driven model of living. Exemplary is the fact that several mourners expressed pleasure in at least briefly being emancipated from their work- and career-dominated lives. Consistent with and perhaps adding to Roberts (2006), present findings indicate that the act of – what is here consumption-laden – online memorialization holds the potential to initiate further – and rekindle ceased – communications between geographically distant mourners. Multiple mourners expressed this emancipatory desire to the point where they vowed to change their lives and stay in closer contact with the social network that Gary's death and online memorialization had reconnected; with this vow seemingly lessening the guilt associated with not staying in contact with once close friends over the years. Consider in this regard the following three verbatim excerpts from postings interactively authored and shared over a five-day period by two successful entrepreneurs.

Gary was an integral player in a closeknit group of friends called the "Brotherhood" in high school … There is a framed photo of the Brotherhood next to my desk from the 10th reunion. I stop and ponder my friends lives now and then – it's been here since 1998. He was among the most brilliant, fun, intense, and interesting people I have ever known. I hope he remembered me as sincere and loyal friend. Until our paths cross again … I will remember you with a smile.

(Tony)

This is my second entry, as I am finding that Gary's death (through the memories of his life) have truly moved me. The class of 1980 (plus those of 1981) was a very close class, and I know that there are many of us that wish we could have been in CA to say goodbye to Gary … So, here is my thought. For those that have been impacted by Gary's passing, and are close enough … perhaps we should get together as a group and say our Iowa goodbyes … All the best to all of you who I think of often, but do a poor job of staying in touch with. What a great thing the internet has become.

(Bob)

I have been reading the entries and clearly see that Gary had a similar charismatic spell and friendship with us all. Bob's gesture is well considered and I would like to meet among friends in Iowa for a memorial … I am not sure when or how we can pull this off. The core group of friends (on and off this memorial) who I know that were tight with Gary are scattered around the country. We should definitely all get together as a broader collective sometime over our 30th reunion for a memorial to Gary (and perhaps other classmates who have passed away) … Seems that Gary and others that we have lost deserve something more than a reading of their names and a brief moment of silence … I'm not sure if others feel the same … but it may help us come to terms with those we have lost. I certainly find it consoling to read how our mutual friend touched us all. I think we all, in our hearts, hope that we have left good memories for each other to draw upon.

(Tony)

Conclusion

The findings of this exploratory research demonstrate that memories expressed via online memorialization of deceased persons can be based heavily upon often vivid shared remembrance of temporally distant product possession and consumption experience. Also exhibited is the potential of products and consumption to (1) enhance the identities and selves – including *extended selves* – of both deceased persons and mourners, (2) perhaps forever link the living to the dead (as forms of socially immortal *linking objects* and *linking phenomena*), and (3) reconnect members of social networks disconnected by time and geographical dispersion (and assuage guilt associated with this disconnection). Further suggested is the ironic potential of products and consumption experiences to – per Kozinets' (2002) conceptualization of "emancipatory communal consumption" – help mourners cathartically escape the unpleasant, dehumanizing, market-driven experience of death and mourning (and, perhaps, at least temporarily escape work- and career-dominated life as well).

This chapter began with allusion to the notion of "cheating death" and a quote from the father of a recently deceased young man discussing his exhilarating experience with the very first online memorialization website. It shall end, in introspective fashion, with summary discussion of my first experience with online memorialization. Like Bo Jonsson, I – and I think I speak for all 38 mourners interactively co-constructing Gary's memorial – also found the act of memorializing a deceased friend or loved one online to be "very special." I too felt that I was "entering a sanctuary" wherein I felt a renewed and enhanced affinity to a geographically dispersed group of people that are now and perhaps forever linked by the common human experience of the loss of someone connected to them with bonds stronger than death. These bonds are significantly based on vivid fond remembrance of products – Gary's childhood cowboy boots, his Kawasaki motorcycle, his Levis blue jean jackets, his Sansui home stereo system, and most notably, his AMC Javelin – and their consumption dating back two to four decades in time. Last, I am confident that death has at least somewhat been "cheated" via our interactive online immortalization of Gary's social – and *extended* – self; he and his products and how he – and we – experienced them may well live forever.

Note

1 Per Kozinets (2010 [chapter 8]), pseudonyms are employed for the deceased and all research participants in an effort to minimize risk and any possible harm. Toward this same end, the name of the "cyber-cemetery" in which the memorial is located is not disclosed. The voluntary consent of surviving family members of the deceased to publish the online memorial-based findings of this research was obtained.

References

Belk, Russell, W. (1988) "Possessions and the Extended Self," *Journal of Consumer Research*, 15 (September), pp. 139–168.

Belk, Russell, W. (2013) "Extended Self in a Digital World," *Journal of Consumer Research*, 40 (October), pp. 477–500.

Carroll, Brian and Katie Landry (2010) "Logging On and Letting Out: Using Online Social Networks to Grieve and to Mourn," *Bulletin of Science, Technology and Society*, 30 (5), pp. 341–349. Available at: http://bst.sagepub.com/content/30/5/341 (Accessed: 14 October 2010).

Clandinin, D. Jean, and F. Michael Connelly (1994) "Narrative, Content, and Semiotic Analysis." In N. Denzin and Y. Lincoln (eds.) *Handbook of Qualitative Research*. Thousand Oaks, CA: Sage Publications, pp. 463–477.

Golden, Tom (2006) "Healing and the Internet," *The Forum*, 32 (4), p. 8. Available at: www.adec.org/AM/Template.cfm?Section=The_Forum&Template=/CM/ContentDisplay.cfm&ContentID=1554 (Accessed: 2 February 2012).

Kozinets, Robert V. (2002) "Can Consumers Escape the Market? Emancipatory Illuminations from Burning Man," *Journal of Consumer Research*, 29 (June), pp. 20–38.

Kozinets, Robert V. (2010) *Netnography: Doing Ethnographic Research Online*. Thousand Oaks, CA: Sage Publications.

Levy, Sidney J. (1996) "Stalking the Amphisbaena," *Journal of Consumer Research*, 23 (December), pp. 163–176.

Lim, Ming (2013) "The Digital Consumption of Death: Reflections on Virtual Mourning Practices on Social Networking Sites." In R. Belk and R. Llamas (eds.) *The Routledge Companion to Digital Consumption*. London: Routledge, pp. 396–403.

Neimeyer, Robert A., Holly G. Prigerson, and Betty Davies (2002) "Mourning and Meaning," *The American Behavioral Scientist*, 46 (Oct.), pp. 235–251.

Roberts, Pamela (2006), "From My Space to Our Space: The Functions of Web Memorials in Bereavement," *The Forum*, 32 (4), pp. 1–4. Available at: www.adec.org/AM/Template.cfm?Section=The_Forum&Template=/CM/ContentDisplay.cfm&ContentID=1554 (Accessed: 2 February 2012).

Ryan, Jennifer Anne (2008) *The Virtual Campfire: An Ethnography of Online Social Networking*. Masters Thesis. Wesleyan University. Available at: http://wesscholar.wesleyan.edu/etd_mas_theses/9 (Accessed: 17 February 2012).

Sofka, Carla J. (1997) "Social Support 'Internetworks,' Caskets for Sale and More: Thanatology and the Information Superhighway," *Death Studies*, 21 (6), pp. 553–574.

Volkan, Vamik D. (1974) "The Linking Objects of Pathological Mourners," in J. Ellard, V.D. Volkan, and N.L. Paul (eds.) *Normal and Pathological Responses to Bereavement*. New York: MSS Information Corporation, pp. 186–202.

Volkan, Vamik D. (1981) *Linking Objects and Linking Phenomena*. New York: International Universities Press, Inc.

Wallendorf, Melanie and Merrie Brucks (1993) "Introspection in Consumer Research: Implementation and Implications," *Journal of Consumer Research*, 20 (December), pp. 339–359.

Walter, Tony (1996) "A New Model of Grief: Bereavement and Biography," *Mortality*, 1 (1), pp. 7–25.

Walter, Tony (1997) "Letting Go and Keeping Hold: A Reply to Stroebe," *Mortality*, 2 (3), pp. 263–266.

Walter, Tony, Rachid Hourizi, Wendy Moncur, and Stacey Pitsillides (2011) "Does the Internet Change How We Die and Mourn? Overview and Analysis," *Omega: Journal of Death and Dying*, 64 (4), pp. 275–302.

Wood, William R. and John B. Williamson (2003), "Historical Changes in the Meaning of Death in the Western Tradition." In C. D. Bryant (ed.) *Handbook of Death and Dying* (Vol 1). Thousand Oaks, CA: Sage, pp. 14–23.

10 Extending the mourning, funeral, and memorialization consumption practices to the human–pet relationship

Phylis M. Mansfield

> *We show our devotion in how we spend. This year Americans will fork out an estimated $53 billion in caring for their pets.*
>
> (Pierce 2012)

This chapter will briefly focus on the human–pet bond when elevated to the level of family member status, and focus on the ways in which humans engage in psychological and consumption practices normally held for human family members after a death. Primarily from an American perspective, the practices of mourning, funeral rites, and memorialization, both as social events and through consuming goods, will be explored as they relate to the loss of one's pet.

The human–pet relationship

One of the canine's first functions was as a food source. Native Americans, the Aztecs, and other people in South and Central America, as well as the Caribbean, relied heavily on dog meat for their animal protein for centuries. In certain areas of Asia and central Europe, both dogs and cats remain a food staple and are highly desirable as a source of meat (Derr 1997, Phillips 2014). However, animals have also coexisted with humans and have played significant roles in society. Anthropologists and archeologists support this latter notion with their findings (Salkind 2005).

As early as 10000 BC in what is now Israel, a puppy was found buried, cradled in the hand of a human, and in 7500 BC a domesticated cat was found buried with a human on the Mediterranean island of Cyprus (Glenn and Larsen 2012). In some ancient civilizations, dogs held cultural significance with regard to death practices, where it was believed that dogs could prevent the death of humans. In Greece, dogs were employed in healing temples as "co-therapists" due to their perceived ability to cure illnesses (Mars 2014). According to Salkind (2005), the Greeks purchased toys for their pets and embalmed their dead cats so they could bury them with the owner when he or she later died. The Chinese Emperor Ling established his dogs as senior officers of the court. Perhaps more bizarre for society's mores today, it was common during the Manchurian LCh'ing dynasty and also in the West Indies and other indigenous cultures, for women to breast-feed puppies along with their children (Salkind 2005).

Historically, animals were domesticated so they could serve their human owners. Animals have been used as protectors and guardians (Derr 1997) and as working partners in rodent control, hunting, herding, and transportation (Grier 2006). Dogs have been used for assistance to the physically challenged, including those who are blind, and in psychological therapy for the elderly, and those who are mentally challenged (Pendergast and Pendergast 2000). While animal and human relationships have long been characterized in society as utilitarian, there is evidence that they held far greater significance to the hierarchy in the familiar unit and interpersonal relationships (Grier 2006; Hirschman 1994).

Photographic artifacts from America in the 1800s provide a glimpse of how pets were esteemed in the familial unit. While society at that time was largely one of an agrarian economy, there remained a distinction between those animals that were utilitarian and those that were companions. It was not uncommon for families at that time to keep wild animals as pets, even inside the house (Grier 2006). Squirrels were the most popular of these, and were kept in cages that included exercise wheels much like the hamster cages today. The squirrel as pet was so common that tinsmiths were employed to make metal cages so the animal could not chew through the wooden bars, and guidelines were published "urging readers to make the cage at least six feet by four feet, with perches like the branches in a tree" (Grier, 2006, from the *Book of Household Pets*, 1866, p. 82). The squirrels were allowed out of their cages to exercise and were occasionally even allowed to play on their owner's bed (Grier 2006). Even though squirrels were very popular wild animals to keep as pets, dogs were the most written-about pets of the time and were often documented in the family diary.

In the late 1800s it was not unusual for families to include their pets (especially dogs) in the family photographs. As early as the 1840s, pets were carried to photographic studios to participate in a social ritual that was very important to people, and by the late 1860s, pets were found in photographs both with their owners and by themselves, even if the pet had died. One study of photographs from that time period showed that dogs were often posed beside, or at the foot of the owner. However, perhaps more evident of the closeness of the relationship between the human owner and the pet was that many were photographed with their heads close together, a composition used for human portraits to imply friendship or love (Grier 2006). The archives of family photographs reveal that the practice of including pets crossed socio-economic levels. One photograph taken in 1887 by an itinerant photographer, Solomon Butcher, depicts an American family in front of their sod house. The photograph includes five adult family members, one infant, and a small dog. It is evident that this family, who were farmers, given the team of horses standing in the background, considered their dog a close companion. Four of the family members, two males and two females, are seated. The fifth family member, a male, stands, and steadies the dog in the chair in front of him, perhaps so that it would stay still while the photograph was taken (Grier 2006).

Views from psychology and sociology

The disciplines of psychology and sociology provide an extensive look into the relationships between animals as pets, and their human owners. Domesticated animals have been regarded as both possessions and companions, with reference made to them by the human perhaps indicating the level of closeness, as either "dog owner" or "dog's human," or even "dog Mom or Dad." Researchers have investigated the relationship of pets and humans as part of the extension of the human's self-identity to the point that another's treatment of the pet is considered to be treatment of the person (Belk 1988). The relationship between pet and owner can affect not only the social interactions of the pet/owner as a singular social unit, but also affect the owner's individual social identity and self-perception as well (Sanders 1990). Psychological studies have addressed the individual's relationship with a pet through the frameworks of personality development and attachment theory (Cameron and Mattson 1972; Voith 1981; Zilcha-Mano, Mikulincer, and Shaver 2011). The unconditional love from pets often serves as a boost to the individual's level of confidence and self worth, sometimes to the degree that the relationship is unhealthy (Cameron and Matson 1972; Zilcha-Mano, Mikulincer, and Shaver 2011).

Attachment theory, originally designed to study the sociological relationship between parent and child throughout the life cycle, has been utilized in the study of human–pet relationships.

Attachment is conceptualized as an affective or emotive state of proximity to someone or some thing, that causes anxiety or discomfort when separated (Ainsworth, Blehar, Waters and Wall; Voith 1981; Zilcha-Mano, Mikulincer, and Shaver 2011). In the human context of attachment, children represent the role of needy, dependent relationship partner, and parents represent the stronger and wiser caregiver (Bowlby 1982). This particular form of attachment can be transferred to the domesticated animal, where pets become the *children* to the human owners. Several studies have addressed the child-surrogate relationship of pets, where they are emotionally and psychologically used prior to a couple's actual addition of human children, or as empty nesters when the children have left the family home (Belk 1988; Cameron and Mattson 1972; Cordaro 2012; Hirschman 1994; Kennedy 2005). The pet and a child–parent bond can work in either direction, as college students in one study revealed close attachments to their pet dogs that equaled the emotional bond to their mothers, best friends, siblings, and significant others (Kurdek 2008). The conceptualization of pets as children is not a new phenomenon. As early as the 1800s pets were often described with affective metaphors, such as beloved children, implying that the pet was treated with care and attention similar as the family's human offspring. This comparison of pets to children was reinforced through an analysis of popular prints and photographs of the time (Grier 2006).

One interesting phenomenon is the report of rising numbers of pet ownership in U.S. households, while at the same time the number of children per household is declining. According to the American Community Survey in 2011, 37 percent of households contained related children, through biological, legal, or other relationship (U.S. Census Bureau 2012a). Between the years of 1970 and 2012, the share of households that were married couples with children under the age of 18 declined from 40 to 20 percent (U.S. Census Bureau 2012b). Alternatively, according to the American Pet Products Association (APPA), the number of households in the U.S. owning at least one pet was 68 percent in 2013. Among a study of dog owners, 22 percent were not, nor had ever been, parents (Pew Research 2010).

This information may reinforce the idea that pets are serving as surrogate children in the U.S.; however, additional data is required to support that notion.

Whether the pet is serving the role of child, sibling, or simply as a companion, many view their relationship with a pet as *family member* (Aylesworth, Chapman, and Dobscha 1999; Belk 1988; Cordaro 2012; Hirschman 1994). Recent studies have reported that between 70 and 87 percent of pet owners viewed their pets as family members (Beck and Katcher 2003; Pew Research 2010). A breakdown by the type of pet indicates that 85 percent of dog owners think of their dogs as family members, while 78 percent of cat owners feel similarly (Pew Research 2010). Pet owners also reported that they tend to hold closer relationships to their dogs or cats than they do to their mothers or fathers. When asked, "Which word best describes your relationship with your dog or cat?" 94 percent of dog owners and 84 percent of cat owners felt "close" rather than "distant." When asked this same question of their relationships with their moms or dads, the same respondents reported that 87 percent felt "close" to their mothers and 74 percent felt "close" to their fathers (Pew Research 2010). Significance testing was not reported.

The role of family member elevates the pet to a level of care similar to that of human children; pets need food, health care, and are showered with gifts. These needs have an impact on the consumer aspect of the human–pet relationship. In 1994, Hirschman identified the human–pet relationship as an area to be considered by consumer behavior scientists. Following her article, a collection of several articles published in a special issue of Society and Animals (1996) was devoted to the "animal as consumer experience" (Aylesworth, Chapman, and Dobscha 1999).

Today, the study of the human–pet relationship has continued to increase in scope to address the psychological aspects of pet ownership, the health benefits of pet ownership, therapy applications, entertainment for and including animals, and various new product and service industries.

The size of the pet-related industry

The consumer implications of the human–pet relationship are vast. In the U.S. today, there are estimated to be 83.3 million dogs owned (not in shelters) and 95.6 million cats (Humane Society 2014). According to The American Pet Products Association (APPA), over half (57 percent) of American households own at least one dog and 45 percent own a cat (2013). In 2013, 68 percent of households included at least one pet, representing 83 million homes (APPA 2013).

This signifies an increase from 56 percent of households in 1988, the first year the study was conducted (APPA 2013).

The dollars spent on pets in the U.S. is estimated to be close to $58 billion, and represents an increase of 344 percent in the last two decades (APPA 2013). Pet owners spent billions of dollars on food ($22.6), supplies and over-the-counter medicines ($13.7), veterinary care ($15.3), purchases of live animals ($2.2), and pet services ($4.7) (APPA 2013). Basic annual expenses for dogs and cats totaled approximately $500 for each pet in 2011 (U.S. Bureau of Labor Statistics 2013).

The expenses for food, shelter, and health care are expected in the everyday care of any pet; however, there are increasingly more unconventional types of consumer purchases that have been showered on pets in the past few years. These are primarily in service industries and include pet insurance, birthday parties, weddings, day care, doggie camp, and funerals. The organization, CouponCabin.com, reports that 9 percent of pet owners currently have pet insurance, and another 19 percent are interested in making the purchase. This represents a 2 percent increase in just one year (APPA 2013).

According to a study by Harris Interactive, more than 20 percent of adults in the U.S. have held or attended a birthday celebration for a pet (PR Newswire 2013). Dog owners are more likely to purchase a birthday cake for their pet than are cat owners, 32 percent and 25 percent respectively, and just under half of the participants at these celebrations reported spending between 1 and 19 dollars in gifts (PR Newswire 2013). The recent study also found that 62 percent of pet owners spent up to $50 per month on their pets, and 15 percent spend over $100. Dog owners are likely to spend more per month than are cat owners; 47 percent of dog owners spend about $50 per month, while only 37 percent of cat owners spend a similar amount (PR Newswire 2013).

The reaction to pet loss

The disciplines of psychology, sociology, and veterinary medicine have studied the relationship between humans and their companion animals, and provide considerable insight to the human's reaction to the loss of one's pet. The study of the human–animal relationship after the loss of a pet was considered to have been undervalued in the field of psychology for many years

(Henry 2008; Sharkin and Knox 2003); however, during the 1980s and 1990s the literature began to see an increase in attention to the phenomenon of post-pet loss and its affect on the human's mental health (Quackenbush and Glickman 1984; Gerwols and Labott 1994; Sharkin and Knox 2003; Sife 2005). Studies have found that the grief felt at the loss of a pet can be similar to that experienced by the loss of a human, and in some cases, even greater (Gerwolls and Labott 1994; Planchon, Templer, Stokes, and Keller 2002; Yonan 2013). One therapist reported that clients often are surprised when they feel grief for their pet stronger than that felt when a parent or sibling died (Yonan 2013). The current trade literature in the subject of *books on pet loss* is expansive, signifying an increased attention to the subject matter by authors, and a demand by pet owners for some insight into their grief. Given the number of publications, this area of grief counseling will not be addressed in this chapter.

Specific numbers regarding the deaths of pets are not readily available; however, given the number of pets in U.S. households, and the average life span of the companion animals, one can extrapolate an estimate. An example of one estimate is that in a single year, a minimum of 13.8 million homes will be affected by a pet's death (Henry 2008). There is also the likelihood that pet owners will experience multiple deaths of pets during their lifetime, due to the shorter life spans of companion animals (Sharkin and Knox 2003). The bond between humans and their pets can be so strong that grief reactions to the loss of a pet can be similar to reactions associated with the death of a human (Gerwolls and Labott 1994). Symptoms of grief reactions at a pet's death have included loss of appetite, difficulty sleeping, visual hallucinations of the pet, loss of control, withdrawal from the rest of the world, preoccupation with the death, depression, and anxiety (Henry 2008; Pierce 2012; Sife 2005).

The reaction to the loss of one's pet is dependent upon several characteristics. These include the age and gender of the owner, the number of previous pet deaths experienced, whether the pet's death was due to accident or illness, guilt, the level of anthropomorphism, and the degree of attachment. The age of the pet owner is related to both the degree of attachment to the pet, and the reaction to the pet's loss, where elderly owners and children are the two groups most affected (Carmack 1991). With regard to gender, females tend to experience higher levels of grief symptoms when compared to males (Gerwolls and Labbot 1994). Pet owners are likely to experience more serious levels of grief when they feel a sense of guilt for the death, such as waiting too long to take them to the veterinarian, or leaving the gate open and then the pet escapes (Sife 2005). Grief may be tempered by timeliness of the death, such as an accident or sudden death. Former president Bill Clinton acknowledged that the death of his dog, Buddy, who was killed when run over by a car, was "by far the worst thing" he had experienced after leaving the White House (Yonan 2013). Additionally, when there is a greater degree of anthropomorphism, i.e., the tendency to attribute humanlike qualities or behavior to the pet, there is likely to be more intense and tangible reaction to the pet's death (Aylesworth, Chapman, and Dobscha 1999; Henry 2008). Finally, the level of attachment, or the emotional state of proximity to someone or something that causes anxiety or discomfort when separated, has been shown to be a predictor of the severity of grief symptoms at a pet's death (Field, Orsini, Gavish and Packman 2009; Zilcha-Mano, Mikulincer, and Shaver 2011). As with human bonds, the attachment to a pet can serve as a buffer to stress, anxiety, and depression (Cordaro 2012), and the loss of that buffer would likely result in increased levels of grief symptoms.

Pet loss is beginning to be considered as a normative bereavement process; however, it carries an increased layer of complexity when compared to that of grieving for a human. The basis for this complexity is the lack of established norms for pet loss grief, and societal attitudes toward the death of a pet (Cordaro 2012). When the grief from a pet loss is left invalidated, or even ostracized by society, the griever experiences an increase in suffering (Doka 2008). There are several forms of unsanctioned losses in society: an extramarital affair, a death by suicide, a miscarriage, or the loss of a pet, and these are typically met with lack of social support and societal norms for mourning (Doka 2008; Worden 2008). When losses are not supported or endorsed by society, this leads to a psychological phenomenon identified as *disenfranchised* grief (Attig 2004). Disenfranchised grief occurs for three reasons: (1) the relationship is not recognized by society, (2) the griever, such as a child, is not socially recognized as a person capable of grieving, or (3) the death is not recognized as a genuine loss (Humphrey 2009). The loss of a pet occurs within each of the three aspects. In American society, pet-related bereavement has typically been considered as unacceptable (Cordaro 2012). One can expect for example, to call an employer and request a minimum of a few days off if a close family member dies as part of the grieving process; however, it is difficult to imagine making the same request for the death of a pet and being met with anything outside of disbelief or even, laughter. Society may also consider the pet owner to be incapable of grieving, and that he or she should get over it and move on, perhaps even replacing the beloved pet (Cordaro 2012). Third, disenfranchised grief can occur because the death of a pet is not accepted in society as a genuine loss (Attig 2004). When the loss of a pet is not viewed by society as legitimate, the owner's grief is unsupported, and perhaps even sanctioned, resulting in complicated or unresolved grief (Worden 2008). An extension of this grief occurs when the owner finds it difficult to talk about the loss due to stigmatization, and further alienates them from speaking up to obtain social support from family or friends. Consequently, bereaved pet owners may find themselves sinking further into depression or anxiety, and perceive their grief an insignificant or inappropriate (Attig 2004). An initial step toward grieving the loss of a pet is to acknowledge the loss (Cordaro 2012), and to find outlets that bring meaning to the owner in the absence of socially supported bereavement norms. These outlets may be in the form of psychological therapy, rituals, or other memorialization processes.

The benefit of rituals: extending the funeral and memorialization process

Often, the grief of losing a pet is complicated by the lack of support one receives from personal friendships and society at large, yet the pet's death can affect the owner both psychologically and physically (Henry 2008; Quackenbush and Glickman 1984). The rituals afforded to those who lose human loved ones provide outlets for grief and mourning, but there is a lack of socially sanctioned rituals for the mourning of the owner/pet relationship (Gerwols and Labott 1994; Sharkin and Knox 2003). Historically, there have been rituals acceptable to society for the honor and mourning of animals. Ancient Egyptians revered their cats and dogs, and ritualized their deaths. When a beloved pet dog died, the owners would shave off their eyebrows, smear mud in their hair, and mourn aloud for days (Brewer 2001). In the early Roman Empire, tombs were built to honor their dead pets (Salkind 2006). In the nineteenth century in America, funerary rituals routinely marked the passing of beloved animals, incorporating some of the same symbols as those in the funerals of people (Grier 2006). "When their dog Carlo was 'murdered' in 1885, the family at Cherry Hill in Albany, New York, went into 'official' mourning, with both animals and people wearing crape" (Grier 2006, p. 107). Often, pets were buried under a weeping willow tree, a symbol of mourning.

The rituals conducted after a pet's death were not done only by women and children. There is a written record from one bachelor farmer in 1851, of the details of a private funeral for his pet dog, Byron.

> My faithful Dog Byron Died this morning, Aged 18 years. I buried him this afternoon, between the hours of three and four o'clock on Mount Lebanon Hill – near a weeping willow. When I had placed his body in the grave, I fired three vollies over it and bade him farewell forever!
>
> Tears rolled down my cheeks like rain. I was alone and I felt as though I had lost one of my best friends. The affections of a dog has made the stoutest hearts melt. Even Napoleon who could dictate the order of battle, where it would cost the lives of ten thousand men, with a dry eye – was once moved to tears, by the affections of a dog!
>
> (Grier 2006, p. 107)

Another ritual during the Victorian era was having posthumous portraits of the deceased pets taken, mostly of pet dogs. It was not uncommon for families to have posthumous portraits taken of their human family members during that era, as many who could not afford the expense of a portrait during the person's lifetime realized that this was a last chance at having a physical representation in the form of a photograph in order to remember the likeness of the person (Gabel, Mansfield, and Westbrook 1994). The majority of the animal portraits mimicked the format of those of the human family members, trying best to present the animal as he or she was in real life; however, many of the photographs also included pictures of angels, clouds, or open gates in the background (Grier 2006, p. 108).

Poetry and obituaries were also often written to commemorate the passing of a pet. In the rural areas, pets were often buried on the family's property, but by the mid-nineteenth century, formal pet graveyards were found in the gardens of many homes. One such instance was found at the former home of the author Harriet Beecher Stowe. An ardent animal lover, her family marked the death of each family dog with a "canine funeral with all the requisite pomp and circumstance" (Grier 2006, p. 108). When one of her homes was sold, the new owner found several small mounds that were puzzling; however, after further investigation, they were found to be dog graves (Grier 2006).

While these rituals appear to have been common during the eighteenth and nineteenth century, many pet owners in more recent years have felt a sense of embarrassment when conducting funerals or memorials for their dead pets. One report from a woman who leads a monthly pet-loss support group in the eastern United States, suggests that this trend may be changing, but some owners are still feeling ostracized.

> It's easier said than done. A few weeks after Red died, some friends from the dog park suggested we have a get-together in his memory. I was grateful for the suggestion, but as I came in and exchanged hugs, I felt a bit sheepish when I pulled out the box of Red's ashes and a recent photo and set them up on the table. Maybe it was my imagination, but I got the feeling that even friends who had gathered for just this purpose would rather say just a quick "I'm sorry; how are you doing?" than truly acknowledge the elephant – or the Doberman – in the room. It wasn't until a couple of hours and drinks later that we finally told a few stories about him.
>
> (Yonan 2012)

In the absence of funeral home options, some owners are creating their own memorial services, such as the one described below.

> The wake for Mico, a terrier-schnauzer mix, was well attended. Mico had been a small but strong-willed animal, and even in death seemed to command the attention of humans. Almost forty people attended Mico's wake, filing through the owners' living room and gazing at Mico's body in an open casket, complete with a blanket, squeaking snowman, and gerbil toy. The group shared memories, laughs, and tears.
>
> (Jamison 2013)

Pet owners are also creating unique memorials for their pets. In some cases, the memorials are created by friends, such as one that was conducted at the burial of a beloved dog named Chica.

While no memorial service was conducted at a funeral chapel, there was a short service conducted at the cemetery prior to the burial of the dog. The owners had invited a close friend, and had brought their surviving dog with them. A short poem was read, and the song "I Did it My Way," sung by Elvis Presley, was played via a smart phone to commemorate the dog's frisky, and sometimes stubborn, personality. After the song, their close friend asked them to look up into the sky, and a small private plane flew over just at that time. The friend's son, who was a private pilot, had told her that he would fly over the service while he was taking a short trip that day as a memorial to the love the owners had for their dog. Later, the friend planted a forget-me-not flower as a tribute to Chica.

(Private interview 2013)

Memorial and death-related consumption

Aylesworth, Chapman, and Dobscha (1999) examined the human and animal companion relationship within a consumer behavior context, providing a framework of the acquisition, consumption, and disposition "lifecycle" to the study of this bond. They posited that after the loss of a pet (disposition stage) an owner's particularly difficult grieving process could result in his likelihood to avoid a future relationship (acquisition) with pets altogether, or avoid forming close relationships with future pets (consumption stage). The consumer behavior perspective can be utilized to further examine the attitudes and behaviors of an individual after a pet dies, especially those activities that result in monetary exchanges. The purchase of memorial objects, such as headstones, monuments, and jewelry, or the purchase of services such as funerary rites or cremation, and the ancillary products that accompany those services, have created a booming consumer market (Choi 2008).

Late in the 1800s, two formal pet cemeteries were established on different continents within approximately three years' of each other signifying an increase in the elevation of the human–pet bond and need for closure at death. The Hartsdale Pet Cemetery was established in 1896 in Hartsdale, New York, and the Cimetière des Chiens et Autres Animaux Domestiques established in 1899 in Paris. The Hartsdale Pet Cemetery is the oldest operating pet cemetery in the world (Hartsdale Pet Cemetery 2014). Begun by a Manhattan veterinarian who offered a grieving pet owner to bury her dog at his upstate farm, it has now grown to contain the remains of over 80,000 animals, and the remains of some of their human owners. It has served as a model for pet cemeteries around the world, and is the only pet cemetery listed on the National Register of Historic Places. The number of pet cemeteries is growing rapidly in the United States, and it is estimated that there are over 600 in the country today (Hornel Animal Shelter 2014).

Many funeral businesses are now beginning to recognize the need for humans to memorialize the deaths of their animal companions and the potential for business. At Pet Passages, the Purdy Funeral Service's newest business in New Hampshire, they offer cremation and memorial services for animals. One such service for a nine-year-old German shepherd is described below.

> After taking their seats in a small, welcoming room, which resembles a common family room, the funeral service owner started a short video. Music quietly played along to photos of the beloved dog. Holding hands and whispering to one another, laughing at some photos and sharing short stories about others, the family members said the service brought them closure and made the grief process easier.
>
> (Kingston 2013, p. 1)

The funeral industry is eyeing the after-death care of pets as a potentially lucrative market, and has been experiencing a considerable growth in recent years. Anderson-McQueen is one of Florida's largest family-owned chain of funeral services, and in 2012, it handled more pets than humans (Jamison 2013). Of approximately 5,700 funerals for both humans and pets, 3,500 were for animals. The majority of pet services were for cremation, a trend that mimics the national statistics. According to the trade association, Pet Loss Professionals Alliance, approximately 1.9 million pets were provided professional death services in 2012 nationwide. The majority were cremated, with only 21,000 buried in traditional cemetery style (Jamison 2013).

Reports of staggering growth have surfaced in the pet-funeral industry. In the U.S. less than a decade ago, there were so few pet aftercare facilities that there wasn't even a list or count; today, there are about 700 nationwide, including funeral homes, crematories, and cemeteries (Spitznagel 2012). The recent growth in the industry is currently untracked, and thus, there are no aggregated financial statistics available. However, the number of traditional funeral homes (for humans) that are turning to the addition of pet aftercare to supplement their income is expected to be growing exponentially, given the various reports of singular businesses. One family-operated funeral home in the business for over forty years, decided to do a pet-only offshoot after conducting marketing research on the topic. Since launching Forever Friends in 2003, the owner claims that sales have risen by 524 percent (Spitznagel 2012).

Another business in southern Indiana reported similar growth. In 2003, the Scott Funeral Home in Jeffersonville, Indiana, opened Faithful Companions, a pet crematory, where they did about 30 cremations in the first year. In 2013, the company did about 100 per month, with an average cost of $130 each (WLKY 2014). The businesses offer comfort to clients in addition to the physical services. A 72-year old widow in the area buried her best friend and companion, a border collie named Buddy, a few years ago. Since she can't drive, she takes a taxi once a month about 60 miles each way, to spend a couple of hours at the cemetery. "I'd do it again," she said. "I'll never find another buddy like him." (WLKY 2014).

Consumer behavior and the pet funeral industry

It is difficult at this time to determine the profile of the consumer who is responsible for the boom in the industry. The increase in the aging of the baby boomers who may have pets after their spouses die could be one reason; however, pet funerals in recent years are reported to be purchased by people in their twenties and thirties, as well as those who have opted not to become parents and treat their pets as surrogate children (Spitznagel 2012). It is possible that the consumer profile crosses demographic lines, and is lifestyle- and personality-oriented as well. Consumers do not seem to be price-sensitive when purchasing pet funeral services (Brus 2010). While the prices for cremation typically run from $300 to $500, including a basic urn and memorial video, the prices for cemetery burial can cost as much as $1,000 to bury a large dog (Macario 2012). There are high-ticket products related to burial such as bronze grave markers ($1,765) and velvet-lined caskets ($1,136). Peternity, an online superstore, sells products such as headstones ($80 to $425), urns (as much as $1,500 for a hand stained version), and stained glass portraits ($200). The site was created in 2003, and according to the owner, sales were up 14,043 percent in 2011, and expected to top close to 30,000 percent by 2012 (Spitznagel 2012).

There are several other more unorthodox memorials that can be purchased to honor a deceased pet. One of these is LifeGem, an organization in Illinois that uses the carbonized ashes from the pet's cremation to create synthetic diamonds (cost from $2,490 to $25,000). The service was initially intended to use the ashes from human cremations to make the diamonds as a remembrance. However, customers began to ask for the service to be done for pets as well. Even though the company does not market its services to pet owners, the segment currently represents for 25 percent of LifeGem's annual business (Spitznagel 2012).

This investigation into the extension of funeral and memorialization services to the death of a pet has uncovered many issues for future research. Since the investigation was from an American perspective, future studies could explore perspectives of pet death and post-death consumption behavior in other cultures. Additionally, several areas of study could be directed toward the differences in how humans memorialize their pets depending on their level of attachment to the pet, their perception of the pet as a family member, the level of disenfranchisement felt at the pet's death, the owner's stage in the family lifecycle, and typical demographics of age, gender, income, and educational levels. From the funeral, cremation, and burial perspective, there is a need to measure the financial impact of this booming industry, and how individuals make their way through the consumer buying decision process, particularly in the American consumer culture.

References

Ainsworth, Mary, Mary Blehar, Everett Waters, and Sally Wall (1978), *Patterns of Attachment: A Psychological Study of the Strange Situation*, Hillsdale NJ: Erlbaum Associates, p. 416.

American Pet Products Association (2013), "Pet Industry Market Size and Future Outlook," retrieved from www.Americanpetproducts.org/press_industrytrends.asp on November 3, 2014.

Attig, Thomas (2004), "Disenfranchised Grief Revisited: Discounting Hope and Love," *Omega*, 49(3), 197–215.

Aylesworth, Andrew, Ken Chapman, and Susan Dobscha, "Animal Companions and Marketing: Dogs Are More Than Just a Cell in the BCG Matrix!" in *NA Advances in Consumer Research Volume 26*, eds. Eric Arnould and Linda Scott, Provo, UT: Association for Consumer Research, pp. 385–391.

Beck, Alan M., and Aaron H. Katcher (2003), "Future Directions in Human-Animal Bond Research," *American Behavioral Scientist*, 47(1), 79–93.

Belk, Russell (1988), "Possessions and the Extended Self," *Journal of Consumer Research*, 15, September, 139–168.

Bowlby, J (1982), *Attachment and Loss: Attachment, Vol. 1*, 2nd ed., New York: Basic Books.

Brewer, Douglas, Terence Clark, and Adrian Phillips (2001). *Dogs in Antiquity: Anubis to Cerebrus, The Origins of the Domestic Dog*. Warminster, UK: Aris and Phillips.

Brus, Brian (2010), "It's a Living: Oklahoma-based Pet Cemetery Owner," *Journal Record*, Oklahoma City, OK, October 12, 2010, retrieved from http://search.proquest.com.ezaccess.libraries.psu.edu on October 30, 2014.

Cameron, Paul and Michael Matson (1972), "Psychological Correlates of Pet Ownership," *Psychological Reports*, 30 (February), 286.

Carmack, Betty. (1991), "Pet Loss and the Elderly," *Holistic Nursing Practice*, 5(2), 80.

Choi, Amy (2008), "Entrepreneurs Reinvent the Funeral Industry," *Bloomberg Businessweek*, June 19, retrieved from www.businessweek.com/printer/articles/219146, November 25, 2014.

Cordaro, Millie (2012), "Pet Loss and Disenfranchised Grief: Implications for Mental Health Counseling Practice," *Journal of Mental Health Counseling*, 34(4), October, 283–294.

Derr, Mark (1997), *Dog's Best Friends: Annals of the Dog-Human Relationship*, New York: Henry Holt.

Doka, Kenneth (2002), *Disenfranchised Grief: New Challenges, Directions, and Strategies for Practice*. Champaign, IL: Research Press, p. 451.

Field, Nigel, Lisa Orsini, Roni Gavish, and Wendy Packman, (2009), "Role of Attachment in Response to Pet Loss," *Death Studies*, 33(4), 334–355.

Gabel, Terrance, Phylis Mansfield, and Kevin Westbrook (1994), "The Disposal of Consumers: An Explortory Analysis of Death-Related Consumption," in *NA – Advances in Consumer Research Volume 23*, ed. Kim P. Corfman and John Lynch, Jr., Provo, UT: Association of Consumer Research, pp. 361–367.

Gerwols, Marilynn and Susan Labott (1994), "Adjustment to the Death of a Companion Animal," *Anthrozoos: A Multidisciplinary Journal of The Interactions of People and Animals*, 7(3), 172–187.

Glenn, Joshua and Elizabeth Foy Larsen (2012), *Unbored: The Essential Field Guide to Serious Fun*, New York: Bloomsbury USA, p. 352.

Grier, Katherine C. (2006), *Pets in America: A History*, Chapel Hill, NC: The University of North Carolina Press, p. 376.

Harris Interactive (2013), "Dog Owners Spend More on Their Pets Than Cat Owners," *PR Newswire*, New York, 22 May 2013, retrieved from http://search.proquest.com.ezaccess.libraries.psu.edu/abicomplete on November 3, 2014.

Hartsdale Pet Cemetery (2014), information retrieved at *www.petcem.com*, September 24, 2014.

Henry, Christine (2008) *Risk Indicators for Grief Symptoms After the Death of a Pet: Does Quality of Attachment Make a Difference?* Unpublished dissertation, Purdue University.

Hirschman, Elizabeth (1994), "Consumers and Their Animal Companions," *Journal of Consumer Research*, 20, March, 616–632.

Hornel Animal Shelter (2014), website www.hornellanimalshelter.org, retrieved November 19, 2014.

Humphrey, Keren (2009), *Counseling Strategies for Loss and Grief*, Alexandria, VA: American Counseling Association, p. 244.

Jamison, Peter (2013), "It's a Dog's Afterlife: Pet Death Care Industry Booms," *Tampa Bay Times*, May 2, 2013, retrieved from www.tampabay.com/features/pets/funeral-homes on November 20, 2014.

Kennedy, Samantha (2005), "More than Man's Best Friend: A Look at Attachment Between Humans and their Canine Companions." Unpublished dissertation, the Department of Sociology, University of South Florida, pp. 16–24.

Kingston, Michelle (2013) "Special Sendoff for Thor: German Shepherd Treated Like One of the Family," *McClatchy-Tribune Business News*, February 22, 2013.

Kurdek, Lawrence (2008), "Pet Dogs as Attachment Figures," *Journal of Social and Personal Relationships*, 25(2), 247–266.

Marcario, Dana (2012), "Pet Funeral Business Beginning to Boom," *TODAY Money.com*, retrieved from www.today.com/money/pet-funeral-business-beginning-boom-998633 on November 12, 2014.

Mars, Inc. (2014), "The Evolution of Pet Ownership," retrieved from http://pedigree.com/all-things-dog/article-library, November 24, 2014.

Pendergast, Sara and Tom Pendergast (2000), *St. James Encyclopedia of Popular Culture*, Vol. 4, Detroit, MI: St. James Press, Gale Group, Cengage Learning.

Pew Research Center (2010), "Gauging Family Intimacy," *Pew Research Social and Demographic Trends*, retrieved from www.pewsocialtrends.org/2006/03/07/gauging-family-intimacy on November 5, 2014.

Phillips, Catherine (2014), "Not Just for Christmas: Swiss Urged to Stop Eating Cats and Dogs," *Newsweek*, retrieved from www.newsweek.com/not-just-christmas-swiss-urged-stop-eating-cats-and-dogs-287378, November 26, 2014.

Pierce, Jessica (2012), "It's Just a Dog. Get Over It. The Death of a Pet is Often Dismissed." *Wall Street Journal (Online)*, New York, December 1, 2012.

Planchon, Lynn, Donald Templer, Shelley Stokes, and Jacqueline Keller (2002), "Death of a Companion Cat or Dog and Human Bereavement," *Society and Animals*, 10(1), 93–105.

Quackenbush, James and Lawrence Glickman (1984), "Helping People Adjust to the Death of a Pet," *Health and Social Work*, 9(1), 42–48.

Salkind, Neil J. (2006), *Encyclopedia of Human Development*, Thousand Oaks, CA: Sage Reference Publications, 990–992.

Sanders, Clinton (1990), "The Animal 'Other': Self-Definition, Social Identity and Companion Animals," in *Advances in Consumer Research*, Marvin E. Goldberg *et al.* (eds.) Provo, UT: Association for Consumer Research, 17, 662–668.

Sharkin, Bruce and Donna Knox (2003), "Pet Loss: Issues and Implications for the Psychologist," *Professional Psychology: Research and Practice*, 34(4), 414–421.

Sife, Wallace (2005), *The Loss of a Pet: A Guide to Coping With the Grieving Process When a Pet Dies*, Hoboken, NJ: Wiley Publishing Company, p. 260.

Spitznagel, Eric (2012), "There's Never Been a Better Time to be a Dead Pet," *Bloomberg Businessweek*, September 7, 2012, retrieved from 222.businessweek.com/printer/articles/70592 on November 3, 2014.

United States Bureau of Labor Statistics (2013), "Average Annual Expenditures for Pets, 2007–2011," *Household Spending on Pets*, retrieved from www.bls.gov/opub/ted/2013/ted_20130529.htm on November 25, 2014.

United States Census Bureau (2012a), "America's Families and Living Arrangements 2012," *U.S. Census Bureau*, retrieved from www.census.gov/prod/2013pubs/p20-570.pdf on November 1, 2014.

United States Census Bureau (2012b), "Households by Type and Selected Characteristics: ACS 2011," *U.S. Census Bureau*, American Community Survey 2011, retrieved from www.census.gov/prod/2012pubs/acsbr11-03.pdf on November 1, 2014.

Voith, Victoria (1981), "Attachment Between People and their Pets: Behavior Problems of Pets that Arise From the Relationship Between Pets and People," in *Interrelationships Between People and Animals*, Bruce Fogle (ed.), Springfield, IL: Thomas, pp. 271–294.

WLKY.com (2014), "Pet Care Industry Sees Rise in Funerals, Related Items," *WLKY.com*, retrieved from www.wlky.com/news/pet-care-industry-sees-rise-in-funerals on November 22, 2014.

Worden, J. William (2008), *Grief Counseling and Grief Therapy: A Handbook for the Mental Health Practitioner*, 4th ed., New York, NY: Springer Publishing Company, p. 314.

Yonan, Joe (2012), "The Death of a Pet Can Hurt as Much as the Loss of a Relative," *The Washington Post*, retrieved at www.washingtonpost.com/national/health-science on March 26, 2014.

Zilcha-Mano, Sigal, Mario Mikulincer, and Phillip Shaver (2011), "An Attachment Perspective on Human–Pet Relationships: Conceptualization and Assessment of Pet Attachment Orientations," *Journal of Research in Personality*, 45, 345–357.

11 Great granny lives on

Pursuing immortality through family history research

Leighann C. Neilson and Delphin A. Muise

It is awful when trying to find someone's footprint and they appear to have not left one.

Introduction

Since the 1990s, research undertaken by historians in the United States, Australia, and Canada, has revealed that many consumers rate knowing about the past of their family as more important than knowing about the past of their nation, ethnic group, or community (Ashton and Hamilton, 2009). In the United States, one-third of respondents to a national survey had worked on their own family history in the preceding twelve months; in Canada, 57 percent were engaged in preparing a family scrapbook and/or writing a family history (Conrad *et al.*, 2013; Rosenzweig and Thelen, 1998). Consumption associated with the pursuit of family history includes subscription to online databases,[1] fees paid to access official documents, purchase of computer equipment and internet access, trips abroad to search for information and visit family, purchase of DNA testing and acquisition of consumer products to reflect ancestry, e.g., Scottish tartans or Irish whiskey.

The expanded place of genealogy and family history in the public consciousness with the advent of television shows like *Who Do You Think You Are?* has given a renewed impetus to the individual pursuit of family history (Kramer, 2011). Demographic trends, such as the aging and retirement of the baby boom generation, indicate that the popularity of family history is likely to increase (Schau, Gilly and Wolfinbarger, 2009; Wilson 2003). Other social and economic indicators, including the convergence of trends associated with globalization – information technology innovations, improved digital access to information resources across national boundaries, increased international travel, and the growing number of individuals who consider themselves to be 'world citizens' (i.e., who maintain attachment to more than one nation) (McAuley, 2004; Cannon and Yaprak, 2002) – also support its growth, making it an important research topic for marketers and consumer researchers alike.

We were interested in learning more about this consumption phenomenon. In particular, we wanted to examine consumers' motivations for conducting family history research and also begin to theorize about the outcomes – what does it all mean for consumers? In this chapter, we discuss the death-defying aspects of family history research, interpreting our results in terms of terror management theory and philosopher Steven Cave's immortality narratives. The chapter is organized as follows: first we briefly review previous research, then we explicate our theoretical frameworks and outline our research methods. Following this, we present our results and interpretation and close with suggestions for further research.

Literature review

Across the social sciences, a fair amount of attention has been paid to the topic of family history research. Sociologists and historians have identified several possible motivations for pursuing family history, including: the search for illustrious ancestors and the corresponding endowment effect (Lambert, 1996, 2002; Andrews, 1982; Hareven, 1978); self-identity formation, that is, developing a deeper understanding of oneself by getting to know one's roots, creating coherence in one's own life by connecting past with present, and self-discovery through adopting the role of family historian (Lambert, 1996, 2002, 2006; Yakel, 2004); family identity formation, or getting to know one's ancestors as people and restoring 'lost' ancestors to the family (Lambert, 1996; 2006); securing one's place in the nation in the face of increasing immigration levels (Lambert, 2002; Redman, 1992); nostalgia and yearning for a (fictional) past (Lowenthal, 1985; Taylor, 1982; Hareven, 1978); dissatisfaction with consumerist culture (Quinn, 1991); and the creation of a gift for future generations (Lambert, 1996).

　Previous consumer research has also engaged with themes related to the pursuit of family history. Belk's (1990, 1988) seminal work on how consumers' sense of self is extended in space and time advances the idea that people and places to which one feels a sense of attachment form part of the extended self, and that these aspects of the extended self do not have to be contemporaneous with the consumer in order to exert an influence. Other research has confirmed that one's sense of self can include various levels of affiliation, such as family, community, and ethnic group (Ahuvia, 2005; Peñaloza, 1994; Hirschman, 1981). Recently, Hirschman's work with Panther-Yates (2007a, 2007b, 2006) on DNA testing has established how reconstruction of one's identity narrative may become necessary in light of test results which reveal unexpected genetic ancestries.

　The importance of family as a central nexus of identity construction has also been well-established (Curasi, Price and Arnould, 2004; Price, Arnould and Curasi, 2000), and Lindridge (2012) has identified the information collated as part of family history research as one form of a family's inalienable wealth. Other consumer researchers, including many in this volume, have investigated rituals and other consumption practices associated with the death of family members (Turley and O'Donohoe, 2012; Zhao and Belk, 2007; Bonsu and Belk, 2003; Gentry *et al.*, 1995).

Although previous research provided some interesting insights and contributed to our thought process, there appeared to be much more to the productive-consumption work being done by consumers. We wanted to know more about the motivations for and outcomes of conducting family history research.

Theoretical perspectives

A core activity of family history research is the accumulation of information; developing an awareness of cultural and historical context is essential to the practice, second only to the discovery and recording of birth, marriage and death dates. Psychologists have argued that reminders of the 'problem of death', such as may occur in person when experiencing the reality of a family member's death, or importantly for this research, at a distance when downloading a copy of an ancestor's death registration from an online database, can create anxiety. Terror management theory, as developed by Greenberg, Pyszczynski, Solomon and colleagues (e.g., Greenberg, Pyszczynski and Solomon, 1986; Greenberg and Arndt, 2011), suggests that individuals deal with this anxiety through both proximal and distal cognitive defense strategies.

Proximal defenses serve as a first line of defense against conscious death-related thoughts (Pyszczynski, Greenberg and Solomon, 1999), and can include suppressing thoughts of one's own death, seeking distractions to banish thoughts of death, rationalization strategies which deny one's current vulnerability (e.g., recalling that one is a non-smoker who maintains a regular work-out schedule) and cognitive distortions such as relocating one's death into a distant future time.

Distal defenses occur when death-related thoughts are accessible but not in current consciousness or of focal attention. They work at a more symbolic level by reassuring the individual that s/he is 'a valuable contributor to a meaningful, eternal universe' (Pyszczynski, Greenberg and Solomon, 1999, p. 839). By making one's life seem meaningful, valuable, and enduring, distal defenses provide a sense of security. This type of defense operates in a more subtle fashion; an example provided by Pyszczynski and colleagues (1999) is forming more favorable evaluations of others who praise one's culture and more negative evaluations of those who criticize it.

Importantly, these researchers relate that although mortality salience has been operationalized in a variety of ways over multiple studies, the focus of research under terror management theory has been on the effects of thoughts about the research participant's *own* death. 'These effects are specific to thoughts of one's own death; parallel effects are not produced by other aversive or anxiety-producing stimuli' (Pyszczynski, Greenberg and Solomon, 1999, p. 836). To the extent that family historians identify motivations closely associated with their *own* lives or identities, terror management theory may provide additional insight into their consumption behaviors.

Philosopher Stephen Cave's work on 'the will to immortality' (2012), overlaps with terror management theory in terms of identifying behaviors that serve to extend one's physical life and beliefs regarding one's spiritual immortality. Cave has distilled the stories of humanity's efforts to deal with the inevitability of death into four 'immortality narratives'. The first narrative, 'Staying Alive', is focused on keeping the body going. Consumption practices associated with this narrative have been discussed in previous research, including the ingestion of 'magic elixirs' produced by the pharmaceutical and natural health industries (Thompson and Troester, 2002), the pursuit of physical fitness (Lehmann, 1987) or chasing physical beauty via plastic surgery (Sayre, 1999).

Faced with evidence that eventually all humans die, the second narrative, 'Resurrection', focuses on the rebirth of the physical body. Traditionally, many religions have embraced the idea of the dead rising again on judgment day, and more recently scientific advances such as cryogenics, offer the hope of preserving the physical body until it can live again. A third narrative, 'Soul', espouses living on spiritually, without the body. Across cultures, many religions hold out the hope of eternal life via a soul which is impervious to death.

The fourth narrative, 'Legacy', is the one with which we are most interested and the path which Cave professes holds out the only real hope for immortality. Living on through one's legacy requires neither a physical body nor an immortal soul. Cave (2012, p. 205) distinguishes between two forms of the Legacy narrative – the *cultural* and the *biological*. The biological legacy narrative depends not only on the passing along of one's genes but also on tracing one's genetic lineage back in time. While the use of DNA testing is certainly a growing part of family history practice (Harmon, 2007), given the space constraints we focus on the cultural form of the legacy narrative.

Cultural immortality is based on the idea that while the individual eventually passes away, the culture of the group to which one belonged lives on. Achieving fame, celebrity or glory during one's lifetime such that one becomes part of cultural narratives is one path to immortality. The creation of cultural works – paintings, poetry, music, literature – also results from the efforts of the individual to claim space within the undying cultural realm. Cave's conceptualization of cultural immortality seems to closely parallel the distal defense mechanism of 'embedding oneself in a meaningful enduring cultural reality' that is postulated under terror management theory (Pyszczynski, Greenberg and Solomon, 1999, p. 838). However, Cave's work has particular import for this research in that he acknowledges the essential role of the scribe or historian in capturing the deeds of the one being immortalized; even if one fails to leave behind a carefully crafted autobiography or photographic image, one can be immortalized through the efforts of others.

To further his argument, Cave (2012, p. 219) makes use of what he terms the 'bundle theory' of the self:

You are just a collection of disparate thoughts, memories, sense impressions and the like, all bundled up together in a package we conveniently label a person ... [W]hat does it mean for 'you' to survive? One answer might be that you survive if enough of these disparate parts survive ... [I] f enough of the bits of the bundle live on, then the person lives on – even if entirely in the world of symbols.

Cave's logic opens the door to thinking about a consumption practice like family history, which seeks to pull together the disparate parts of a life (birth certificates, wedding photos, locks of hair) into a semblance of the 'whole' person, as a means by which one's descendants might render one immortal.

Method

We employed multiple data collection methods including participant observation and depth interviews followed by a nation-wide survey. Since December 2006, the lead author has been involved in a participant observation study which has included becoming a member of a local family history society, attending regular meetings, training workshops and conferences as well as a course in writing life history, reading family history journals and undertaking the creation of her own family history. 'Cultural immersion' allowed the researcher to develop an emic understanding of the culture under study, acquire fluency in the genealogical vernacular, and better understand discourses associated with the pursuit of family history, benefits highlighted in previous research (Thompson and Troester, 2002; Kozinets, 1997). Further, it facilitated the development of deeper insights into the value system of the culture, allowed the researcher to establish herself as a knowledgeable and trusted member of the community, facilitated recruitment of interview and survey respondents and provided the opportunity for member-checking our emerging interpretation.

The second author was a co-investigator in a Canadian study of attitudes toward the past (Conrad *et al.*, 2013) and facilitated an early round of data collection through interviews with genealogists in the context of a graduate seminar in Public History. During the summer of 2007, a series of interviews with family historians was conducted by a graduate student research assistant under the supervision of both authors. An important outcome was the determination that family historians, regardless of age, had ready access to computing equipment, internet connections and a comfort level operating in an online environment; this made the use of a web-based survey instrument possible.

During the summer and early fall of 2011, a web-based survey – the Canadian Genealogy Survey[2] (CGS) – collected data from over 2,700 people. Although responses were received from 27 countries, most respondents listed Canada as their country of residence (72 percent), followed by the United States (21 percent).[3] The use of both closed ended and open-ended questions allowed respondents to expand on their reasons for doing genealogy and its impact on their lives. The survey built on the foundation laid by sociologist Ron Lambert's (1996) study of family historians in Ontario, Canada, but was extended to include questions covering new internet-based technologies and constructs of interest to this research.

Since previous researchers had identified low response rates and confidentiality concerns as possible disadvantages to web-based surveys (Healey, Macpherson and Kuijten, 2005; Grandcolas, Rettie and Marusenko, 2003), special efforts were made to drive traffic to the survey website. Participants were recruited through announcements in family history blogs and websites, and by soliciting the cooperation of genealogical societies to announce the survey at meetings and in their newsletters. Posters advertising the survey were mailed out to archives across the country and personal visits were made to archives and museums in our provinces of residence (Ontario and Nova Scotia) to deposit posters and flyers and solicit the assistance of staff to notify their summer visitors of our survey. Because potential respondents may have considered some of the data we sought to collect to be of a sensitive nature (e.g., country of origin, immigration date, last visit to country of origin), we took extra effort to reinforce the confidential nature of the survey and the security of their responses in our communications.[4]

Responses to the open-ended questions were analyzed following accepted methods for interpreting qualitative data (Spiggle, 1994). An undergraduate research assistant and the lead author worked through the 2,000 Canadian responses question by question, iteratively generating a coding structure. As each new coding category was created, a description was generated along with examples of what responses would and what would not be considered to fall within the meaning of the category. The coding structure typically firmed up after approximately one-quarter of the responses to a question had been analyzed (e.g., 350–500 out of 2,000). Up to this point, we returned to re-code earlier responses in light of the creation of later coding categories. In the section which follows, we report on the most frequently stated responses. This does not mean that infrequent responses were not theoretically interesting, simply that given space limitations, we chose to discuss what might be considered more 'typical' responses for the consumers and phenomenon being researched.

Findings and discussion

We report, first, a description of our Canadian-resident respondents in order to provide a profile of the typical family historian. The largest proportion of respondents was in the 50–65 year age group (48.4 percent of those who answered the question), followed by those aged 66–76 (35.3 percent) and those aged 30–49 (9.1 percent). Women outnumbered men by almost two to one (65.3 percent to 34.7 percent). Overall, respondents were highly educated, with 77.5 percent having college, undergraduate or postgraduate degrees or professional qualifications. This compares with the Canadian average of 35.42 percent (Statistics Canada, 2009). On average, both male and female respondents had been interested in family history for the same length of time, about 27 years, although the men described themselves as being 'actively' engaged for a slightly longer period of time (18.47 years), than did the women (16.88 years).

Although our sample was not representative of the Canadian population overall, it did align with previous surveys of family historians conducted in Canada. For example, in Lambert's 1996 study of Ontario Genealogy Society members, 63 percent of respondents were female, 54 percent were 60 years of age or older, 50 percent had a university degree, and the median time of involvement in family history research was 14 years. The demographic profile of family historians appears to have remained relatively consistent over time.

We now focus on the reasons given for setting out to do genealogy work. When we asked people to identify the primary reason that they started researching their family history, the predominant response was a desire to learn about their roots. 'To learn about my family, my ancestors, myself' was the response provided by 22 percent of people completing the survey. The following quote from a 53 year old man with 25 years of experience is typical, 'I wanted to know more about where my ancestors came from and who they were.' The second most common reason was the influence of a family member. Thirteen percent of respondents provided this response, with 5 percent identifying their parents as the primary influence. A 75-year-old woman, actively researching for 8 years, commented,

> Mother was approaching 90 yrs. old and she had a briefcase full of data. When she was in her declining years, she talked a lot about her family. It stirred my interest. I inherited the briefcase when she died at 93 yrs. of age. Our roots are very exciting. I now have a passion (addiction) to researching our families.

Similar to previous research, informants spoke of 'personal traumas' such as the death of a parent (Lindridge, 2012) or 'trigger events', like planning for a family reunion (Schau, Gilly and Wolfinbarger, 2009) as the stimulus for their interest in family history. One woman stated, 'After the death of my parents I found scattered notes and bits of info on my grandparents and their siblings and decided to sort them out so as to leave them for my children, if they were interested.' Motivations stemming from intergenerational trauma, such as death in childbirth and adoption (Lindridge, 2012) were present in our data. However, other forms of intergenerational trauma reflected the Canadian context; for example families rent asunder and cultural continuity disrupted through the experience of attending residential schools by aboriginal peoples.

Other motivations reflected broader societal changes; storytellers from previous generations are no longer living in the same home as their children and grandchildren. Accordingly, a 58-year-old woman identified her reason for starting family history research as, 'To research and record our family history for posterity. Elders in the family were dying and with them the stories and knowledge of the history of our family.' Another mechanism for keeping the family's story alive is needed. The family history, organized and recorded, provides a bridge from past to future family members.

Some of the reasons that scholars had identified in previous research also appeared in our data, but with much less frequency. For example, only 2 percent of respondents reported that qualifying for ancestral society membership stimulated their research, while tracing the existence of a medical condition, or learning whether such a condition existed, was important to only 1 percent of respondents. A comparatively small proportion of respondents (0.6 percent) identified religious requirements as a motivating factor, while finding links to rich or famous people inspired only 0.3 percent of the family historians who took part in our survey. Recognizing that the Canadian Genealogical Survey was conducted in the lead up to the 200th anniversary of the war of 1812, we probably had more responses dealing with establishing United Empire Loyalist ancestry than we would have received had the survey been conducted at another time. But it is interesting to note that the motivations commonly attributed to family historians were some of the least mentioned reasons provided by family historians themselves.

Given the time and financial investment many family historians were making, it was interesting to explore the role that family history played in their lives. For some, it was described as a 'nice hobby' (5.3 percent of respondents), or an activity that 'filled up the time', often in retirement (2.2 percent). Simply knowing more about family, in terms of the typical birth, marriage and death information recorded in family trees, was the outcome recorded by 5.3 percent of respondents. But for others, researching their family history had become central to their identity, both as individuals and members of larger family networks. Developing a better sense of 'who I am', with the emphasis on the focal individual, was noted by 6.7 percent of respondents, while a 'sense of connection and belonging' within an extended network of kin was the most common outcome identified (9.6 percent of respondents).

The second most common outcome expressed was a feeling of gratitude and deep respect for the life experiences of their ancestors, mentioned by 8.3 percent of respondents. Typical comments include, 'It has given me a great deal of pleasure in knowing who I am, [and] where I came from. And an appreciation of my ancestors whose hard work and personal sacrifices made it possible for me to be here!!' (62-year-old man). Learning about the hardships endured by their immigrant ancestors in order to provide them with a better life had a profound impact on many informants. When paired with informants' pride in how their families had contributed to their new country, we can see evidence of the distal defense mechanisms theorized by terror management theorists. For example, a 52-year-old female informant stated that working on her family history, '...has helped me to understand our history and how my family played a part in the building of our Canada.' The idea that one's family has contributed in a meaningful way to something valuable and enduring, is one way that family history research may lend symbolic reassurance in the face of one's inevitable mortality (Pyszczynski, Greenberg and Solomon, 1999).

However, another major theme emerging from our analysis of the data is the idea that while researching and recording ancestors' names and tombstone data (typically considered the 'genealogy' component) plus learning about the social context in which ancestors lived (the 'family history' part) is a way of getting to know one's extended family (in other words, communing with the dead), it can also serve to make those ancestors immortal. It does so through practices which reflect Cave's (2012) 'bundle theory' of the self: by recording their 'dates' (birth, marriage and death), gathering photographs, stories and other mementoes, and using them to write their life histories.

The 'legacy' route to immortality works because the connection that family historians feel often extends back several generations, in spite of the lack of a living, emotional linkage (Lindridge, 2012). A 41-year-old woman said, '[It] makes me feel more connected to my family which is spread around the country and also to my family that I never got to know because they were gone before I was born.' Another woman discussed how the people she has researched are present in her thoughts, 'It puts real people into the bigger stories and trend of history, so when I read a history book, I am always thinking about "where was this person when that was happening?" or "how did that impact on that person?"' Finally, a 64-year-old woman commented that doing family history, 'keeps lively a community which has largely disappeared now'.

Family historians aren't just concerned with the past but also with the future. When we invited informants to tell us about any steps they were taking to preserve special family objects, an overwhelming number of respondents indicated that they had adopted digital technologies to ensure the family's inalienable wealth is protected. Typical of their comments was this one from a 55-year-old woman, 'I am making sure that many family members have digital images of things that I have found. Share the wealth.' A 67-year-old woman has compiled a scrapbook, for a relative who was a missionary in Japan for 30 years. She said, 'I have many articles and photos from Japan all retained for future generations.' In this manner, ancestors live on through the legacies family historians produce for them.

In our research, 42 percent of informants had recorded their own reminiscences for posterity, but an equal proportion (41 percent) had not and a further 17 percent said they didn't plan to do so. These results accord with Lambert's (1996) finding that the focus of most family historians is less on perpetuating their own self and their own legacy through time than on ensuring the family unit's narrative or the story of a 'special' other (e.g., an uncle who went off to war) continues to be told, although the role of family historian is still important to self-image. Hence our opening quote which highlights the sadness family historians feel when they can't find, much less bundle together, the pieces of an ancestor's legacy.

We would be remiss if we did not discuss how the belief system of adherents to the Church of Jesus Christ of Latter-day Saints (LDS, commonly referred to as the Mormons) also works to immortalize ancestors. Central to LDS doctrine is the idea of recovering family members to the faith through proxy baptism. In the words of LDS prophet, Joseph Smith, members of the faith, '...have the privilege of being baptized for those of their relatives who are dead, whom they believe would have embraced the Gospel, if they had been privileged with hearing it...' (quoted in Akenson, 2007, p. 51). Thus can the faithful 'overcome not only their own death, but that of their children, and of their ancestors' (Akenson, 2007, p. 53), resulting in eternal life. Central to the project is establishing the family's lineage. This has resulted in the creation of an enormous database of the essential stuff of family history (see familysearch.org); though most users of the data are not adherents to the Mormon faith (Akenson, 2007).

Limitations and conclusion

Terror management theory has been used effectively in past research to understand consumption behavior after the death of a family member (Bonsu and Belk, 2003). Our research extends its application into a more broadly practiced consumption practice – family history. Using Cave's (2012) 'cultural legacy' immortality narrative as an interpretive lens helps us to better understand the meaning at the heart of family history practice.

Although our study was national in scope, it was offered only in the English language, resulting in under-representation of the French-speaking population. Further, our recruitment efforts resulted in over-representation from our two home provinces. However, our immersion in the culture, the large number of respondents, and the fact that the average time taken to complete the survey was almost 63 minutes, allows us to feel confident that we have faithfully captured the essence of the experience of Anglophone Canadian family historians.

While past research has focused on the possession of consumer goods (e.g., motorcycles in Schouten and McAlexander, 1995), or membership in consumption communities (e.g., Star Trek fans in Kozinets, 2001) as the materials from which consumers symbolically construct and reconstruct their identities, this research has examined how information resources are also 'marketer-generated materials' from which consumers construct personal and familial identities within the structural limitations of the marketplace (Arnould and Thompson, 2005). In doing so, it challenges consumer culture theory to move away from an emphasis on material culture (Epp and Price, 2010; Bradford, 2009; Curasi, Price and Arnould, 2004) and embrace an important, and timely, consumption domain often missing from our literature – information (cf., Lindridge, 2012).

Notes

1 The largest online database, Ancestry.com, has seen the number of its subscribers grow from almost one million in June, 2009 to 2,125,000 as of September 30, 2014 and its revenues grow from $122.6 million in 2004 to $540.4 million in 2013.
2 The survey research was supported by a grant from the Social Sciences and Humanities Research Council of Canada.
3 Many American respondents reported Canadian ancestry and extensive connections with family still resident in Canada.
4 Our university's research ethics committee required us to engage a survey firm that could guarantee the data would reside on a Canadian server, outside the reach of the US Homeland Security Act. Using a service located within another branch of the university lent credibility and reassurance – the both the survey URL and the landing page carried the university's name.

References

Ahuvia, A. (2005) 'Beyond the Extended Self: Loved Objects and Consumers' Identity Narratives', *Journal of Consumer Research*, 32 (June), pp. 171–184.

Akenson, D.H. (2007) *Some Family: The Mormons and How Humanity Keeps Track of Itself*. Montreal and Kingston: McGill-Queen's University Press.

Andrews, P. (1982) 'Genealogy: The Search for a Personal Past', *American Heritage*, 33(5), pp. 10–16.

Arnould, E.J. and Thompson, C.J. (2005) 'Consumer Culture Theory (CCT): Twenty Years of Research', *Journal of Consumer Research*, 31(4), pp. 868–882.

Ashton, P. and Hamilton, P. (2010) *History at the Crossroads: Australians and the Past*. Ultimo, New South Wales, Australia: Halstead Press.

Belk, R.W. (1990) 'The Role of Possessions in Constructing and Maintaining a Sense of Past', in Goldberg, M.E., Gorn, G. and Pollay, R.W. (ed.) *Advances in Consumer Research*, vol. 17. Provo, UT: Association for Consumer Research, pp. 669–676.

Belk, R.W. (1988) 'Possessions and the Extended Self', *Journal of Consumer Research*, 15(Sept), pp. 139–168.

Bonsu, S.K. and Belk, R.W. (2003) 'Do Not Go Cheaply into That Good Night: Death-Ritual Consumption in Asante, Ghana', *Journal of Consumer Research*, 30(1), pp. 41–55.

Bradford, T.W. (2009) 'Intergenerationally Gifted Asset Dispositions', *Journal of Consumer Research*, 36(June), pp. 93–111.

Cannon, H.M. and Yaprak, A. (2002) 'Will the Real-World Citizen Please Stand Up! The Many Faces of Cosmopolitan Consumer Behavior', *Journal of International Marketing*, 10(4), pp. 30–52.

Cave, S. (2012) *Immortality: The Quest to Live Forever and How it Drives Civilization*. NY: Crown Publishers.

Conrad, M., Ercikan, K., Friesen, G., Letourneau, J., Muise, D., Northrup, D. and Seixas, P. (2013) *Canadians and Their Pasts*. Toronto: University of Toronto Press.

Curasi, C.F., Price, L.L. and Arnould, E.J. (2004) 'How Individuals' Cherished Possessions Become Families' Inalienable Wealth', *Journal of Consumer Research*, 31(December), pp. 609–622.

Epp, A.M. and Price, L.L. (2010) 'The Storied Life of Singularized Objects: Forces of Agency and Network Transformation', *Journal of Consumer Research*, 36(February), pp. 820–837.

Gentry, J.W., Kennedy, P.F., Paul, C. and Hill, R.P. (1995) 'Family Transitions During Grief: Discontinuities in Household Consumption Patterns', *Journal of Business Research*, 34(1), pp. 67–79.

Grandcolas, U., Rettie, R. and Marusenko, K. (2003) 'Web Survey Bias: Sample or Mode Effect?' *Journal of Marketing Management*, 19, pp. 541–561.

Greenberg, J. and Arndt, J. (2011) 'Terror Management Theory', in Van Lange, P.A.M., Kruglanski, A.W. and Higgins E.T (eds.) *Handbook of Theories of Social Psychology*, Vol. 2. Los Angeles: Sage, pp. 398–415.

Greenberg, J., Pyszczynski, T. and Solomon, S. (1986) 'The Causes and Consequences of a Need for Self-Esteem: A Terror Management Theory,' in Baumeister, R. F. (ed.) *Public Self and Private Self*. New York: Springer-Verlag, pp. 189–221.

Hareven, T.K. (1978) 'The Search for Generational Memory: Tribal Rites in Industrial Society', *Daedalus*, 107(Fall), pp. 137–149.

Harmon, A. (2007) 'Stalking Strangers' DNA to Fill in the Family Tree', *The New York Times*, 2 April. Available at: www.nytimes.com/2007/04/02/us/02dna.html?_r=2&oref=slogin& (Accessed: December 13, 2014).

Healey, B., Macpherson, T. and Kuijten, B. (2005) 'An Empirical Evaluation of Three Web Survey Design Principles', *Marketing Bulletin*, 16, Research Note 2. Available at: http://marketing-bulletin.massey.ac.nz/V16/MB_V16_N2_Healey.pdf (Accessed: December 13, 2014.)

Hirschman, E.C. (1981) 'American Jewish Ethnicity: Its Relationship to Some Selected Aspects of Consumer Behavior', *Journal of Marketing*, 45(3), pp. 102–110.

Hirschman, E.C. and Panther-Yates, D. (2007a) 'Designer Genes: DNA Testing Services and Consumer Identity', Paper presented at 2nd Consumer Culture Theory Conference, York University, Toronto, Ontario, May 25–27.

Hirschman, E.C. and Panther-Yates, D. (2007b) 'Suddenly Melungeon! Reconstructing Consumer Identity Across the Color Line', In Belk, R.W. and Sherry, J.F., Jr. (ed.) *Research in Consumer Behavior: Consumer Culture Theory*, vol. 11. Oxford: Elsevier, pp. 241–259.

Hirschman, E.C. and Panther-Yates, D. (2006) 'Romancing the Gene: Making Myth from "Hard Science"', in Belk, R.W. (ed.) *Handbook of Qualitative Research Methods in Marketing*. Cheltenham, UK: Edward Elgar, pp. 419–429.

Kozinets, R.V. (2001) 'Utopian Enterprise: Articulating the Meanings of Star Trek's Culture of Consumption', *Journal of Consumer Research*, 28(June), pp. 67–88.

Kozinets, R.V. (1997) '"I Want to Believe": A Netnography of the X-Files Subculture of Consumption', in Brucks, M. and MacInnis, D.J. (ed.) *Advances in Consumer Research*, vol. 24. Provo, UT: Association for Consumer Research, pp. 470–475.

Kramer, A.M. (2011) 'Mediatizing Memory: History, Affect and Identity in *Who Do You Think You Are?*' *European Journal of Cultural Studies*, 14(4), pp. 428–445.

Lambert, R.D. (2006) 'Descriptive, Narrative, and Experiential Pathways to Symbolic Ancestors', *Mortality*, 11(4), pp. 317–335.

Lambert, R.D. (2002) 'Reclaiming the Ancestral Past: Narrative, Rhetoric and the "Convict Stain"', *Journal of Sociology*, 38(2), pp. 111–127.

Lambert, R.D. (1996) 'The Family Historian and Temporal Orientations Towards the Ancestral Past', *Time and Society*, 5(2), pp. 115–143.

Lehmann, D.R. (1987) 'Pumping Iron III: An Examination of Compulsive Lifting', In Wallendorf, M. and Anderson, P. (ed.) *Advances in Consumer Research*, vol. 14. Provo, UT: Association for Consumer Research, pp. 129–131.

Lindridge, A. (2012) 'Inalienable Wealth and Trauma Resolution: An Explanation of

Genealogy Consumption', In Dahl, D.W, Johar, G.V., and van Osselaer, S.M.J. *Advances in Consumer Research*, vol. 38. Duluth, MN: Association for Consumer Research, pp. 641–642.

Lowenthal, D. (1985) *The Past is a Foreign Country*. Cambridge: Cambridge University Press.

McAuley, A. (2004) 'Seeking (Marketing) Virtue in Globalisation', *Marketing Review*, 4, pp. 253–266.

Peñaloza, L. (1994) 'Atravesando Fronteras/Border Crossings: A Critical Ethnographic Study of the Acculturation of Mexican Immigrants', *Journal of Consumer Research*, 21(June), pp. 32–53.

Price, L.L., Arnould, E.J. and Curasi, C.F. (2000) 'Older Consumers' Disposition of Special Possessions', *Journal of Consumer Research*, 27(September), pp. 179–201.

Pyszczynski, T., Greenberg J. and Solomon, S. (1999) 'A Dual-Process Model of Defense Against Conscious and Unconscious Death-Related Thoughts An Extension of Terror Management Theory', *Psychological Review*, 106(4), pp. 835–845.

Quinn, P.M. (1991) 'The Surge of Interest in Genealogy Reflects a Populist Strand of Society with Important Implications for Our Culture', *Chronicle of Higher Education*, 37(36), p. B2.

Redman, G.R. (1992) 'Archivists and Genealogists: The Trend Toward Peaceful Coexistence', *Archival Issues*, 18(2), pp. 121–132.

Rosenzweig, R. and Thelen, D. (1998) *The Presence of the Past: Popular Uses of History in American Life*. NY: Columbia University Press.

Sayre, S. (1999) 'Using Introspective Self-Narrative to Analyze Consumption: Experiencing Plastic Surgery', *Consumption, Markets and Culture*, 3(2), pp. 99–127.

Schau, H.J., Gilly, M.C. and Wolfinbarger, M. (2009) 'Consumer Identity Renaissance: The Resurgence of Identity-Inspired Consumption in Retirement', *Journal of Consumer Research*, 36(August), pp. 255–276.

Schouten, J.W. and McAlexander, J.H. (1995) 'Subcultures of Consumption: An Ethnography of the New Bikers', *Journal of Consumer Research*, 22(June), pp. 43–61.

Spiggle, S. (1994) 'Analysis and Interpretation of Qualitative Data in Consumer Research', *Journal of Consumer Research*, 21(December), pp. 491–503.

Statistics Canada (2009) Population 15 years and Over by Highest Degree, Certificate or Diploma, by Province and Territory (2006 Census). Available at: www.statcan.gc.ca/tables-tableaux/sum-som/l01/cst01/educ41a-eng.htm (Accessed: April 7, 2012).

Taylor, R.M., Jr. (1982) 'Summoning the Wandering Tribes: Genealogy and Family Reunions in American History', *Journal of Social History*, 16(1), pp. 21–37.

Thompson, C.J. and Troester, M. (2002) 'Consumer Value Systems in the Age of Postmodern Fragmentation: The Case of the Natural Health Microculture', *Journal of Consumer Research*, 28(4), pp. 550–571.

Turley, D. and O'Donohoe, S. (2012) 'The Sadness of Lives and the Comfort of Things: Goods as Evocative Objects in Bereavement', *Journal of Marketing Management*, 28(11/12), pp. 1331–1353.

Wilson, I, (2003) 'First Person, Singular … First Person, Plural: Making Canada's Past Accessible', *Canadian Issues*, October. Available at: www.collectionscanada.gc.ca/about-us/012-213-e.html (Accessed: December 13, 2014).

Yakel, E. (2004) 'Seeking Information, Seeking Connections, Seeking Meaning: Genealogists and Family Historians', *Information Research*, 10(1), paper 205. Available at: www.informationr.net/ir/10-1/paper205.html.

Zhao, X. and Belk, R.W. (2007) 'Desire on Fire: A Naturalistic Inquiry of Chinese Death Ritual Consumption', In Borghini, S., McGrath, M.A. and Otnes, C. (ed.) *Advances in Consumer Research – European Conference Proceedings*, vol. 8. Duluth, MN: Association for Consumer Research, pp. 245.

12 Physician-assisted suicide at the crossroads of vulnerability and social taboo

Is death becoming a consumption good?

Françoise Passerard and Xavier Menaud

Though science and medicine have made the idea of death more and more remote, to some it remains terrorizing. To others immortality has become more fascinating since it seems to be reachable – they perceive death as a voluntary choice, denying the ultimate and traditionally sacred frontier.

In developed countries, the question of the end of life remains a sensitive topic with virulently opposing viewpoints. The study of physician-assisted suicide (PAS) is not only a case in point but it raises a question of rights, specifically in France, which has historically been the country of human rights. The intellectual debate that pits partisans against detractors of a chosen death must consider this statistic: French people are the third largest nationality to commit PAS in Switzerland (Gauthier *et al.*, 2014, p. 3).

The objective of the research herein is to examine PAS from the perspectives of three profiles of participants who have a stake in its aftermath: the medical expert, patient and relative. The research question at hand asks whether or not death is a consumption good; the authors posit that PAS stands at the crossroad of vulnerability and social taboo when it comes to the stream of end of life research. End of life has been communicated in the following way:

> The issue of end-of-life cannot be reduced to the sole time of the "very end of life". End of life strikes as soon as the severe disease is announced. It progressively remains present all along the duration of the disease or the aging. It is felt during the very last moments, and it goes on after death within the process of funerals and mourning. The issue if end-of-life has a global dimension and, to be understood, it must be seen as a more or less long process, punctuated with breaks, during which individuals try, more or less easily, to face death.
>
> (French National Observatory on End of Life Care, 2011, p. 14)

To better understand the dilemma posed by PAS requires an understanding of the differences between certain words that are frequently misunderstood: suicide, physician-assisted suicide and euthanasia. Suicide is a major concern that has been extensively researched by the Sociology of Health and Illness. Durkheim's (1952) seminal works, for example, are still fundamental references due to their timeless topicality. Durkheim defined suicide as "all cases of death resulting directly or indirectly from a positive or negative act of the victim himself, which he knows will produce this result" (Durkheim, 1952, p. 44). This definition underscores the fact that committing suicide is the personal choice of the participant. Suicide is classified into one of four categories depending upon whether it is an excess or a defect of integration or regulation. Durkheim considers integration the social interaction of a person and integration describes whether the person is integrated into the community or living marginally.

The degree of integration leads to two specific forms of suicide. *Selfish suicide* is the result of individuation that is too strong. The participant has not integrated into the community very well and death is not perceived as lacking in the group. *Altruistic* suicide is caused by little individuation. The victim perceives her death as a necessary sacrifice to protect the community: the general interest prevails over the individual interest.

Contrary to integration, regulation refers to the social context within which the person evolves. Here, it is suitable to regard the person as evolving in a society that holds its members to certain standards, standards whose level of vividness have a direct impact on the nature of the suicide being performed. These suicides can take one of two forms:

- *Anomic suicide* is caused because of a defect of regulation. In this case, society allows extensive freedom that leads to a loss of reference.
- *Fatalistic suicide* is the result of excess regulation. In this case, society creates excessive standards that must be respected at the cost of expressing any form of passion.

According to its Greek etymology, *euthanasia* means *good death*. A more contemporary approach to the word regards legitimizing euthanasia as a form of killing in the participant's own interest. The main difference between euthanasia and PAS depends on whether the person comprehends the act leading to death. In the case of PAS, the patient self-administers the lethal drink; in the case of euthanasia, it is the doctor who carries out the act even though the decision is motivated by the same factors as PAS, to reduce the suffering of a patient fighting an incurable pathology.

Table 12.1 Synthesis of Durkheim's classification of suicide

	Defect	*Excess*
Integration	Selfish suicide	Altruistic suicide
Regulation	Anomic suicide	Fatalistic suicide

This research is dedicated to the concept of PAS that is defined in this way: "In physician-assisted suicide the patient self-administers medication that was prescribed intentionally by a physician." (Onwuteaka-Philipsen, 2012, p. 908).

PAS integrates four components:

- The context of the end of life: physical suffering or declining state without any hope of improvement.
- The person making the decision is the patient.
- The means to ending life are lethal products provided by the medical profession.
- The person who causes the act leading to death is the patient.

Very few countries sanction assisted suicide and/or euthanasia: "Euthanasia and assisted suicide have been legal in the Netherlands and Belgium since 2002; assisted suicide has been permitted in Switzerland since 1948; Oregon since 1997; Montana and Washington since 2009; and Vermont since 2013" (Gamondia *et al.*, 2014, p. 127). Still, several specifications for its implementation exist. For instance, in 2014, Belgium extended the right to self-requested euthanasia to terminally ill minor patients without a minimum age limitation. The terms were reinforced, and insisted that "the issue of capacity for discernment, which should be assessed carefully by a multidisciplinary pediatric team, including a clinical psychologist. The parents must agree to the request." (Dan *et al.*, 2014, p. 672). In Switzerland, euthanasia is not legal but, since 1942, the Helvetic penal code allows for the provision of PAS, but only if the request is not for a selfish suicide. In the U.S., physician-assisted suicides are mainly organized by associations that give minor roles to the medical profession. In Oregon and Washington, the Death with Dignity Act is dedicated to terminally ill patients who have less than six months to live. They are allowed to end their own lives instead of succumbing to their illnesses. They can do so by taking physician-prescribed lethal drugs. While an act does not exist in Montana that legalizes PAS, in 2009 the state officially allowed patients to request medical aid in dying. More recently, in 2013, the government of Vermont adopted the Patient Choice and Control at End of Life Act. Oregon, Washington and Vermont legalized PAS but demand two medical opinions before allowing it to be carried out.

These countries represent a pioneering approach to what is widely regarded as a sensitive ethical issue. Indeed, while PAS is viewed by many as medicine supporting the right to die with dignity, the role of the doctor remains complex. Because physicians take oaths to care for their patients and cure them, it is difficult to assimilate the idea that providing them with lethal products in an effort to aid their suicides is part of their medical ethics in general, and deontology in particular. Still, PAS is commonly associated with the hope of a good death.

Death remains taboo in France. An overview of the laws concerning end of life issues in France shows how they have evolved and reveals PAS as a timely issue despite its status as a societal taboo. In 2002, a pivotal law was passed that integrated the notion of Patients' Rights. Its impact remains paramount because it allows patients to access their own complete medical records and aims to reduce the informational gap between patient and doctor. In 2005, a specific legal framework was designed that prohibits clandestine euthanasia. It integrates points that improve patients' rights in managing their end of life. They now have the right to ask for the cessation of treatment once they are made aware of the consequences of this decision, and to write advance directives that are valid for three years but are revocable at any time. In 2012, the Sicard report contended that the 2005 act is misunderstood and does not adequately resolve the problem. Indeed, patients regard this act as a way to legally protect doctors during palliative care. Further, French physicians can reject advance directives because of their deep attachment to the Hippocratic Oath, which is their commitment to care for their patients regardless of their health. They refuse to consider that prescribing life-ending medication is a medical act, claiming that they have not been trained to kill.

In 2015, the French government launched a project to restructure the 2005 law, with the goal of maintaining the illegality of euthanasia and PAS. However, medical staffs now have the right to deeply and continuously sedate patients in phases of terminal illness until they die. Further, advance directives are now valid indefinitely but are revisable and revocable at any time, and physicians are obligated to respect them.

This study relies on two main theoretical streams. First, the approach to this very sensitive topic relied upon Paul Ricœur's philosophy of "little ethics" (Ricoeur, 1992), which elaborates on ethical intention, or seeking a good life, as a three-fold design that is built upon self-esteem, dialogical structure and fair institutions. Selfhood is related to being faithful to oneself, willing to stick to one's involvements or keeping a promise. The notion of an end is seen as the way it is articulated, whether each action owns an end or happiness is the ultimate end. Ricœur identified a need to dialectalize fundamental questions in an effort to seek coalition between what appears to be the best choice and the one that governs. Here, a dimension is reached that is both ethical and dialogical. Ricœur considered the concept of solicitude to be the fundamental heart of ethics. Seen as spontaneous benevolence, solicitude is "an intimate union with the flesh of feelings" (Ricœur, 1992). The suffering being is the one whose ability is diminished. Solicitude comprises pity, compassion and sympathy. According to Ricœur, solicitude is the reason we forbid – it is the refusal of an others' indignity. Casuistry should therefore be used to make individualized decisions.

Second, this study is based on Jean-Pierre Boutinet's anthropology of projects (Boutinet, 2005). The notion of project means to contemplate a goal, an intention, a prevision, an anticipation, an agenda, the ends, a programme, a prevention, a prospective … project is also synonymous with the ability to create and manage change. It is essentially a paradigm that symbolizes a preexisting and fugitive reality. It is linked to anticipation behaviours that make something happen. Time is central; it is the prospective to control, the potential time to dominate, the future time to explore and domesticate.

The notion of project focuses on the way individuals, groups and cultures experience time. The concept of project only reveals itself through realized intention. Yet, by being realized, it stops existing as such. So the concept of project is dedicated to living in a discontinuous way since it destroys itself by the fact that it happens. PAS is part of what Boutinet calls "existential situations with a project" which appear at different stages of life. If we consider PAS as a project, then it corresponds to any kind of project within its specific context:

- It searches a lost meaning and tries to be meaningful.
- It coincides with the growing individualisation of culture.
- It represents the myth for transparency.
- It stands for the contributing symptom of the individual or the group.
- It is a way of expressing a defence against fundamental anxieties linked to nonsense.
- It aims to create a new "social link." (Boutinet, 2005, pp. 364–365)

PAS is twofold. On the one hand it is still taboo. It is also difficult to find people to interview about the topic. On the other hand, most people who admit to their desire for PAS belong to mediatized associations. This biases the selection of informants. To overcome these obstacles, an exploratory and qualitative study was conducted using a convenience sample of informants. One of the co-authors of this chapter previously worked as a communications manager in a French public hospital, which afforded access to three profiles of respondents: experts, sick people and relatives.

The decision was made to conduct interviews within these profiles because they echo the core participants in the doctor/patient relationship. We therefore conducted 12 semi-structured interviews during the first four months of 2015:

- The first group of respondents consisted of four French medical experts: two physicians, a nurse and a sociologist. They were U.S. trained in Clinical Ethics methodology in the early 2000s but all currently belong to different French medical ethics committees.
- The second group of respondents was composed of four sick people who had been diagnosed with incurable diseases.
- The third group of respondents was comprised of four people who had recently lost a sick relative to a severe illness.

One interview guide per interviewee profile was elaborated (see Table 12.2). The goal was to obtain insights into the self-perceived value of life, the dissymmetry in the patient/doctor relationship, the patients' families' lived experiences, and the impact PAS has on the mourning process. Questions arose that required the exploration of individuals' own ethics in terms of health and care. How are they experienced in different situations? What do they express about them?

When bioethics experts were interviewed, they revealed their deep trust in palliative care when it is progressively implemented and is in agreement with both patient and relative.

The nurse explained how deeply she believes in the value of palliative care as it is linked to deontology:

> The palliative care relies on the humanist values of Medicine such as supporting and accompanying our patients. The goal is to relieve physical and moral pain. When palliative care is well implemented, then euthanasia and medically assisted suicide are no longer relevant. A curing hand cannot be a killing hand!

The collegial thinking around clinical ethics helps these professionals experience decision making that is better aligned than before with their professional deontology. Sharing the deliberation process as well as the resulting decision appeases the situation. The general practitioner expounded on the collegial committee as a regular help in the face of difficult moments in his practice:

> It helps us think about the clinical case with different points of view, and it makes us feel as good as possible with the decisions we make. Before joining this committee, I was continuously wondering if I had taken the right decision and where was the frontier between the care, the cure, the relief and the death. And I had nobody to share these thoughts with. Whereas, now, I feel peaceful.

Similarly, the sociologist relayed the fact that each expert can share different arguments and state their positions on a global level: "We are together to defend the patient's voice and make it heard through the lenses of our multidisciplinary statements, in full respect of the law."

Interviews with the sick illuminated their fear of agony … without actually naming it. What they described was the fear of a long, slow, suffering death lasting several days, several weeks or even several months. Surprisingly, they did not express strong wills to maintain their dignity; what they mainly expressed was their fear of being in agony, especially those who had witnessed at least once the loss of relatives or friends. The sick are deeply traumatized by the narratives they have heard in the past or during their illnesses. The way the dying are portrayed in the media these days does nothing to provide reassurance. All told, the sick cannot help imagining the end of their lives as similar to those testimonies.

Ophelia constantly referred to her familial experiences when projecting herself into her own end of life:

> I hope I will be able to decide by myself when the end gets closer. I remember my mother when she was dying ... I took the decision to welcome her at home and I was the one who took care of her. And our doctor helped her ... He let her go ... I don't know how, but we all agreed that she was enduring unbearable pain. She was so weak. So it was very sad, but it was fine. It is important to plan one's very end. I don't want to see myself get weaker and weaker. I am convinced that palliative care should be the best solution but I hope it won't last too long. Long pain is a torture. I've heard about assisted suicide ... For religious reasons, I should be against such practices. Yet, in reality, I think I am capable to do it for myself. I would regret to have reached that extreme decision, but I think I could choose it. For ethical reasons, I'm against it because I see it as a very expensive business.

A death plan helps eliminate the uncertainty of the way in which a person might die. It helps the dying gain confidence that they have control of this process, and essentially allows a person ultimate control over what is normally an unpredictable natural phenomenon. Still, it was observed that the dying intended to let their relatives choose to be present on the day of their deaths – or not. All of them expressed that they would rather be surrounded by their relatives, but none of them wanted to impose their own choices on their loved ones. Zack explained that having a death plan in mind, such as PAS, reinforced his sensation of being alive and in better control of the potential evolution of his illness.

Sandra expressed her awareness of her own mortality:

> I've realised that I've been close to death several times, and I know that my relatives are aware of my own vulnerability. But we have never talked about my death, about the way I want to die. They don't know. Yet, I fear loneliness, I am scared to die alone and to suffer. What I would like is a peaceful path toward death. I plan to choose medically assisted suicide because I want to be free to decide how and when I am going to die. If I can anticipate, then I can control the moment of my death. I already know how to access medically assisted suicide in Switzerland ... It costs around 8000 euros, but I can save money for it. I also found out how to get lethal medicines in other European countries and how to self-administrate them whenever I feel ready. But I hope it will be legalized in France before I need it because I don't want to feel stressed or guilty because of clandestine practices.

Indeed, "the phenomenon of suicide tourism unique to Switzerland can result in amendment or supplementary guidelines to existing regulations in foreign countries." (Gauthier *et al.*, 2014, p. 6).

The notion of vulnerability raised in the latter paragraph by Sandra echoes Mary's experience:

> I feel vulnerable because I feel fragile ... My fragility makes me vulnerable! I believe in God, I'm catholic, and I believe in eternity. To me, death is not an end but a passage toward another form of life. I was born after the Second World War and my dad used to tell us what he had been through as a prisoner in Germany. And since I was a little girl I associate the notion of death to the notion of courage. I think it sounds unusual but I can't help wondering if I will be courageous enough to face it. This is why I'm divided about assisted suicide. I experienced several weeks of coma twenty years ago, and I remember that, when I woke up, the pain was so unbearable that I kept asking to die. And I know, for sure, that I would have taken lethal drugs myself if it had been possible then. But I feel perturbed because it is at the opposite of my religious faith...!

Interviews with relatives revealed their ambivalence toward the deaths of others. They all expressed a strong ambiguity when it came to their expectations about the experience. On one hand they understood and shared the fear of agony expressed by their sick relatives and expressed their beliefs that PAS is a peaceful solution to preparing for one's death. On the other hand, as relatives, they tended to consider PAS to be a rather violent alternative to turn to themselves. It was hard for them to imagine the context, the moment of the PAS. The idea of it sounded so strange and improbable that they felt perplexed by it. They all mentioned their fears that they may not be courageous enough to care for their dying relatives until the very end. What is striking is that they all focused on the "suicide" part of PAS and not at all on the "assisted" part. Faustina referred first to her sister's suicide attempt when they were younger and then to her uncle's long and impressive agony. Violence occurred in different forms in both cases, and both were traumatising on several levels – to the individual participants, to the affected family and to the surrounding group of relatives and friends. Past experiences still influenced her attitude and explained her ambivalence. Olivia admitted that, in her eyes, "Assisted suicide is a suicide hard to support for the caretakers. They keep their hands clean, but their conscious is surely heavier as years go by."

Relatives were the ones who expressed the most about the consumption aspects of death in general, and about assisted suicide in particular. Emily explained that she went to a funeral home to get an idea of the prices:

> All in all, funerals cost around 8000 euros if you don't want to take the bottom-of-the-range ... Funerals are a terrible business, the market is wide! And if you travel to Switzerland to die of assisted suicide, then you can at least double the price.

The fieldwork undertaken for this study shed light on the interpersonal relationships between doctors and patients, and highlighted the major roles played by patients' relatives: "where trust and consciousness meet." Two conscious states exist here: one is personal and the other is professional. Both are at the crossroads of medical and social ethics and both feature a form of vulnerability. Though it is less mediatized, it is clear that professionals can also experience vulnerability. Patients often see their doctors as superhuman and expect miracles from them. Yet doctors are still vulnerable and the paradox between vulnerability and power remains the central reflexion, adding to it the notions of taboo, identity, authority and trust. As Ricœur said, "to believe that I can is already to be capable" (Ricoeur, 2001, p. 90).

Recognizing that each individual is important reduces the initial dissymmetry in the relationship, hence supporting the care.

All respondents saw three advantages to PAS compared to traditional euthanasia:

- The lethal action is the patient's deliberate choice and gesture.
- The physical presence of the doctor guaranties the required professional assistance.
- The action of putting an end to one's life is taken from a purely ethical point of view, so is thus much less constraining and more similar to the decision to give up futile treatments.

These results also show the importance of parenthood in the PAS project. The informants clearly stated their visions of their deaths to be different depending on whether or not they had children. PAS was seen as a way to remain autonomous until the very end; thereby prohibiting the alternate possibility of children and relatives being present but powerless during one's long and slow death. However, the nagging question remained: "How does one know when it is the right moment, neither too early nor late to commit assisted suicide?"

Another striking result of this process was the patients' fear of agony. Because being in agony is seen as the worst way to die, people consider PAS as the one and only alternative to dying a slow death. This is true for people who have seen and accompanied relatives through agony before death, but it is also true for people who have never witnessed it but are aware of it due to social representations. For all respondents, death was not so frightening as the end of life itself – its duration, the quality of life during that period of time, the degree of suffering, the harshness of treatments and care, the dignity or the loss of it, and the loneliness.

All in all, some respondents did indeed anticipate their deaths using PAS as projects. They explained that they consider death to be part of life. Life plans and death plans are then intrinsically linked. And this link occurs when the feeling of social taboo is the weakest. Indeed, death is then seen as a part of life, and it seems normal, or at least does not seem so shocking, to anticipate it when it is still well into the future. However, part of our respondents could not mentally associate death with life. For them, the associated taboo was really strong and deeply rooted in their past experiences.

The qualitative study revealed that PAS has three components:

- Death appears to be the patient's choice; she knows that the patient is informed about the irreversibility of her situation and will not only refuse futile treatments, but will do so until the very end.
- The doctor's role should first be limited to informing the patient and providing her with the means to end her life and second to assisting her in the steps leading up to death so it happens with certainty and without pain.
- The main motivation that makes the doctor's intervention legitimate and compulsory is a rigorous and pitiless sense of duty to respect the patient's will and autonomy.

Contemporaneous debate has focused on the issue of PAS as it is relates to euthanasia. Two major arguments in favour of these issues supports their legislation. The first demands the patient's autonomy and judges that any individual has the right to control, as much as possible, the course of his/her own death. The other relies on what is called pity or nonmaleficence. It states that any individual has the right to proceed to one's own death when no solution exists that can avoid or weaken one's fatal sufferings.

Two counter arguments oppose the legislation of PAS. The first argument states that the act of killing someone is morally wrong. Hence, it is wrong for doctors to facilitate or carry it out. The second states that legislating PAS makes the act of killing too easy, and leads society to involuntary murder. The perceived peril is that doctors may prescribe suicide for biased reasons, avidity, or impatience or frustration when a patient has reached a medically unresponsive state. Allowing PAS affords a dangerous model for people who feel vulnerable but not yet concerned that their disease is incurable. In societies where elders, the disabled, racial minorities and many others groups are still strongly stigmatized and where financial concerns are great in healthcare systems that do not guaranty equity in access to care, death may be imposed upon these vulnerable individuals, ostensibly by choice but not truly voluntary. In such circumstances, suicide would become a social expectation or even an imperative.

Arguments in favour of the PAS/euthanasia debate ask for more comprehensive examination of suicide as a way to reduce psychopathologies and provide enhanced information about these kinds of situations. By unveiling ancient and clandestine practices, legislation could guaranty authenticity in patients' choices and rigorous control in the process.

Some say that medical innovation provides hope for pain management and that PAS will no longer be relevant. Others say that modern societies are experiencing a transition from Christian values regarding death to more stoic attitudes that enable individuals to wisely control their lives until the very end.

Studying PAS as a project corresponds to studying its structure. Results show that this project is actually a quest for an inaccessible ideal. In concert with Boutinet's work, it was found that PAS contains three dimensions: vital, psychological and existential. PAS appears to be a solution to the search for one's own existence as an answer to averting fate. It is a way to cope with social taboo and vulnerability.

The generalized use of Clinical Ethics methodology is recommended. It originated in the US, and is now applied in several hospitals around the world via Clinical Ethics Centers (Chicago, Paris, Toronto, etc.) This methodology is used as a tool to help medical decision-making when the solution to a sensitive situation cannot gain consensus among a team of practitioners, or when practitioners' and patients' points of view differ. A multidisciplinary team of experts in the field of health practice Clinical Ethics by giving consultative advice. Practitioners and/or patients and/or relatives can ask for this guidance when the relationship between doctor and patient reaches an impasse. The goal is to then craft arguments that require consideration based on the circumstances and the individual context, and to ultimately reunite doctors, patients and relatives:

> The context of a case is determined by multiple social factors, including (among others) the dynamics of the family, the living situation of the patient, and cultural and religious beliefs of the patient and the family. In addition, it is important to be aware of who the major caregivers are for the patient and how the various medical choices will affect the caregivers' ability to provide care.
>
> (Schumann, 2008, p. 40)

Clinical Ethics present pioneering thought regarding the practice of medicine. Its etymology comes from the Greek *klinikos, at the sickbed*, which dictates that medical care should not only be practiced using the doctor's theoretical knowledge but also by observing one's patient. But Clinical Ethics is not just a question of words. It challenges the need to judge each unique case on its own basis. According to Jonsen, Siegler and Winslade (2002), this casuistic methodology should be employed when a conflict occurs between two or more of the four intermediary principles of respect: Beneficence and Nonmaleficence, Autonomy and Justice. The team of experts has to answer a set of precise questions through the lenses of the four ethical principles. First, the principle of nonmaleficence explores the medical indications and asks how the patient can benefit from medical and nursing care, and how harm can be avoided in balance with the benefits of treatment. Second, the principle of respect for autonomy is linked to the patient's ability to make reasoned and informed choices, and investigates whether the patient's right to choose is being respected to the greatest extent possible within ethics and the law. Third, the principle of beneficence considers quality of life by asking whether the patient's present or future condition is such that his or her continued life might be judged undesirable. Last, contextual features are examined through the principle of justice in order to fairly distribute benefits, risks and costs, and to ensure that patients in similar positions be treated in similar manners.

The limitations of this study are linked to the difficulty of the field and the fact that the subject is inherently taboo. Conversely, exploratory and qualitative studies would gain much insight if extended into several different cultures and countries and contained a mix of qualitative and quantitative investigations.

Methodological contributions show how important it is to cross three different profiles of participants who are linked by the same challenges. Here the fieldwork demanded that the opinions of the participants in each category who were concerned with PAS be considered, regardless of the stage of the process they were in. In a way, the choice of informants replicated the trio that constitutes the heart of the relationship between health and care: doctors, patients and their relatives.

Methodological contributions aid Social Marketing in understanding the need for pedagogical information that concerns health practitioners and the general public. Every citizen needs to know what PAS is and what it is not. All voices deserve to be heard. Practitioners need to say how difficult it is for them from a deontological point of view to have patients ask them for death. The sick need to express their anxieties, fears of agony, and need to be informed and reassured that their anguish and pain will be considered and relieved in the care process.

From a theoretical standpoint, it is apparent that Durkheim's classification of suicide is both modern and eternal; revealing that mixing theories from different eras to approach the timeless and eternal topic of death can be rich and enlightening.

New insights might be gained by longitudinally and interculturally extending this study. Light might further be shed on this topic by extending it to studies that compare it with research from other fundamental moments in life like birth. Indeed, birth is related to many bioethical features: abortion, medically assisted procreation, etc. Recent innovations in medical research promise new inroads into this field that will surely pose further ethical debates and questions. For example, deciphering the human genome can inform physicians about what they are looking for in the moment, but also about future latent chronic, degenerative or fatal diseases. This innovation in the field of medical research leads to an ethical standoff that begs an answer to the question of what to do: to tell or not to tell? What kind of life is liveable once an individual knows the specific sword of Damocles that rests in his hand?

Table 12.2 Information on informants

	Name	Age	Profession	Family status	Short presentation
Medical experts		47	Nurse, specialized in intensive and palliative care.	Married, 2 children	She considers herself as an "old nurse now" because she has been working for 18 years. The harshness of her daily work led her to train in clinical ethics because she felt the need to reassess her life and gain ethical tools that enabled her to think about her profession.
		58	Sociologist, specialized in Health and Illness	Single, no child	His role in the committee is to bring fundamental and theoretical roots to the cases being studied. He is a professor at a French university.
		55	Oncologist	Married, 4 children	He is deeply concerned with the deontological frontiers of his profession when faced with patients who request dying assistance. He works in a French public hospital.
		47	General practitioner	Single, no child	He came to ethics as a result of his passion for bioethical issues, which are linked to his professional practice in a French public hospital.
Sick people	Sandra	42	Front office employee	Single, no child	At the age of 20, she was diagnosed with feminine cancer, which has since become chronic. She considers PAS a concrete option for her own end of life.
	Ophelia	71	Retailer	Married, 1 child	Her first cancer was diagnosed when she was 30. She now suffers from several chronic cancers.
	Mary	65	Clinical psychologist	Married, 3 children and 5 grandchildren.	She was diagnosed at the age of 40 with a severe form of autoimmune disease.
	Zack	37	Economist	Single, no child	He found out at the age of 32 that he was HIV positive and has decided to ask for PAS if his illness gets too devastating.
Relatives	John	71	Retired – former executive manager	Married, 3 children and 5 grandchildren	He is a former executive manager. He took care of his mother during the last eight years of her life.
	Emily	24	Baker	Single, no child	Her mother died of breast cancer three years ago. She had looked after her from the time she was just a little girl when her mother was first ill.
	Olivia	69	Retired – former consultant in corporate strategy	Divorced, 2 children and 3 grandchildren	She took care of several friends and siblings who all died of cancer
	Faustina	38	Communications manager	Married, 1 child	A couple of years ago, she took care of her uncle who was dying of a generalized cancer.

References

Baude-Heymans, C., Hannicq, M., Hélin, V., Wouters, B. (2001) L'avis des consommateurs? [Consumers' opinion?]. *Revue internationale de soins palliatifs [International Review of Palliative Care]* 16 (3). pp. 31–36.

Boutinet, J. P. (2005) *Anthropologie du projet [Anthropology of projects]*. Paris: Presses Universitaires de France.

Dan, B., Fonteyne, C., Clément De Cléty, S. (2014) Self-requested euthanasia for children in Belgium, *The Lancet*. 383 (9918). pp. 671–672.

Durkheim, E. (1897) [1952] *Suicide: a study in sociology*. London: Routledge and Kegan Paul.

French National Assembly (2015) *Société: nouveaux droits en faveur des personnes en fin de vie [Society: new rights in favor of the people at the end of life]*. Available from: www.assemblee-nationale.fr/14/dossiers/nouveaux_droits_personnes_fin_vie.asp. [Accessed: 20th May 2015].

French National Observatory On end of life care (2011) *Fin de vie: un premier état des lieux [End of life: a first report]*. Available from: www.onfv.org/wp-content/uploads/2014/10/Rapport_ONFV_2011.pdf.

Gamondi, C., Borasio, G. D., Limoni, C., Preston, N., Payne, S. (2014) Legalisation of assisted suicide: a safeguard to euthanasia? *The Lancet*. 384 (9938). p. 127.

Gauthier, S., Mausbach, J., Reisch, T., Bartsch, C. (2014) Suicide tourism: a pilot study on the Swiss phenomenon, *Journal of Medical Ethics*. Published online August 20, 2014, doi: 10.1136/medethics-2014-102091.

Jonsen, A.R., Siegler, M. and Winslade, W. J. (2002) *Clinical ethics: a practical approach to ethical decisions in clinical medicine*. 5th Ed. New York: McGraw-Hill.

Mallet, D. and Jacquemin, D. (2013) Le rapport Sicard: une étape au milieu du gué [The Sicard report: a midstream stage], *Revue d'éthique et de théologie morale [Journal of Ehics and Moral Theology]*. (274). pp. 53–90.

Marchesini, S. M. (2012) Le suicide assisté: la nouvelle 'peine de mort' induite par la société contemporaine? Une analyse à la frontière entre droit et psychanalyse [Assisted suicide: the new 'death penalty' induced by the contemporaneous society? An analysis at the frontier between law and psychoanalysis], *Études sur la mort [Death Studies]* (141). pp. 37–53.

Onwuteaka-Philipsen, B., Brinkman-Stoppelenburg, A., Penning, C., de Jong-krul, G., van Delden, J., van der Heide, A. (2012) Trends in end-of-life practices before and after the enactment of the euthanasia law in the Netherlands from 1990 to 2010: a repeated cross-sectional survey. *The Lancet*. 380 (9845). pp. 908–915.

Ricoeur, P. (1992) *Oneself as another*. Chicago: University of Chicago Press.

Ricoeur, P. (2001) *Le juste II [The Just II]*. Paris: Éd. Esprit.

Schumann, J. H. and Alfandre, D. (2008) Clinical ethical decision making: the four topics approach. *Seminars in Medical Practice*. (11). pp. 36–42.

Sicard, D. (2012) *Penser solidairement la fin de vie [Thinking of the end-of-life in terms of solidarity]*. Report to François Holland, President of the French Republic, by the Commission on reflection on the End-of-Life in France. Available from: www.elysee.fr/assets/pdf/Rapport-de-la-commission-de-reflexion-sur-la-fin-devie-en-France.pdf.

Steck, N., Egger, M., Maesen, M., Reisch, T., Zwahlen, M. (2013) Euthanasia and Assisted Suicide in Selected European Countries and US States: Systematic Literature Review. *Medical Care*. 51 (10). pp. 938–944.

World Health Organization. Preamble to the Constitution of the WHO as adopted by the International Health Conference, New York, June 19–22, 1946; signed on July 22, 1946 by the representatives of 61 States. Official Records of the World Health Organization, no. 2, p. 100 and entered into force on April 7, 1948.

13 Dispatches from the dying

Pathographies as a lens on consumption *in extremis*

Darach Turley and Stephanie O'Donohoe

Introduction

For Bury (2001:264), 'universal, cultural and individual levels of human existence are tied together with narrative threads'. Consumer researchers have long acknowledged this, drawing consumption stories from interviews, comics and novels, and personal introspection (Belk 1987; Brown 1995; Gould 1991).

For all their salience in everyday life, stories acquire particular urgency *in extremis*. Serious illness and impending death are common yet extraordinary circumstances that cause physical and emotional havoc, trailing 'narrative wreckage' (Frank 1995) in their wake. Individuals experiencing such adversity 'often feel a pressing need to re-examine and re-fashion their personal narratives' (Bury 2001: 264). Telling stories of illness and loss, Frank suggests, is a way of reclaiming agency, transforming fate into experience, and crystallising or rebuilding disrupted identity projects.

Many such stories are crafted in conversation, and the consumer research literature has been enriched by studies drawing on interview accounts with people facing serious, life-limiting or life-threatening illness (Kates 2001; Pavia and Mason 2005; Botti *et al.* 2009; Dunnett *et al.* 2011; Tian *et al.* 2014). Prior to undertaking interviews with women about breast cancer, Pavia and Mason (2004) read published memoirs as they sought to orient themselves to this sensitive topic. In this chapter, memoirs of illness and dying move from this supportive, orienting, role to centre stage, just as they appear to have done in the publishing industry.

Pathographies are a form of popular culture, a genre of autobiographical literature describing an author's experiences in facing or witnessing serious or terminal illness, or grieving for the loss of a loved one (Hawkins 1999). For all the debate about the extent to which modern society is death-denying (Aries 1981; Walter 1991), there appears to be considerable consumer demand for musings on mortality; Lane (2000) notes that '[t]he death memoir was the cultural and publishing sensation of the past decade'. Challenging views of death as taboo in Western culture, O'Neill (2012) asks '...how many times does a taboo have to be broken before we stop calling it a taboo?

Because writing about one's own malady, especially if it's cancer, is actually pretty commonplace these days'. O'Neill (2012) attributes the contemporary popularity of pathographies to a morbid, disease-obsessed and titillation-seeking culture; others attribute it to more profound reader concerns and point to hundreds of letters thanking authors for the consolation or inspiration of their words and for sharing their own stories of illness, dying and loss (Small 1998; Armstrong-Coster 2012; Berman 2012).

Illness narratives not only offer accounts of how disease affects individual lives; they may also offer important insights into 'the links between identity, experience and "late modern" cultures' (Bury 2001). Such links are central to the consumer culture theory agenda (Arnould and Thompson 2005). Clearly, the authors of pathographies do not set out to foreground consumption issues. Nonetheless, we suggest that deep and detailed accounts of serious or terminal illness, particularly when furnished by accomplished writers, offer a powerful lens for examining the role of consumption and consumer culture *in extremis* – how consumers in distressing circumstances use an array of goods and services in their struggle to make sense of illness and loss. As extended, uninterrupted, narratives of illness trajectories, these accounts also minimise the risk of researcher-led fragmentation (Gilbert 2002).

In this chapter, we highlight the contribution of pathographies to understandings of consumption *in extremis*, using as exemplars two influential cancer memoirs written by British journalists. We suggest that these authors' journalistic training, coupled with the heightened sensitivity bestowed on them by illness and decline, suffuse their memoirs with deep insights into the interplay between markets and mortality.

A pathographical lens on mortality and the marketplace

1998 saw the publication of two books that began as newspaper columns by well-established, popular, British journalists documenting their responses to progressively more pessimistic cancer diagnoses. Offering insights into lives lived in the knowledge of possible and then certain impending death, their devastating accounts are leavened with wit and gallows humor. Ruth Picardie's *Before I Say Goodbye* (1998), published posthumously, incorporates her seven eponymous newspaper columns documenting the ten months before she died at age 33; her breast cancer, initially misdiagnosed (Boseley 2011), spread to her liver, lungs and brain despite several rounds of chemotherapy. It also includes email correspondence between Picardie and a small group of friends, postscripts from her husband and sister, and a selection of letters from readers of her column. John Diamond's *C: Because Cowards Get Cancer Too* (1998) bears witness to a throat cancer diagnosis in his mid-forties, leading to chemotherapy, radiotherapy and surgery that cost him his tongue, his voicebox, and his broadcasting career as his prognosis plummeted from a 92 per cent chance of survival to imminent death. Occasionally incorporating extracts from his newspaper columns, Diamond offers a more detailed, sole-authored account of declining health than does Picardie.

The publication of these two books was the point where 'cancer commentary took off' in Britain (O'Neill 2012). Indeed, journalism professor, former newspaper editor and colleague of Diamond, Roy Greenslade (2011), argues that '[t]heir work, and the resulting publicity that it generated, was praised by doctors and resulted in enormous, and positive, feedback from the public'. As discussed below, many of the experiences recounted by Picardie and Diamond were inextricably linked to the marketplace. Some of their stories resonate with Pavia and Mason's (2005) account of consumers *with* cancer, but others were written as consumers *of* cancer treatment.

Consuming treatment: contrasting paths through the healthcare system

Both Picardie and Diamond found themselves navigating the UK healthcare system, four-fifths of which is run under the auspices of the NHS, the world's largest publicly funded health service (Nuffield Foundation 2014). NHS treatment is, with few exceptions, offered free at the point of use to all permanent UK residents (NHS 2013). It coexists with a private healthcare system which is generally accessed by individuals through private health insurance schemes, although individuals may pay directly for particular consultations or treatments. In practice, the relationship between public and private health provision is complex, with personnel, equipment and buildings often shared between the two systems.

Although both Picardie and Diamond were writing around the same time and in the same metropolis (London), they present us with contrasting health-consumption profiles as each author took a different path through the UK healthcare system. In market positioning terms, the profiles of our two authors could be plotted on the twin axes of public versus private healthcare, and orthodox versus alternative medical regimes.

John Diamond remains resolutely in the orthodox/private quadrant for most of his book. His distaste for all things complementary was due primarily to his conviction that, in scientific terms, they simply do not stand up, a conviction reinforced by a brief and futile dalliance with an alternative practitioner as a 30-something bon-vivant suffering the effects of excessive tobacco and junk food intake. Electricity-disrupting allergens were prescribed on the basis of tests which Diamond identified as fundamentally flawed. By the time he comes to write his memoir, he is in his mid-forties, diagnosed with throat cancer and pinning his hoped-for bodily survival unapologetically to the mast of orthodox medicine. His stance on alternative medicine at this point is 'roughly where the Pope stands on getting drunk on the communion wine and pulling a couple of nuns' (p. 98).

Diamond's choice of private over public healthcare system seems to have been a matter of pragmatism over principle. He recounts that his father's 'political puritanism didn't quite approve of individual home ownership', so regardless of his parents' professional occupations, 'I and both my brothers were born on council estates[1] and lived in them until we were teenagers' (p. 47). Despite enjoying a successful media career and marrying into a wealthy and well-connected family, Diamond retained a sense of solidarity with working class communities. He had seen his father wait two years for an angiogram with the National Health Service before paying for it privately. On the day his father paid up, Diamond took out BUPA (private health) insurance for himself. The trajectory of his book is one of an ambivalent private patient dealing with an array of consultants, surgeons, therapists and nurses as a paid-up BUPA member. This is a world where dropping consultants' names is the stuff of health consumption entrées and social capital. One of the notable features of 'going private' for him is that this system shrouds the whole process of disease and dying with the architectural, sartorial and decorative veneer of non-medicalised everyday life. Consultants sport pin-striped suits, medics wear 'Calvin Klein lab coats' and nurses pose in air-hostess uniforms. Hospital room fittings and ersatz framed posters remind him of a hotel chain. Specialists show a practiced ability to dissemble, mollifying clients by pasteurising their 'rooms' of any distasteful or disturbing contaminants. Surgeries morph into sitting rooms or studies:

> God forbid that a Harley Street consulting room should look like a doctor's office; they are laid out as old-fashioned drawing rooms or studies: a leather-topped oak desk, a couple of button-back chairs, some anodyne reproduction paintings … And there in the corner, hiding away, will be a tray full of stainless-steel specula or a discreet X-ray light box or a tasteful little ultrasound machine, as often or not stored behind doors in the way they store TV sets in the Home Counties.
>
> (p. 20)

The suppression and shrouding of medical cues may be interpreted as material support for the death denial thesis, but there may be a simpler, market-driven explanation: many surgeons and consultants work in both private and public clinics, so the fees charged to private patients cannot be justified by expertise alone. Framing private medical treatment as an elite, discreet professional service recasts patients as discerning clients who 'get what they pay for'.

In any case, Diamond submits to this dissembling and domesticated mise-en-scène in return for prompt access to the world of 'I need it now' medical ministration. He admits to harbouring lingering reservations about it, especially 'if anything went wrong', since in his view private institutions come 'second best in extremis'. Occasionally, he finds himself back in the public health domain, highlighting the tensions involved for patients who straddle or indeed cross the delicate fault lines between both health provision sectors. One evening, for example, he found himself – a private patient – in a public ward in St. George's hospital, having waited all day to be admitted for the removal of a cyst. Reflecting on his irate interaction with a staff nurse, he notes:

> ...I feel so crass doing the 'What the hell do I pay BUPA all that money for if I can't have a room to myself' shtick in front of a row of patients who have probably been hanging around for months on waiting lists hoping to get a bed in the NHS lottery. But anger overcame crassness...
>
> (Diamond 1998: 30)

In contrast to the studied argumentation of Diamond's discourses on medics and medicine, Picardie's allusions to her illness and symptoms tend to be brief and often brutal. By the time she came to write the first e-mail reproduced in her book, she was already receiving chemotherapy for breast cancer, misdiagnosed two years previously (Boseley 2011). So, a somewhat jaundiced view of orthodox medicine is hardly surprising, as is her openness to complementary alternatives. From the outset she leaves both friends and readers in no doubt that she is 'going public'. Over time, however, a sizeable portion of the savings accruing from this principled stand is spent on alternative therapies. Far from being an unquestioning evangelical devotee, Picardie acknowledges that heterodox regimes boast their fair share of quackery, snake-oil peddlers, and 'money grabbing wankers'. Her descriptions of encounters with alternative practitioners and their adherents are shot through with humour, wry scepticism, irreverence, and fulsome admissions that she's 'clutching at straws', admissions that beg the question of why she engaged with this collection of complementary purveyors for so long. Patronage of particular complementary therapies is fickle and promiscuous, with new options shared by word of mouth among her circle of friends. Her investment in these alternative alternatives seems predicated primarily on the belief that she owes it to herself, and those she loves (including her toddler twins) to at least give them a try.

> I started in October by visiting a so-called complementary guru whom I'm sure won't mind being called Dr Charlatan (his swish London clinic closed down overnight; he has now disappeared). First, he got me on the aforementioned supplements ... plus a £275 drink called Yeastone which filled up half the fridge. Then he got my blood analysed by a German professor who advised me that refined sugar was poison and urged me to go on a complicated diet (vinegar bad, trout good, three-day-old eggs best of all). Finally, he got me hooked up with a computer expert-cum-homeopath for a course of 'Bicom' therapy which meant being wired up to a laptop which positively recharged my cells. All this may sound ridiculous; but when the hospital baldies have told you, aridly, that such-and-such treatment only has a '50:50 survival benefit', you desperately want to lengthen the odds ... the desperate hope of a girl with cancer knows no bounds.
>
> (p. 76)

Here Picardie rides a roller coaster of complementary therapies, reflexively aware how absurd it all sounds and yet asking her readers to understand why, given the shoddy treatment and sober prognosis she had received from oncologists, she could hardly have done otherwise. Indeed, as de Mello and Mac-Innis (2005) note, having hope can be a goal in itself and even a coping mechanism, since it uplifts and energises. Furthermore, 'the marketplace affords customers myriad ways to buy and have hope' (p. 49). In Picardie's case, when particular marketplace offerings failed her, the possibility that the next one might not sustained her through bleak times. Ultimately however she was left with the bitter sense that her desperate need to hope had been exploited.

The ambivalence of patient empowerment

Although both authors differ on the optimal health-provision and therapeutic approaches for cancer, they have much in common. Both are unashamed denizens of the risk society (Giddens 1999; Lupton 1997; Giesler and Veresiu 2014), refusing to be cowed when confronted with professional pomposity or the foibles and fallibilities of medics. They seek to exert personal agency in the diagnosis, understanding, and management of their respective conditions. In Diamond's case this goes as far as acknowledging quite openly that his smoking had been tantamount to playing Russian roulette with his immune system. Sharing a passion to know exactly what was going on, both authors saw the internet as a wellspring of information and empowerment for those living with cancer.

A related motif for both authors is a studied reliance on self-diagnosis and a resolve to ensure that they listened as carefully to their own bodies as they did to the medics. This is particularly pronounced in Picardie's case, as she recounts numerous 'I told you so' incidents. Indeed, her husband, Matt describes 'a pattern in which she always knew the bad news before the hospital tests confirmed it' (p. 105). At one stage Diamond receives an official all-clear, but, whenever he is asked if he still has cancer admits presciently: 'I feel as if I ought to say that I haven't because the truth is that there is no cancer anyone can find. But when it comes to saying the words, I can't do it. I hedge, and fudge, and bluster' (p. 238).

As Lupton (1997: 374) notes, the increasingly popular notion of 'the patient qua consumer', like that of the reflexive actor, assumes an individual who is 'actively calculating, assessing and, if necessary, countering expert knowledge and autonomy with the objective of maximizing the value of services such as health care'. Dunnett *et al.* (2011) document how a multiple myeloma support group enabled its members to reclaim a degree of agency and become skilled healthcare consumers. Indeed, Giesler and Veresiu (2014: 841–2) refer to a process of 'consumer responsibilization' through which consumers 'are reconstructed as free, autonomous, rational, and entrepreneurial subjects who draw on individual market choices to invest in their own human capital…' in contexts including healthcare decisions. Various sociological studies highlight the interpersonal complexities of health encounters as well as the 'tensions, ambivalences and contradictions' that are often involved (Lupton 1997). Indeed, when parents confronted tragic end-of-life decisions in neonatal intensive care units, those who were 'empowered' to make the choice themselves appeared to suffer more than those who saw medical staff decide to withdraw life support (Botti *et al.* 2009). These issues are foregrounded in our two pathographies.

The internet's democratic and egalitarian ethos lends itself to untrammelled expression, leading Diamond to view it as the site where the battle lines between traditional and heterodox treatments are most vividly evidenced. The more he browsed, the more he became aware of a vast corpus of scientific research studies on cancer outcomes and, although he was unable to adjudge their relative merit, their collective import for his survival odds was somber and 'really scaring'.

The tensions and ambivalence of a 'consumerist' stance (Lupton 1997) are evident in other parts of Diamond's account. Having made rational choices about orthodox, private medicine, he acknowledges that this requires him to compromise on both comprehension and control over his condition, in contrast to the sense of empowerment afforded the alternative aficionado:

> How much better it would be if I could do something for myself … which would allow me to take control of my cancer. How wonderful it would be to decide for myself which of the dozens of equally valid remedies from around the world was most suitable for my personality, my cancer, my birth sign.
>
> (p. 104)

Picardie also alludes to the 'dark side of empowerment' in medical contexts (Dunnett *et al.* 2011). For those who lack the requisite physical and emotional stamina, empowered consumer health choice can prove a burden rather than a bonus. At the outset of her treatment, she emails a friend who is also seriously ill:

> Like you say, the fact that you have done so much research and are making treatment decisions must make you feel good. Have yet to get a web browser and find breast cancer site. Part of me is so exhausted by all the appointments and X-rays and tears that I want to switch off from the subject completely.
>
> (p. 7)

Nonetheless, she finds herself having to be on guard, alert to the options and obtaining second opinions. Comparing what she knows about chemotherapy regimes at two hospitals, she notes the Marsden reviews treatment after four cycles, 'whereas Guy's seem to let you suffer for the whole whack, regardless of efficacy, unless you take control' (p. 7). Concerns about secondary bone cancer lead her to 'shop around', but 'The Marsden pretty much said what Guy's said, so I won't be transferring there' (p. 9).

Confronting cancer: contested control

Both authors are at pains to confront their condition by putting a tolerable distance between them and their cancer. The very process of penning a pathography can be viewed as such an enterprise (Hawkins 1999). Both texts are replete with accounts documenting the size, location and progression of the authors' respective tumours and cancer cells. That these well-informed accounts are couched in conversational terms underscores how normalisation can serve as a means of control and empowerment. Diamond's narrative includes particularly vivid examples of exerting control through objectification and externalisation. In one instance he asks his radiotherapist for a slide of sections of his cancer and brings a radiotherapy mask home as a souvenir. Later, in an equally fetishistic vein, he uploads as a screen-saver a photograph of a squamous cell cancer of the neck. Finally, given his experience in broadcasting, he agrees to making a documentary for the BBC featuring his undergoing and recuperating from major surgery – all in the hope 'that by rendering the cancer an objective spectacle I could distance myself from it' (p. 214).

The contestation for control between cancer and patient is played out in several additional arenas in both books. On some occasions the pendulum swings in cancer's favor as when Diamond finds himself in a hospital waiting room and comes face to face with a plethora of momento mori: leaflets on how to register a death, contact details for religious ministers when death is imminent. These sober reminders were disconcerting enough without his being further ambushed by a barrage of glossy magazine headlines: an article on weekend breaks titled 'When you've got to go GO'. Other headlines leap out of pieces on the mundanities of travel, cooking and wine: 'A GRAVE SOLUTION, NO HOPE OF RETURN, HEAVEN CAN'T WAIT' (31). When it came to double entendres, the darker side seemed to win out every time.

If cancer commands attention and colours perception in this way it can also impose itself on the individual in more tangible and explicit ways. Daily routine in both narratives becomes dominated by rosters of consultations with medics, dosage regimes for medication, and dates of hospital appointments and discharges. 'My whole life seems to have been taken over by illness', complains Picardie before detailing her diary for the following week; Thursday is her only day off. Cancer also exercises control by imposing itself on their physical surroundings and both authors proffer multiple lists of pharmaceutical prescriptions, patient paraphernalia and cancer accoutrements, goods that are increasingly populating and dominating their personal living space. Diamond hammers home this point by devoting over three pages of his book to rattling off a litany of his 'latest collection of cancer victim takeaway gear'. At one level such exhaustive inventories betoken consumers essaying to manage their illness by auditing what exactly is going on, at another they mirror in external matter the physical progression of the cancer within.

Keeping cancer at bay?

One notable feature of both books is the juxtaposition of harrowing detail and what might appear banal consumption-related stories. This may reflect the role of everyday consumption in keeping those facing serious illness woven into the fabric of everyday life (Mason and Pavia 2005). Indeed, when a friend worries that she should purge her messages of such things, Picardie emails 'PLEASE keep the so-called trivia coming: the last thing I want to do is spend 23 (instead of 22) hours a day thinking about cancer' (p. 17). Picardies' entreaty epitomises the resolve on the part of both authors to resist any diminution in their roles as parents, partners, and friends and to restate their enfranchisement and empowerment as consumers.

Over the course of her book, Picardie loses much of her hair; initially she asks her friends to send her hats, and makes multiple hairdresser appointments, first to cut her hair into a manageable bob, and then, once clumps start falling out, to have her head shaved. Weight gain from treatment and her response to that treatment are constant themes in Picardie's book; she impishly ascribes the extra weight to eating opportunities such as the chocolate biscuits at the cancer support group and the sandwiches consumed to kill time in hospital. She accommodates to her expanding girth by entering into 'fashion bimbo' mode:

> ...yesterday bought pair of linen trousers (elasticated waist) and linen shirt from Hobbs (my new favourite shop, though size 16 jacket was too tight) and new pair of (brown, three strap) Birkenstocks. What is happening to me? But it is such good therapy.
>
> (p. 26)

Diamond, on the other hand, loses a considerable amount of weight. He too decides to take action. On finding that most of his clothes were now two sizes too large, he chooses not to behave as men are supposedly wont to behave; he purchases a £299 leather jacket on impulse on his way home from a hospital appointment.

> What sort of world was this where a man with cancer couldn't buy himself a leather jacket?... It was bad enough that I had cancer without having to have cancer and be dressed in clothes two sizes too big. And, what the hell, we could pay the Amex bill next month.
>
> (p. 118)

Both refer to being cheered by what Picardie labels 'retail therapy'; indeed both report some delight in making various purchases which in their 'normal' lives they would have considered extravagant or excessive. There may have been more than a momentary psychological fillip at play here, however. Accommodating to physical increments or decrements by changing one's wardrobe, by not throwing in the towel, can be seen as an instance of turning a physical loss into a psychological and morale gain. Refusing to continue wearing ill-fitting clothes can thus represent an attempt to neutralise at a sartorial level what cancer was doing to their appearance at a physical level. It may also be read as an act of defiance, following the poet Dylan Thomas's command to '[r]age, rage, at the dying of the light'.

Other consumption accounts suggested however a more measured, gentle going into Thomas's dark night. Pavia and Mason (2004) refer to 'green banana' syndrome among cancer sufferers, reflecting a degree of anxiety about tempting fate by investing in products that presume a longer lifespan than they might be granted. Towards the end of both these books, however, the authors *know* their fate is sealed and goods have more to do with the duration and tone of time remaining than any hope of recovery. Picardie muses whether her jar of face cream will see her through to the end and Diamond's last words in his book refer to acceptance of impending death rendered through an act of consumption:

> As I write this we have just returned from buying a basket for the spaniel we are due to collect in a couple of days time. A friend e-mailed me when she heard this to tell me about how it's a denial of what's happening and what's about to happen. It isn't at all: I know what's happening. But a dog is a happy thing, and it will be happy for me for whatever time I've got left and as happy as things can be for the family when I've gone.
>
> (p. 256)

Conclusion

Accounts of dying date back to the medieval and Renaissance eras, when the Church sought to instruct the faithful into the ways of a good death, drawing on examples of those who departed this world in a state of grace (Hawkins 1999). The two pathographies featured here are devoid of spiritual searching or metaphysical musing. Nonetheless, they support Berman's (2012: 295) argument that in our contemporary consumer culture, end-of-life memoirs constitute 'a secular example of the long tradition of *ars moriendi*, the art of dying', offering readers opportunities to learn from others' experiences so that they feel less isolated and afraid. Clearly, in a crowded market not all pathographies will be written in such a way as to strike a responsive chord with readers confronting illness, mortality or bereavement, but many do reach heady heights in both literary and humane terms.

Perhaps one of the most striking insights offered by Diamond and Picardie is that dying well entails sustaining as good a life as possible, for as long as possible, and that consumption is intimately interwoven into the fabric of that life. Their accounts show two people going about their business, engaging with the marketplace as consumers of cancer care and consumers with cancer, and they illuminate for readers the light, shade and even the routine involved in performing both roles, the many tensions involved, and the ambivalence of agency in medical extremis.

The detailed, granular accounts provided in pathographies may be particularly valuable for future cross-cultural studies of healthcare consumption. This literary genre may also lend itself well to analyses of consumer experiences in the course of particular illnesses or traumatic events, or of how illness or bereavement have been experienced within consumer culture in different eras or for different groups of consumers. Overall, there seems to be a great deal of analytical life remaining in this literary genre devoted to illness, dying and death.

Note

1 As tenants in public housing schemes.

References

Aries, P. (1981) *The Hour of our Death*, New York, Oxford University Press, trans. H. Weaver.

Arnould, E. and Thompson, C. (2005) Consumer culture theory (CCT): twenty years of research, *Journal of Consumer Research*, 31:4, 868–82.

Armstrong-Coster, A. (2005) In morte media jubilante [2]: a study of cancer-related pathographies, *Mortality*, 10:2, 97–112.

Belk, R. (1987) Material values in the comics: a content analysis of comic books featuring themes of wealth, *Journal of Consumer Research*, 14:1, 26–42.

Berman, J. (2012) *Dying in Character: Memoirs on the End of Life*, Amherst, MA, and Boston, MA: University of Massachusetts Press.

Boseley, S. (2011) Surgeon who missed Ruth Picardie breast cancer struck off by GMC, *The Guardian*, December 30, www.theguardian.com/society/2011/dec/30/ruth-picardie-cancer-doctor-struck-off.

Botti, S., Orfali, K. and Iyengar, S. (2009), Tragic choices: autonomy and emotional responses to medical decisions, *Journal of Consumer Research*, 36, 337–53.

Brown, S. Sex 'n' shopping: a 'novel' approach to consumer research (1995). *Journal of Marketing Management*, 11, 769–83.

Bury, M. (2001) Illness narratives: fact or fiction? *Sociology of Health and Illness*, 23:3, 263–85.

de Mello, G. and MacInnis, D. (2005) Why and how consumers hope: motivated reasoning and the marketplace, in S. Ratneshwar and D.G. Mick (eds), *Inside Consumption: Consumer Motives, Goals and Desires*, London and New York: Routledge, 44–66.

Diamond, J. (1998) *C: Because Cowards Get Cancer Too*, London: Vermillion.

Dunnett, S., Brownlie, D. and Hewer, P. (2011) From patient to agent: collective practices and identity work in an emotional community, in D. Dahl, G. Johar, and S. van Osselaer (eds), *Advances in Consumer Research*, Volume 38, Duluth, MN: Association for Consumer Research, 26–7.

Frank, A. (1995) *The Wounded Storyteller: Body, Illness and Ethics*, Chicago: University of Chicago Press.

Giddens, Anthony (1999) Risk and responsibility, *Modern Law Review*, 62:1, 1–10.

Giesler, M. and Veresiu, E. (2014) Creating the responsible consumer: moralistic governance regimes and consumer subjectivity, *Journal of Consumer Research*, 41:3, 840–57.

Gilbert, Kathleen R. (2002) Taking a narrative approach to grief research: finding meaning in stories, *Death Studies*, 26: 223–39.

Gould, S.J. (1991) The self-manipulation of my pervasive, perceived vital energy through product use: an introspective-praxis perspective, *Journal of Consumer Research* 18:2, 194–207. DOI: 10.1086/209252.

Hawkins, A. (1999) *Reconstructing Illness: Studies in Pathography*, West Lafayette, IN: University of Purdue Press.

Kates, S. (2001) The disposition of possessions among the 'chosen' families of people living with AIDS, *Psychology and Marketing*, 18:4, 365–87.

Lane, H. (2000) Two funerals and a book deal, *The Observer*, February 13, www.the-guardian.com/books/2000/feb/13/biography.harrietlane.

Lupton, D. (1997) Consumerism, reflexivity, and the medical encounter, *Social Science and Medicine*, 45:3, 373–81.

NHS (2013) About the National Health Service (NHS), www.nhs.uk/NHSEngland/thenhs/about/Pages/overview.aspx.

Nuffield Trust (2014) UK spending on public and private health care, www.nuffield-trust.org.uk/data-and-charts/uk-spending-public-and-private-health-care.

O'Neill, B. (2012) Cancer memoirs are growing like, well, tumours, *VICE*, 13 September 2012 http://brendanoneill.co.uk/post/31449632613/cancer-memoirs-are-growing-like-well-tumours.

Pavia, T. and Mason, M. (2004) The reflexive relationship between consumer behavior and adaptive coping, *Journal of Consumer Research*, 31, 441–54.

Picardie, R. (1998) *Before I Say Goodbye*, London: Penguin Books.

Small, N. (1998) Death of the authors, *Mortality*, 3:3, 215–28.

Tian, K., Sautter, D., Fisher, D., Fischbach, S., Luna-Nevarez, C., Boberg, K., Kroger, J. and Vann, R. (2014) Transforming health care: empowering therapeutic communities through technology-enhanced narratives, *Journal of Consumer Research*, 41:2, 237–60.

Thomas, D. (1952) 'Do not go gentle into that good night', in *The Poems of Dylan Thomas*, New Directions.

Walter, T. (1991) Modern death: taboo or not taboo?, *Sociology*, 25:2, 293–310.

Part IV

Death and the body

14 The role of body disposition in making sense of life and death

Courtney Nations Baker, Stacey Menzel Baker and James W. Gentry

Upon the loss of a loved one, individual and social sentiments often focus toward the body, ritual ceremonies may revolve around the body and decision making related to death-care consumption is affected by biological aspects of the body. Beyond making logistical decisions about the remains, bereaved loved ones must also somehow make sense of what it means to no longer have the physical presence of the deceased as part of their lives. Even after death, the body of the deceased passively experiences many additional sentiments. People touch it, talk to it, dress it, style it, display it, carry it, honour it and use symbolic items to represent it. Despite its passive contribution toward the observances, the body of the deceased often becomes the centerpiece of attention.

The bereaved must make pragmatic decisions about how to handle the physical remains. This has both practical and emotional aspects. Practically, the decomposition process begins rapidly, and a reality of death is that the body cannot be maintained permanently. Emotionally, the disposition may be imbued with meanings somehow related to the deceased individual. Whether practical or emotional, decisions about body disposition affect how those impacted by the death make sense of life and death.

The present research seeks to understand how individuals make sense of life and death in the context of disposition of the physical body. The chapter first reviews relevant literature on disposition and liminality. Next, the study context and methods are described. After we present four emergent themes from the data, we conclude with a discussion on the theoretical and practical implications of sense-making in the context of body disposition.

Theoretical background

Disposition

Disposition research focuses on tangible material objects that have outlived their functional or symbolic usefulness and that are voluntarily relinquished (Jacoby, Berning and Dietvorst, 1977); on objects that have been involuntarily surrendered, as in the case of theft or disaster (Sayre, 1994); on how objects impede or facilitate role transitions (McAlexander, 1991; Schouten, 1991); or on how families and groups of people make sense of possessions in the face of mortality (Bradford, 2009; Price, Arnould and Curasi, 2000). We know that in everyday life possessions have implications for self-definition and self-continuity/change (Kleine and Baker, 2004; Belk, 1988). We also know that possessions serve as a semiotic link between possessions and the memories of their owners, thus legitimizing consumers' past experiences (Grayson and Shulman, 2000). Therefore, because possessions may hold deep meanings, disposition of them can be difficult, or even impossible.

A distinct type of special possessions, those objects that people should not give away or sell but pass down through generations and keep within the group, is deemed inalienable wealth (Curasi, Price and Arnould, 2004). Specific qualities related to possessions considered as part of a family's inalienable wealth include the group's commitment to preserving them, the items' ability to affirm social order and reality, the creation and affirmation of inalienable wealth across generations, the development of myths surrounding heirlooms, the role of a guardian to protect and maintain the objects, the necessity that inalienable wealth remains in the family, and the fragility of these possessions (Curasi, Price and Arnould, 2004). Other important traits of inalienable wealth include possessions' influence on kin keeping, the maintenance of these assets, the ability of objects to transition from alienable to inalienable, and the coexistence of inalienable and alienable wealth (Bradford, 2009).

To this point, disposition literature has remained largely silent on the disposal of deceased persons. Yet, the literature on disposition and special possessions provides a theoretical foundation from which to explore how people make sense of the body after death. The body becomes a tangible vessel, no longer full of life and, metaphorically, a special object which requires disposition. A theoretical vantage point from which to view how people make sense of the body as it transitions from full-of-life to lifeless also is needed. This perspective is afforded through sociological theory on role transitions and liminality, reviewed next.

Role transitions, liminality and identity negotiation

The transition from life to death can be described as a rite of passage (Turner, 1969; Van Gennep, 1909), in which an individual or group experiences a progression through the stages of separation, liminality and reintegration (Van Gennep, 1909). Separation, a response to crisis, is the distancing of the individual or group from usual activities, relations and conditions. Crisis occurs with a change in place, state, social position or age. Liminality is the suspension of notions regarding identity, time, and space, and often is described as 'betwixt and between.' Finally, reintegration occurs when the individual or group is somehow reincorporated back into social participation (Van Gennep, 1909).

In the present case, death is the crisis. Because the deceased can no longer participate actively in the social interactions associated with life, a tangible separation occurs. The deceased experiences a change in status by transitioning from life to death, and the bereaved must separate from a life in which the lost loved one had a physical presence. Liminality is present for the bereaved as they try to make sense of the past identity and the present state of the deceased, as well as what death means for all their lives (Gentry *et al.*, 1995a). The bereaved must construct and understand what role the deceased plays in their new lives void of the deceased's physical presence, which eventually leads to a reintegration of the deceased into the current social world of those left behind.

Crises, life transitions, and rites of passage demand the reconstitution of identities and roles. During a life transition, individuals may engage in identity play or reconstruction of self-concepts (Schouten, 1991). In this chapter, we explore the value of tangible, physical remains in helping people make sense of the deceased's life and death. We now turn to the method we use to understand how people make sense of body disposition, beginning with a description of the study context.

Method

Study context

The study context is death-care services in the U.S., where, in recent years, new products and services related to body disposition have emerged. Current trends in funeral services include the rising popularity of cremation, personalization, advanced funeral planning, new technologies enabling new services, and green funerals (National Funeral Directors Association, 2013). Beyond this, the national cremation rate was at 9.7 per cent in 1980, 24 per cent in 1998, 42 per cent in 2011, and is projected to hit 50 per cent by 2017 (Sanburn, 2013). These figures suggest a momentous shift in the way Americans understand and handle body disposition.

Data collection

To gain insights into how consumers make sense of body disposition, phenomenological interviews and projective techniques (Belk, Fischer and Kozinets, 2013) were employed. Twenty-three interviews with 24 individuals were conducted, including 12 consumers who had planned funeral and burial services for their own future needs and 12 consumers who had planned these services for a deceased loved one. These individuals hailed from 16 different states and ranged from 37 to 78 in age. Twenty participants were female, and four were male. Participants identified with 12 different religious or non-religious organizations or sentiments, including referencing themselves as spiritual, Catholic, non-practicing Catholic, Jewish, Buddhist, Unitarian, non-religious and a variety of Protestant faiths.

Two alternative burial service providers, Eternal Reefs and Memorial Ecosystems, assisted in the recruitment of participants. The first provider, Eternal

Reefs, allows consumers to have their cremated remains mixed with PH-neutral concrete in order to form reef balls that mimic natural reef formations and become part of the ecosystem at the bottom of the ocean. The second provider, Memorial Ecosystems, provides consumers the option to be buried naturally into a hand-dug grave with no embalming fluids, no synthetic caskets or vaults, no artificial flowers, and no unnatural tombstones. These two body disposition alternatives were chosen because they provided contrasts to more traditional funeral service providers, and were different from each other in significant ways (e.g. body disposition, ritual processes). Often, valuable insights can be gleaned from exploring extreme cases (Price, Arnould and Moisio 2006).

Participants were chosen because of their valuable insights into both the traditional and the newer alternative types of disposition methods. Due to the sensitive nature of the subject, potential informants were provided with the contact information of the first author so they could initiate communication to participate if desired. Contact information was given to potential participants via a provider Facebook page, a provider newsletter, and personal contact by the provider with its customers. For those who had lost a loved one, at least three months' time had passed between the death and the interview (Gentry *et al.*, 1995a,b).

Each interview lasted between 60 and 90 minutes. Interviews included questions related to personal funerary experiences, end-of-life preferences, decision-making processes, funerary expenses and personal values. An interview guide was employed, but a conversation-style approach allowed participants to share their stories and approach subjects as they felt comfortable doing so (Schouten, 1991). The first author developed rapport via email conversations and during initial interview questions related to personal background. This was a crucial step, especially since interviews were conducted via Skype or telephone. All interviews were recorded and transcribed verbatim for analysis purposes. In addition to completing an interview, some interview participants shared photos, memorial webpages, and other resources, which have been retained by the research team. Interview participation was voluntary, and no informants received payment for their participation.

Data analysis

Data analysis took place throughout data collection with iterations between the data and the relevant literature streams (Belk, Fischer and Kozinets, 2013). Interview files were reviewed and a close reading of transcripts took place. Themes within interviews were identified throughout the process, relationships between the themes were identified, and these connections were abstracted to relate to theory and practice. A list of ideas about emerging themes was maintained and updated after each interview. Handwritten notes during each interview allowed for insights into thematic relationships between interviews as more data were collected. The findings below seek to offer insights into how the physical body of a deceased person may influence the process of sense-making related to life and death for the living.

Making sense of the body in the context of death

Our interpretation of the data is structured around four major themes: inseparable notions of life and death, type of disposal as an expression of identity, physical remains as inalienable wealth, and viewing the body. We discuss each in turn.

Inseparable notions of life and death

Informants have difficulty separating notions of life from notions of death. This applied to both consumers who were discussing deceased loved ones and those who were projecting themselves into a future deceased state. In particular, many informants expressed aversion to being buried upon their deaths. These people could not seem to separate their ideas about physical occurrences that may happen to a dead body from their understandings about how those same occurrences might make them feel in life. One informant, who chose cremation, expressed concerns about his current claustrophobia:

> I guess a part of it is I'm claustrophobic, slightly claustrophobic. The thought of being eight feet under with all that earth on top of me is stressful. And the attraction to having ashes spread or having ashes interred in a reef, that's a very comforting thought.
>
> (Lloyd [male, 61])

This informant has experienced what it is like to feel a sensation of claustrophobia when he is in small spaces, so he is projecting his living ideas of claustrophobia onto his future deceased self.

Another facet of how individuals may be unable to separate life from death can be found in their continued interactions with their loved ones, even after they have passed. Many informants who had lost a loved one, discussed occasions on which they talked to the dead, wrote to the dead, and celebrated the birthday of the dead. These individuals know that they can no longer have physical interactions with their loved ones, but they feel they can continue to interact with them in more transcendental ways. These interactions facilitate the relationship between the bereaved and the deceased, despite the fact that physical interactions are no longer a part of their communication processes. One participant, whose mother was cremated, held on to her remains while trying to decide how best to dispose of them. In the meantime, she would talk to the remains:

> Mother's ashes were in my back closet that's in my office, and I'd walk by there every day, 'Hey girl! I'll take care of you this year [*laughter*]. The

right place is going to show up. I know the right thing is going to show up.' Well, this went on forever.

(Rita [female, 75])

It took a while for the right disposition option to come along, so this informant held on to these remains for 10 years. During that time she would speak to the box of remains as if her mother were sitting in that closet just waiting for interaction.

Finally, some participants felt that the deceased continue to have tangible influence in their lives. This seems to exist on a continuum. On one end, it could be participants having unique gut-feelings about the deceased somehow guiding them by showing them something. On the other end, informants have even expressed beliefs about the possibilities of spirits and ghosts.

When that happened, I said to my husband, 'You know, [our son] said he wanted to be buried at sea. That's not possible, so what we'll do is just have him cremated, and we'll spread his ashes out in the ocean.' So that's what we decided to do. And then I went online to look for a cremation urn, like a dolphin or something because he loved the water so much. And I typed in cremation urn, and the very first website that came up was Eternal Reefs. And I looked at it, and I'm like, 'Eternal Reefs? What is that? It doesn't sound like an urn company.' And I clicked on it, and as soon as I saw it, I knew it was [our son]. I even said out like, 'Oh my gosh, [son], I know you're letting me know this is what you want because you can't be buried at sea.'

(Olivia [female, 56])

This participant was unable to give her son the full-body burial at sea that he desired, but she believed her son led her to another option that would allow her to better fulfill his wishes.

Without a physical body, it seems that bereaved individuals must find ways to redirect their feelings toward the deceased. When people die, they cannot simply be detached from the lives of the bereaved in one fatal swoop. The deceased are only tangibly removed, and their memories, identities, and relationships with others live on. The living individuals who continue to interact with the deceased or feel specific influences from the deceased are finding ways to continue their relationships with the deceased in meaningful, intangible ways. This continuance of the relationship plays a critical role in the sense-making process.

Type of disposal as an expression of identity

As informants explained their disposition choices, they revealed that the type of disposal option they chose allows them to extend their identities beyond life. For example, the decision to use cremation, either for the self or for a loved one, allowed for unique expressions of self that might be impossible with a decision to have full-body burial. First, with cremation, remains can be divided so that it is not necessary for all remains to end up in the same location as a final resting place. The bereaved can share the remains by giving each family member a portion of the ashes. Cremated remains may be scattered in a single location or dispersed to numerous locations. Remains in this form can also be retained by loved ones within their homes, housed in a decorative urn or simple cardboard box. One informant shared how she was able to memorialize her husband in a special way, through scattering his remains in multiple meaningful locations:

> He died in October of 2010 and we did the Eternal Reefs ceremonies in January of 2012. Now in between that, we had scattered his ashes at several other places. In the week or so before he died, he and I talked about it quite a bit, and there were places where he knew he wanted to have his ashes … We agreed that they would be scattered on our favorite beach in Hawaii. And so, after his death, I took my son and two of our grandsons, and we went to Hawaii, and we scattered him there. And then another bunch of the kids and grandkids came to our place in Virginia, and we scattered him in Virginia. But the third place that we talked about that he wanted his ashes scattered was with Eternal Reefs … It was near Ft. Lauderdale, Florida … The fourth place is actually in Wisconsin, and that's going to happen in three weeks. Almost three years later, we're finally getting together in Wisconsin to scatter his ashes up there … He just loved Green Lake, Wisconsin.
>
> (Ulyssa [female, 66])

This quote demonstrates how much people relate to specific places and how powerful their connections to those places can be. Ulyssa scattered her husband's remains in four different locations, all of which had specific personal meanings in his life.

The option of cremation also has allowed for the development of creative new alternatives in disposition, such as the use of remains to create diamonds, fireworks, ammunition, synthetic reefs, hourglasses, and vinyl records. Of course, none of these are quite feasible with a fully intact body. Cremation also grants the ability to mix the cremated remains with other entities. With cremation, an individual may have their remains mixed with the remains of a loved one or pet so that they may spend eternity truly together.

The mixing of remains is not limited to people and pets, but it also extends to possessions. Meaningful objects may be placed within remains in their final container, or special objects may actually be used as the final container. Again, one might argue that loved ones may spend eternity together with side-by-side burial or that meaningful possessions may be placed in a casket with the full body, but the physical blending of these remains indicates self-extension (Belk, 1988), even after death. One participant describes how she was given a photo by her partner's mother to be placed with his remains:

But if you talked to him, he would have nothing but complaints about his mother, and he'd say she wasn't very nice to him ... and yet he called her every single week ... But his sister told me [his mother] was like wracked with guilt, that she was upset, and that she was crying. When I went to see her, she gave me a photo of him as a little boy and said, "Can you find a way to put this in with his ashes?" She said, "This is how I think of him when I think of him as my son."

(Shirley [female, 62])

In this case, cremation allowed for placing a symbolic photo into the man's remains in order to help his mother in her sense-making process. Some notions that may have been tied to that photo for his mother include guilt, memories, and a sense of contribution. While she may not have been as involved with his life or end-of-life ceremonies as she may have liked to have been, she was still able to contribute this old photo as a means of reaching some closure.

Finally, the act of choosing cremation may, in itself, have implications for expressing something about the individual. Some examples of this idea could be how the choice of alternative disposition relates to the frugality, spiritual beliefs or environmental conscientiousness of the deceased person. One participant shared how her choice to be cremated expresses her beliefs and gives insights into her faith:

Well, [my husband] and I are devout Catholics, and the church now has no objection for people being cremated, but they do not want people scattering their ashes. My plan had been to be taken out on a fishing boat and be dumped, but I'm not going to go against the church. So I found this Eternal Reefs, and that is the solution.... Like I said, I don't want to go against the Church's teachings, if they don't want your ashes scattered. And I think that's just disrespectful is how they figure it. Because, I mean, if I'm dumped in the Gulf and God wanted to put me back together again, I'm sure He could.

(Hanna [female, 64])

On one hand, Hanna wants to closely follow the teachings of the church, but on the other hand, she has faith that her God is capable of doing what He wants. So she opted for a compromise that allowed her to be cremated but also keep all of her remains together in one location.

In regards to body disposition, these informants are concerned with leaving life in a more personal and expressive way than traditional death services allow. Cremation, because of its unique characteristics, allowed the informants the desired freedom to dispose of their bodies in ways that are more representative of who they were in life and more consistent with their self-definitions and desire for continuity (Kleine and Baker, 2004). Because cremation allows remains to be divided, shared, scattered, retained and mixed with other entities, it affords informants more freedoms in their disposition methods and expressions. Cremation also allows people to become part of tangible objects. An avid hunter can be turned into ammunition that friends use for their next hunt, a lifelong musician can become a vinyl record that his children play to remember him, and a passionate scuba diver can become part of a reef that supports the marine life she loved. Cremation has created an opportunity for consumers to symbolically, or even literally, go out with a bang.

Physical remains as inalienable wealth

The physical remains, the final resting place, and others' lingering memories of a deceased person all have the potential to become a part of the family's inalienable wealth. For those who hold viewing and funeral services before the deceased is cremated or interred, the physical body is a part of the 'beautiful memory picture' (Slocum and Carlson, 2011). It is the family's last image of the deceased person, so death-care service providers work to make this a beautiful, or at least acceptable, image. Further, cremated remains may be retained in a container to be passed down from generation to generation, so that the deceased person continues to be part of their descendants' lives. This container, which would most likely be considered sacred, placed in a safe location, and maintained by the family, is a priceless heirloom that becomes part of the family's heritage. Remains interred into the ground could also be considered part of a family's inalienable wealth, despite the fact that they are not physically retained by the family. Occasionally an individual will be buried on family land, but more typical is an interment in a cemetery. Still, because the family has access to visit the site, and the physical grave has become part of the story of the family's history, these become part of the family's inalienable wealth.

The memories, stories and evidences of someone's existence in the past have implications for family and individual identity, meaning and legacy. Because remains, resting places, and memories play such critical roles in telling the story of a family and its history, these may be valued as priceless. In fact, in the U.S., the only mail service that will ship cremated remains from one location to another is the United States Postal Service (Cremation Association of North America, 2013). The fact that most providers of mail services will not even accept cremated remains for shipment speaks to the fact that people find it difficult or even impossible to put a price on human remains for insurance purposes.

The location at which physical remains are placed is also of value for some:

> When we scattered my dad's ashes, wherever we were in the ocean, his sister, my aunt, was very distressed. She's ninety-something now and a different generation, but she said, 'I just hate the fact that there's no grave for me to go and visit.' And I felt bad for her because she had not really

said that until it was way too late, and I felt bad for her because it meant so much to her to have a place to go and put flowers on the grave on Memorial Day or whatever. And that didn't mean anything to me.

(Ulyssa [female, 66])

While a site or location did not provide value for Ulyssa, she described how additional stress was added to her aunt's grieving process because of her inability to visit a physical site to memorialize her brother. Ulyssa believes the differences in burial site preference reflect generational differences; however, another participant, who was even younger than Ulyssa, seemed to also find value in a site or location, as Ulyssa's aunt had:

I have been the one who visits the graveyards, pulled the weeds, and brought flowers all these years. I wanted to respect my husband's wishes but in the same time give myself something to hold onto. That is my GPS coordinates. I have the satisfaction that he has an eternal resting place but not traditional in the ground. I have since then learned how to scuba dive to visit his final resting place. I am scheduled to dive it this summer.

(Gertrude [female, 55])

This respondent's husband really wanted to be returned to the sea because of his love for the ocean and his background in the Navy, which they both thought would mean scattering his cremated remains in the ocean. Still, Rita longed for a specific location to visit her husband if she so desired. She decided on a compromise by selecting a reef burial for him, which would allow him to return to the sea and give her a site to visit.

For some, a site may be more than just a place for them to visit. It may mean having a location for future generations to visit, especially those interested in family history:

I thought, 'You know something? What's the number one thing that helps genealogists? Tombstones!' I found one of my relatives the other day that lived in 1774, and his tombstone is still out there ... Well, it's priceless. It's just priceless.

(Rita [female, 75])

For this participant, who was interested in genealogy, it was important to have a physical gravesite for her mother that was beside her father's grave. Shirley selected to place her mother's cremated remains in a specific, marked location in addition to an alternative reef burial, despite the additional costs and efforts associated with having two different types of dispositions. Having a tombstone and site for her parents meant future generations would be able to trace the family story and see evidence that these people existed.

It is not uncommon for individuals to want to leave some sort of legacy to prove to the world that they existed. In fact, how disposition occurs may be a tool to 'live on' in some way:

> She was an indomitable woman, and given the kind of existence she lived, her tenacity for life was incredible … She was up against some terrible odds, and yet, she clung, clung, clung to life … But my mother never threw up her hands, despite living in this sensory deprived world that she was in. She had this stubborn will … I think it's what makes me so happy about Eternal Reefs, because she is in a place and doing something that kind of takes care of that problem of her not wanting to leave this world no matter what.
>
> (Natalie [female, 78])

Natalie found value in giving her mom a way to 'live on' in the world through a reef burial. The mother, who loved life and never wanted to leave, is now a part of a coral reef habitat that will live on through the creation of new marine growth.

Finally, for some participants, the stories, legacies and symbolically continued lives of the deceased are displayed and memorialized on certain days imbued with symbolic meanings.

> This is just a graveyard, and they have balloon releases and stuff like that at Christmas, and I have participated in that. You go stand by their grave. Sometimes they'll have candlelight and you'll light the candle for him one year. And several years they've had the balloons and where you, at a certain time, everybody's on the grave, you release the balloons … The candlelight I liked more. I really didn't care about releasing balloons. To me, that's more pollution in the environment, but out of respect for him, I did it.
>
> (Wanda [female, 61])

Significant dates of remembrance are an important part of the family's story because they signify individual lives and collective beliefs that revolve around special days. Days like Memorial Day and Veteran's Day help the bereaved legitimize the lives of the deceased.

The physical body of a deceased person impacts the inalienable wealth of a family in many ways. The remains or the final resting place become part of the overarching story and heritage of a family. Marking where the body rests provides evidence for generations to come that a person's life was lived and that they played a role in setting up the family for the future. Physical indications that a person lived provides others with a clear 'memory picture' of the deceased, a basis for genealogical research, and reinforced ideas about collective identities, memories, and meanings. For the deceased, the ability to leave a legacy or maintain symbolic immortality gives them the freedom to die at peace, knowing their living was not in vain. The physical traces remaining from a person's life provide benefits for the deceased, for the living, and for future generations.

Viewing the body

A major debate related to body disposition relates to whether or not the corpse should be viewed before cremation or interment. Many funeral directors assert that viewing the body is a critical aspect of healing during the grieving process (Slocum and Carlson, 2011). As of 1998, over 68 per cent of American funerals featured an open casket (Mitford 1998). Of course, the rate of cremation has increased since that time, and under that circumstance, just over 15 per cent of consumers associate a traditional funeral ceremony with occurring prior to cremation (National Funeral Directors Association 2014). Still, if you ask a group of individuals, you would most likely receive a plethora of different opinions, including some who want or need to see the body and others who wish to remember the person as they were in life.

For one informant, who had also experienced a traumatic loss early in life, the intense yearning to stand and stare at the body was almost captivating:

> Certainly the first funeral I ever went to was very memorable. And that's because I was around 12 or 13 years old. And it was a friend of mine who died of leukemia. And so, it was a very traumatic thing to have someone who was your friend … I had known him ever since kindergarten … And he got leukemia and died. And I went with my parents to the funeral, and I remember going up to the coffin to look at him with my father. And I kind of just wanted to stand there and stare. And to this day, I can picture what he looked like … But what I remember is my father taking my arm and pulling me away, because I guess I was standing there too long staring … And he never said a word to me but I got this very strong message like, 'You're not supposed to stand there and stare so long.'
>
> (Shirley [female, 62])

One can almost envision this participant as a young girl, frozen in place with eyes affixed on her deceased friend. Something made her feel this need to stare intently at the body of her young, lifeless friend, and yet, something else pulled her away from her fixation. On the surface, one might say that her father guided her away from this fixation as he certainly enacted the physical act of leading her away from the casket. On a deeper level, cultural norms prescribing appropriate behaviour directed her father to pull her away. This norm, and the way it contradicted her innate urge to look, created a lasting memory, imbued with meanings about appropriate interactions with the dead.

One informant reiterated the idea that funeral attendees should act in a certain way in interacting with physical remains:

> I can't see doing the suits and ties and everybody uncomfortable, stiff and sitting in chairs, chatting, trying not to talk about the fact there's a dead body in the room. There's a white elephant called a dead body sitting right there, but we're supposed to be chatting and having a great time.
>
> (Francis [female, 52])

These individuals attempted to act naturally and carry on casual conversation because they felt it was the appropriate way to commence. Yet, Francis exposes them by highlighting how truly unnatural and awkward this is. By exposing the irrationality of their actions, Francis is really calling into question the cultural norms of continuing a seemingly ridiculous ritual. Also, the 'elephant in the room' metaphor was employed here to describe the group's willful disregard of the corpse in the room.

The corpse is certainly a critical part of sense-making for individuals, but it does so in many different ways. Early experiences can be captivating or distressing, but most of all, they leave a memory trace. Another issue that arose was the influence of cultural norms on appropriate interactions with the body. Prescriptions about how to behave are based on cultural understandings and agreements related to the ritual at hand, but there was also evidence in these interviews that consumers may be calling into question the norms that hold no meaning for them. Finally, the urge to view or avoid the body is often based on personal preferences. For some, it is comforting to see that the person is actually deceased, to obtain a sense of closure, or to have that final glimpse of a loved one. For others, it may be discomforting to have the corpse as the final memory, to see others interact with the body, or simply to be in the room with a dead person. In any case, the deceased's body plays a major role in human understanding of the meaning of life, death and the physical body.

Discussion

This study explores how people make sense of life and death in the context of body disposition. Our work has several implications for theory and practice. First, it extends our understanding of disposition. Physical bodies that were once full of life are rendered lifeless; their value-in-use has expired. As the value of tangible bodies diminishes or expires, people, who have claims to physical remains, must make decisions about disposition. Yet, survivors must address body disposition at a time when decision-making is impaired because of grief (Gentry *et al.*, 1995b). In addition, much like the disposition of a special possession, disposition of the body requires both spatial and emotional detachment (Kleine and Baker, 2004). Attachment to the body can be transferred to attachment to a burial site or a virtual space where communication with the deceased continues to occur. The transference allows for a continued relationship between the living and the deceased. In addition, attachment to the body can be shared. Remains can become part of the inalienable wealth of the family, as when ashes are divided among the living. Disposition is a process that occurs in stages and requires detachment (Kleine and Baker, 2004), and, in the case of the body, transference from one vessel to another.

Second, the study extends our understanding about transitions, in this case the transition between life and death for both the deceased and the bereaved. The body transitions between states, leaving memory traces that are central as the living make sense of the life and death of loved ones, as well as their future selves. Memory traces can be found in places, material objects and even other people, as in the case of organ donation. These traces become part of the inalienable, and therefore priceless, wealth of families, and symbolically allow the deceased to live on.

Third, disposition choices impact identity, which is fluid even after death (Bonsu and Belk 2003). Some alternatives to body disposition allow for a unique form of psychological appropriation and self-extension (Belk, 1988). For example, by 'becoming one' with other people, pets, objects or places, the identity of the deceased is symbolically intermingled and extended into other entities. Here, the individual identity of the deceased crosses a porous boundary and becomes part of the collective (Lastovicka and Fernandez, 2005). In this way, places and objects serve to tangibilize the deceased's identity and thereby facilitate reconstitution and fluidity of the deceased's self into the future.

Acknowledgements

The authors appreciate the death-care service providers at Eternal Reefs and Ramsey Creek Preserves for helping to recruit participants and for allowing the first author the opportunity to observe their services. We also are indebted to the informants for sharing their stories. This research was funded in part by a grant from the Association for Consumer Research and the Sheth Foundation in support of Transformative Consumer Research (TCR).

References

Belk, R.W. (1988) 'Possessions and the extended self,' *Journal of Consumer Research*, 15(2), pp. 139–168.

Belk, R.W., Fischer, E. and Kozinets, R.V. (2013) *Qualitative Consumer and Marketing Research*. Thousand Oaks, CA: Sage Publications.

Bonsu, S.K. and Belk, R.W. (2003) 'Do not go cheaply into that good night: death-ritual consumption in Asante, Ghana,' *Journal of Consumer Research*, 30(1), pp. 41–55.

Bradford, T.W. (2009) 'Intergenerationally gifted asset dispositions,' *Journal of Consumer Research*, 36(1), pp. 93–111.

Cremation Association of North America (2013) *Transport of Cremated Remains.* Available at: www.cremationassociation.org/?page=Transport (Accessed: 8 September 2013).

Curasi, C.F., Price, L.L. and Eric J. Arnould (2004) 'How individuals' cherished possessions become families' inalienable wealth,' *Journal of Consumer Research*, 31(3), pp. 609–622.

Gentry, J.W., Kennedy, P.F., Paul, C. and Hill, R.P. (1995a) 'Family transitions during grief: discontinuities in household consumption patterns,' *Journal of Business Research*, 34(1), pp. 67–79.

Gentry, J.W., Kennedy, P.F., Paul, C. and Hill, R.P. (1995b) 'The vulnerability of those grieving the death of a loved one: implications for public policy,' *Journal of Public Policy and Marketing*, 14 (Spring), 128–142.

Grayson, K. and Shulman, D. (2000) 'Indexicality and the verification function of irreplaceable possessions: a semiotic analysis,' *Journal of Consumer Research*, 27(1), pp. 17–30.

Jacoby, J., Berning, C.K. and Dietvorst, T.F. (1977) 'What about disposition?' *Journal of Marketing*, 41(2), pp. 22–28.

Kleine, S.S. and Baker, S.M. (2004) 'An integrative review of material possession attachment,' *Academy of Marketing Science Review*, 2004(1), pp. 1–35.

Lastovicka, J.L. and Fernandez, K.V. (2005) 'Three paths to disposition: the movement of meaningful possessions to strangers,' *Journal of Consumer Research*, 31(4), pp. 813–823.

McAlexander, J.H. (1991) 'Divorce, the disposition of the relationship, and everything,' *Advances in Consumer Research*, 18, pp. 43–48.

Mitford, J. (1998) *The American Way of Death Revisited*, New York: Knopf.

National Funeral Directors Association (2013) *Trends in Funeral Service.* Available at: http://nfda.org/media-center/trends-in-funeral-service.html (Accessed: 28 August 2013).

National Funeral Directors Association (2014) *Consumer Preference for Cremation Expected to Surpass Burial in 2015.* Available at: http://nfda.org/news-a-events/all-press-releases/4046-consumer-preference-for-cremation-expected-to-surpass-burial-in-2015.html (Accessed: 9 April 2014).

Price, L.L., Arnould, E.J. and Curasi, C.F. (2000) 'Older consumers' disposition of special possessions,' *Journal of Consumer Research*, 27(2), pp. 179–201.

Price, L.L., Arnould, E.J. and Moisio, R. (2006), 'Making contexts matter: selecting research contexts for theoretical insights,' In Belk, R.W. (ed.) *Handbook of Qualitative Research Methods in Marketing*. Northampton: Edward Elgar Publishing, pp. 106–125.

Sanburn, J. (2013) 'The new American way of death,' *Time Magazine*, June 2013, pp. 30–37.

Sayre, S. (1994) 'Possessions and identity in crisis: meaning and change for victims of the Oakland firestorm,' *Advances in Consumer Research*, 11, pp. 109–114.

Schouten, J.W. (1991) 'Selves in transition: symbolic consumption in personal rites of passage and identity reconstruction,' *Journal of Consumer Research*, 17(4), pp. 412–425.

Slocum, J. and Carlson, L. (2011) *Final Rights: Reclaiming the American Way of Death.* Hinesburg, VT: Upper Access, Inc.

Turner, V.W. (1969) *The Ritual Process: Structure and Anti-Structure.* Chicago: Aldine.

Van Gennep, A. (1909) *The Rites of Passage.* London: Routledge and Kegan Paul.

15 Consumer acceptance of radical alternatives to human disposal

An examination of the Belgian marketplace*

Louise Canning, Isabelle Szmigin and Cathy Vaessen

The environmental challenge

With the growing recognition of the consequences of man's negative impact on the earth's finely balanced ecosystem, people are encouraged to adopt behavioural patterns to minimise the use of natural resources. In a move towards more mindful consumption (Sheth, Sethia and Srinivas, 2011) we might be asked to eschew excess consumption, relinquish product ownership, or at the very least engage in recycling activities. Such actions are intended to limit, if not eliminate, demand for products that draw from finite natural resources. However, in some markets, demand is unlikely to drop and the notions of reuse and recycling bring with it particular challenges. One such sector is the funeral market place. In 2010 the world population stood at 6.9 billion and is expected to reach at least 9.7 billion by 2100 (Anonymous, 2014). As the world becomes increasingly populated, so the removal of human remains becomes a fundamental environmental issue with regards land use, material and resource consumption, waste and emissions (Canning and Szmigin, 2010). There is a substantial body of literature on death and dying within sociology and anthropology (e.g. Hockey and Hallam, 2001), but much of this draws from practices in Britain, North America and Australia to comment specifically on Anglo-Saxon death rituals (Vandenporpe, 2000). Added to this is the fact that there is a paucity of consumer research which examines disposal of the dead (Gentry, Hill and Kennedy, 1994; Gabel, Mansfield and Westbrook, 1996; Bonsu and Belk, 2003). Our chapter addresses these gaps by considering consumer response to cremation altern-atives, focusing specifically on the Belgian marketplace and in doing so, drawing from selected literature on identity, sequestration (Mellor and Schill-ing, 1993) and disposal (Rumble *et al.*, 2014) in relation to death. Belgium represents a particularly interesting setting because of the institutional and cul-tural differences between the Flemish and French-speaking regions of the country. We start by introducing the institutional setting of mortuary practice in Belgium, factors driving interest in disposal alternatives and we give a brief description of two processes that might substitute existing cremation technology. We then consider French-speaking consumer responses to these alternatives and the implications for those in the funeral industry wishing to present cremation substitutes in Belgium.

Institutional setting

The institutional setting in which funeral rites are enacted is significant because it determines consumer access to body disposal. In Belgium, a hybrid model of service provision exists in which a mixture of commercial organisations and public bodies (at the level of regional communes) operate cemetery and crematoria, while funeral directing is undertaken by profit-making entities. With regards crematoria in particular, there are 12 cremation sites in Belgium managed by 4 societies (Anonymous, 2011a). Irrespective of the nature of the disposal service, cemetery and crematoria operators must comply with legislative requirements, which in Belgium (compared to other European countries) is unique in that this can vary. At the start of the twenty-first century, and particularly in relation to cremation for example, strict environmental regulations were in place in the northern region of Flanders, while in the Brussels commune, emissions filtering systems were advised (but not obligatory) and Wallonia encouraged continuous improvement in emissions reductions, but did not mandate target reductions or systems installation (Davies and Mates, 2005).

How body disposal is dealt with in terms of the structure of service provision and within specified legislative requirements obviously has some bearing on funeral consumption, but it is cultural and religious norms that are significant given the influence of these in shaping consumer disposal practices and the likely acceptance of alternatives. Historically, Belgian mortuary tradition has been dominated by the Catholic Church (Davies and Mates, 2005), and burial the only disposal option until the latter half of the twentieth century. As an alternative to this, cremation was promoted from the late nineteenth century by non-Catholic individuals motivated in part to create funeral rites adapted to the requirements of atheists. However, Belgium was a relative latecomer compared to other parts of Western Europe, as it was not until the Catholic Church recognised cremation as an approved disposal method in 1966, and it entered the Belgian legal system in 1971, that the Belgian population were free to consider it as a suitable alternative to burial. Cremation was initially associated with the rejection of religion and while this historical connection is important, it does not necessarily hold, given that practicing Catholics might opt for cremation and atheists burial. Indeed, the growing acceptance of cremation as a suitable disposal method (in a country where 80 per cent of the population are baptised according to the Catholic ritual and the majority of social groups want a priest as the celebrant in the funeral ritual – Vandenporpe, 2000) is evidenced by disposal statistics that recorded 383 cremations in 1969 (Davies and Mates, 2005), compared to 49,201 by 2009, this representing 47 per cent of all deaths in Belgium that year (Anonymous,

2011a). Such growing popularity might be explained by a number of factors: for example the capacity for the bereaved to maintain the memory of the deceased (avoiding thoughts associated with the material decomposition of the corpse), the removal of obligations to visit and tend a burial plot (in favour of more personalised and private memorialisation alternatives) and lower costs for cremation compared to those that burial incurs such as plot purchase and extended maintenance fees (Vandenporpe, 2000).

Mortuary ritual is performed according to the customs and traditions of a particular cultural context. As a remote practice in most peoples' lives it is not one where the mantra of reduce, reuse or recycle is easily applicable even if the bereaved endeavour to make funeral decisions based on their perceptions of the deceased's values and environmental consciousness. For many, bereavement presents the individual with a situation in which distress purchase decisions are made regarding rites prior to actual body disposal, for example body preparation, sending of funeral invitations and the farewell ceremony itself. Funeral consumption presents the bereaved with decisions of considerable psychological and financial consequence, but the conditions of urgency and emotional vulnerability under which decisions are frequently made means that such purchases can be impulsive and irrational (Baumeiser, 2002; Gentry, Hill and Kennedy, 1994). This is different where the deceased (and/or close family members) engage in an explicit and deliberate funeral planning process ahead of death and in which conscious efforts to minimise environmental consequences of disposal consumption could be made. Such attempts are significant given that pre-disposal rites (such as body preparation or farewell ceremonies) are thought to be more environmentally damaging than the disposal act itself (typically burial or cremation) (Krijzer and Kok, 2011). However reluctant individuals might be to participate in funeral ritual decisions, consumerising of market provision is well-established and now includes choices that are presented in the marketplace by funeral directing businesses as being more environmentally benign; for example, coffins made from alternative materials such as banana leaves, cardboard, wicker or wool.

Body disposal: the environmental challenge

In moving toward a more sustainable form of existence, each of the elements in a particular consumption system need to be examined in order to identify and encourage behavioural patterns that are of reduced environmental consequence. This is critical for three reasons – first it is embedded in the cultural context and practices of a social group; second, the means by which a corpse is physically transformed is something with which individuals do not readily engage (Vandenporpe, 2000); and third, the disposal act brings with it environmental consequences both in terms of resource consumption and pollution. Our intention is not to argue the environmental benefits of one disposal method over another. Nevertheless, it is important to consider some of the challenges posed by traditional mortuary practices of burial and cremation to understand better how alternatives might reduce the environmental impact.

Starting with burial, as the dominant disposal method in Belgium (representing 53 per cent of deaths in 2009 (Anonymous, 2011a), its principal negative environmental impacts centre on land-use and human toxicity (Krijzer and Kok, 2011). Regarding land-use, even if plots within a cemetery are kept for a finite period of time, areas reserved for burial retain that purpose as other land uses change or develop; and this is certainly the case in densely populated areas in Belgium. In Brussels, for example, expansion of the city along with its population since the 1800s means that the cemetery of Ixelles now stands in the heart of the student quarter. In Grez, in the region of Wallonia, the cemetery has been expanded by taking over agricultural land nearby, while in Doiceau, a public park has been converted into a cemetery. Besides land use, environmental consequences of burial are associated with human toxicity, centring around decomposition and the potential contamination of nearby soil and water supplies by viruses, bacteria and toxic substances such as dental fillings as well as nitrogen and phosphorous releases (Krijzer and Kok, 2011).

While burial might still be the predominant disposal method, the shift to cremation is expected to continue in Belgium and along with it the need to increase capacity by building new crematoria facilities (Anonymous, 2009a; Anonymous, 2011b). The impacts normally associated with cremation centre on energy consumption (used to reach temperatures in excess of 800°C during the two-hour incineration process), and emissions. According to a 2002 study undertaken in Flanders, healthcare costs resulting from atmospheric pollution stood at 2.3 billion Euros (Anonymous, 2009b) and it might be expected that cremation contributes to this, given, for example, that hydrofluoric acid and sulphur dioxide would be pumped back into the atmosphere, and cremation is estimated to account for 8 per cent of mercury emissions in Belgium (Anonymous, 2011c). With regards disposal of ashes, Belgians are not permitted to retain the urn, and instead have two options, to either scatter ashes (over a cemetery lawn or at sea) or bury them in a grave or columbarium. While, the majority of ashes are scattered on cemetery lawns (Vandenporpe, 2000), with commemorative plaques on cemetery walls the only visible trace of the deceased, a shift to placing ashes in columbariums has started to emerge in recent decades (Coenegrachts, 1999). This trend also brings with it negative environmental consequences of land-use associated with crematoria (Krijzer and Kok, 2011).

Cremation alternatives

Two substitutes for the existing cremation process consist of technology based on cryogenics and alkaline hydrolysis. Cryomation (the patented process based on cryogenic technology) involves freezing the body to −196 °C using liquid nitrogen. Subjecting the body to controlled pressure then reduces it to smaller pieces from which non-organic materials (e.g. metal and plastic prostheses) can be removed. The remaining organic materials undergo a further fragmentation process, followed by freeze-drying, and the final treatment to reduce pathogens results in a sterile, odourless mix of fragments equivalent to one third of the original weight of the body and coffin (Krizjer and Kok, 2011). Resomation (the patented process involving alkaline hydrolysis) comprises submerging the body in a strong alkaline solution (a mixture of potassium hydroxide and water) – the solution is heated to 180 °C and circulated continuously, after which the liquid is cooled and drained. The skeletal remains are removed and dried, and materials (such as plastic and metals) separated, leaving the bones to be crushed into a white powder in a processor (similar to cremulators used at the end of the incineration process).

These alternative processes and cremation are similar in that each provides rapid transformation and reduction of the corpse. However, the cremation substitutes represent fundamental shifts (away from combustion) in the nature of the transformation processes and their developers suggest that they offer improved environmental performance through reduced energy consumption and emissions. Independent evaluation of different disposal technologies does in fact suggest they are more environmentally benign compared to cremation and burial (Krizjer and Kok, 2011).

Changes in legislative provision to accommodate these cremation alternatives (currently being pursued in Flanders as well as in Holland, Banks, 2014) and acceptance by religious bodies are important to allow their introduction. This latter point is significant given the symbolic connection of the body and soul for Roman Catholics and the breaking of this link when the body is destroyed. Deliberation by the Catholic Church over the destruction of the corpse would be necessary just as it reflected on cremation before its acceptance as an appropriate disposal method (Walter, 2005). Besides legal and religious factors, of critical importance to any eventual launch of either cryomation or resomation is consumer recognition of these technologies as suitable substitutes for cremation technology, and it is to this that we now direct our attention.

Belgian consumer acceptance of cremation alternatives

The exploratory nature of our investigation into Belgian consumer funeral decision-making regarding disposal method and responses to the cremation alternatives led us to use focus groups to develop descriptive data. The inherently sensitive nature of funeral practices might lead researchers to use in-depth interviews. However, while all participants had prior funeral involvement, we did not seek to probe respondent funeral experiences in such a way that the loss of a loved one might bring highly emotional responses to the fore. Rather our intention was to specifically examine the action of disposal and in using focus groups, to provide a setting in which participants could share experiences and discuss their responses to the proposed cremation alternatives. Three focus group discussions were conducted, with the 23 participants being drawn from the predominantly French-speaking regions of Brussels and Wallonia, these representing approximately

40 per cent of the Belgian population (Sketch, 2005). An inductive exploratory approach was used (Miles and Hubermann, 1994), in which thematic
analyses were undertaken of the verbatim transcripts created from the recording of each focus group discussion. We now direct our attention to the examination of these findings.

Choice of disposal method: burial or cremation

Looking first at existing disposal practices, selection of burial or cremation can
be considered both in terms of choice regarding the decision made on behalf of
the deceased (at time of need) or one's own disposal (and which might therefore be expressed in advance). With regards burial, besides religious beliefs,
factors contributing to respondent preference for this disposal rite included the
desire for individuals to have a site in memory of the deceased and for some, as
a way of dealing with the sudden and unexpected loss of a loved one.

> I didn't want to have my husband cremated, and I'm not sure that I can
> explain why ... but it was very difficult, and very sudden and you say to
> yourself that (*if he was cremated*) ... he would disappear completely ... so I
> wanted somehow to keep a little part of him.
>
> (Anna)

Anna's explanation surrounding the choice of burial for her husband exemplifies the anxiety and emotional instability felt at this sudden loss. It might
also suggest that while cremation for her would have meant a final and brutal
'rupture' in this relationship, burial on the other hand enabled her to maintain a connection to her husband and thus sustain in some way her own self-
identity (Mellor and Schilling, 1993).

The finality to a relationship and to the physical presence of the deceased
which Anna felt cremation imposed, was mirrored by those respondents who
had experienced cremation as part of the funeral ritual. Respondent reflections
on their experiences of cremation exemplify perhaps the tension between the
emotional connection with the deceased and the bodily remains of that individual which require disposal (Rumble *et al.*, 2014). At the point where the
farewell ceremony ends and the corpse is given over for incineration, respondents felt a sense of abruptness in this early stage of the bereavement process.

> Incineration, or cremation, let's say, is difficult psychologically ... the fact
> that you're there and you see the coffin disappear.
>
> (Beatrice)

> When my Mum died, it was difficult ... having chosen (she decided
> beforehand), the moment when you're faced with it, my God, it makes
> you shiver.
>
> (Sandrine)

There is a distinction however, between the experience during the grieving process immediately following bereavement and once some time has passed. This is evidenced by the fact that, notwithstanding the emotional difficulty with the perceived abruptness of cremation, it offered seemingly practical benefits. A number of factors led respondents to prefer cremation, our findings reflecting previous studies conducted in other countries. This includes, for example, discomfort with the image of putrefaction connected with natural decomposition of the body (Davies and Shaw 1995; Kellaher *et al.*, 2005). Besides such imaginings, more seemingly practical motivations were apparent, including physical, financial and emotional burden associated with burial and memorialisation, such as engaging in plot maintenance or marking death anniversaries with cemetery visits.

> (*The thing with burial*) is having to go every year and to relive the death twice a year – the anniversary of the death and on 1st November, on All Saints day.
>
> (Sandrine)

An important point in relation to this preference is that whilst cremation might offer practical benefits for body disposal, it does not mean that respondents dissociate themselves from the deceased. In fact, as observed by Vandenporpe (2000), individuals opt to direct feelings of grief and memorialisation acts in alternative personalised and perhaps more private ways.

> Me, I think that the person who has died is still alive in your heart and head, not anywhere else … and I think that's the best homage you can pay someone … you keep their memory alive through others … ashes don't serve any purpose … there isn't anybody there.
>
> (Virginie)

Despite factors being identified favouring either of the established disposal methods, the dominant preference amongst respondents was for cremation over burial. This is significant in that it is consistent with prior research (Hiernaux and Vandendorpe, 2000), reflects the move away from burial, which in turn could theoretically lessen the environmental burdens associated with burial. Moreover, the historical and predicted future growth in cremation opens up opportunities for comparable disposal methods where a society has already accepted technologies that involve the rapid transformation and reduction of a corpse.

Interpretation of cryomation and resomation process descriptions

In focus group sessions, descriptions of the two cremation alternatives were closely aligned to the information presented in the respective company websites, in which words that might be deemed as sensitive or inappropriate for association with funeral rites (such as 'basin' in the case of alkaline hydrolysis or 'compost' for cryogenics) were either contained or absent from those companies' material content.

The most common responses expressed by focus group participants relating to the alkaline hydrolysis technique were

- discomfort with the notion of a corpse being dissolved,

'I don't want to end up like a soup'.

(Eric)

'oh it disgusts me ... reminds me of horror films'.

(Jean-Paul)

- the association with the Pastor Pandy Case (in 1997, Pastor Pandy and his daughter Agnès were arrested in the Belgian capital for having killed six members of their family and placing them in an acid bath to dissolve the corpses),
- dislike of the idea that the solution used in the process can be disposed of via normal water treatment systems,

'...couldn't we end up drinking this if it goes into the water system and the normal treatment process?'.

(Edith)

Regarding points one and two, associations were made with acid despite explicit explanations being given that the process is alkaline based. Such an interpretation is not uncommon and is something which the technology suppliers seek to counter via, for example, their online explanations of the process. Consumer acceptance and commercial operation of resomation in North America since 2011 clearly indicates that initial interpretations can in fact be countered. However, in this investigation, references made to the Pastor Pandy criminal case are obviously specific to the cultural context of French-speaking parts of Belgium and might arguably prove more challenging to overcome. Besides this culturally specific reference, there is an apparent difficulty in disassociating the bodily representation of an individual's identity (Mellor and Shilling, 1993) from the remains or waste that a cadaver represents (Rumble *et al.*, 2014). Furthermore, leaving aside further explanations necessary to correct misinterpretation of this process, responses might also imply less inclination towards dispersal of human remains within environments inhabited by the living in Belgium compared to other countries (Rumble *et al.*, 2014).

Compared to alkaline hydrolysis, the cryogenic process drew an overall more favourable response, namely that

- it was perceived as being more natural

  'it's a more natural way of preserving things ... mmm ... in some way, cold seems more logical'.

  (Alicia)

  'it's natural ... fire exists elsewhere, and so does ice...'.

  (Virginie)

- it was considered cleaner

  'it seems less polluting, cleaner ... so maybe it's an OK alternative to cremation'.

  (Jean-Paul)

- it would fit better from a cultural perspective (there being no negative associations with criminal cases).

  'it seems to fit better with our traditions ... with what we already know'.

  (Sarah)

Factors that might explain the response and interpretation of the process descriptions could include understanding of the processes used for body disposal as well as closeness of fit with the incumbent combustion method. Focus group observations indicated that participants did not have difficulty in understanding the principles of the alternative technologies although technical knowledge of the chemical and engineering processes as well as their environmental impact was limited. So for example, prominent questions in focus group discussions related to

- the nature of the treatment of the alkaline hydrolysis solution before this mixture returns to the natural water cycle

  'can this really be better for the environment ... the liquid must have to be treated before going into the water cycle, so that requires energy...'.

  (Philippe)

- the carbon footprint of liquid nitrogen production

  'what happens to the gases emitted in the process ... don't they themselves cause pollution?'

  (Robert)

- the texture and appearance of ashes resulting from each of these processes.

'with normal cremation, we know what we're getting – ashes... but what would we get at the end of this (alkaline hydrolysis)?'

(Guilllaume)

'so what you'd get at the end this (*cryomation*) would be bigger than ashes from cremation?'

(Maude)

'how much would we be left with after Cryomation compared to ashes from cremation?...because we know where we are when it comes to ashes...'

(Anna)

With regards 'closeness of fit' with the current incineration technology, clearly all three processes involve rapid transformation of the corpse. While each involves different chemical and engineering systems, common to all three is the fact that treatment of the corpse is undertaken in units in which the process is not readily visible. This reflects the overall sequestration of death in modern society (Mellor and Schilling, 1993) including the act of dis-posal in which there is an element of removal or distance from the trans-formation process (Vandenporpe, 2000). Yet in being introduced to cremation alternatives, respondents are required to consider what actually happens to the body, and it is arguably the exposure to this part of the funeral rite that creates discomfort (irrespective of the method used). Such considera-tion is seemingly less problematic when respondents reflect on the technology and process without associating these with the identity or indeed the death of someone to whom they are closely connected.

For me the crematorium is the house of disappearing ... Whether it is in a basin, via freezing or incineration ... you're prepared in the same way as for cremation and you come out the same. What is going on in between ... it takes about two hours ... well we don't actually care.

(Robert)

If you aren't the family member who has to make the choice, you wouldn't know which technique was used, if for example, the three techniques were housed in the same building. So I don't see where the problem is.

(Jan)

Here, both Robert and Jan appear to be able to consider the body as separate from the identity of the deceased, as matter which requires treatment. The fact that the transformation process is hidden allows respondents to distance themselves from the physical destruction of the corpse and its rendering into substances that enable disposal.

From considering disposal preferences and respondent interpretations of resomation and cryomation, we now examine how these cremation alternatives might be introduced in the marketplace, focusing specifically on communication activities and pricing. The logic in touching on only these two aspects is that the disposal methods involve fixed technologies (but which would be part of services offered by a funeral director or crematorium) and could only be accessed through legally recognised crematorium sites.

Presenting cremation alternatives in the marketplace

To consider either resomation or cryomation as cremation alternatives requires that individuals be aware of and understand these technologies. There is consequently both an educational and informational aspect to communication activities which has to precede any promotional work that might be used to guide body disposal decisions. This might include public relations and journalistic items featured in, for example, news and current affairs programmes or printed publications in which the reasons for the alternatives and the principles of the technologies can be presented. Such presentations could feature around 1 November, All Saints day, which as an annual event commemorating the dead, triggers extensive media coverage and much more open discussion surrounding death and dying. An important factor is message content and its presentation. Consistent with the sequestration of death (Mellor and Schilling, 1993) and dissociation from corpse transformation (Vandenporpe, 2000) respondents expressed preference for communications that explained the broad principles of the processes and the associated benefits rather than providing technical or graphic details of the systems.

> I suppose the fact that no one here knew that (after cremation) bones are ground to reduce them to powder shows our ignorance on the subject, and we don't really try to find out more. And it would the same here, knowing that the process involves freeze-drying or dissolution and that it's more ecological, that's all that's needed.
>
> (Robert)

Communication activities containing rational messages at pre-time need, and access (via social media sites) to video content featuring the environmental benefits of the processes as part of news items, discussions or documentaries would at least go some way to generating awareness and placing cremation alternatives in the possible choice set of individuals as part of advanced and explicit funeral planning.

As part of funeral planning undertaken by the bereaved faced with at time-need decisions, funeral directors would be essential both in presenting cremation alternatives as disposal options and explaining the processes. This however presumes that the bereaved wish to consider disposal alternatives when making distress purchase decisions, rather than reverting to disposal methods practiced within their social group. Nevertheless, funeral parlours might list resomation and cryomation as possible disposal choices within their service provisions and provide very brief descriptions of the methods. The content and tone of communication in this situation requires the balancing between the provision of some factual content but more critically a message that empathises with the bereaved during a period of extreme emotional vulnerability. In North America where the resomation process is in commercial operation, this is offered by one funeral parlour as part of its cremation service and presented as 'Flameless Cremation', with the operator providing a very short description of the process and environmental benefits alongside coastal, water and sky-based photographic images.

Such summative introductions and evocations of this cremation alternative are important to bring this into an individual's choice set. However, as with other aspects of the funeral business, information provision, explanation and even guidance is centred very much on one-to-one discussions between undertaker representatives and the bereaved who must either put in place the decisions previously expressed by the deceased or make choices themselves.

> It's very similar to selling funeral cover ... because these are subjects where really the discussion is between the company representative and um, the person concerned ... if you've got somebody there to answer your questions, then it's much easier. You couldn't really do a big communications campaign. That would be a bit strange. Well in Belgium at least.
>
> (Robert)

In terms of pricing of alternative technologies, respondents believed that products positioned as more environmentally benign are typically set at higher prices. However, with regards the cremation alternatives, respondents felt that prices for these should be comparable to those charged for cremation, given the reduced energy consumption associated with both. This is the strategy adopted in North America by the funeral parlour Anderson-McQueen, where the first commercial installation of resomation technology (under the name Flameless Cremation) has been in operation since 2011.

Conclusion

This chapter has added to understanding of death rituals by examining consumer acceptance of cremation alternatives in French-speaking parts of Belgium. The chapter introduces the reader to the process involved in body disposal and possible future practices. Results from the empirical investigation suggested that cryomation might be more readily accepted than resomation especially in terms of cultural sensitivities in Brussels and Wallonia. Interestingly however, as a method of disposal, resomation is already in commercial operation in some states in North America and this presents other countries and the funeral industry with evidence of recognition by religious bodies (Mirkes, 2008) and consumer acceptance. Add to this the environmental impact analysis commissioned by the Dutch funeral group Yarden (Krizjer and Kok, 2011) in which resomation was concluded to be the most environmentally benign and one can understand the recent drive by the Flemish Funeral Council to seek changes in legislative provision in Flanders and the Netherlands to allow for resomation (under the brand name Bio-Cremation – Banks, 2014). Even if legislative changes are introduced in Flanders, regulatory differences in Brussels and Wallonia, and consumer interpretations of the resomation process and associations with the Pastor Pandy criminal case, present particular challenges for the funeral industry in these two French-speaking parts of Belgium. Perhaps more time must elapse and a more extensive process of information exchange and communication must be played out before consumers in Brussels and Wallonia consider resomation as a suitable cremation alternative and in preference to cryomation.

Note

★ This chapter draws from postgraduate research undertaken by Cathy Vaessen.

References

Anonymous, (2009a) 'Projet création d'un crematorium au sein de la région du centre', La Louvière: Espace Environnement.

Anonymous, (2009b) 'Pollution de l'air: quels impacts sur la santé', Réseau Intersyndical de Sensibilisation à l'Environnement.

Anonymous, (2011a) 'International cremation statistics 2010', *Pharos International*, 76 (4), pp. 26–38.

Anonymous, (2011b) 'Un crematorium pour les provinces de Namur et du Luxembourg', Namur: Bureau Economic de la Province de Namur.

Anonymous, (2011c) 'Arrêté du gouvernement Wallon déterminant les conditions sectorielles relatives aux crématoriums et modifiant l'arrêté du gouvernement Wallon du 30 juin 1994 rélatif aux déchets d'activités hospitalières et de soins de santé'. Available at http://environnement.wallonie.be/legis/pe/pesect062 (Accessed: 24 July 2011).

Anonymous, (2014) 'World Population Prospects: the 2010 Revision Population Database', United Nations Department of Economic and Social Affairs, 14 September. Available at: http://esa.un.org/unpd/ppp/Documentation/highlights.htm (Accessed: 19 April 2015).

Banks, M. (2014) 'Belgium and Netherlands plan to approve "bio-cremations"', *The Telegraph*, 5 October, Available at www.telegraph.co.uk/news/worldnews/europe/belgium/11141960/Belgium-and-Netherlands-plan-to-approve-bio-cremations. (Accessed: 21 November 2014).

Baumeiser, R.F (2002) 'Yielding to temptation: self-control failure, impulsive purchasing, and consumer behaviour', *Journal of Consumer Research*, 28 (4), pp. 670–676.

Bonsu, S. K. and Belk, R. W. (2003) 'Don't go cheaply into that good night: death-ritual consumption in Asante, Ghana', *Journal of Consumer Behaviour*, 30 (1), pp. 41–55.

Coenegrachts, K. (1999) 'Cremation in Belgium', *Pharos International*, 65 (1), pp. 32–37.

Davies, D.J. and Mates, L.H. (2005), *Encyclopaedia of Cremation*. Aldershot: Ashgate.

Gabel, T. Mansfield, P. and Westbrook, K. (1996), 'The disposal of consumers: an exploratory analysis of death-related consumption', *Advances in Consumer Research*, 23 (1), pp. 361–367.

Gentry, J.W. Hill, R.P. and Kennedy, P.F. (1994) 'The vulnerability of those griev-ing the death of a loved one', *Journal of Public Policy and Marketing*, 13 (2), pp. 128–142.

Hiernaux, J.P. and Vandenorpe, F. (2000) 'Deux générations face à la mort: acteurs de recompositions symboliques contemporaines', *Recherches Sociologiques*, 1, pp. 111–122.

Kellaher, L. Prendergast, D. and Hockey, J. (2005) 'In the shadow of the traditional grave', *Mortality*, 10 (4), pp. 237–250.

Keizjer, E.E. Kok, H.J.G. (2011) 'Environmental impact of different funeral technol-ogies', TNO report TNO-060-UT-2011-004142.

Mellor, P. A. Schilling, C. (1993) 'Modernity, self-identity and the sequestration of death', *Sociology*, 27 (3), pp. 411–431.

Miles MB, and Huberman MA (1994) *Qualitative Data Analysis: An Expanded Source-book*. Thousand Oaks: Sage.

Mirkes, R. (2008), 'The mortuary science of alkaline hydrolysis: is it ethical?' *The National Catholic BioEthics Quarterly*, 8 (4) pp. 683–696.

Rumble, H. Troyer, J. Walter, T. and Woodethorpe, K. (2014) 'Disposal or disper-sal? Environmentalism and final treatment of the British Dead', *Mortality*, 19 (3), pp. 243–260.

Sheth, J.N., Sethia, N.K., and Srinivas, S. (2011) 'Mindful consumption: a customer-centric approach to sustainability', *Journal of the Academy of Marketing Science*, 39 (1), pp. 21–39.

Sketch, M. (2005), *Encyclopaedia of the World's Minorities*. Abingdon: Routledge, pp. 202–204.

Vandenporpe, F. (2000) 'Funerals in Belgium: the hidden complexity of con-temporary practices', *Mortality*, 5 (1), pp. 18–33.

Vandenporpe, F. (2003), 'Practices surrounding the dead in French-speaking Belgium: rituals in kitlike form', in Bryant, C.F. Edgley, C.K. Leming, M.R. Peck, D.L. and Sandstrom, K.L. (Eds.). *The Handbook of Death and Dying*, Vol. 2, Thousand Oaks: Sage Publications, pp. 619–630.

16 Theatre of the abject

Body Worlds and the transformation of the cadaver

Kent Drummond and Eric Krszjzaniek

Introduction

> No, as in true theater, without makeup or masks, refuse and corpses *show me* what I permanently thrust aside in order to live. These bodily fluids, this defilement, this shit are what life withstands, hardly and with diffi-culty, on the part of death.
>
> There, I am at the border of my condition as a living being. My body extricates itself, as being alive, from that border. Such wastes drop so that I might live until, from loss to loss, nothing remains in me and my entire body falls beyond the limit – *cadere*, cadaver.
>
> (Kristeva, 1997: 3)

In her landmark essay, *Powers of Horror: An Essay on Abjection*, renowned post-modern theorist Julia Kristeva ruminates on what repulses humans most: blood, pus, excrement, decaying food. These are items that disgust the senses and nauseate the body. We throw them away – and sometimes throw up as we do so. While the word *abject* is usually used as an adjective meaning utterly hopeless or miserable (e.g., 'abject poverty'), Kristeva uses it as a noun ('*the* abject') to objectify the utterly repulsive.

And among the litany of the repulsive, Kristeva saves her greatest revulsion for the cadaver. Why? Because, at its deepest level, the cadaver transcends representation. It *shows* all of us what we are not yet, but will eventually become. In the presence of the cadaver, we press up against the border of our humanity. There, we know ourselves by what we *are not*, by what we must relentlessly *throw out*.

And yet, living bodies often place themselves in close proximity to dead ones. Those working in the medical profession do so out of obligation. But millions of us do so by choice. We read Patricia Cornwell novels, binge-watch 'The Walking Dead,' blog about where we'll hide when the Zombie Apocalypse hits, and listen to *Thriller* 30 years on. Like Kristeva, we may be repulsed by dead bodies, but we're obsessed with them as well.

The great conundrum

Into this imbroglio of impulses walks the museum blockbuster *Body Worlds*. Now in its twentieth year, *Body Worlds*, the exhibit featuring 'real human bodies,' has become the most successful touring show in the history of the world. It has appeared in more than 90 cities globally, attracted more than 40 million visitors, and made its creator, Dr. Gunther von Hagens, very wealthy. In two decades, *Body Worlds* has become the world's most popular site for the consumption of dead bodies. To understand how – and why – this has happened is to understand much about the contemporary consumption of death.

In this chapter, we apply Kristeva's theory of the abject to the case of *Body Worlds*. We ask: What is it about *Body Worlds* that transcends the abject? How have the producers of this exhibit persuaded millions of consumers to stand in the presence of dead bodies, and pay for the privilege?

To answer this question, we offer an interpretive, impression-based analysis of the exhibit. We visited six *BW* exhibits in four cities in five years, closely observed the behavior of hundreds of visitors to these exhibits, interviewed curators, security guards, and museum-goers, collected artifacts from museum gift shops, and collected notes, quotes, and information on the persona of the inventor of *Body Worlds*. Our data base meets the requirements of a market-based ethnography (Arnould and Wallendorf, 1994). Here, we offer primarily cultural-based explanations, as seen through Kristeva's lens of the abject. Following the call issued by Firat and Venkatesh (1995) 20 years ago, we focus as much on what producers display as what consumers apprehend. We begin by taking the reader on a typical tour of *Body Worlds*, describing the sights, sounds, and interactions that tend to take place there.

Welcome to the black parade

Immediately upon entering a *Body Worlds* exhibit, the visitor is greeted by waves of black velvet drapes. Stretching from the floor to the ceiling, they muffle sounds and block light. Voices are hushed accordingly.

In the center of the first gallery sit three giant light boxes, projecting human faces that morph swiftly and silently from young to old, male to female, black to white. Spectators witness the passing of time in these unrecognizable faces, yet they are powerless to do anything about it. There's something sad and elegiac about this tableau. The message on a nearby placard does little to lighten the mood. 'The exhibit focuses on the nature of our physical being, not on providing personal information on private tragedies.' The tone here, possibly translated from the German, is oddly foreboding. What private tragedies? Whose personal information? By stating what it won't be focusing on, the exhibit calls our attention to that very thing. Are the cadavers, soon to be encountered, somehow linked to the faces on the light boxes? A high-spirited young couple giggles and walks past the boxes without pause.

After a short, dark passage, the path opens into a room focused on conception, entitled *It Starts With a Single Cell*. Lines of text, arranged into stanzas of free-form poetry, greet the visitor.

They explain how cells combine to form a unique human who has never existed and who will never be recreated. An endless-loop video narrates the story of conception, backed by piano and flute accompaniment. Six fetuses in different stages of development line the walls. They look like plastic babies a child might play with, because they have undergone the process of plastination, the preservation procedure invented by Dr. Gunther von Hagens. But, the spectator cannot help but recall, they were once dead babies. The objectification of life, at its most nascent, is especially striking. Usually, this exhibit is placed off to the side with a sign warning visitors that they may find the subject matter and contents offensive.

Despite the somber ambiance, there is more giggling from other spectators. A man tells his date (most *Body Worlds* shows are open on Friday nights for that very purpose) that at the treatment center, he learned a lot about fetal alcohol syndrome. A woman in a separate group approaches the plastic placentas, saying, 'Ewww. What *is* this?' After a pause, 'Lovely. Let's keep walking.' She giggles her way into the next gallery.

There, shafts of track lighting pierce the dark, exposing white bones; the skeletal system is featured next. Various casements display different arrangements of bones. Some are arthritic, and many visitors grimace as they view them. Short personal narratives pierce the silence, accompanied by small gestures. One spectator moves close to the shoulder joint, explaining to friends that his shoulder pops a lot and wants to see what's going on. Another straightens his spine as he encounters a casement containing a healthy spine. Another says, 'I have a herniated disk in my back. I haven't talked to my doctor about it since I was nine, my cousin caused it.' Still another worries to a companion that the exhibit will leave him with the impression that youth is fleeting, and that by the end, he'll be saying, 'No, youth! Come back!' This is certainly the impression given by the light boxes at the exhibit's beginning.

In fact, the theme of *tempus fugit* – and the personal choices we make as time flies – is developed early and repeated often. Posters and placards with various titles – some ominous, others reassuring – persuade us that 'Good health is a highly fragile condition.' Skin ages, we are shown, but what ages the skin is largely determined by the choices we make. Ultraviolet rays, smoking, stress levels, and amount of sleep are all within our control, one poster reminds us. Another poster contains a less didactic, more poetic message. Featuring an Asian boy caught in a contemplative moment, the quote is from Lebanese poet Khalil Gibran:

> Your body is the harp of your soul. And it is yours to bring forth sweet music from it or confused sounds.

Other quotes follow from philosopher-kings such as Abraham Lincoln, Gandhi, the Dali Lama, and Albert Einstein. In contrast to the informational posters, these messages serve to soften the grit of the exhibits and take the spectator to a higher plane. Great thinkers and great humanitarians elevate the discourse, in sharp contrast to the finely detailed anatomical displays.

As visitors move through the galleries, bodily systems complexify. Sinew, muscle, ligaments, and tendon are added to the skeletal system. It is at this moment that visitors encounter their first whole-body plastinate, *The Baseball Player*.

Power to the plastinates

Whole-body plastinates are the stars of *Body Worlds* shows. Although almost every item on display is plastinated – such as body parts, organs, and tissue – only a dozen full-body plastinates will populate a medium-sized show. This is because they are extremely expensive to make (each one costs about as much as a Rolls Royce) as well as time-consuming (at least one year). At some point in the show, a cursory and inconspicuous explanation of the plastination process is offered. It usually consists of these five steps:

> In Phase One, the cadaver is embalmed with formalin to prevent decay. Then the skin, fat, and connective tissues are removed.
>
> In Phase Two, body water and soluble fats are further dissolved when the cadaver is placed in an acetone bath.
>
> In Phase Three, the central step of plastination takes place. The body is filled with a reactive polymer (silicone rubber) then placed in a vacuum chamber. The vacuum removes the acetone and replaces it with the polymer, which penetrates every last cell within the specimen. This is how von Hagens is able to render his plastinates in such high detail. It also gives the cadaver – if it can still be called that – a plastic quality that allows it to be formed in whatever way von Hagens chooses.
>
> In Phase Four, the plastinate (no longer a cadaver) is positioned. Running, standing, sitting, reclining – all positions are possible for the plastinate to assume, but only with the help of a myriad of wires, needles, clamps, and foam blocks. And all of these are eventually hidden from view.
>
> Finally, in Phase Five, the plastinate is cured by the application of light, gas, or heat. Only then is it ready for an exhibit.

Star studs

As *The Baseball Player* illustrates, full-body plastinates are oddly captivating. Visitors crowd around the figure isolated in a large acrylic casement. Bat swung far to his left, torso dynamically twisted, *The Baseball Player* has just hit what looks like a home run. (Plastinates are invariably winners.) With muscles of bright red and connective tissue of pale cream, he strides like a fat-free god, daring spectators to ignore him. They can't. After all, his mouth is agape as his glass eyes follow the arc of an imaginary ball. Body bent back and feet improbably balanced, he is frozen, like most plastinates, in a moment of great physical exertion. At any moment, it seems as though he could topple over, but he doesn't. The dozens of wires, clamps, and blocks needed to sustain his precarious position are all hidden from view. What the spectator sees is a paragon of Man.

And what a man! Hanging between *The Baseball Player's* legs is a generous endowment of genitalia, drawing fleeting, embarrassed glances from the spectators pressed up against his casement. Whatever their status in real life, in the after-life all plastinates (with the exception of the effete *Flamenco Dancer*) are awarded perfectly-formed breasts, taut buttocks, large penises, and fulsome vaginas that draw giggles from some, admiring glances from others. And as onlookers press up against the casements, a curious thing happens. Since all casements are highly reflective in the track lighting set against the black drapery, spectators see their reflections overlaid onto the plastinates. They can literally see themselves in von Hagens's creations. This subtle but profound act of what Burke would call identification (1945) takes on an ask-not-for-whom-the-bell-tolls quality. That cadaver was once a man or woman, and s/he was probably a lot like you. But now, something's happened to them and not you. And yet you could be – *will* be, if you wish – this transformed being, this cyborg. But given how oddly poised, powerful, and popular the plastinates are, would that be such a bad thing? It could prove to be the ultimate makeover. It is here that postmodern consumer researchers might sense that Kristeva's theory is very much in play. What is usually most revolting has been stylized into something strangely appealing. The proof is in the behavior of the consumers: they're not pulling back; they're being drawn in.

And in fact, until recently, *Body Worlds* allowed visitors to donate their bodies for plastination simply by completing a form at the end of their tour. This moment in the exhibit was accompanied by its own plastinate, *The Supplicant*. Posed on one knee, head bowed as if in prayer, *The Supplicant* was bathed in a shaft of light. Salvation? Enlightenment? It was difficult to tell. But one thing was made clear by a placard accompanying *The Supplicant*: the show could not go on without the generosity of living subjects who had willed their bodies to the exhibit. *Body Worlds* used to depend on some of its consumers in a very demanding way. Now, however, the supply of bodies exceeds demand. *The Supplicant* and the permission form are no longer part of the show.

His dark materials

And so the show continues, from one gallery to another, one system to another, one plastinate to another. Although length and focus of *Body Worlds* exhibits vary, visitors must always follow a pre-determined path through the exhibit, and back-tracking is not encouraged. Nor are visitors likely to tarry long, as the temperature is relatively cool. The plastinates cannot get overheated, or they might disintegrate.

After *The Baseball Player* comes *The Runner*. He is posed mid-stride, with all of his muscles peeled back to reveal key junctures of the skeleton beneath. Next is *Nerve Leonardo*, a plastinate referencing da Vinci's famous drawing, *Vitruvian Man*. Other prominent plastinates include *Body of Open Doors* (revealing how all internal organs are packed tightly into the body by displaying them outside it), *The Hockey Players* (wielding hockey sticks, two plastinates contend for a puck), and *The Winged Man* (wearing a hat, this plastinate is accompanied by a quote from von Hagens's: 'I put the hat on this plastinate to make it look more lively and humorous. Beauty and humor motivate learning, while horror hinders it.').

In fact, Dr. von Hagens is never far from the exhibit; his presence is felt from start to finish. Beginning with banners announcing the exhibit's title (officially, 'Gunther von Hagens' *Body Worlds'*), and ending with a benedictory photograph of the inventor backlit by the sun, spectators cannot escape knowing that a single man is responsible for this singular display. Von Hagens' flamboyant persona is enacted boldly, both within the show and beyond it.

Variously described as concentration camp survivor, prison escapee, precocious medical student, savvy entrepreneur, and diabolical provocateur, von Hagens embraces whatever descriptors are leveled at him, for it gives him the chance to further fan the flames of controversy. He bears more than a passing resemblance to Dr. Victor Frankenstein, decked in an omnipresent hat and, occasionally, a white smock. He wears a fedora, he explains, because all the great anatomists do. Quite deliberately, he seems the living embodiment of one of the figures in his favorite painting, Rembrandt's *The Anatomy Lesson of Dr. Nicolaes Tulp*.

Operating rooms were originally surgical theaters, and von Hagens is nothing if not theatrical.

Yet none of von Hagens' adventures or opinions would matter if he weren't, first and foremost, a brilliant anatomist. Here is how one museum curator, a biochemist by training, describes him:

> I've been to his workplace in Germany, and I can tell you, he's brilliant. His knowledge of biochemistry is remarkable.
>
> That's how he was able to develop plastination. Rather than infusing the body with a preservative substance, which is what embalming does, he discovered a way to draw the fluid in. No one had ever done that before.

Once von Hagens' perfected this process, he decided to take his show on the road. The impetus, according to the same curator, was political rather than financial.

> Most people don't realize this, but von Hagens refers to himself as a medical socialist. He wants to put the information in the hands of the

people and let them decide. That's why so many of the preserved parts show pathologies. You see this, and you make the choice. Is this how you want to end up?

Many religious leaders, outraged by what von Hagens has done with human bodies, have protested the presence of *Body Worlds* within their communities. Their inclination is to bury the plastinates out of respect for the dead. And this concern raises the question of von Hagens' own perspective on religion and spirituality. The final placard in the exhibit, written by von Hagens, is typically and strategically ambiguous:

> The presentation of the purely physical reminds visitors to *Body Worlds* of the intangible and unfathomable. The plastinated post-mortal body illuminates the soul by its very absence.
>
> Plastination transforms the body, an object of individual mourning, into an object of reverence, learning, enlightenment and appreciation. I hope for *Body Worlds* to be a place of enlightenment and contemplation, even of philosophical and religious self-recognition, and open to interpretation regardless of the background and philosophy of life of the viewer.

This message, only recently added to *Body Worlds* shows, represents a sea-change in von Hagens' world view. In earlier exhibits, he would not have considered any reference to a 'soul' or 'religious self-recognition.' Now, he encourages a peaceful interchange of these ideas.

Kristeva and consciousness

By experimenting on dead bodies rather than allowing them to take center stage in an accepted death ritual – such as internment, cremation, or sky burial – von Hagens has crossed a line that shocks some consumers and intrigues others. The reasons for this go beyond 'mere religion,' prompting questions about the ego and its boundaries.

As Freud and Jung observed – and Kristeva herself expresses – individual and collective consciousness abhors death. It remains an obstacle we, as mortals, cannot overcome.

Embalming processes from ancient Egypt to the present day, as well as faces on coins, talismans, burial tombs and embalmed corpses in silk-lined coffins speak to the profound denial of our mortality. Despite the expense, the waste, the illogic of it all, consumers in the Western world, at least, spare no effort to preserve the departed and ensure their comfort on whatever journey they believe they will take – knowing, at a profound level, it is a journey we ourselves will take.

The visceral feeling of abhorrence has a basis, Kristeva argues, in the breakdown of boundaries that allow us to function on a day-to-day basis without thinking about mortality and the chaos that exists beyond our lingual structures. Kristeva posits that there is something that exists beyond our understanding of the world, that there are experiences that exist outside our civilized boundaries. This 'other' which is not a part of us, nor a part of that which we can control – neither subject nor object. This is the abject. Different from a theory recognizable to the social scientist, Kristeva's theory of the abject is more of a generalized world view that gives voice to our (ultimately ineffable) fear of the repulsive. As such, it provides an especially nice fit with a museum exhibit that deals in cadavers.

Kristeva posits that the power of the abject lies in its inability to be categorized. It exists as a repugnancy that haunts us, but which also possesses a sublimity that transforms us. The most concise, and wholly incomplete, way to define the abject for quick reference is that it is the opposition of the self – in whatever form that may take – but it also a recognition of a dichotomy that allows for an 'I' or a self to exist. The revelation of this boundary is the feeling of abjection. Small wonder, then, that the abject surrounds us and has the ability to drive our creative endeavors. Art becomes 'that catharsis par excellence ... which is rooted in the abject it utters and by the same token purifies' (Kristeva, 17). If the consumer experiences something akin to a religious awakening from *Body Worlds*, it is no accident, because religion and the abject are entwined. 'The various means of *purifying* the abject – the various catharses – make up the history of religions.'

Divine invention

As Kristeva would predict, that's how consumers typically react after they've seen the *Body Worlds* exhibit. A sampling of comments in the guestbook show the extent to which the abject has been diminished, even eradicated:

> An amazing show! What a piece of work is Man!

> God surely knew what He was doing when He created us! Only God could have created so complicated a being!

> Talk about a miracle. Truly beautiful!

> If this doesn't make you believe in God, I don't know what will!

The vast majority of visitors are awestruck by what they see at *Body Worlds*. And the comments, brief and ebullient, tend towards the spiritual. Thanks and praise to a Higher Being abound. Intelligent design is often invoked. Visitors marvel at the wonders of the human body as revealed by von Hagens, but the ultimate attribution is divine.

This may not be surprising, for several reasons. One is that *Body Worlds* deals in human bodies that were once human beings. Most attendees of the exhibit are willing to assign a spiritual dimension to the bodies. If the body is the temple of the spirit, as many people believe, then the body is still sacred, even if the spirit has left. Respect, if not reverence, is required. This is why the more vehement critics of *Body Worlds* ask that the plastinates be buried rather than displayed.

Another reason is that, when standing before a cadaver-presented-as-plastinate, almost all viewers are awe-struck by the intricacy, the fragility, and – strangely enough – the beauty of the systems on display. It's like seeing a photo of the Milky Way. One simply cannot conceive of putting together something so complicated, on such a grand scale. Where the human attribution falls short, the divine steps in, for most viewers.

In Kristeva's terms, *Body Worlds* succeeds brilliantly at purifying the abject. The special revulsion reserved for the cadaver has been controverted to admiration and affiliation. The spectators hung out with 'real human bodies,' and it wasn't so bad. The spiritual presence so many visitors acknowledge contains a sense of relief, as if to say, 'I *knew* we came from God!'

Other comments, gleaned from dozens of brief interviews with visitors as they left the exhibit, reveal a deep personal connection with particular body parts, based on a health crisis that affected a loved one, or themselves:

> When they showed the blackened lungs from the smoker, I knew that's what killed my dad.

> My uncle drank too much, and his liver must have looked like that one they showed with cirrhosis.

> Seeing all that fat … I've got to start exercising!

Many respondents perceive the exhibit as a cautionary tale. Marbled fat in a leg, blackened tissue in a lung become the object lessons of lives carelessly led, of loved ones lost too soon. The resolution: turn from your wickedness and live (healthfully), so that you'll be around for your children's children. At least in that moment, visitors commit to a path of clean living that will ensure their longevity.

However, a distinct minority of comments expressed reservations with the exhibit itself, as well as with plastination. Artists, as well as those who have worked in the medical professions, took a more jaundiced view:

> He wanted to turn a dead body into a work of art, and he failed at both.

> He says he used real human bodies, but there's maybe 3 percent of anything human left in these figures. It's mostly synthetic.

> This is like no cadaver I've ever worked with. Real cadavers smell like formaldehyde, and their skin is gray. Their muscles are darker. And they need ventilation.

He's removed the sight and the smell of the cadaver. He's taken away the stigma and the taboo.

Respondents wise to the ways of anatomical preservation almost grudgingly acknowledge his technical brilliance, while questioning the intention:

I see what he's trying to do here. It's a purposeful attempt to blend art and science. Art meets pop-science. For most people, he's succeeded.

In other words, experts in the medical profession and those concerned with aesthetics focus less on the outcome and more on the process and its creator.

Abject lessons

By the numbers alone, *Body Worlds* continues to occupy a significant and sustained cultural moment. But numbers alone cannot explain the show's overwhelming success.

Rather, our cultural-interpretive findings demonstrate that, through a brilliant application of technology and a fluid application of theatrical effects, *Body Worlds* controverts the abject into something palatable, even desirable. In this context, consumers tolerate the presence of the cadaver because most of them do not recognize it as such. Hence, a potentially horrific experience becomes an hedonic one (Andreasen and Belk, 1980; Hirschman and Holbrook, 1982). More significantly, *Body Worlds* offers an alternative to the cadaver, and by extension, to death. The plastinate, which offers the possibility of never-ending life.

Along the way, *Body Worlds* animates and engages consumers in a way that few museum exhibits do. In one oft-repeated interaction pattern, a man points to a body part in a casement, then explains to a woman how that part functions. He does so by showing her where it is on his body. This theater of mimesis and exhibitionism, set against the sublimity of the abject, crosses a bridge without burning it. Touch, flex, trace: one body responds to another in pre-verbal, pre-conscious ways.

Male consumers seem particularly energized by *Body Worlds*, as though they've finally found a museum exhibit they can relate to. The naked body posed in idealized glory: what's not to love? Part Greco-Roman locker room, part Playboy Mansion of the departed, *Body Worlds* titillates as it educates. And many men respond accordingly: softly chortling, peering and pointing. The experience is intoxicating for many of them. But it can also be overpowering, inducing a kind of hyperfocus that goes beyond flow (Csikszentmihalyi, 1991). The security guards we interviewed noted that that at least three people faint every day at *Body Worlds*, and two of those three are men.

By any measure, *Body Worlds* is intense and immersive (Firat, 2001). The theatrical effects of black velvet drapes, laser-sharp lighting, clear acrylic casements, slick videos, and stylized posters profoundly shape the consumption experience (Pine and Gilmore, 1999, 2011). As sound is muffled, sight is heightened. Any type of odor is, understandably, nonexistent. The sense of touch is denied. Yet consumers appear to compensate for this lack of sensorial input by touching themselves, flexing their muscles, and tracing the outline of the plastinates with their hands. Strangely enough, *Body Worlds* is an embodied experience (Joy and Sherry, 2003). Although consumers' senses are attenuated, their living bodies relate to their once-living counterparts in pre-conscious ways.

Undeniably, von Hagens' technical brilliance and flamboyant persona help build a bridge between the living and the non-living. His success in preserving cosmetized cadavers that will last for decades means that he and his plastinates are welcome in the most prestigious museums of science and nature around the globe. This legitimation is an achievement (Humphreys, 2010) that helps pre-figure consumer perceptions about the exhibit itself (i.e., If this is showing at the Museum of Science and Industry in Chicago, it must be okay). One need only visit knock-off exhibits in discount shopping malls to experience the illegitimate, which in this context becomes the freakish and the macabre.

Beyond these effects, *Body Worlds* promotes a fascinating, if subtle, politics of the body. A few areas within the exhibit display political biases, in spite of the expected equality created by the skinless plastinates. Some Euro-centrism is probably to be expected, given *Body Worlds* German origins, but the underlying exaltation seems to be for visitors to strive towards becoming the Übermensch.

For instance, the posters feature quotes from great thinkers, artists, and leaders. In each of these instances, the individual's nationality is linked to their words or accomplishments – except for Monet and Degas, the only prominent French nationals featured. And all the quotations focus on power, leadership, and self-determination. Throughout the exhibit, *Body Worlds* makes it clear that the consumer's preference should always be towards strength. An underlying jingoistic message pervades even the signage titles, such as 'Battle the Radicals' (cancer) or 'Too Much of a Good Thing' (obesity). Consumers see an Alzheimer-riddled brain and are told that, because they live so long in the First World, by 2050, 14 million Americans will have Alzheimer's. Then the consumer is told how to live as long as possible. The message is not always consistent, nor is it always clear.

In the exhibit's only direct acknowledgement that humans, and thereby consumers, will die, a post-mortem photo of a body in a casket adorns a sign that explains what happens when the brain dies. However, in a subtle undermining, directly adjacent to this message is a plastinate skeleton emerging from a grave. This theatrical positioning harkens back to old beliefs about the dead dancing at night, reinforcing the theme, however crudely, that death is not an end.

These contradictions aside, the brilliance of *Body Worlds* is that von Hagens has created a giant safety lens through which consumers can gaze upon the boundless and feel the sublimity of the abject without being consumed by it. A bridge has been built, but not burned; consumers can still go back. In that sense, plastination is the modern-day equivalent of Victorian post-mortem photography: an application of a new technology that gives the grieving the solace of immortality – for the departed, and perhaps for themselves.

Kristeva observed that the presence of the abject drives creative powers. We make things to show that we are still alive. But sometimes those things take on a life of their own and come back to haunt us. Like Frankenstein's monster, *Body Worlds* circles the globe and haunts consumers, but in a form most of them can handle. The cadaver is back, but in a sleek, plastinated package, a theatrically produced palliative that seems ready to accompany us on that most excellent adventure, whenever we're ready. In the case of *Body Worlds*, the return of the repressed is what drives both producers and consumers on.

References

Andreasen, A., and R. Belk. 1980. Predictors of attendance at the performing arts. *Journal of Consumer Research* 7, no. 2: 112–120.

Arnould, E., and M. Wallendorf. 1994. Market-oriented ethnography: Interpretation building and marketing strategy formulation. *Journal of Marketing Research* 31, no. 4: 484–504.

Csikszentmihalyi, M. 1991. *Flow: The psychology of optimal experience.* New York: Harper & Row.

Firat, F. 2001. The meanings and messages of Las Vegas: The present of our future. *Management* 2, no. 3: 101–120.

Firat, F., and A. Venkatesh. 1995. Liberatory postmodernism and the reenchantment of consumption. *Journal of Consumer Research* 22, no. 3: 239–267.

Hirschman, E., and M. Holbrook. 1982. Hedonic consumption: emerging concepts, methods, and propositions. *Journal of Marketing* 46, no. 3: 92–101.

Humphreys, A. 2010. Semiotic structure and the legitimation of consumption practices: The case of casino gambling. *Journal of Consumer Research* 37, no. 3: 490–510.

Joy, A., and J. Sherry. 2003. Speaking of art and embodied imagination: A multisensory approach to understanding aesthetic experience. *Journal of Consumer Research* 30, no. 2: 259–282.

Kristeva, J. 1982. *Powers of horror: An essay on abjection.* Tr. by Roudiez, L. New York: Columbia University Press.

Pine, B., and J. Gilmore. 1999, updated 2011. *The experience economy: Work is theatre and every business a stage.* Boston, MA: Harvard Business Press.

Part V
Alternate endings

17 The 'mortal coil' and the political economy of death

A critical engagement with Baudrillard

Ai-Ling Lai

> At the very core of the 'rationality' of our culture, however, is an exclusion that precedes every other: ... the exclusion of dead and of death. There is an irreversible evolution from savage (pre-modern) societies to our own: little by little, the dead cease to exist. They are thrown out of the group's symbolic circulation.... Strictly speaking, we no longer know what to do with them, since today, it is not normal to be dead, and this is new. To be dead is an unthinkable anomaly; nothing else is as offensive as this. Death is a delinquency, and an incurable deviancy ... The cemetery no longer exists because modern cities have entirely taken over their function: they are ghost towns, cities of death. If the great operational metropolis is the final form of an entire culture, then, quite simply, ours is a culture of death.
>
> (Baudrillard (1993), *Symbolic Exchange and Death*, pp. 126–127)

Introduction

This chapter provides a critical engagement with Jean Baudrillard's (1993) *Symbolic Exchange and Death* by discussing how the concept of 'symbolic exchange' challenges the modernist account of 'death denial' in Western societies (Becker, 1973; Aries, 1974). The 'denial of death' thesis is premised on the assumption that culture emerges as a wellspring of human activities to cope with the anxiety of death; to the extent of its radical extradition from life (Baudrillard, 1993; Bauman, 1992). Baudrillard (1993: 147) is highly contemptuous of the exclusion of death in modern societies, claiming that this constitutes a 'phantasm' that is concealed through various cultural institutions. Specifically, Baudrillard observes how culture has put in place various survival policies to foster an 'imaginary' transcendence (p. 131), as evident in the promise of (1) *religion* in securing immortality in the 'afterlife' (p. 128); (2) *scientific rationality* in mastering the materiality of death (p. 152) and (3) *capitalist political economy* in cultivating 'fantastic secularisation' through the production and accumulation of capital (p. 129). This chapter focuses its discussion on (2) and (3).

In particular, I discuss how the mortal body emerges as a locus of social control and a target of marketplace intervention (Turley, 2005). Baudrillard explains that this pre-occupation with the body is rooted in the cultural redefinition of death as a biological phenomenon – a concept he calls 'punctual death'. Tierney (2012; 1997) argues that 'punctual death' reflects modernity's attempt to rationalise death in a scientific manner. Elsewhere, Bauman (1992) contends that the bid for (im)mortality in modernity is poignantly marked by the paradoxical struggle with the body, which is at once a conduit of life and a potent reminder of death. For Baudrillard, as for Bauman, death infiltrates the very fabric of modern lives as individuals invest in various body projects (Shilling, 1993) and cultural practices[1] to come to terms with the ephemerality of their mortal coils. Baudrillard argues that such investments create an 'illusion' that masks the symbolic absence of death (Perniola, 2011), while simultaneously re-establishes it as an *equivalent* 'presence' in the everyday praxis of life. As Baudrillard argues, modern (consumer) culture is profoundly a 'culture of death' (p. 127).

Drawing on the writings of Bauman (1992), Turley (2005: 74) argues that 'much of consumption is a crusade against the eventualities of death' and that consumer culture ascends in power by providing individuals with avenues to 'buy their way out of deconstructed death'. Elsewhere, Turley (1997) concurs with Baudrillard, stating that death cannot be conceptualised as a punctual *terminus ad quem*, which marks the omega point of consumption. Instead, he argues that death is everywhere present in the consumption landscapes and thus needs to be 'reinstated on an equal footing with living' (p. 352). He therefore suggests that interesting insights can be gleaned by exploring consumption contexts where death is *non-imminent*.

To date, death studies in consumer research have tended to focus on the role of consumption and (dis)possession that take place during the 'fateful moment' (Giddens, 1991) when death is *imminent* (Turley, 2005). For instance, these studies explore the role of mortuary rituals in the consumption of funerals (Bonsu and Belk, 2003; Gabel *et al.*, 1996; Ozanne, 1992), the role of possessions for the bereaved (O'Donohoe and Turley, 1999; Gentry *et al.*, 1995; Young and Wallendorf, 1989; Turley, 1995), the experience of dispossession among dying consumers (Pavia, 1993; Stevenson and Kates, 1999) and the posthumous memorialisation of the departed (O'Donohoe and Turley, 2006). While these scholars pave the way for the exploration of mortality in consumer research, their studies are nevertheless restricted to the conceptualisation of death as an end-of-life event. This chapter endeavours to broaden the study of death by exploring its concealed presence in consumer culture.

This chapter will commence with a review of Baudrillard's critique of modernity and how this leads to his exploration of 'symbolic exchange' as a counter-narrative. The next section revisits the 'denial of death' thesis from Baudrillard's perspective and discusses his deconstruction of the theory. The final sections draw on Baudrillard's observation to analyse how modern societies construct a culture of hygiene, longevity and security around the mortal body and how the concept of 'symbolic exchange' is implicated within these contexts.

Baudrillard and the turn to symbolic exchange

Baudrillard has often been described as a provocateur (Kellner, 1994) since his writings are often intended as a provocation to induce his readers into considering an alternative vision of modern life (Bogard, 1990). In *The Mirror of Production* (1973/1975), Baudrillard mounted a systematic attack on classical Marxism (Kellner, 1994), arguing that Marx's productivist ideology is counter-revolutionary. He explains that the privileging of production as a central principle in the organisation of society is inadequate since it merely reinforces the agenda of capitalism (Kellner, 1974). According to Poster (1975: 3), Baudrillard is particularly concerned with Marx's rationalisation of social wealth as a universal activity of men, since this convinces 'men that they are alienated by the sale of their labour power; hence it censors the much more radical hypothesis that they do not have to be labour power, the "unalienable" power of creating value by their labour.'

Symbolic Exchange and Death reflects Baudrillard's radical break from Marx's political economy (Kellner, 1994). Inspired by Marcel Mauss' (1950/2002) study of gift economies, Baudrillard turns to the concept of 'symbolic exchange'[2] (which characterised the organisation of life in pre-modern societies) to offer an emancipatory alternative to Marx's production logic (Kellner, 1994). Baudrillard proposes that it is through the reinterpretation of death as symbolic exchange that we can begin to destabilise the totalised value system of capitalist political economy (Hegarty, 2004; Groom, 1996). As Baudrillard (1993: 187) remarks, 'if political economy is the most rigorous attempt to put an end to death, it is clear that only death can put an end to political economy.'

Baudrillard defines the 'symbolic' as 'the cycle of exchanges, the cycle of giving and returning, an order born of reversibility' (p. 136). Here, death is offered as a counter gift in the symbolic exchange with the living. By conceptualising death in terms of symbolic exchange, Baudrillard hopes to rekindle the reciprocal relationship between the dead and the living since 'death is *given* and *received*, and is therefore reversible in the social exchange, soluble in exchange' (p. 132).

In pre-modern societies, the dead is embraced by the living as a continuous presence who still has a role to play (Tierney, 1997). As Baudrillard (1993: 159) observes, symbolic exchange dictates that 'life is given over to death and death continues to articulate life and exchange with life' by infusing it with meaning. As such, symbolic exchange challenges the modern idea of life as a *biological linearity* that begins with birth and ends with death. Rather birth and death are to be understood as a *social cycle* that perpetually sustains itself. From this perspective then, the boundaries between the living and the dead are permeable since they are mutually enriching, interdependent and reversible[3] (Tierney, 1997).

According to Baudrillard, modern culture has severed the social relation between the dead and the living. He explains that this is due to the way in which modern culture operates, which is predicated on the process of accumulation at the expense of symbolic exchange. He contends that the primary engine that drives the rationality of capitalist political economy is the abolishment of death through the accumulation of *time-as-value* (longevity). However, as *time* accrued through the postponement of (biological) death can no longer be symbolically exchanged; it becomes objectified as a currency to be converted into life-capital (e.g. life span). Concomitantly, the dead and the dying are divested of their value as social beings and are therefore precluded from engaging in a reciprocal exchange with the living. In other words, the dead has nothing 'valuable' to offer the living and thus must be exiled from society and 'thrown out of the group's symbolic circulation' (Baudrillard, 1993: 126). In sum, capitalist political economy reduces 'life to an *absolute-surplus value* by subtracting death from it' (p. 127).

When Baudrillard bemoans that we have witnessed an irreversible evolution from the pre-modern age of symbolic exchange to the modern age of political economy, it is easy to dismiss his thesis as a nostalgic longing for a fusional utopia (Turley, 1997). Baudrillard refutes this, stating that the return to the pre-modern age cannot be considered as nostalgia since it does not constitute a 'rediscovery of some miraculous innocence where the followers of "desire" roam freely and the primary processes are realised without prohibition' (p. 137). However, he acknowledges that his conceptualisation of 'symbolic exchange' is deliberately utopian. By stressing its extreme, Baudrillard hopes to offer 'symbolic exchange' as a counter-myth (Tierney, 1997) that challenges the metanarrative of modernity. According to Hegarty (2004: 16), Baudrillard is not entirely opposed to modernist progress, but he is disenchanted by its distortion under capitalism where death 'becomes the object of a perverse desire' (p. 147) invested in the separation of life and death. *Symbolic Exchange and Death* can therefore be read as a deconstruction of modern culture (Groom, 1996), and in so doing, engender a conceptualisation of death that is reversible, reciprocal and inseparable from life. Baudrillard's analysis therefore provides a useful interpretation of the 'denial of death' thesis currently dominating the social sciences.

Revisiting the death denial thesis

According to McManus (2013), the 'denial of death' thesis is deeply entrenched in the metanarrative of modernity. Proponents of the thesis have often described modern death as 'offensive' (Becker, 1973), 'a taboo' (Gorer, 1955/1965), 'remote and imminent' (Aries, 1987) and 'an embarrassing encounter' (Elias, 1985). The thesis has gained increasing prominence within the social sciences (especially in sociology) as a canonical body of work (Stanley and Wise, 2011). The theory has its roots in the psychoanalytic analysis of Ernest Becker (1973: 33), who argues that culture is a manifestation of man's creative life-ways to defend against the anxiety of death. Meanwhile, Berger (1967/1990) contends that society is a product of human activities where men come together to construct a meaningful 'sacred canopy' to shield against the terror of anomie. Yet, despite occupying a dominant position within the discipline, the 'denial of death' thesis is not without its criticisms.

Becker and Berger have been criticised for their over-psychologised, universalised and ahistorical views on death (Seale, 1998; Shilling, 1993; Moore and Williamson, 2003). McManus (2013) argues that the 'denial of death' thesis does not allow for the exploration of marginal experience and a nuanced understanding of death and dying. Similarly, Baudrillard (1993: 159) posits that death must be understood as 'a nuance of life; and life is a nuance of death'. As such, he considers it absurd that modernity should negate death as an 'unthinkable' anomaly – i.e., a deviant 'other' of life. Indeed, Baudrillard proclaims that:

> The irreversibility of biological death, its objective and punctual character, is a modern fact of science. It is specific to our culture. Every other culture says that death begins before death, that life goes on after life, and that it is impossible to distinguish life from death.
>
> (1993: 159)

While Baudrillard may have over-generalised the inseparability of life/death in 'every other culture', he nevertheless highlights the unique way in which modernity has repressed the symbolic potency of death once enjoyed by the dead (Tierney, 1997). He contends that pre-modern societies do not have a concept of biological death as a punctual termination of life. He does not dispute that death can be terrorising in these societies; rather the exigency of death is 'soluble' in symbolic exchange as it conjures away 'the double jurisdiction, the repressed psychical agency (and) the transcendent social instance' (p. 136).

In other words, it is because death is de-socialised that modern individuals come to experience it as a 'mortal' danger' since 'what cannot be symbolically exchanged becomes that which haunts us' (Hegarty, 2004:43). Baudrillard provides a historical-social interpretation of Freud, claiming that modern society has transformed death repression into *death drive*; its psychical energy becomes amplified as a hidden, subterranean psychological power (Perniola, 2011: 347). Consequently, life in modernity is a life lived in the shadow of death – as the repressed drive materialises as a sense of 'uncanniness' (*Unheimlich*) that takes the form of death anxiety. For Baudrillard then, the denial of death is a manifestation of the 'social repression of death, (which in turn) facilitates the shift towards the repressive socialisation of life' (p. 130).

Meanwhile, sociologists such as Seale (1998: 3) argue that the 'social organisation for death in late modernity is remarkably active, realistic and death accepting'. He distinguishes the psychological 'denial of death' from the sociological perspective, postulating that death is not so much 'denied' as it is 'sequestered' and systematically managed. According to Giddens (1991: 48), individuals create 'an ontological reference point as an integral aspect of 'going on' in the context of day-to-day life'. Ontological security must therefore be maintained through the routine 'bracketing' of death if one is to realistically immerse in the practicality of everyday life.

Sequestration therefore involves the relocation of death from the intermundane space of public life to the private sphere, where death is often understood as institutionalised dying (Stanley and Wise, 2011; Howarth, 2007). The latest ONS statistics (2013) documented that 50 per cent of deaths in England and Wales took place in NHS hospitals and another 28 per cent took place in care homes and hospices while only 21 per cent died in their own home. Baudrillard (1993) attributes the institutionalisation of death to the progressive medicalisation of the dying/dead body, which 'no longer has any place (to go) but within a technical milieu' (p. 183). By relegating the management of the dying/dead body to the functional space/time of the hospital, the symbolic difference that identifies the deceased/patient's personhood is then neutralised and objectified.

Consequently, an impenetrable veil of silence has begun to form around the dying, whose social death[4] precedes their biological death (Mulkay and Ernst, 1991). Elias (1985: 85) observes that dying has become a lonely affair since 'never before have people died so noiselessly and hygienically as today ... in social conditions fostering so much solitude'. Baudrillard (1993: 163) concurs, stating that the 'third age', and by extension, the 'dying', has become a 'dead weight' on society, whose social existence has ceased to be symbolically recognised.

Stanley and Wise (2011: 948) dispute the sequestration thesis, stating that institutionalised dying does not necessarily replace the importance of domestic figuration as 'people continue to respond to dying and death, not as unconnected individuals, but as members of a network of interpersonal relationships'. In Baudrillard's term, the living and the dying continue to engage in a reversible social relation through symbolic exchange, where the shared experience of death/dying is reciprocated through the revitalisation of kinship. As Walter (1999) observes, the dead remain socially present through wills, ashes and graves as well as through memories, in the ongoing biography of the living (Bauman, 1992). In addition, Stanley and Wise (2011) argue that death is equally present in the public domain as it is in the private sphere, as demonstrated by public mourning practices such as roadside shrines. More recently, the advent of social media has fuelled the emergence of a new form of public commemoration in which private deaths are collectively shared online. Walter (2014) argues that online memorial culture has transformed the social relationship between the dead and the living that is reminiscent of the pre-industrial modes of mourning, which, as Baudrillard argues, is predicated on symbolic exchange. Here, the sharing of online memorials is akin to the social exchange of gift, which rejuvenates the reciprocal bond between members of the mourner's community. At the same time, the social presence of the dead is kept alive as they continue to impart lessons to the living in the form of collective memories (Tierney, 1997). While Walter (2014) considers online memorial culture as a new chapter in the history of mourning, Stanley and Wise (2011) suggest that there is a pluralisation in death practices, in which institutionally sequestered death exists alongside domestic figuration. Following Baudrillard, Tierney (1997) argues that the institutionalisation of death is not simply an act of sequestration; rather it constitutes the very foundation upon which power is established. As Baudrillard (1993) argues:

> Power is possible only if death is no longer free, only if the dead are put under surveillance ... The economic operation consists in life taking death hostage. This is a residual life which can from now on be read in the operational terms of calculation and value.
>
> (p. 130)

The mortal body emerges as a fundamental site where the struggle for power is enacted. If political economy operates on the basis of keeping death under surveillance, the body then constitutes the ground on which the battle to pre-serve life-as-value is fought. In the next section, I will discuss how modern societies localise their effort to manage the mortal body. In particular, I will illustrate how a network of industries has spawned around the mortal body by turning (1) sanitisation (2) longevity and (3) security into valuable investments in a capitalist political economy.

Sanitisation and the hygienic culture

> Our whole culture is hygienic, and aims to expurgate life from death. The detergents in the weakest washing powder are intended for death. To sterilise death at all costs, to varnish it, cryogenically freeze it, air con-dition it, put make-up on it, design it, to pursue it with the same relent-lessness as grime, sex, bacteriological or radioactive waste.... Death must therefore be *naturalised* in a stuffed simulacrum of life.
>
> (Baudrillard, 1993: 180–181)

Baudrillard observes how modern culture has made 'hygiene' its business, one that is intended to police, sterilise and expunge death from the realm of the living. From detergents to disinfectant, from food hygiene to sexual hygiene, from pest control to border control, from waste management to sewage man-agement – the task of modern culture is to ensure the living is hermetically sealed from the contagion of death.

McManus (2013) observes that a globally co-ordinated network of disease surveillance has been established to cope with the onset of emergent infec-tions. This is perhaps most notable in the 2003 SARS (Severe Acute Respira-tory Syndrome) outbreak in Southeast Asia, where affected and neighbouring countries joined forces to set up a series of regional disease surveillance net-works to control the cross-border transmission of the deadly virus and to facilitate the global exchange of information (New Straits Times, 2003;

Caballero-Anthony, 2005; Curley and Thomas, 2004). The scale of the SARS outbreak reflects the distance and rapidity in the global flows of people (McManus, 2013), and thus necessitates a surveillance approach that targets the moving body of travellers. Border checkpoints became the vanguard in the global policing of epidemic. Here, travellers were ushered through thermal imaging scanners where they were scrutinised and monitored for signs of infection (New Scientist, 2003). Compulsory quarantine and forced medical treatment were also imposed to isolate the 'infected' body from the 'uninfected' body (McManus, 2013). In isolation, the 'infected' body can then be *neutralised* within the sterilised space of the clinic and medical laboratory (Baudrillard, 1993). Meanwhile, the streets of Asian cities swarmed with surgically masked faces (Cohen, 2003), creating a foreboding atmosphere of death as civilians sought to stave off the risks of infection. Interestingly, the surgical mask has since attained a fetishised status in Asia as a fashion symbol, with chic designer and character imprinted masks widely available for consumption (Yang, 2014). As such, the facemask veils the unsettling presence of hazards by turning the culture of hygiene into a stylisation of death, or what the media has termed 'Smog-Couture' (RT News, 29 October 2014). More recently, the Ebola outbreak in West Africa has transformed the way in which the 'infected' body is handled and managed, as evident in the following BBC News article:

> Ebola relies on intimate social interaction to ensure its continued survival – it is passed on through close contact with the bodily fluids of infected individuals … The most simple human touch – a handshake or a hug – was quickly discouraged across the three worst affected countries. Liberia lost its traditional finger-snap greeting. And the fabric of the final goodbye changed too. Traditional burial ceremonies were re-written, mourning practices – such as washing the bodies of the deceased – were banned. Now a family can expect an Ebola response team to turn up, in full spacesuit-like gear, to take bodies away in the most dignified way possible in the circumstances. At the height of the outbreak, entire communities were quarantined. And for some in Sierra Leone, Christmas was cancelled.
>
> (BBC News, 23 March 2015)

The Ebola and SARS outbreaks have heightened the culture of hygiene, which prohibits the physical contact between those who are infected and those who are not. The leaky boundaries of the infected/deceased bodies are deemed dangerous and 'unhygienic' since they threaten to contaminate the uninfected/healthy bodies (Douglas, 1966; Baudrillard, 1993). Consequently, the body is pathologised as a potential repository of disease and a source of death, which must be managed and contained (Armstrong, 1987; Foucault, 1973).

Indeed it is the concern for public health and improved sanitation (in the late nineteenth century) that have led to the emergence of professional deathcare industry (Metcalf and Huntington, 1991). As McManus (2013) observes, medical and mortuary experts have taken over the tasks of managing and caring for the deceased, which were once the responsibility of the community. As a result, modern individuals have become increasingly de-skilled in the handling of the deceased body. By conceding the body to the care of mortuary experts, the deceased can then be transported to the techno-clinical space (morgue, crematorium, embalming room), where various pseudo-scientific techniques are employed to safely contain the decomposing potential of the flesh (Hallam *et al.*, 1999; McManus, 2013).

Baudrillard (1993) is especially perturbed by the modern practice of sar-cophagic rituals – such as embalming (and more recently the freezing of the body through cryogenics) – in which the body is artificially preserved to take on the 'appearance of life'. For instance, embalming is orchestrated to mask the signs of death and to return the decomposing body to the 'naturalness of life' (Baudrillard, 1993). In imitating life, the body is 'made to lie' (Hallam *et al.*, 1999) and in so doing, reinforces the modern binary that privileges life as 'natural' while death is problematised as an 'offence' against nature. The embalmed body is therefore a 'stuffed simulacrum of life' (Baudrillard, 1993), which conceals the scandal of death (Bauman, 1992).

Once again, Baudrillard urges us to return to pre-modern societies, where there is no ambiguity between the living and the dead. Instead of preserving the body, pre-modern societies embrace the decaying matter as a signifier that marks the deceased's rite of passage from the realm of the living to the realm of the dead. As such, they do not see the need to 'make the dead play the role of the living' (p. 181) for the dead are conceded their differences through their putrefying flesh, which is bequeathed to the living in symbolic exchange.

According to McManus (2013), a new archetype of death management is beginning to take shape in modernity. Most notably, bespoke funerals call for greater collaborations between mortuary experts, the deceased and their next-of-kin to 'negotiate the symbolic content, the meaning and the terms-of-passage for those who are transitioning from life to death' (p. 105). The return to the symbolic is also observed in emerging eco-friendly disposal practices such as natural burial and new cremation practices. Rumble *et al.* (2014: 244) demonstrates how these disposal practices constitute a de-sequestration of death by reclaiming the communal space where the dead and the living intermingle. Here, the dead enters into a *reciprocal* symbolic exchange with the living through the act of gifting' or 'giving something back', and thus nourishes the interconnection between them, the environment and the future generation. Eco-friendly disposal practices also transform the association of the decomposing body as 'unhygienic' and 'resource con-suming' to that which is 'purifying' and 'productive', as depicted in the dis-course of natural burial:

> In natural burial discourse, human remains nourish nature and become
> part of the natural world that sustains the living (West, 2008). Such

rhetoric invokes an animate gifting to nature, to fecundity, and to future generations ... Such views make the naturally buried dead 'valuable' to the living and to the planet – by fertilizing the soil, they propagate new life for the benefit of nature and enjoyment for the living. In this way, the corpse is no longer a *toxic* body to be disposed of but rather a *fertile* body to be dispersed back into the soil to nurture new life from its very decomposition.

(Rumble *et al.*, 2014: 247, *italics* in original)

While emerging cultural practices are beginning to revive the symbolic value of the dead/dying body, Baudrillard argues that modern societies are deeply invested in the maintenance of the 'living' body. In the next section, I discuss how modern societies capitalise on the prolongation of biological life and how the amassing of biological capital becomes tantamount to the convertibility of *time as value*.

Time as value: natural death and longevity

According to Baudrillard (1993), modern societies put a premium on the absolute '*value of life*', which must be preserved through the accumulation of *time*. As such, the '*value of life*' espouses the '*value of time*'. As living becomes a process of accumulation, the prolongation of life comes to be equated with the attainment of longevity (Tierney, 1997) accomplished through the biological deferment of death. According to McManus (2013), a new culture of death is emerging and becomes embedded in a consumer-based culture of longevity, where there is an expectation that the process of ageing can be delayed (if not reversed). Baudrillard argues that science and technology, in particular biomedicine, plays an important role in progressively pushing back the temporal frontiers of death and towards a linear infinity of time-as-value.

Consequently, the accumulation of time constitutes the marker of modern progress, which necessitates its quantification since it elevates scientific knowledge as objective truth. The quantification of *time-as-value* is most notable in statistics charting patterns of life expectancies, mortality rates, birth rates, morbidity rates, and success rates in medical treatments. According to Baudrillard (1993), the prolongation of life is predicated on localising death in a precise point in time and space, and in modernity, this is directed at the maintenance of the body as a machine:

But our modern idea of death is controlled by a very different system of representations: that of the machine and the function. A machine either works or it does not. Thus the biological machine is either dead or alive.... The mind-body duality ... is death itself, since it objectifies the body as residual, as a bad object which takes its revenge by dying.... Therefore the mortal body is no more 'real' than the immortal soul: the idealism of the soul and the materialist idealism of the body, prolonged in biology.... The subject needs a myth of its end, as of its origin, to form its identity.

(Baudrillard, 1993: 159)

The 'body-as-a-machine' is a Cartesian metaphor predicated on the laws of mechanical causation and mathematical reasoning as its epistemological foundation (Crossley, 2001). A dead body, like a 'broken' machine is nothing but a 'bad object' that has irreversibly exhausted its functional value. The body-as-machine metaphor therefore corresponds with the modern conception of death as a punctual cessation of biological life (Tierney, 2012). Thus, one is either alive or dead; the machine is either working or not working. Meanwhile, the vitality of the biological machine rests on optimising its function. In addition, Baudrillard acknowledges that the body is central to the construction of self-identities in modernity (Mellor, 1993). Since death is de-socialised in modernity, individuals require the myth of biological death to rationalise the 'demise' of the self (Tierney, 2012). Equally, such a myth also heightens the quest for modern individuals to work on the body as part of their identity constructions (Shilling, 1993).

Bauman (1992) remarks that the pursuit of health – in the form of self-care projects (e.g. dieting and exercise) – has become a pre-occupation for individuals in modern societies. The health and fitness industry is asserting an increasing hold on the consuming body by offering a plethora of health-care products/services aimed at disciplining and optimising its biological function. Consequently, fitness becomes objectified as biological capital, which must be measured and monitored in terms of body mass index, optimal heart rate, cholesterol level etc. By building-up one's biological capital (fitness), one is also amassing time-as-capital, which is quantified in terms of life expectancy. As such, consumers can 'buy time' by buying into the 'culture of fitness' (Sassatelli, 2010).

Bauman (1992) claims that the participation in self-care regimes is tied to the moral discourse of self-responsibility. By managing one's health, one also plays a personal role in controlling the unmanageable 'problem' of death. However, Baudrillard (1993) is concerned that the cultural insistence on preserving 'life-as-absolute-value' has compelled individuals to adhere to the moral 'duty' to 'stay alive and healthy'. For Baudrillard, such a moralistic discourse conceals the expansion of State control across an individual's entire lifespan, in which he/she is stripped of the freedom to exercise personal choices over matters of life and death:

From birth control to death control, whether we execute people or compel their survival, the essential thing is that the decision is withdrawn from them, that their life and their death are never freely theirs, but they live or die according to a social visa.

(Baudrillard, 1993: 174)

In modernity, death as a result of biological causes is seen as a 'natural' way of dying since it 'comes under medical care and finds us in good health and old age' (Baudrillard, 1993: 175). Consequently, 'natural death' is idealised as 'good death' as it comes 'at life's proper term' (Baudrillard, 1993). On the contrary, premature, suicide and violent deaths are designated as 'unnatural' or 'bad death' as they defy the orthodoxy to preserve 'life-as-value'. Indeed, dying at a young age is 'scandalous' since it signifies the failure of scientific rationality to prolong the biological capital of life. Violence, and, in particular, suicide, are considered the ultimate sabotage to 'life-as-value' as it involves the wilful destruction of biological capital, and thus subverts State monopoly over death (Baudrillard, 1993).

Tierney (1997) argues that suicide is a subversive form of freedom that calls into question our dependence on modern medicine in deciding when and how we should die. This is especially acute in recent years as we witness an increase in public demands for legalised euthanasia and physician-assisted suicide (*Guardian*, 18 July 2014). McManus (2013) alludes that the 'right-to-die' movement signals a shift in power, in which medical professional are no longer seen as figures of authority; rather they must negotiate with the dying (as opposed to dictating) the manner of death that is deemed appropriate. Tierney (1997) is less optimistic, and instead concurs with Baudrillard, arguing that the legalisation of the 'right to die' will merely reinforce the social control of death by medical authorities. Baudrillard questions as to whether it is possible to integrate death as a social service that is made available for consumption as part of the healthcare system. He is, however, sceptical of such a prospect, postulating that by allowing individuals to exercise the freedom to die, modern societies must also renounce the idea of preserving life-as-absolute-value (sanctity of life). Such an idea contravenes the vested interest biomedicine has placed in governing the biological body as a site of natural death.

> And if your death is conceded you, it will still be by (medical) order ... death proper has been abolished to make room for death control and euthanasia ... it is no longer even death but something completely neutralised that comes to be inscribed in the rules and calculations of equivalence. It must be possible to operate death as a social service, integrate it like health and disease under the sign of the Plan and Social Security. This is the story of 'motel-suicides' in the USA where, for a comfortable sum, one can purchase one's death under the most agreeable conditions (like any other consumer good) ... Why did death not become a social service when, like, everything else, it is functionalised as individual and computable consumption in social input and output? In order that the system consents to such economic sacrifices in the artificial resurrection of its living losses, it must have a fundamental interest in withdrawing even the biological chance of death from people.
>
> (p. 174)

As modern society continues to privilege 'natural death', it inevitably suffers from a 'collective paranoia' where 'unnatural deaths' such as accidents, murder, terrorism etc. threatens to undermine social order. This engenders the marketisation of 'security' as a form of commodity.

Security and disaster capitalism

Baudrillard (1993, p. 177) argues that security is an industrial business predicated on turning accident, disease and pollution into capitalist surplus profit. This observation is reflected in Naomi Klein's (2007) depiction of 'disaster capitalism'. In *The Shock* Doctrine, Klein (2007) reveals how private corporations capitalise on the collective trauma in the aftermath of catastrophic events by turning it into commercial opportunity (McManus, 2013). She argues that the rise in neoliberal free market policies have led to the privatisation of aid, which sees corporations taking over the task of disaster management contracted to them by government agencies, thereby shifting considerable wealth from the public sector to the private sector. Following the devastating impact of Hurricane Katrina, Klein observes how New Orleans' public infrastructures such as housing, hospitals and schools have been demolished – in the name of the city's clean-up operation – to pave way for the development of private housing, which potentially generates considerable revenue for the developers. As such, disaster capitalism has reinstated the class divide between the wealthy and the poor and segregates those who can afford to pay their way out of death and those who cannot:

> The Red Cross has just announced a new disaster-response partnership with Wal-Mart. When the next hurricane hits, it will be a co-production of Big Aid and Big Box. This, apparently, is the lesson learned from the US government's calamitous response to Hurricane Katrina: businesses do disaster better. 'It's all going to be private enterprise before it's over,' Billy Wagner, emergency management chief for the Florida Keys, currently under hurricane watch for tropical storm Ernesto, said in April. 'They've got the expertise. They've got the resources.' But before this new consensus goes any further, perhaps it's time to take a look at where the privatisation of disaster began, and where it will inevitably lead … One year ago, New Orleans's working-class and poor citizens were stranded on their rooftops waiting for help that never came, while those who could pay their way escaped to safety. The country's political leaders claim it was all some terrible mistake, a breakdown in communication that is being fixed. Their solution is to go even further down the catastrophic road of 'private-sector solutions'.
>
> (*Guardian*, 30 August 2006)

While 'disaster capitalism' emerges in the aftermath of a catastrophic event, Baudrillard (1993) observes how security is manufactured and built into the production line of consumer goods, thereby creating an artificial milieu of death. From crash test dummies to aviation black boxes, from health warnings on cigarette packaging to the regulation of sexual health, from life insurance to eco-friendly offerings, consumer culture operates as a colossol armour, safe-guarding the consuming body. Indeed, Baudrillard contends that the 'biologisation of the body' goes hand in hand with the 'technicisation of the environment' and the materiality of 'techno-security' becomes an extension of the embodied self (Belk 1988). Baudrillard (1993, pp. 177–179) illustrates this in his example of car manufacturing:

> 'Belt up' says an advertising slogan for seatbelts … Thus car safety: mummified in his helmet, his seatbelt, all the paraphernalia of security, wrapped up in the security myth, the driver is nothing but a corpse, closed up in another, non-mythic death, as neutral and objective as technology, noiseless and expertly crafted. Riveted to his machine glued to the spot in it, he no longer runs the risk of dying, since he is *already* dead … the protective armour is just death miniaturised and become a technical extension of your own body.… After having exalted production, today we must therefore make security heroic. At a time when anybody at all can be killed driving any car whatsoever, at whatever speed, the true hero is he who refuses to die.

For Baudrillard, the consuming body is always '*already a corpse*' whose death is momentarily suspended within the technological milieu that makes up material culture. Just as the driver is a suspended 'mummified cadaver', the holder of life insurance policy is nothing but a 'corpse in the making.' Security, for Baudrillard, is an 'industrial prolongation of death' made possible by the material production of 'safety'. The car in this instance is a technologised hearse, manufactured to cocoon the body, and thus act as a protective skin against the potentiality of accidental deaths.

In addition, Baudrillard observes how 'safety' is made heroic through the moral discourse of responsibility where 'belting up' comes to be regarded as an act of a good citizen. In a similar vein, the breaching of 'safety' norms is regarded as a rebellious act. This is best encapsulated in Schouten and McAlexander's (1995) study on Harley Davidson subculture. They observe how Harley riders abhor the mandatory wearing of helmets, which they see as a symbol of confinement. This facilitates the emergence of a market for products that allow riders to subvert the legislation of safety and embrace the spirit of freedom.

Still, the chink in the armour of security invokes 'terror' as it signifies a breakdown in social control, leaving the consuming body unarmed and vulnerable. As Baudrillard (1993) proclaims, accidents (including catastrophe) are *sabotage* and identifying the causes of accidents is imperative in modern societies since accidental deaths do not abide by the law of rationality. The recent disappearance of the Malaysian MH370 flight is disturbing precisely because the incident brings to home a false sense of security society placed on modern technology: a sentiment best encapsulated by the following headlines: 'The Malaysia Airlines Disappearance Shows Technology's Limits' (*Wall Street Journal*, 11 March 2014). Yet, it is to technology that modern societies turn in the aftermath of disasters. As evident in the multinational search for the missing plane, the world responded by deploying a paraphernalia of technologies – ranging from satellite imaging charting the southern Indian Ocean, to search vessels documenting the underwater topography of the seabed (BBC News Asia, September 2014). This ensures that 'security' remains a technologised operation that continues to feed into the myth of scientific progress. While the headlines were dominated by news locating the 'cause' of the airplane disappearance, the casualties (with the exception of the pilots) were reduced to statistics of missing nationalities, whose deaths (while mourned) were depersonalised as objective facts, inflaming the ensuing political tension between Malaysia and China.

In addition, Baudrillard argues that modern consumer culture does not only prosper through the material production of security. Rather, consumer culture is perpetuated through an ongoing 'manufacturing' of risks. According to Giddens (1991), manufactured risk is a consequence of the modernisation process and as such is a product of human activity. In particular, Giddens observes that rapid technological changes have produced unanticipated ramifications, which become materialised as 'high-consequence risks'. Due to its emergent character, there is a lack of (concrete) experience as to what the risks are and how they can be eliminated, which therefore renders 'high-consequence risks' largely unpredictable. Environmental hazards (e.g. Chernobyl, BP Oil Spill), biomedical side-effects (e.g. Dolly the Sheep), genetically modified food, and deep space mining (e.g. asteroid mining), are examples of 'high-consequence risks' that have contributed to this unsettling atmosphere of insecurity in modernity. As Beck (1992: 20) proclaims, modern society is a risk society, where there is a heightened reflexivity of risks, in which the 'promise of security grows with the risks and destruction and must be reaffirmed over and over again to an alert and critical public through cosmetic or real interventions in the techno-economic development.' According to Baudrillard, the ongoing production of risks begets the growing demand for solutions. As such, it has created a society where individuals must fight for their rights to security. Baudrillard regards the industrialisation of security as 'social blackmail', since it acculturates consumers into believing that they need to insure against risks that are manufactured by the industry in the first place.

Conclusion

In this chapter, I have discussed how Baudrillard's conceptualisation of symbolic exchange poses a challenge to the modernist account of death. In particular, this chapter sheds light on Baudrillard's vision of capitalist political economy, which is sustained through the accumulation of *time-as-capital* by exerting social control over the mortal body. Consumer culture emerges as a powerful institution since it facilitates the process of accumulation and provides resources for the biological prolongation of life. In other words, we are made 'survivors' through our practical immersion in consumer culture, and through which we become socialised into a culture of hygiene, longevity and security. Yet, Baudrillard argues that our survival through (consumer) culture is ultimately futile since the act of accumulation reduces life to an *absolute-surplus-value* (p. 127), which is continuously held ransom by death. As such, the preservation of *life-as-value* begets the *equivalent* production of death.

Baudrillard is convinced that the return to the symbolic will abolish the demarcation between life and death, and in doing so, restores the social significance of death. More recently, the emergence of new death practices (e.g. natural burial, online memorial) suggests a return of the symbolic. Yet, the extent to which such practices are able to revolutionise modern death practices remains to be seen. For Baudrillard, revolution is possible if modern societies embrace the raw encounter with life and death in an immediate and reversible manner. After all, as Baudrillard alludes, we are *always* already a 'dead man walking'.

Notes

1 The bid to deconstruct mortality can be observed through body projects such as health and fitness, sports, cosmetic surgeries, etc., as well as through cultural practices such as the seeking of peak experiences, nationalism, relationships, wealth, just to name a few.
2 Baudrillard uses the term 'symbolic exchange' to refer to a 'form of transaction in which the exchange of objects cannot take place in any system without threatening that system with imminent collapse' (Groom, 1996: 689).
3 Baudrillard draws on the rite of initiation to demonstrate the reversibility between birth and death. Here, the initiate symbolically transverses the rite of passage, which marks the death of childhood and the transition into adulthood. Initiation is therefore a *simulation* of death (Perniola, 2011) as well as a *second birth* that facilitates the initiate's entry into the symbolic reality of exchange (Baudrillard, 1993).
4 Social death occurs when an individual has been stripped of his/her personhood and thus 'ceases to exist as an active individual agent in the ongoing social world of some other party' (Mulkay and Ernst, 1991: 178).

References

Aries, P. (1974). *Western Attitudes Towards Death: From the Middle Ages to the Present*, Baltimore: John Hopkins University Press.
Aries, P. (1987). *The Hour of Death*, London: Penguin.
Armstrong, D. (1987). Silence and Truth in Death and Dying. *Social Science and Medicine*, Vol. 24(8): pp. 651–658.
Baudrillard, J. (1973/1975). *The Mirror of Production*. St. Louis: Telos Press.
Baudrillard, J. (1993). *Symbolic Exchange and Death*, London: Sage.

Bauman, Z. (1992). *Mortality, Immortality and Other Life Strategies*, Standford: Stanford University Press.

BBC News Asia (8 September 2014), Missing Malaysia plane MH370: What we know. www.bbc.co.uk/news/world-asia-26503141. Accessed on 1 October 2014.

BBC News. (2015). How Ebola Changed The World. *BBC News.* 23 March 2014. www.bbc.co.uk/news/health-31982078. Accessed on 10 April 2015.

Beck, U. (1992). *Risk Society: Towards a New Modernity*, Sage Publication: London, Thousand Oak and New Delhi.

Becker, E. (1973). *The Denial of Death.* New York: Free Press, 1973.

Belk, R. W. (1988). Possessions and the Extended Self. *Journal of Consumer Research*, Vol. 15(9): pp. 139–168.

Berger, P. L. ([1967]1990). *The Sacred Canopy, Elements of a Sociological Theory of Religion*, New York: Anchor Books.

Bogard, W. (1990). Closing Down The Social: Baudrillard's Challenge to Contemporary Sociology. *Sociological Theory*, Vol. 8(1): pp. 1–25.

Bonsu, S., and Belk, R. W. (2003). Do Not Go Cheaply into That Good Night: Death Ritual Consumption in Asante, Ghana. *Journal of Consumer Research*, Vol. 30(June): pp. 41–55.

Caballero-Anthony, M. (2005). SARS in Asia: Crisis, Vulnerabilities, and Regional Responses. *Asian Survey*, Vol. 45(3): pp. 475–495.

Cohen, J. (2003). Do Surgical Masks Stop SARS? *Slate Magazine.* 7 April 2003.

Crossley, N. (2001). *The Social Body: Habits, Identity and Desire*, London: Sage.

Curley, M. and Thomas, N. (2004). Human Security and Public Health in Southeast Asia: the SARS Outbreak. *Australian Journal of International Affairs*, Vol. 58(1): pp. 17–32.

Douglas, M. (1966). *Purity and Danger: An Analysis of Concepts of Pollution and Taboo*, London: Routledge and Keegan Paul.

Elias, N. (1985). *The Loneliness of Dying*, Oxford: Blackwell.

Foucault, M. (1973). *The Birth of the Clinic*, trans. A. M. S. Smith, London: Tavistock.

Gabel, T. G., Mansfield, P. and Westbrook, K. (1996). The Disposal of Consumers: an Exploratory Analysis of Death-Related Consumption, in K.P. Corfman and J.G. Lynch Jr. (eds.), *Advances in Consumer Research*, Vol. 23, Provo, UT, Association for Consumer Research: pp. 361–367.

Gentry, J. W., Kennedy, P. F., Paul, C., and Hill, R. P. (1995). A Family Transitions During Grief: Discontinuities in Household Consumption Patterns. *Journal of Business Research*, Vol. 34(September): pp. 67–79.

Giddens, A. (1991). *Modernity and Self-Identity: Self and Society in the Late Modern Age*, Cambridge: Polity Press.

Gorer, G. (1965 [1955]). *Pornography of Death. In Death, Grief and Mourning Garden City*, NewYork: Doubleday.

Groom, N. (1996). Review: Symbolic Exchange and Death. *The Modern Language Review*, Vol. 91(3): pp. 689–691.

Guardian (2006). Disaster Capitalism: How To Make Money Out of Misery. 30 August 2006. www.theguardian.com/commentisfree/2006/aug/30/comment. hurricanekatrina. Accessed on 7 April 2015.

Guardian (2014). House of Lords Debate Evenly Split Over Assisted Dying Legislation. 18 July 2014. www.theguardian.com/society/2014/jul/18/assisted-dying-legalisation-debate-house-lords. Accessed on 7 April 2015.

Hallam, E., Hockey, J., and Howarth, G. (1999). *Beyond the Body: Death and Social Identity*, London: Routledge.

Hegarty, P. (2004). *Jean Baudrillard: Live Theory*, London and New York: Continuum.

Howarth G. (2007). *Death and Dying*, Cambridge: Polity.

Kellner, D. (1994). Introduction: Jean Baudrillard in the Fin-de-Millenium, in D. Kellner (ed.). *Baudrillard: A Critical Reader*, Cambridge and Oxford: Blackwell, pp. 1–24.

Klein, N. (2007). *The Shock Doctrine: The Rise of Disaster Capitalism*. London: Penguin.

McManus, R. (2013). *Death in a Global Age*, Palgrave Macmillan: London.

Mauss, M. (1950 [2002]). *The Gift: The Form and Reason for Exchange in Archaic Societies*, trans. W. D. Halls, London: Routledge Classics.

Mellor, P. A. (1993). Death In High Modernity: The Contemporary Presence and Absence of Death, in D. Clark (ed.), *The Sociology of Death: Theory, Culture and Practice*, Oxford: Blackwell Publishers, pp. 11–30.

Metcalf, P. and Huntington, R. (1991). *Celebrations of Death: The Anthropology of Mortuary Ritual*, Press Syndicate, University of Cambridge Press: Cambridge.

Moore, C. and Williamson, J. B. (2003). The Universal Fear of Death and The Cultural Response, in *Handbook of Death and Dying*, Sage Publications: Thousand Oaks, CA, pp. 3–14.

Mulkay, M., and Ernst, J. (1991). The Changing Profile of Social Death. *European Journal of Sociology*, Vol. 32: pp. 172–196.

New Scientist, (2003). Airports Scan For SARS victims' Flushed Faces. 24 April 2003. www.newscientist.com/article/dn3656-airports-scan-for-sars-victims-flushed-faces.html#.VVzBYvlViko. Accessed on 5 April 2015.

New Straits Times, (2003). Pre-travel Checks for ASEAN. 27 April 2003.

O' Donohoe, S., and Turley, D. (1999). Consumption, Identity and Coping Strategies in Times of Crisis, in E. J. Arnould and L. M. Scott (eds.), *Advances in Consumer Research*, Provo, UT, Association for Consumer Research, Vol. 26: pp. 421–423.

O'Donohoe, S. and Turley, D. (2006). Compassion at the Counter: Service Providers and Bereaved Consumers. *Human Relations*, Vol. 59 (10): pp. 1429–1448.

ONS Statistics (2013). National Survey of Bereaved People (Voices), Office for National Statistics.

Ozanne, J. L. (1992). The Role of Consumption and Disposition During Classic Rites of Passage: The Journey of Birth, Initiation and Death in J. F. Sherry Jr. and B. Sternthal (eds.), *Advances in Consumer Research*, Vol. 19: pp. 396–403.

Pavia, T. (1993). Dispossession and Perceptions of Self in Late Stage HIV infection, in L. Mcalister and M. L. Rothschild (eds.), *Advances in Consumer Research*, Provo, UT, Association for Consumer Research: pp. 425–428.

Perniola, M. (2011). Being-Towards-Death and The Simulacrum of Death: Heidegger and Baudrillard. *Cultural Politics*, Vol. 7(3): 345–358.

Poster, M. (1974). Translator's Introduction, in J. Baudrillard, *The Mirror of Production*, St. Louis: Telos Press: pp. 1–20.

RT News. (2014). Smog Couture: Facemasks on catwalk at China's Fashion Week. 29 October 2014, http://rt.com/news/200443-china-facemask-catwalk-pollution/. Accessed on 5 April 2015.

Rumble, H., Troyer, J., Walter, T. and Woodthorpe, K. (2014). Disposal or Dispersal?: Environmentalism and Final Treatment of the British Dead. *Mortality*, Vol. 19(3): pp. 243–260.

Sassatelli, R. (2010). *Fitness Culture: Gyms and The Commercialisation of Discipline and Fun*, Basingstoke and New York: Palgrave Macmillan.

Schouten, J. W. and McAlexander, J. H. (1995). Subcultures of Consumption: An Ethnography of the New Bikers, *Journal of Consumer Research*, Vol. 22(1): pp. 43–61.

Seale, C. (1998). *Constructing Death: The Sociology of Dying and Bereavement*, Cambridge: Cambridge University Press.

Shilling, C. (1993). *The Body and Social Theory*, London: Sage.

Stanley, L. and Wise, S. (2011). The Domestication of Death: The Sequestration Thesis and Domestic Figuration. *Sociology*, Vol. 45(6): pp. 947–962.

Stevenson, G. and Kates, S. M. (1999). The Last Gift: The Meanings of Gift-Giving in the Context of Dying of Aids, in E.J. Arnould and L. M. Scott (eds.), *Advances in Consumer Research*, Provo, UT, Vol. 26: Association for Consumer Research: pp. 113–118.

Tierney, T. F. (1997). Death, Medicine and The Right to Die: An Engagement With Heidegger, Bauman and Baudrillard. *Body and Society*, Vol. 3(4): pp. 51–77.

Tierney, T. F. (2012). Punctual Selves, Punctual Death and the Health-Conscious Cogito: Descartes' Dead Bodies. *Economy and Society*, Vol. 41(2): pp. 258–281.

Turley, D. (1995). Dialogue With The Departed, in F. Hansen (Ed.), *European Advances in Consumer Research,* Provo, UT, Association for Consumer Research, Vol. 2: 10–13.

Turley, D. (1997). A Postcard from The Very Edge: Mortality and Marketing, in S. Brown and D. Turley (eds.), *Consumer Research: Postcard From The Edge*, London and New York: Routledge, pp. 350–377.

Turley, D. (2005). Death, Where is thy Sting? Mortality and Consumer Motivation in the Writings of Zygmunt Bauman, in S. Ratneshwar and D. G. Mick (eds.), *Inside Consumption: Consumer Motives, Goals and Desires*, London and New York: Routledge pp. 67–85.

Wall Street Journal Online (11 March 2014), The Malaysia Airlines Disappearance Shows Technology's Limits: Radar, Satellites Are Powerful Tools but Still Have Limited Reach. http://online.wsj.com/articles/SB10001424052702304250204579 433581873448554. Accessed on 1 May 2014.

Walter, T. (1999). *On Bereavement*. Buckingham: Open University Press.

Walter, T. (2014). New Mourners, Old Mourners: Online Memorial Culture as a Chapter in the History of Mourning. *New Review of Hypermedia and Multimedia*, Vol. 21(1): pp. 1–15.

Yang, J. (2014). A Quick History of Why Asians Wear Surgical Masks in Public. Quartz. 19 November 2014. http://qz.com/299003/a-quick-history-of-why-asians-wear-surgical-masks-in-public/. Accessed on 5 April 2015.

Young, M. M., and Wallendorf, M. (1989). Ashes to Ashes, Dust to Dust: Conceptualizing Consumer Disposition of Possessions. In T. L. C. E. Al. (ed.), *American Marketing Association Winter Educators' Conference*, Chicago, American Marketing Association: pp. 33–39.

18 The spectre of posthumanism in technology consumption

The death of the human?

Margo Buchanan-Oliver and Angela Gracia B. Cruz

The marriage of reason and nightmare that dominated the 20th century has given birth to an ever more ambiguous world. Across the communications landscape move the spectres of sinister technologies.

(J. G. Ballard)

Our machines are disturbingly lively, and we ourselves frighteningly inert.

(D. J. Haraway)

Introduction

In the context of 'technology-intensive markets' (John, Weiss, and Dutta 1999: 78), a latent cultural concern has emerged about the location of agency and the death of human subjectivity. While the notions of nightmare, disturbance, and fright evoked by the 'spectres of sinister technologies' (Ballard 1973: 96) have long been a theme in interdisciplinary discourses of science, technology, and society (Clarke 2002; Helman 1988; Virilio 1997), marketing scholars and marketing communications texts have remained largely silent on the deep-seated disturbance evoked by these ontological concerns. The purpose of this chapter is to illuminate and illustrate these concerns.

This chapter contributes to the stream of marketing literature known as posthuman consumer culture. Posthuman consumer culture has been conceptualised as both an epistemology and an aesthetic mode. Previous studies have examined visual representations of posthumanism as represented by the figure of the cyborg (Campbell, O'Driscoll, and Saren 2005; Giesler 2004; Giesler and Venkatesh 2005; Schroeder and Dobers 2007; Venkatesh, Karababa, and Ger 2002). Scholars have further traced the linkage between posthuman epistemologies and cultural production (Venkatesh and Meamber 2006). In addition, while not explicitly linked with posthumanist concerns, explorations of technology consumption have also illustrated how consumers experience technology with a degree of ambivalence (Mick and Fournier 1998), identity tension (Schau and Gilly 2003), and anxiety (Meuter, Bitner, Ostrom, and Brown 2005; Mick and Fourner 1998). More recently, marketing scholars have begun to link posthuman visual aesthetics and consumer ambivalence to the wider 'context of context' (Askegaard and Linnet 2011: 381) in which these representations and responses are shaped (Buchanan-Oliver, Cruz, and Schroeder 2010; Buchanan-Oliver and Cruz 2011; Campbell and Saren 2010). These studies are beginning to uncover a genealogy of socio-historical and ontological disquiet in how humans face their technologies.

Building on this initial foundation, this chapter further explores ontological disquiet in human–technology interactions by drawing on the concept of abjection (Kristeva 1982) and illustrating how three forms of abjection play out in a marketing communications text to underline a profound and at times inarticulable horror concerning the potential of technology to disintegrate human subjectivity. We will examine recent theoretical assumptions about human interaction and relationship with machines, conceptualised as posthumanism. In particular, we show that abjection – the fear of losing what makes us human – permeates posthumanist discourses. Such fears arise out of the erosion of clear-cut boundaries between human/nonhuman, between organic/mechanistic, and between agency/dependency. We further illustrate various forms of abjection through a close examination of Playstation 3's 'Baby' advertisement. Anxieties over the death of human subjectivity, while ordinarily repressed in marketing representations of technology advertising, constitute a significant and palpable cultural concern which accompanies the emergence of technology-saturated markets. Given the simultaneously disturbing and arresting power of these ontological concerns, we interrogate the efficacy of addressing such ontological anxiety in the marketing communication of technology brands.

The spectre of posthumanism in technology consumption

Posthumanism posits a state of human/machine intersection where no separation exists between the human body and the machine. As Hayles (1999: 3) explains:

> In the posthuman, there are no essential differences or absolute demarcations between bodily existence and computer simulation, cybernetic mechanism and biological organism, robot teleology and human goals.

Posthumanism arises in opposition to the concepts of Enlightenment Humanism and Modernism. Posthumanism acknowledges the limitations of a humanist concept of 'man' in control (Gane 2005) and encourages a hoped-for transcendence of materiality (Wolfe 2010) which 'embraces the possibilities of information technologies without being seduced by the fantasies of unlimited power and disembodied immortality' (Hayles 1999: 5). In this vein, Venkatesh *et al.* (2002: 446) write that the emerging posthuman paradigm 'views the intersection of human and machine as a postmodern possibility in contrast to the received view under modernist thinking which considers these two entities as distinctly separate.' Throughout these conceptualisations is a repeated challenge to modernist dichotomies which demarcate clear boundaries between humans and their machines. Hence, posthumanist discourses offer new possibilities for rethinking human subjectivity. Posthumanist discourses highlight the constitutive role of technology in allowing consumers to 're-code' and 're-configure' themselves and dissolve the traditional boundaries of modernity (Firat and Venkatesh 1993). To counteract the cultural displacement of Humanism, Posthumanism considers necessary the rapid evolutionary human development in this technologically informed age through mechanical, biotechnical, or digital modification of the human body. These modifications range from the use of simple prosthetic devices such as spectacles and contact lenses to enhance body motor and sensory functions, to the building of technological environments around the body, to the incorporation of technology into the body as in the case of cosmetic surgery (Featherstone 2000).

Posthumanist discourses engender tensions between celebratory fascination and ontological anxiety. As Hayles (1999: 283) posits, 'the prospect of becoming posthuman both evokes terror and excites pleasure'. Such an intersection gives rise to a key tension in the cultural zeitgeist; what Haraway (1991: 150) calls the 'border wars', in which modernist boundaries and distinctions between humans and machines are simultaneously contested, blurred, and reaffirmed. Associated with these border wars is a crisis of human subjectivity. Bukatman (1993: 2) observed that the rise of electronic technology provokes 'a set of crucial ontological questions regarding the status *and power* of the human' (emphasis in original). As Bukatman (1993: 5) further explains, 'a desire for the extension of power that technologies permit is accompanied by the concomitant fear of a *loss* of power and the weakening of human control.'

These conflicts and confusions are vividly embodied in the hybrid and liminal figure of the cyborg, characterised by ambiguity, indeterminacy, contradiction, incoherence, and porosity of boundaries. The cyborg, Haraway (1991: 149) notes, is a liminal and contradictory figure: both material and metaphorical, both 'a creature of social reality as well as a creature of fiction'. The figure of the cyborg is used to underline and celebrate the hybridity, contingency, partiality, and incoherence of embodied subjectivity. A figure which is both human and machine, both flesh and metal, both spiritual and material, and ambiguous in gender, the cyborg for Haraway (1991) is the embodiment of liminality in its juxtaposition of contradictory opposites and in its inherently hybrid nature. The figure of the cyborg highlights the potential to break down traditional dichotomies between human and animal, organism and machine, physical and non-physical. The notion of the thirdspace (Campbell *et al.* 2005) – a space of heterogeneity and impurity which resists the dualistic separation associated with modernist conceptions – is particularly relevant here, as it erupts in the liminal figures of the superhuman, the robot, and the cyborg. These are creatures which embody the thirdspace by confounding traditional dichotomies and straddling the boundaries between human/nonhuman, subjective/ objective, living/nonliving, organic/artificial, spiritual/material, ambiguous/ mechanistic and empowered/enslaved.

However, such ambiguities are commonly coded in abject terms. Kristeva (1982) introduces the term abjection to describe a state of ontological liminality and paradox which is simultaneously fascinating and repulsive. Beyond their liberatory promise (Venkatesh *et al.* 2002), posthumanist discourses paradoxically harbour dangers, threats, and anxieties. Indeed, such liminal states of being do not fit in easily with regular narratives or extant categories and tend to be conceived as polluted, taboo, and associated with impurity, alterity, exclusion, danger and Otherness. In this vein, Derrida (1978: 293) writes of

> the as yet unnameable which is proclaiming itself and which can do so, as is necessary whenever a birth is in the offing, only under the species of the non-species, in the formless, mute, infant and terrifying form of monstrosity.

Clarke (2002: 35) similarly observes that 'liminal beings are [...] perceived as polluting [...] and are more often than not characterized as monstrous, diseased, queer, marginal, black, insane or female.' This is unsurprising because what 'dies' in the human–technology interaction as framed by posthumanist lenses is the idea of a coherent human subject as defined by modernist conceptions. The cyborg is a dramatic visual representation of fusions of the body and technology, with non-biological material literally piercing, merging with or entering the 'biological skin-bag' (Clark 2003).

The cyborg figure commonly invokes notions of Otherness, the abject and the unnatural, carrying with it mythic resonances with Frankenstein's monster and anxieties around pollution, contamination, recombination, and miscegenation (Helman 1988). This union of the artificial, unnatural, nonhuman, and Other with human being is a problematic and uneasy merger, raising concerns around the dilution or pollution of human identity. In particular, the concept of the abject is associated with feelings of anxiety, fear, and horror. The abject suffuses Virilio's (1997: 20) depiction of

> this citizen-terminal soon to be decked out to the eyeballs with interactive prostheses based on the pathological model of the 'spastic', wired to control his/her domestic environment without having physically to stir: the catastrophic figure of an individual who has lost the capacity for immediate intervention along with natural motricity and who abandons himself for want of anything better, to the capabilities of captors, sensors and other remote control scanners that turn him into a being controlled by the machine with which, they say, he talks.

In a similar vein, Woodward (1994: 62–63) writes that 'most of us fear the future prospect of frailty as a cyborg, "hooked up" ... to a machine.'

Such anxieties around posthuman abjection have been widely explored in cultural sites. Within popular culture, literary texts (e.g. 'Neuromancer', 'I, Robot', 'Brave New World', and 'Nova Express') and popular films (e.g. 'The Terminator', 'Blade Runner', 'The Matrix', 'Her', 'Lucy', and 'Transcendence') represent a liminal vision of human–machine interactions and their psychological and socio-cultural tensions and repercussions. Within the academy, scholars from media and communications studies, cognitive neuropsychology, cultural studies, and critical theory have explored these posthuman tensions. These perspectives are continually 're-visioning' technology and influencing how consumers think about and experience technology products, raising questions of identity, immortality, and the death of the human. To closely illustrate how abjection erupts in cultural expression, we now focus our attention on an eruption of posthuman abjection through a close analysis of a marketing communications text.

Tracing the death of the human in the Playstation 3 'Baby' advertisement

The Playstation 3 'Baby' advertisement, which originally aired in 2006, is the first of a series of television commercials which promoted Sony's launch of its Playstation 3 gaming console. This 30-second advertisement opens from a brief state of initial darkness to the sight and sound of bright fluorescent lights flickering to life. The establishing shot reveals a clinical white room, perhaps a laboratory or an interrogation room. The *mise-en-scène* presents an unclothed and ungendered Baby, sitting in one corner of the room, facing a black box (the Playstation 3) in the opposite corner. The soft-fleshed Baby is positioned with both arms extended towards the machine. As deep, rumbling, and foreboding music slowly rises in intensity in the background, shots of the Baby are interspersed with shots of the Playstation 3. In these shots, the image of the Baby is reflected in the Playstation 3's shiny surface. Suddenly, the Baby opens its eyes to the sound of a camera click and exhibits a range of life-like yet competing and incongruent emotions. The Baby makes cooing noises and lifts up its hands towards the Playstation 3, as if reaching for the machine (*in propria persona* the Baby's mother?).The Baby blinks several times while smiling, and we hear the laughter of an innocent baby. We then see the Baby's smile transform into a frown and then a cry, but this is eerily juxtaposed against the sound of a mechanical adult laugh. The Baby then opens its mouth wide while we hear a screeching and mechanical gasp. Its eyes display an expression of surprise, or perhaps fear. A close up of the Baby's eyes shows different gaming scenes flashing through its eyes. We hear the sound of crying and see tears running down the Baby's cheeks. Suddenly, these tears run back up the Baby's cheeks and into its eyes, which then turn fiery red. We are returned to the original establishing shot of the white room. Here, the Playstation 3 slowly levitates above the floor as the Baby utters, in a mechanical and distant voice, 'Ma–ma'. The final title features a frontal shot of the Playstation 3 and reads 'Play Beyond'. Finally, the screen fades out to black and features the symbols '*III7*'.

This advertisement provides a useful text for illuminating the horror of posthuman abjection and thinking about the death of human subjectivity in the context of the omnipresence of human–technology encounters. While advertising texts tend to favour representations in which technology is cast in the role of the helpmeet – a benevolent, enabling, and emancipatory assistant of human life, the Playstation 3 'Baby' advertisement uniquely addresses posthuman fears concerning how human–technology interaction might denaturalise human subjectivity and render the human obsolescent. Indeed, the controversial reception of this advertisement at the time of its release suggests that, in the technology marketplace, there is an expectation that such fears are to be repressed in advertising representations. In confronting and vivifying these issues, this advertisement represents an eruptive moment in the media representation of technology and a stark exception in the landscape of technology advertising. It is precisely because this advertisement is an outlier that it forms the object of our close analysis. This advertisement is not intended to be a representative exemplar of normative marketing communications practice or an expression of the privileged intentionality of a cultural producer (Barthes 1977), but a useful platform for thinking about and illustrating key tensions within the cultural zeitgeist shaping technology consumption.

This advertisement heightens these concerns through intertextual references to both dystopic science fiction texts (for example, the Playstation 3 console resembles Hal, the powerful black monolith from the film '2001: A Space Odyssey') and horror texts (for example, the Baby resembles Chucky from the film 'Child's Play'). In drawing on the Gothic tradition, this advertisement represents unspeakable fears (Bruhm 2002: 171) which remain latent in human interactions with technology. In particular, this advertisement raises questions about what it means to be human in the context of increasing similarities, role reversals, metaphorical conflations and boundary breaches between humans and their machines, signalling deep-seated anxieties surrounding the human–nonhuman boundary. In the following analysis, we show how this advertisement illustrates the posthuman abjection of human agency in accordance with the following three themes: abjection of human autonomy, abjection of the human body, and abjection of human emotion.

Abjection of human autonomy

Several elements in the advertisement animate the abjection of human autonomy. The idea of human agency and free will is contested and denatured in the face of issues of unhealthy dependence on technology and surveillance societies, both of which are increasingly enabled within technology-saturated markets. Many posthumanist theorists (Bukatman 1993; Postman 1993; Virilio 1997) see humans as increasingly imprisoned by and rendered helpless in the face of their machines. In contrast to the metaphor of technology-as-helpmeet, that which is supportive of human life, machines are seen to control and delimit human activity, thereby inverting the master–slave dialectic which would ideally characterise human–machine interactions. This inversion is provocatively illustrated towards the end of the advertisement, in the image of the Playstation 3 rising above the floor. On one level, this can be read as the elevation and worship of machines – an ironic underscoring of their godlike status within technology-saturated markets. This can also be read as an intertextual reference to the seminal science fiction and popular cultural text '2001: A Space Odyssey', wherein the reverence of technology as a harbinger of human progress is symbolically enacted in an initial scene in which the primitive apes elevate a bone (the first tool) by throwing it into the sky. Indeed, the level of hype surrounding new product releases such as the Playstation 3, or in more recent times, the iPhone 6, provides real-world testimony to widespread consumer fascination with, and reverence of, new technologies. On another level, the Playstation 3 closely resembles Hal, the black monolith from '2001: A Space Odyssey'. In the original film, the monolith is an advanced machine built by an otherworldly species which triggers human evolutionary progress at key points in history. In the final scene of the film, the human (Dave) ages drastically and at the point of his death, has his consciousness merged with the machine (the monolith). Here, the posthuman singularity is born at the moment of the death of the human being. By making intertextual references to the monolith, the Playstation 3 advertisement evokes fears of technologies which are alien and superior to human understanding, but also fears of transforming the human being into something other-than-itself.

In addition, the figure of the naked and unarmoured Baby, (*qua* the consumer), sits imprisoned in the white laboratory and is transfixed by the machine, evoking fears of human dependency, vulnerability, defencelessness, and infantilisation in the face of totalising technologies. These images suggest the colonisation of the human mind by the demands and rhythms of the machine, whereby human imagination and cognition are dictated and distorted by our technologies. This mirrors Postman's (1993) contention that we have allowed technology to dominate all aspects of human life to the extent that technology has effectively eliminated all alternatives to itself. In 'Technopoly', Postman (1993) provides an account of how technology structures and dominates our sociocultural institutions and knowledge structures to an unhealthy extent. Here, Postman (1993) constructs a narrative of a tool-using culture, where technology is born as a benign enabler under humanity's power and control, but then shifts towards a technocracy, where technology attacks the culture, ultimately becoming a Technopoly, a totalitarian and all-consuming technocracy. Such is the most current zeitgeist explored in the movies 'Her', 'Lucy', and 'Transcendence'. Other extreme forms of vulnerability and a pathology of dependence can occur when consumers become addicted to technologies such as video games, cell phones, or social media and find themselves unable to live without these technology-mediated inter-actions. Bukatman (1993: 17) characterises this phenomenon as 'image addic-tion'. While the machine can be characterised as a drug, delivering an intensely pleasurable experience, being 'under the influence' connotes a loss of agency, with the human addict seen as the ultimate embodiment of a being controlled by and dependent on the machine (Virilio 1997).

Fears of technology-enabled surveillance further contribute to the abjec-tion of human autonomy. These fears are coded in this advertisement through the setting of a white room with no doors, suggesting that the room could be the site for a scientific experiment or an interrogation room in which the Baby is to be read as a Benthamite being who is constantly surveilled. This reflects an atmosphere of entrapment and paranoia, a sense in which there is no escape from an all-encompassing technological network. Downey and Dumit (1997: 5) underline the suffocating and pervasive force of technology when they write:

> [W]e cannot say No to the medical complex that appropriates our bodies, defines our state of health, and positions us in a continuum of fitness from the temporarily abled to the permanently disabled. We cannot say No to the corporate/government information complex that wires our social security numbers, driver's licenses, bank accounts [...] and other technological vectors of identity. We cannot say No to the experience of science, technology, and medicine collectively as a disciplining center that polices other meanings and orders power relations in contemporary life.

Technology can indeed be seen to facilitate a panoptic mode of constant sur-veillance, for example in minute-by-minute monitoring of how employees spend time at their workstations, or how internet shoppers spend their time and money online. Indeed, the increasing blanketing of information commu-nication technologies over the globe leads to concerns around the close scrutiny of personal information by governments and corporations. Thus, technology emerges as an apparatus for the production and control of 'docile bodies' (Foucault 1977) and is implicated in the totalising power of govern-mental and economic institutions over individual bodies.

Abjection of human embodiment

The uncanny figure of the Baby/robot provokes further anxieties associated with the abjection of the human body. The figure of the Baby is firmly entrenched within the genre conventions of body horror. As Hurley (1995: 203) explains:

> Body horror seeks to inspire revulsion – and in its own way, pleasure – through representations of quasi-human figures whose effect/affect is

produced by their abjection, their ambiguation, their impossible embodiment of multiple, incompatible forms. Such posthuman embodiments are liminal entities, occupying both terms (or rather, existing in the slash between them) of the opposition human/not-human.

In the Playstation 3 advertisement, the core of the uncanniness stems from the uncertainty of how to read the figure of the Baby. Is it human? Is it a robot? Is it a doll? Is it a child? Is it an adult? While the Baby could simply be read as a mechanised robot or a lifelike doll given the plastic appearance of its skin and its mechanised movements, this reading is contradicted by other elements: the Baby's skin at times appears soft and plastic, resembling a human baby (in contrast to the armoured metallic figures seen in films such as 'I, Robot' or 'The Terminator'); the Baby's eyes and face are highly expressive and display a range of human emotions including delight, sadness, and fear. The Baby further dispels biological fluids in the form of tears, which are then reversed and absorbed back into the Baby's eyeballs. These highly transgressive acts denaturalise and destroy the coherence of the child's body, denying its human life and potentiality. In these ways, the figure of the Baby is simultaneously coded as both human and not-human. In contrast with stereotypical representations of the metallic and mechanistic robot, the Baby/machine defies simplistic categorisation and straddles the boundary between human and nonhuman; it is difficult to read. In straddling these contradictions, the mutable figure of the Baby's body is unsettling and monstrous in its continuous slippage between human and machine embodiment.

In addition, the figure of the Baby/robot/doll evokes fears of endowing machines with qualities that are considered exclusive to human beings, thereby challenging the innateness and specificity of human embodiment. A border war is being played out in the boundary between human and machine bodies. In displaying elements of human embodiment, the figure of the Baby blurs the boundary between what is alive and what is not. The uncanniness of the Baby reflects wider concerns about humans animating their technologies in various ways and conferring the properties of higher beings onto inanimate objects. Indeed, toy baby dolls which open their eyes, talk, eat, and breathe often blur the line between living and non-living embodiment in attempts to offer 'lifelike' baby experiences to children. This advertisement takes the uncanniness of this interaction to a different level. As Zuboff (1988) observes, machines are increasingly exhibiting complex intelligence, simulating human emotion, and taking on 'human' tasks to the extent that technology can be seen to take on a life of its own and confound these clear-cut dichotomies. As humans increasingly divest their agency onto machines (Clark 2003), the boundaries which distinguish humans and machines are blurred as agency appears to no longer be an exclusive feature of human being. Luke (2000) coins the term 'zombiosis' to describe the ways in which 'dead' commodities are activated by 'undead labour' and thus possess 'artifactancy', the ability to act. He argues that we breathe life onto our machines, such that 'All effusions of objectivity crackle with subjectivity' (Luke 2000: 48).

Despite Luke's (2000) optimistic slant, such developments also provoke anxieties around the replication of brain function in non-biological, man-made artefacts to the extent that any differences between human and machine embodiment are negligible (Haugeland 1985). In this vein, the uncanny valley theory describes extremely negative emotional responses when non-living beings such as prosthetic hands, dolls, and robots that seem 'almost human' are animated and exhibit anthropomorphic behaviours (Mori 1970). Such extreme reactions are clearly based on modernist discourses of bodies and machines as distinct entities, and an association of hybrid beings such as 'almost-human' robots and cyborgs with the abject, the polluted or the taboo. The Frankensteinian myth, for instance, sees science and technology as breeding the unnatural 'Other', a pervasive and perpetuating myth which constructs technology and human spirituality as oppositional (Helman 1988).

Abjection of human emotion

Further issues surrounding the abjection of human emotions and human relationships are suggested by the structuring absence of the Baby's mother or any human caregiver in this advertisement. What are we to make of the enigmatic ending, in which the Playstation 3 is elevated and the Baby utters the word 'mama'? What does it mean that a machine seemingly replaces the mother's teat becoming a site of behavioural and affective nourishment? These images can be read as a representation of wider fears about the ways in which human-technology interactions are supplanting and polluting human relationships. Machines increasingly 'stand in' for people and play important roles in social scripts. For example, there is a trend towards the use of self-service technologies such as ATMs and kiosks (Meuter *et al.* 2005), which can be seen as central 'actors' in routine service encounters. Within the home, the television can be used to 'babysit' children (Morley 1986), raising concerns around the increasing use of machines for social instruction, arbitration and gratification. Moreover, technology may reduce the quality of interpersonal communication or result in increased isolation, which has been shown with internet use (Kraut *et al.* 1998).

Beyond making humans increasingly redundant in contemporary socio-technical networks, such developments also carry ramifications for the phenomenology of human emotion, perception, and memory. Because the Baby/robot/doll exhibits human emotions which are simultaneously recognisable and alien, this raises and problematizes the idea that human emotions can be programmed and replicated, and thus rendered irrelevant; a mere carapace or performance of a 'real' emotion. As Botting notes (2005: par. 17): 'humans glimpse themselves in the machine, the same and yet different, duplicatable and dispensable, replicatable and replaceable.' Futhermore, the figure of the Baby/robot evokes fears of rendering the consumer into an emotion-producing-machine, a mere terminus or appendage in a network of other machines. In this vein, Baudrillard (1988) observed the human subject as rendered into a 'terminal of multiple networks'. Woolgar (1991) similarly sees technology as configuring users whose behavioural repertoires are regimented by the requirements of the machine. In the Playstation 3 advertisement, the Baby becomes a metaphor for the human transformed into an image-processing and emotion-producing machine. As Musk (2014) has recently forewarned: 'Hope we're not the biological boot loader for digital superintelligence. Unfortunately, that is increasingly probable'. Ballard (1984: 96) also foreshadowed, in this vein, the 'death of affect' in which the human capacity to emote is denatured in the face of over-stimulation. The Baby represents a 'hollow body, emptied of qualities associated with personality and affect' (Scheer 2002: 85).

Moreover, the speed at which the images flash through the Baby's eyes and the speed at which the Baby's emotional expressions change echo wider cultural concerns about the colonisation of human perception and emotion. As argued by Virilio (1991) and Lash (2001), the relentless speed of the information network threatens the capacity for meaningful human engagement and, indeed, diminishes the usefulness of human contemplation in the cacophony of accelerated information. Here, the human faculty of contemplation, judgement, and reflection is thwarted by the relentless flow of machine input, diminishing the human into a response creature. Despite the innocence suggested by the edenic nakedness of the Baby, and the fact that it is a baby, the potentiality of this life is disturbingly denied as the Baby is rendered into an empty vessel, lacking in memory or history, merely awaiting the next technological input in order to produce the next emotional reaction.

Discussion

Drawing on the concept of abjection, our close analysis has shown how human-technology interaction provokes fears associated with the abjection of human autonomy, embodiment, and emotion. In the Playstation 3 advertisement, the death of human subjectivity coincides with the birth of the machine. The figure of the Baby, born a posthuman, denies the Romanticism associated with modernist conceptions of humanity. The figure of the Baby, semiotically signifying birth and new life, is simultaneously polluted in this rendering as the ultimate programmable machine. This represents the techno-social realities that the consumer is 'born' into: a posthuman reality in which the human no longer connotes a privileged position. It is a world in which the human itself has been transformed into something other-than-itself. This advertisement evokes Burroughs' (1964) concept of 'terminal identity'. As Bukatman (1993: 9) explains, terminal identity is 'an unmistakably double articulation in which we find both the end of the subject and a new subjectivity constructed at the computer station or television screen'. By conflating metaphors of birth and death, the Playstation 3 advertisement vividly exemplifies the spectre of terminal identity

– of the death of the human – associated with the cultural zeitgeist of posthumanism. In illuminating these concerns, this chapter extends the paradigm of posthuman consumer research and uncovers a deep-seated ontological disquiet concerning technology consumption which touches on issues of human materiality, identity and, ultimately, immortality.

A discussion of posthumanist abjection and its relation to ontological anxiety remains to be more fully articulated in marketing theory. Certainly, marketing scholars have discussed linkages between posthuman epistemologies and the postmodern decentering of human subjectivity (e.g. Buchanan-Oliver and Cruz 2009; Buchanan-Oliver *et al.* 2010; Giesler and Venkatesh 2005; Venkatesh and Meamber 2006). Marketing scholars have additionally explored the shift from modernist dichotomies to posthuman ambiguity as vivified in cyborgian representations (Campbell *et al.* 2005; Giesler 2004; Schroeder and Dobers 2007; Venkatesh *et al.* 2002). However, scholarly engagements with the fundamental disquiet associated with technology consumption have been limited (for exceptions, see Buchanan-Oliver and Cruz 2011; Campbell and Saren 2010). We note that Campbell and Saren's (2010) work, which traced associations between the primitive and horror in marketing representations of posthuman embodiment, was not published in a marketing journal.

Why is the horror of technology not being discussed in marketing theory? Given the recent turn in consumption research towards the 'dark side' of consumption phenomena, as evidenced in studies of addictive consumer-brand relationships (Buchanan-Oliver and Schau 2012), and recent explorations of the agency of objects (Epp and Price 2010), the current repression of fears around the death of human subjectivity in the face of technological pervasiveness is surprising. This shift from modernist views of technology to posthumanist views (and fears) of technology is an important area of study because it represents an important cultural movement which forms the wider 'context of context' (Askegaard and Linnet 2011) for technology consumption. What do these eruptions of disquiet teach us about the cultural zeitgeist of technology consumption? To what extent do these ontological fears, clearly prevalent in the cultural zeitgeist, inform consumers' technological imaginaries? We hope that this chapter sparks further discussion in this area.

In addition, we have previously observed that the juxtaposition of horror and technology representation – as evidenced in the Playstation 3 'Baby' advertisement – constitutes a stark exception in the landscape of posthuman aesthetics, in which cyborgs are more often framed in servile, celebratory, or non-threatening terms. This contrasts with popular culture representations, in which a tension between fascination and repulsion towards technology are frequently played out. Bukatman (1993: 10) argues that 'Science fiction constructs a *space of accommodation* to an intensely technological existence' (emphasis in original). Featherstone (2000: 2) also notes how science fiction literature such as Gibson's (1986) descriptions of cyberspace in 'Neuromancer' extends the 'horizons of expectations of human–machine fusions,' transforming common understandings of the body and technology and impacting business and research practice.

Why is this 'space for accommodation' (Bukatman 1993: 10) seemingly absent in the landscape of marketing communications? Why do most marketing communications texts of technological brands repress the unrest associated with human abjection in technology consumption? Where do these eruptions appear, and why? One could surmise that this is congruent with Podoshen, Venkatesh, and Jin's (2014) recent observation that utopia is a more popular topic of writing in consumer culture than dystopia. However, the current dearth of death in the landscape of technology branding is particularly surprising given two arguments in the marketing communications literature. One argument suggests that advertising should reflect wider cultural concerns in order to achieve resonance with its intended audiences (McCracken 1986). As Meamber and Venkatesh (2006) more recently argue, 'A cultural product that provides symbolic benefits consistent with cultural priorities is more likely to be accepted than the one that does not'. As reflected in the entrenchment of posthumanist discourses in both theoretical discourses of science, technology, and society, as well as popular culture texts, the death of human subjectivity is a key tension in the cultural zeitgeist. A second argument has shown that, in contrast to being likeable and conventional, marketing communications texts can deploy grotesque and macabre imagery to arrest and achieve engagement with viewers (Phillips and McQuarrie 2010). Why aren't there more examples which parallel the captivating, repulsive, and enigmatic figure of the Baby in contemporary marketing communications? In such an *aporia*, the puzzling Playstation 3 'Baby' advertisement is a significant marketing communications text which, in our view, gives voice to ontological tensions which underlie human–technology interactions.

Bukatman (1993: 281) observes a dialectic between death and immortality in popular cultural imaginaries of human–technology interaction: 'in science fiction the death of the subject is continually acted out in a form that yields a rebirth on another plane'. For example, in Rudy Rucker's novel 'Software', a human mind is 'uploaded' into a robotic body. In '2001: A Space Odyssey', the moment of Dave's death gives way to a re-incarnation in a new form: the merging of the human and the machine. More recently, in Big Hero 6 (2015) the machine reproduces a video capture of the protagonist's dead brother (and its own creator) which both memorialises and immortalises its progenitor, and perpetually vivifies its genesis: a perpetual re-birthing and interaction of both human and machine. As Featherstone (2000: 10) writes, 'technoscience [...] allows us to create bodies which escape the fatefulness of both DNA and God.' Indeed, aspirational marketing messages tend to reinforce the perfection, infallibility, and capability of technology to extend human capacity (Salomon, Perkins, and Globerson 1991) and in some cases, extend human life (Munson 2002; Olshansky, Carnes, and Grahn 1998). If the relentless advance of technology in contemporary consumer cultures indeed constitutes the next stage of human evolution, what are the implications of these technological advances on human subjectivity? Does a Faustian bargain permeate our relationship with technology – do we exchange our humanity for immortality? Posthumanist theories begin with these questions.

References

Askegaard, S., and Linnet, J. T. (2011). Towards an Epistemology of Consumer Culture Theory: Phenomenology and the Context of Context. *Marketing Theory,* *11*(4), 381–404.

Ballard, J. G. (1973). *Crash.* London: Cape.

Ballard, J. G. (1984). Introduction to Crash. *Re/Search, 8/9.*

Barthes, R. (1977). Death of the Author. In Heath, S. (ed.) *Image, Music, Text.* London: Fontana Press.

Baudrillard, J. (1988). *The Ecstasy of Communication.* Brooklyn, NY: Autonomedia.

Botting, F. (2005). Reading Machines. *Gothic Technologies: Visuality in the Romantic Era.* www.rc.umd.edu/praxis/gothic/botting/botting.html.

Bruhm, S. (2002). Contemporary Gothic: Why Do We Need It? In J. E. Hogle (Ed.), *The Cambridge Companion to Gothic Fiction.* Cambridge: Cambridge University Press.

Buchanan-Oliver, M., and Cruz, A. (2009). The Body and Technology: Discourses Shaping Consumer Experience and Marketing Communications of Technological Products and Services. *Advances in Consumer Research,* Duluth, MN.

Buchanan-Oliver, M., and Cruz, A. (2011). Discourses of Technology Consumption: Ambivalence, Fear, and Liminality. *Advances in Consumer Research,* St Louis, MO.

Buchanan-Oliver, M., and Schau, H. J. (2013). Consuming Spirituality and the Spirituality of Consuming Media Narratives. In D. Rinallo, L. M. Scott and P. Maclaran (Eds.), *Consumption and Spirituality* (pp. 81–94). New York: Routledge.

Buchanan-Oliver, M., Cruz, A., and Schroeder, J. E. (2010). Shaping the Body and Technology: Discursive Implications for the Strategic Communication of Technological Brands. *European Journal of Marketing, 44*(5), 635–662.

Bukatman, S. (1993). *Terminal Identity: The Virtual Subject in Postmodern Science Fiction.* Durham: Duke University Press.

Campbell, N., and Saren, M. (2010). The Primitive, Technology and Horror: A Posthuman Biology. *Ephemera: Theory and Politics in Organization, 10*(1), 152–176.

Campbell, N., O'Driscoll, A., and Saren, M. (2005). *Cyborg Consciousness: A Visual Cultural Approach to the Technologised Body.* Paper presented at the European Advances in Consumer Research, Goteborg, Sweden.

Clark, A. (2003). *Natural-born Cyborgs: Minds, Technologies, and the Future of Human Intelligence.* New York: Oxford University Press.

Clarke, J. (2002). The Human/Not Human in the Work of Orlan and Stelarc. In J. Zylinska (Ed.), *The Cyborg Experiments: The Extensions of the Body in the Media Age* (pp. 33–55). New York: Continuum.

Derrida, J. (1978). *Writing and Difference* (A. Bass, Trans.). Chicago: University of Chicago Press.

Downey, G. L., and Dumit, J. (1997). Locating and Intervening: An Introduction. In G. L. Downey and J. Dumit (Eds.), *Cyborgs and Citadels: Anthropological Interventions in Emerging Sciences and Technologies* (1st ed., pp. 5–29). Santa Fe, NM: School of American Research Press.

Epp, A. M. and Price, L. L. (2010). The Storied Life of Singularized Objects: Forces of Agency and Network Transformation. *Journal of Consumer Research, 36,* 820–837.

Featherstone, M. (2000). Body Modification: An Introduction. In M. Featherstone (Ed.), *Body Modification* (pp. 1–14). London: Sage.

Firat, A. F., and Venkatesh, A. (1993). Postmodernity: The Age of Marketing. *International Journal of Research in Marketing, 10,* 227–249.

Foucault, M. (1977). *Discipline and Punish: The Birth of the Prison* (1st American ed.). New York: Pantheon Books.

Gane, N. (2005). Radical Post-humanism: Friedrich Kittler and the Primacy of Technology. *Theory, Culture and Society, 22*(3), 25–41.

Gibson, W. (1986). *Neuromancer.* London: Grafton.

Giesler, M. (2004). *Consuming Cyborgs: Researching Posthuman Consumer Culture.* Paper presented at the Advances in Consumer Research, Valdosta, GA.

Giesler, M., and Venkatesh, A. (2005). *Reframing the Embodied Consumer as Cyborg: A Posthumanist Epistemology of Consumption.* Paper presented at the Advances in Consumer Research, Duluth, MN.

Haraway, D. J. (1991). A Cyborg Manifesto: Science, Technology, and Socialist-Feminism in the Late Twentieth Century *Simians, Cyborgs, and Women: The Reinvention of Nature.* New York: Routledge.

Haugeland, J. (1985). *Artificial Intelligence: The Very Idea.* Cambridge, MA: MIT Press.

Hayles, N. K. (1999). *How We Became Posthuman: Virtual Bodies in Cybernetics, Literature, and Informatics.* Chicago: University of Chicago Press.

Helman, C. (1988). Dr Frankenstein and the Industrial Body: Reflections on 'Spare Part' Surgery. *Anthropology Today, 4*(3), 14–16.

Hurley, K. (1995). Reading Like an Alien: Posthuman Identity in Ridley Scott's *Alien* and David Cronenberg's *Rabid.* In J. Halberstam and I. Livingston (Eds.), *Posthuman Bodies* (pp. 203–224). Bloomington: Indiana University Press.

John, G., Weiss, A. M., and Dutta, S. (1999). Marketing in Technology-Intensive Markets: Toward a Conceptual Framework. *Journal of Marketing, 63*(4), 78–91.

Kraut, R., Patterson, M., Lundmark, V., Kiesler, S., Mukophadhyay, T., and Scherlis, W. (1998). Internet Paradox: A Social Technology that Reduces Social Involvement and Psychological Well-Being? *American Psychologist, 53*(9), 1017–1031.

Kristeva, J. (1982). *Powers of Horror: An Essay on Abjection.* New York: Columbia University Press.

Lash, S. (2001). Technological Forms of Life. *Theory, Culture and Society, 18*(1), 105–120.

Luke, T. W. (2000). Cyborg Enhancements: Commodity Fetishism and Human/Machine Interactions. *Strategies, 13*(1), 39–62.

McCracken, G. (1986). Culture and Consumption: A Theoretical Account of the Structure and Movement of the Cultural Meaning of Consumer Goods. *Journal of Consumer Research, 13*(June), 71–82.

Meuter, M. L., Bitner, M. J., Ostrom, A. L., and Brown, S. W. (2005). Choosing Among Alternative Service Delivery Modes: An Investigation of Customer Trial of Self-Service Technologies. *Journal of Marketing, 69*(April), 61–83.

Mick, D. G., and Fournier, S. (1998). Paradoxes of Technology: Consumer Cognizance, Emotions, and Coping Strategies. *Journal of Consumer Research, 25*(September), 123–143.

Mori, M. (1970). The Uncanny Valley. *Energy, 7*(4), 33–35.

Morley, D. (1986). *Family Television: Cultural Power and Domestic Leisure.* London: Comedia Publishing Group.

Munson, R. (2002). *Raising the Dead: Organ Transplants, Ethics, and Society*. New York: Oxford University Press.

Musk, E. (2014). @elonmusk. Retrieved 21 November 2014, from https://twitter.com/elonmusk/status/496012177103663104.

Olshansky, S. J., Carnes, B., and Grahn, D. (1998). Confronting the Boundaries of Human Longevity. *American Scientist, 86*(1), 52.

Phillips, Barbara J., and Edward F. McQuarrie. (2010). Narrative and Persuasion in Fashion Advertising. *Journal of Consumer Research, 37*(3), 368–392.

Podoshen, J. S., Venkatesh, V., and Jin, Z. (2014). Theoretical Reflections on Dystopian Consumer Culture: Black Metal. *Marketing Theory, 14*(2), 207–227.

Postman, N. (1993). *Technopoly: The Surrender of Culture to Technology* (1st Vintage Books ed.). New York: Vintage Books.

Salomon, G., Perkins, D. N., and Globerson, T. (1991). Partners in Cognition: Extending Human Intelligence with Intelligent Technologies. *Educational Researcher, 20*(3), 2–9.

Schau, H. J., and Gilly, M. C. (2003). We Are What We Post? Self-Presentation in Personal Web Space. *Journal of Consumer Research, 30*(3), 385–404.

Scheer, E. (2002). What Does an Avatar Want? Stelarc's E-motions. In J. Zylinska (Ed.), *The Cyborg Experiments: The Extensions of the Body in the Media Age* (pp. 81–100).

Schroeder, J. E., and Dobers, P. (2007). Imagining Identity: Technology and the Body in Marketing Communications. *Advances in Consumer Research*, Duluth, MN.

Venkatesh, A., and Meamber, L. A. (2006). Arts and Aesthetics: Marketing and Cultural Production. *Marketing Theory, 6*(1), 11–39.

Venkatesh, A., Karababa, E., and Ger, G. (2002). *The Emergence of the Posthuman Consumer and the Fusion of the Virtual and the Real: A Critical Analysis of Sony's Ad for Memory Stick*. Paper presented at the Advances in Consumer Research, Valdosta, GA.

Virilio, P. (1991). *The Aesthetics of Disappearance* (1st English ed.). New York: Semiotexte Books.

Virilio, P. (1997). *Open Sky*. London and New York: Verso.

Wolfe, C. (2010). *What is Posthumanism?* Minneapolis: University of Minnesota Press.

Woodward, K. (1994). From Virtual Cyborgs to Biological Time Bombs: Technocriticism and the Material Body. In G. Bender and T. Druckrey (Ed.), *Culture on the Brink: Ideologies of Technology* (pp. 47–64). Seattle: Bay Press.

Woolgar, S. (1991). Configuring the User: The Case of Usability Trials. In J. Law (Ed.), *A Sociology of Monsters* (pp. 58–99). London and New York: Routledge.

Zuboff, S. (1988). *In the Age of the Smart Machine: The Future of Work and Power*. New York: Basic Books.

19 Poetically considering death and its consumption

Terrance G. Gabel, Editor

> To communicate the essence of some of our most meaningful consumer experiences, the precise, linear language of science and academia may be, in and of itself, unsuitable ... Perhaps emotional truths are best communicated emotionally. Perhaps we know certain things are true and valid because, like good poetry, they resonate within us, expanding and enriching our consciousness.
>
> (Sherry and Schouten, 2002, p. 219)

> Often, in death, everything else fails. We are left only with the music and meaning of poetry.
>
> (Young, 2010, p. xv)

Among the most veiled and emotionally charged of life's experiences are those related to death. Given that poetry has long been recognized as an unparalleled means of expressing and understanding the most complex and emotional aspects of life (Sherry and Schouten, 2002), it is of little surprise that few poets regarded as the finest of all wordsmiths have not, since time immemorial, grappled with death.

Recently, within marketing and consumer research, poetry has slowly but progressively come to be recognized as a means by which to understand, express, celebrate, and/or confront that which defies scientific or other more "scholarly" explanation (Canniford, 2012; Wijland, 2011; Sherry and Schouten, 2002). This "poetic turn" has manifested itself most notably within the nascent realm of Consumer Culture Theory (CCT); mainly in poetry reading sessions held – with published chapbooks in hand – in concurrence with the annual CCT symposium. Death-related poetry penned by marketing and consumer researchers has there entered – albeit randomly – the CCT circuit (see, for example: Arnould, 2014; Steinfield, 2014; Gabel, 2013, 2010; Downey, 2011, 2010a, 2010b, 2010c).

This chapter represents the first formal, organized attempt to better understand death-related consumption experience and meaning via the creation and dissemination of original works of poetry. The chapter's title reflects the broad, eclectic perspective of death and consumption herein pursued. We consider funerary and other – good, service, and ideological – product consumption activities and experiences transpiring in the context of death. We also embrace the notion that death often brutally consumes those dealing with it; a "consumption of consumers by death." In turn, as vividly expressed in several of the poems in this chapter, consumption acts or experiences and/or memories thereof may be instrumental in cathartically coping with "being consumed by death."

Toward this end, gathered together and presented here is a small collection of death-related poetic utterances from regular contributors to the CCT poetry dialogue as well as those of several kindred-spirit "new recruits." Ordering of the poems is based on loose categorization into four emergent and not necessarily mutually exclusive themes/types. Appearing first are those wherein the author considers and/or alludes to what it feels like to deal with the death of friends and loved ones. We then transition into works in which the poet contemplates his or her own death. Following that are poems that do not focus on the death of a particular person as much as they do on culturally prescribed death-related consumption ritual and/or consuming *some thing or things* as a consequence of systemic, macro-level market forces shaped by decisions made by global economic and political elites (e.g., the marketing of war and traditional mass religion and the endless cycle of work, death, grief, healing, and work associated with dominant energy production and consumption practices). Finally, in closing, two epitaph poems are offered.

Consuming Love and Death

By Sidney J. Levy

Culture Theorists study the Consumers,
Converting into facts all those rumors
About what they buy and what they sell,
Interpreting for journals what subjects tell.

Lately we see that Death is a commodity
Like anything else in the market vicinity
As a branded idea and its attendant gear,
The medical care, interment, and all we fear.

Death is the biggest, most successful vendor;
Its service is huge, of all ills the greatest mender.
It needs to advertise to absolutely no one
Because its total market segment is everyone.

Anyway, this is my chance to be a subject,
A case study that reviewers won't reject,
About my personal actions in this culture
Where Death waits my turn with its nurture.

The ads nagged at me, have you a will?
As if writing one was like taking a pill.
So I did it, not that I had much to leave;
Maybe it gave me a sense of reprieve.

We also bought policies for cremation,
Feeling planful and a virtuous sensation.
And, oh, yes, another for long term care,
As if to tell Death, Ha, you better beware.

Did these consumer acts do much good?
That is a research question I still brood.
Many folks don't make plans this way.
Their philosophy lets them ignore or pray.

The old song says, Love is everywhere,
Its magic perfume fills the air. Ah, there!
But so too does Death pervade one's life.
I know too well: it took my son and my wife.

Last night I dreamed the word "Anodyne"
As if repeating it cured ills of mine.
Yet too it means do not offend;
How then can such obsequy mend?

Such contradictions stir my mind.
Old eyes can see but are also blind.
To cleave may mean to cut in parts
And also says we join our hearts.

Bobette was ill, I cared for her at bedside.
I said, "I love you," as her eyes opened wide.
She smiled, moved hand to her heart, and died,
And then, as now, I cried, I cried, I cried.

Thus, you are dead and have left me
Dear Ones, why have you bereft me?
Ever since I'm a man so bereaved,
Left alone to pine, and ever grieved

I search to find the opposing side,
Seeking reasons why I should abide.
You said I must stay and still find joy
When my impulse is all to destroy.

I thought to help my sad dreary head:
What about death had great poets said?
I found that Conrad Aiken shared my fate;
He said, "I am without you, all is desolate."

I can with Keats think of my last breath,
With him "half in love with easeful Death,"
Enjoying Browning as were I high on meth,
"I shall but love thee better after death."

But no, better to buy what Thomas sold
To counter the allure of the endless Cold
And continue to wage the living fight
And "rage against the dying of the light."

So, is all this as if life were a business?
Can we buy and sell both ease and stress?
The mundane world says it must be so,
Promoting how to prepare and get ready to go.

To see a son die, to see a wife die, I must confess,
To say what I feel there's no way to express.
At the slightest hint of memory all I do is weep;
As a consumer of love, O, the price is so steep!

Things ... I Do Not Ask

By Terrance G. Gabel

I do not ask
why
you did
what you did

I do not ask
why
I remember you
through material things
of 30 and 40 years past...

Levis jackets;
    weathered shades
    tattered blue
    reeking of smoke
    throughout school

the Javelin;
    faded a dull piss yellow
    broken down
    or parked
    as often as not

Budweiser cans;
    the exploding tabletop pyramid
    you flew atop me through
    rolling, clanging, howling
    across the dusty wooden floor

I do not ask
why
I relive these things
every time I see a train
roll by

I do not ask
why
I come here
beside bloodless tracks
where you did not just stand
with defiant determination
and as if these things
meant nothing

I do not ask
why
I find myself here
so often
so near
tons of screaming steel
to feel the gritty breeze
to face the ghosts
of these things
so grandly
so boldly
consumed.

I do not ask why.
I laugh.
I cry.

Tears Apart

By Pilar Rojas Gaviria

In honor of Patricia Garcia-Prieto

Part I

The sand clock has run down,
It is all now just a matter of remaining awake...
Endless time
In a shared life-part,
When falling apart,
My heart,
Being in the world,
When you are my world.
Being with you,
Your breath,
My blessing.
Next to my soul,
You laugh,
Music and Armagnac
Thrilling me,
And we are "chronically ill"
In this last, glamorous, dance.
Not much time to say good-bye.
How much I would have loved
Just to be there,
And there again,
Different shoes and hairstyles,
Passing through the hard and the good times,
Getting old and perhaps fat.
Telling you, tears apart,
When life gets tough,
How much I would have loved
Making you smile,
That one last time.

Part II

If we had just one more day
Back in Greece:
A blue ocean
And a deep breath.
It's all about to close,
Time to decide on the magical box.
No possible replacements,

They said.
Running out of pieces,
No new lungs, heart or kidneys.
Is this how far they can go?
Not impressed, while collecting the pieces
Of a heart once again falling apart.
You may feel:
The cold inside,
The grey outside,
You will have ups and downs,
As you improvise your way through life!
And then you may have a look
At our magical box,
Where I treasured for you,
Among other valuables:
My hello kitty angels,
One pink and one blue,
You never know which dream will come true.
A quill pen,
Waiting for your first alphabet.
A hair tie,
To see how close you are to me
On the days you ask:
How strong is my love for you?
My favorite paragraph,
On Kafka's Metamorphosis,
A must read in busy life days!
Some random notes and letters, testaments
Of as much anticipated love as I can give to you.
Closing the box,
Outside,
You and me,
We managed to take out
Those auxiliary ties,
On the red and black bike,
Rolling all around,
We laugh and jump,
Tears apart,
You are doing great for someone of your age!
All this as my end draws vividly near.
Holding you one last time,
Wishing you a sweet, endless ride,
Loving you,
My cherished child,
Forever.

Changling

By Hilary Downey

I noticed, when out of character
Your voice slipped in, *you* must
Attend that lilac tree; the *you*
Had a finality I would not share,
Hostility hung, a barrier created
That could not be overcome,
I mulled it over and over, before
Raking it up again; as one might
Give life to dying embers in the blackened
Grate, I called back, sure *you* will make certain
Of that; not awaiting the response, I gabbled
Over cracks now created in conversation,
Banter and babble, the order of the day

It was a first toe-dipping into a reality,
A future life; where loss and laughter
Of a voice singed, tinged and cherished since
Childhood, is lost. A blanket from the big outdoors,
A well in which I swim, swam and want to, always,
Is slowly silting in. Now I hear in every turn
Of phrase, that uncertainty, my unwillingness
To see, frailty-falling, fading as autumnal
Light, burnt ochre now upon us

To acknowledge, I have to accept,
That door will hold tight against brush
Of down and flesh. My mouth *will not*
Sound out sickening-syllables, cast out,
Cage-caught in the air, pressing, pulsating,
Day on day. You are not welcome now,
Or ever to share these rooms of home
You have *no* legitimacy here, clad in
Raiments of sleep. I will watch for you
Come steeling down on night beams
And halt your stare

You grapple with *i gcróilí an bháis*,[1]
Unwieldy roots, shoots of clinging clematis
Honeysuckle and fibrous ivy, sewn deep in red
Brick. You master the unruly, untamed growth
Battling to quell the uprising that strikes

At will, and tries to still, your love of life.
I follow from the kitchen window, your soft
Footfall through wild grass; a footstep
I hear and know, fight-falling

From the garden to the bedroom
Clearing as you go, bags bulging with
Cobbled charity treats; too big, we keep
Too much, such urgency in the clearing
Heightens my vulnerability. I question this
Chaos; aggression, annoyance for an absence
To come. I am all but drowning in sorrow
For my changling

Five poems on the recent death and dying of my parents

The Thought

By Terrance G. Gabel

the thought
initially came hard to me
somewhere between too late and too soon

that perhaps
it would be better
for it to come sooner
to see no more
what has been seen these last months

that technology, expectations, and fears
have rendered living
however unimaginably miserable
more possible
more acceptable
more important
than dying a good death

of what I would do
if she
my mother
were to ask me
to end it for her
right here
now

that it is no longer
too soon or too late
or wrong
to be
at least considered

This is It

By Terrance G. Gabel

I know
even before I see the area code of my birth

this is it

the time has come
one you are not supposed to hope for
that I have
many times

I do not answer...

I pace
a darkened room
recalling how I wondered
how I might react
when the time would come
thinking
"not like this"

I shower
a long, tearful cleanse
up against the wall...

ready the car

return the call

yes...

my angelic mother
peacefully and quietly
singing *Amazing Grace*
with the nurse
to which I speak

two hours past
in a hospital one hour away
and I was not there...

there was work I "had to do"
sixty-plus – but never-enough – hours
each of her lonely last weeks...

and those undying scenes
I wished to avoid more of
closing acts from the final three of her 87 years
"lived" in a "nursing home"
positioned as "health center"
fading bruising forgetting bleeding rotting
paralyzed and harnessed
mechanically hoisted out of bed
like the cow in *Apocalypse Now*
to be fed and medicated
profitably prolonged
amidst the endless dirge of muffled screams and babblings and moans
which she will so patiently and without protest
suffer no more...

this is it

I must go.

Weeks Passed

By Terrance G. Gabel

three weeks have passed
since you left

I thought that by now
it would be better
but there is nothing
that is

no bottle or pill or road or place or show or song or poem or person
or other thing
material or not
is as capable as I had hoped

three weeks
fighting feelings

that I should feel
a certain, expected way

three weeks
expecting nothing
three weeks
telling myself
I did all I could

oh how I lie
...
I notice the calendar
and through tears see
it has been six weeks
instead of three

Keeping Dad

By Terrance G. Gabel

now I try to help
keep dad alive
out of harm's wide market way...

though he now seems to want to live
as little as I
wish to see him die

he wants nothing
to do
with anything
old or new
he does not understand
or hear or eat or call
or want to do much of anything
but twist thoughts
theorize conspiracies
into self-fulfilling worst-case scenarios

I haul him to lawyers and banks
fill out run-on forms
back and forth to doctors
for teeth and hearing aids
that cost far too much
and that he knows will not work

I make dead-end automated-away calls
fighting insurance
and the impoverished state
he worked so hard for so long for
so that his last years might be consumed
defending against the offensive
secret parallel world
fine people
just doing their jobs
what they have to do
legalizing
justifying
monetizing
the vulnerable
dying old

Bought In

By Terrance G. Gabel

you bought me
into the world
of having
of wanting
my own

taught me too
of the world
of enough
of appreciating
how to not forget

like the red, white, and blue
10th birthday basketball
and the 1st Black Sabbath cassette on #15
that play no longer
yet still function

thanks
to both of you
for all this
never to be
not here with me

Goodbyes to Nelson Mandela

By Laurel Steinfield

Jozi skies
Grieved
Madiba
As he left our earthly world
Grey soberness
Hung heavily for days
In lifeless clouds
Coldness seeped into the summer air
The mourning sun did not shine

The unsettled night skies
wept rain storms
whipped bemoaned winds
ending the human celebrations
of the freed man who
danced up in townships
and chanted out side the black barred house gates

Man celebrated Madiba's life
while nature lamented
the departed royal spirit
or perhaps
as African lore avows
it was the gods
raining down their joy
welcoming our Tata home

The Finest Flour

By John Schouten

Somewhere on a mountain, you said,
maybe at the roots of a big Doug fir.
But I chose a giant hemlock instead
a few minutes' walk into the woods.
The firs are majestic, but the hemlock
knows to bow its head.

How tired and saggy we became,
how loath to let an evening pass
without a bottle of wine and something

on the television, a foot in my lap
hungry to be rubbed, toes pulled
until they snapped.

I regret the pangs of shame we shared
over all those hours of sameness,
the hours of well-earned flab
slabbed off in hammocks of cool skin,
the groans of laughter
at some darkly funny line.

I've stopped watching, you know.
The set sits dark and holding
half-watched seasons of HBO
and Showtime. The screen
projects an empty room
and glimpses of a passing ghost.

I have a new habit.
You might approve.
I bake bread, a small loaf
every week on Sunday afternoon.
By Thursday it's gone.
I never share it with anyone.

When I finally got the urn
I let it sit for the longest time
on the kitchen counter,
next to the Mixmaster
that followed us around
the world and back again.

In the fall I finally opened it
and sifted you
through a fine strainer.
The coarser bits I took to the hemlock.
That was a Sunday afternoon.
By Thursday you were gone.

The finest flour I transferred
to a crockery jar.
I have two recipes I like best,
one that takes pumpkin seeds
and another with cherries and hazelnuts.
To every loaf I add a pinch of delicate ash.

When that is gone I'll bake no more,
but I'll return to the hemlock
and ask it to compare notes
on nutritional value and flavor
knowing full well before I go
that I got the very best of you.

Observations at My Own Funeral[2]

By John Schouten

What is this place?
A sea wall?
People gathered at a pier?
I sense water here, and salt.

I have no eyes, no ears.
No fingertips.
Emotional contours shape the air:
a granite fist lodged in ancient ice,
the mineral smell of unfinished business,
burrowing worms of fear.

I begin to understand.
This is not the shore.
There is no boat.
No cry of gulls.
What I imagined to be floating here
is just a box of souring bones.

My flesh and blood,
are you also in this place?
Which of these huddled shapes are yours?
I sift through them and try to trace
your emotional signatures.

Here a woman holds a picture
of me, only younger
and crueler.
I get fraying paper, broken glass,
sand at the heart of a misshapen pearl.

And here a rage of muscle,
a tongue-tied brain,
a flash of sugar in flame.

In him I hear my own voice,
the bass line in a song
of hope, despair, disdain.
My son, grow strong.

And you.
I would know you anywhere.
You are my open country.
I know your every stream and every wood.
Every blade of grass.
I would inhabit, if I could,
this empty space, this sparrow's nest
filling up with snow.
I see you have kept secrets.
Jewels wrapped in papery leaves.
I will let them be.
You have done as much for me.

heart attack

By John F. Sherry, Jr.

a crinkling like uncrumpling cellophane, like splashed
tabasco prickling that cramped space beneath the ribs,
a latticework of sharp and low volt jolts and spiky probes and fullness.
curled like a shrimp atop an unmade bed, holding myself
against the buzz of radiant current coursing through clenched jaw,
so far from home, so far from all I love,
feeling foolish to have picked this place
to misread signs I never should have seen,
wondering if widowhood becomes you.

Symbols for Sale: A Case Study

By Sidney J. Levy

Flowers serve the culture of consumer mental fitness.
'Though not food, clothing, shelter, they are big business
An industry of twenty-eight billion dollars a year,
With many floral customs that help allay our fear.

At each cycle of life floriculture means a lot to us
Whether scattered or set inches apart as we fuss
We buy some seeds and plant them in the earth.
And lovingly watch them as the seedlings give birth.

They poke up with strength despite their fragility,
Soaking up water, facing the sun with their ability,
Putting out their stems and their fledgling leafing
And greening our thumbs with credit for achieving.

Next come the buds, those dear plump harbingers,
With anxious nurture and hope that nothing injures
A promise that points up like hands held in prayer
The burgeoning blooms they're about to declare.

The wonder of flowers whether grown or bought:
With emotional intensity they are also fraught,
Delighting the senses as colored, delicate, fragrant,
With their symbolism they are laden and flagrant.

In vases around the house they serve as bright décor,
Or they come shyly as a gift for an error they deplore.
The tulips and the iris announce that spring is here,
And a single rose may say that I love you my dear.

When sick they say we're sorry and please get well;
They surround wedding altars and make events swell.
They congratulate promotions, can express our thanks,
And even bring a smile to the face of grumpy cranks.

But alas! We also know that in flowers an evil lurks:
They say that life is short despite beauty and good works.
Like Albright's wreath on the funereal door we rue:
"That which I should have done I did not do."

The flowers die in days, rotting, moldering in their vases,
Dropping their dead leaves on their doilies or laces.
Like ultimate respirators or meds, measures brutal,
Those pennies, sugar, vodka, and bleach are all futile.

So! Flowers speak aesthetically of the pleasures in life'
We buy them and we give them to express less strife.
They symbolize the consumption of our span of days,
Telling with fragrant breath of certain death in subtle ways.

Coal Town Hospice

By Robert Neimeyer

On the banks of the Ohio,
far from the namable places,

the town squats, wounded.
The sturdy girders
of the bridges carry cars
away, away,
across the brown expanse of river
bleeding these hills,
across the tracks of the C&X coursing
with their loads of coke
and steel. In the pre-dawn drizzle
Main Street stands empty
as the stores, their vacant eyes
leaking the dreams
of grandfathers.

On either end of town tower
the Goliaths of the plant, the refinery.
They announce the descent
into this valley, bar the exit,
squelch hope with belching fumes.
Between them the town crouches,
subservient.

There is still work here,
deposits to be made
to bank accounts,
    to lungs.
The cancer sends its metastases
winding down the wide streets,
the back alleys.
The eager tendrils find the unstopped
cracks under doors, the open
windows, mouths. For the young,
there is one sure way
out.

It is here that hospice
does its dark work,
lays its light hand
on laboring chests.
The plants have set down roots
in the furrowed brows,
sewn seeds of need
in the fertile flesh. Questions seep
like oil from the pores.

Like history,
nurses have no answers to give.
They fill the beds, fill the bags
hanging on steel poles,
coax the anodyne
into collapsing veins.
With each loss, chaplains
suture the wounds with familiar verse,
lay the dead to rest in the scarred soil.
Social workers apply their gentle press
to the bereaved, nudge them back to life,

back to the factories. In the end,
the survivors carry the memory
on their bent shoulders,
feel the heavy hand of obligation
that follows them to the furnaces,
to their homes,

like grief.

Pious Men

By Gregory W. Boller

Slothful...

Gluttonous,

These cadgers
Of heaven's prurience.

Stealing desperate prayers in secret
While belching their salvation with smug, pretentious wooliness;
Even raptured copulations with itinerant angels cannot slake their thirst
for murdering
    innocence.

Gleefully stoking hell's pyres of the eternal inquisition,
Pissing piety for wrath's fuel,
These saved celebrants
Know no
Penitence.

Scraping
Clutching
Covetous
Sinners all...
Girded with greed,
Fettered astride death's pale steed,
"To war," they cry, and "Stay the course,"
Lifting shattered flesh and burnt lives in
    fetid sacrifice to their god's decadence.

Dark fears nourish malignant loneliness in their envy,
Starving innocents of emotional intimacy
With bulimic rituals
To purge
Femininity.
Terrified
Tortured
Testosterone
Surges angrily.
God the Father,
The Son and Holy Ghost
Dress as warriors for Sunday's ménage à trois,
And hopeful minds are devoured of dreams by hosts of the Holy Pestilence.

Not the Funeral for a Friend

By Gregory W. Boller

Late winter's pallid morning sky,
Rudely carved from cold lead beckons;
Black leaves glare meanly and fly.

Grasping chants in this House of lies –
Ancient timbres offered a god,
Gathering sorrow and cries.

I am raped with tales of rapture;
Abused, unwilling, by Jesus;
Gavaged with pure manufacture.

My celebration of her time,
Now bent for medieval purpose,
Instead vomits hate writ benign.

Covetous hollow lips feign praise –
Ministered emptiness with psalms,
While lovers recall her days.

Marchers' grim agonies pass near,
Fleeing the soft petaled caisson;
Seared dreams' dark glows sigh with fear.

EPITAPH

By Hilary Downey

I return to dull memories, flamed by fresh
Finality, a culling of splintered craft-making
Tinted rose in the gathering gaze,
Hot spots of hunger-held highlights
Play my mind, soft-soothe in
A gossamer bind; kaleidoscopic snapshots
Of hedonic consumption times

Fresh final flame, the
Turning down of day, awakening
Of yester year, the shimmering of
Youth now awash with spume,
Frivolous fervour, bated breath,
Upon bás's drum, I beat; a retreat
On rhythmic consumption desires

an epitaph invoking nine muses and norm denzin

By John F. Sherry, Jr.

weathering seven moments,
awakening in our eighth day of creation,

mourning the golden age
beyond blurred genres and
the representing crises
of our contested methods,

seeking right and to avert
the hidden consequence
of needing, wanting, having,
publishing and perishing
and publishing again,

we long for that ninth moment,
the number of circles of hell
we've seen freeze over,
our lucky number nine,

we conjure a ninth life
where each of us can go
the whole nine yards
dressed to the nines,
perhaps retire on cloud nine,

as if history weren't a weapon
being written by the victors,
as if our moments weren't
as savory in their melting,

as if nine of ten doctors
could ever agree

Notes

1 i gcróilí an bháis= throes of death.
2 An earlier version appears in *Advances in Consumer Research*, Vol. 32, p. 9, 2005.

References

Arnould, Eric (2014) "To My Father (Whose Birthday I've Forgotten)" In Sherry, J.F., Jr., J.W. Schouten, and H. Downey (eds.) *Caribou Coracle Tera*. St. Bathans (New Zealand): University of St. Bathans Press, pp. 36–37.

Canniford, Robin (2012) "Poetic Witness: Marketplace Research Through Poetic Transcription and Poetic Translation," *Marketing Theory*, 12 (4), pp. 391–409.

Downey, Hillary (2010a) "Suppressing the Medical Model" In Wijland, W., J.W. Schouten, and J.F. Sherry, Jr. (eds.) *Canaries Coalmines Thunderstones*. St. Bathans (New Zealand): University of St. Bathans Press, p. 16.

Downey, Hillary (2010b) "Family at War" In Wijland, W., J.W. Schouten, and J.F. Sherry, Jr. (eds.) *Canaries Coalmines Thunderstones*. St. Bathans (New Zealand): University of St. Bathans Press, p. 17.

Downey, Hillary (2010c) "The Fallenness of Humanity" In Wijland, W., J.W. Schouten, and J.F. Sherry, Jr. (eds.) *Canaries Coalmines Thunderstones*. St. Bathans (New Zealand): University of St. Bathans Press, p. 18.

Downey, Hillary (2011) "The Last Gift" In Wijland, R. (ed.) *Coyotes Confessions Totems*. St. Bathans (New Zealand): University of St. Bathans Press, p. 20.

Gabel, Terrance G., (2010) "End Products" In Wijland, W., J.W. Schouten, and J.F. Sherry, Jr. (eds.) *Canaries Coalmines Thunderstones*. St. Bathans (New Zealand): University of St. Bathans Press, pp. 21–22.

Gabel, Terrance G., (2013) "The Wrong Time" In Sherry, J.F., Jr., J.W. Schouten, and H. Downey (eds.) *Cardinal Cuento Tianda*. St. Bathans (New Zealand): University of St. Bathans Press, pp. 16–17.

Sherry, John F. and John W. Schouten (2002) "A Role for Poetry in Consumer Research," *Journal of Consumer Research*, 29 (2), pp. 218–234.

Steinfield, Laurel (2014) "Goodbyes to Nelson Mandela" In Sherry, J.F., Jr., J.W. Schouten, and H. Downey (eds.) *Caribou Coracle Tera*. St. Bathans (New Zealand): University of St. Bathans Press, p. 10.

Wijland, Roel (2011) "Anchors, Mermaids, Shower-Curtain Seaweeds and Fish-Shaped Fish: The Texture of Poetic Agency," *Marketing Theory*, 11 (2), pp. 127–141.

Young, Kevin (2010) "Introduction" In Young, K. (ed.) *The Art of Losing: Poems of Grief and Healing*. New York: Bloomsbury.

20 Examining death and learning about life

Jeffrey Podoshen

In terms of understanding death consumption and its trajectory, the authors in this volume have paved a path of deep examination, introspection and reflection that offers significant insight into humanity and how the living deal with death. In these times of increased uncertainty, economic strife, and global unrest, the prospect of death may be more at the forefront of our minds. This means that death, and in some cases, associated violence and/or historic violence or distress is permeating our everyday lives and our consumption practices in ways we haven't really reflected on in the past number of decades. Further, it is clear from these chapters that there is increasing attention on the "performance" of the spaces (as we see in McKenzie's and Hackley and Hackley's chapter) and practices related to death, giving us more opportunity to understand the discourse surrounding death in tourism, rituals and consumption. In some cases, performance becomes interconnected with the horrors of death or the abject, as in Drummond and Krszjsaniek's work. In other cases, death and its related materiality deals with the symbolic and/or relational (see Dobscha, *et al.* 2012). This increase in what has become more salient, as well as more acceptable to witness, engage in and discuss, in itself, indicates a cultural shift towards an environment whereby humans are forced to confront more tangible realities of death in consumption practices. Death and the abject has been a topic of increased interest in recent history as humans appear to make sense of the violence that surrounds them and has become ever-so-present in the global media (Podoshen, *et al.* 2015) – a media which is reporting on mass and serial death and violence at an alarming rate – whether it be ISIS, gun violence or public unrest. No longer are images sanitized by the news media, but rather images and stories, in raw form, are available to everyone in seconds via social media. In fact, it is nearly impossible to simply "turn off" media and its associated images in the digital age.

Consuming death and related activities beyond the traditional funeral or religious ritual reflects a transformation in our search for answers and explanations that go beyond the limits of mere religiosity or cultural mores. Further, as demonstrated by some of the work in this volume, the concept of death and dying finds itself as a central ethos in a myriad of consumption activity, tourism and materialistic sensemaking. Once centered on ritual, religion and community, death as a consumption practice and consumer culture construct has transcended previous boundaries, prejudices and beliefs. Death consumption and interest has rapidly begun to remove itself from being viewed as merely a transgressive consumption activity. Schadenfreude labels of this type of consumer activity are being replaced by more introspective thoughts and feelings. Death is not something that we avoid (or can try to avoid) like we once did. As Marketing academics, many of us probably use the product of life insurance as the exemplar of the unsought good. The reality is that death-related products and services are not really as unsought as they once were and how we deal with the materiality of our bodies is one that takes on even more significance as our planet gets more crowded and more tumultuous.

Death consumption today continues to further blur lines of acceptability and mortality as evidenced by Welch's work in this volume and might even find itself blending and bridging themes we don't "normally" associate with death, such as renewed and deeper understandings of erotica, art and sex. As evidenced in the recent literature (Venkatesh, *et al.* 2015) global underground and extreme subcultures have used sex and gender issues to make provocative statements not just about death and dying, but about the living, culture(s) and subcultures(s) and attempts to deny or defy death. This falls into line with Stone and Sharpley's (2008) assertions that activities such as dark tourism and death-related consumption really tell us about humans currently living and breathing, their thoughts, feelings and dispositions, and not necessarily so much about the dead. This focus on the needs, wants and desires of the living based on the dead has manifested itself in increasingly popular quests for understanding ancestry as evidenced by Neilson and Muse or through mythologizing deceased celebrities to bring living fans closer to them as seen in Radford and Bloch's piece.

It should come as little surprise that while we are producing this text, Silicon Valley scientists, investors, bankers and billionaires are attempting to find ways to live forever and that death, violence and environmental concerns about the body are at the forefront of popular culture and consumption activity. As Dobscha mentions in the Introduction, embarking on the study of death and consumption is one that causes discomfort for many, yet appears in the public and non-public discourse more and more. This all creates an interesting amalgam that makes a sharp statement about the current state of neoliberalism, consumer behavior and what lies beyond. Will economic power really allow us to escape death? Will there be such a thing as "terminal illness?" How will death rituals and traditions change when we run out of space for the earth's bodies? How will the digital world preserve the memories of the dead – and better yet – how will the dead become "resurrected" in the digital realm? I might argue that underlying all of this is the issue of control – control of our bodies, our identities and our environment – in an era filled with uncertainty, economic strife and never-ending war. For some, death is one of the few things we can control, or at least better prepare for, and, as such, the implications of this reality are unsurprisingly manifest in consumption.

References

Dobscha, S., Drenten, J., Drummond, K., Gabel, T., Hackley, C., Levy, S., Podoshen, J., Rook, D., Sredl, K., Tiwaskul, R.A. and Veer, E. (2012). Death and all his friends: The role of identity, ritual, and disposition in the consumption of death. In Z. Gurhan-Canli, C. Otnes, and R. Zhu (Eds.), *Advances in Consumer Research Volume 40* (pp. 1098–1099), Duluth: Association for Consumer Research.

Podoshen, J., Venkatesh, V., Wallin, J., Andrzejewski, S., and Jin, Z. (2015 in press). Dystopian dark tourism: An exploratory examination, *Tourism Management.*

Stone, P., and Sharpley, R. (2008). Consuming dark tourism: A thanatological perspective. *Annals of Tourism Research, 35(2)*, 574–595.

Venkatesh, V., Wallin, J. J., Walschots, N., Netherton, J., and Podoshen, J. (2015 in press). "Giving head to the dead": Penetrating, defiling and polluting the ethos of death in necrophilic death metal. In Aggrawal, A., Hickey, E. and Mellor, L. (eds.), *Necrophilia: A Global Anthology.* San Diego, CA: Cognella, Inc.

Index

Page numbers in *italics* denote tables, those in **bold** denote figures.